INTERNET TECHNOLOGIES AND INFORMATION SERVICES

Joseph B. Miller

Library and Information Science Text Series

A Member of the Greenwood Publishing Group

Westport, Connecticut • London

Library of Congress Cataloging-in-Publication Data

Miller, Joseph B., 1952–
Internet technologies and information services / Joseph B. Miller.
p. cm. — (Library and information science text series)
Includes bibliographical references and index.
ISBN 978–1–59158–626–5 (alk. paper)
ISBN 978–1–59158–625–8 (pbk. : alk. paper)
1. Libraries and the Internet. 2. Libraries—Information technology.
I. Title.
Z674.75.I58M55 2009
020.285'4678—dc22 2008037448

British Library Cataloguing in Publication Data is available.

Library of Congress Catalog Card Number: 2008037448
ISBN: 978–1–59158–626–5
978–1–59158–625–8 (pbk.)

First published in 2009

Libraries Unlimited, 88 Post Road West, Westport, CT 06881
A Member of the Greenwood Publishing Group, Inc.
www.lu.com

Printed in the United States of America

The paper used in this book complies with the Permanent Paper Standard issued by the National Information Standards Organization (Z39.48–1984).

10 9 8 7 6 5 4 3 2 1

To my wife Susan, for a lifetime of love and support

Contents

Preface

Why another book about the Internet? The simple answer is that although there are a number of excellent books on networking, the Internet, HTML, Web design, Web programming, XML, and Web searching, there is not a single survey text that explores these topics holistically in the context of the knowledge and skills needed by those preparing to enter information technology (IT) intensive fields such as library and information science (LIS), business and management information systems (MIS), and decision science (DIS). Many professions are increasingly dependent on these technologies, and this book is intended to serve as a text for a survey course introducing these interrelated Internet technologies and applications. It provides an overview of how they work, how they are evolving, and why they are important to technology-intensive professions. My goal is to support courses in LIS or other disciplines developed for students who are not technology experts but who find their chosen field mandates a more complete understanding of many technical topics that they may not have encountered in their previous studies. I have drawn on 15 years of experience teaching technology topics to nontechnical audiences at a level of depth that sufficiently addresses the subject without overwhelming those lacking a background in IT. Thus, this book provides an overview of these technologies and builds the foundation necessary to enable the student or practitioner to explore them more fully in subsequent courses or in professional practice.

Obviously, because all these technologies have themselves been the subject of entire books, it is clear that this text cannot reflect the full depth to which each could be explored. There are places where this text is deliberately more “horizontal” than “vertical” and therefore tends to be a “mile wide and inches deep” (well, perhaps “yards” deep). Such an approach is in keeping with both its survey nature and its intended nonexpert audience.

In my field of Library and Information Science, there is a clear need for a broad, holistic understanding of these technologies. Roy Tennant, formerly of the California Digital Library, decried the "Digital Librarian Shortage," noting that although not everyone needs to be able to code software, "they should know what software is capable of doing, when a program could be easily written to accomplish a task, and what skills someone needs to write one" (2002, p. 32). He concluded this knowledge is crucial to professional success, and I wholeheartedly agree. I would argue his statement is relevant not just to librarians but to all preparing for careers dependent on the extensive use of IT. This text addresses these topics from that point of view, acknowledging that not everyone in these fields needs to become expert with every technology but that understanding what they are, how they work, and what they are capable of doing is critical to future professional success.

This book is organized around three main areas. Part 1 is on network and Internet technologies, covering computing and information technology fundamentals, networking and connection technologies, and Internet protocols. Part 2 considers Web design and the technologies of Web publishing, focusing on graphics, HTML, CSS, Web programming, and XML. Part 3 is on Internet content, information retrieval, and search engines covering the documentary formats for Internet content, a brief overview of information retrieval (IR) models and issues, and the use of search engines in the retrieval process. Part 3 concludes with a discussion of the impact of Web 2.0 and beyond in the context of the information professions. For those who might benefit from additional background on computing there is an appendix with a brief primer on binary numbers and the binary nature of digital computers; a glossary of terms is also provided.

Much like the potential buyer of a computer who knows that they can always find something better, faster, and cheaper if they wait until tomorrow, I enter this effort knowing that the area of Internet technologies is a rapidly moving target, and tomorrow there will be something new I will wish had been included. However, I believe the foundations discussed here will continue to be relevant even as new technologies continue to emerge. The goal of this text is to develop a frame of reference and the "eye for detail" that these future technologies will demand. The desired outcome of this process is an enhanced understanding and appreciation of these technologies that will support the life-long learning demanded of all working in these rapidly changing fields.

The conventions used in the text include the use of italics (except for their occasional use for simple emphasis) to denote terms found in the glossary and the use of bold font to represent commands, filenames, and tag references within the narrative. In addition to the sources I consulted for this text, each chapter may list other recommended sources or Websites for those desiring more information on the topics discussed.

A final note is to acknowledge that portions of two chapters are derived from articles I previously published in *Kentucky Libraries*, which are used here with permission. Parts of Chapter 1 are loosely based on "The Internet has changed, like *everything*" (Miller, 2006). Chapter 6 makes use of portions of "PC security in a networked world" (Miller, 2003).

REFERENCES

Miller, J. B. (2003). PC security in a networked world. *Kentucky Libraries, 67*(4), 18–22.

Miller, J. B. (2006). The Internet has changed, like, everything. *Kentucky Libraries, 70*(2), 4–6.

Tennant, R. (2002). The digital librarian shortage. *Library Journal, 127*(5), 32.

Acknowledgments

I have a colleague who compares writing a book to giving birth. I am somewhat skeptical of this comparison, but continuing with that metaphor, it does appear to "take a village" (at least in my case). I am extremely grateful to those who encouraged, assisted, and otherwise supported my efforts in writing this book. Several School of Library and Information Science (SLIS) colleagues provided helpful reviews that shaped and sharpened my thinking about topics that are in their areas of expertise. Professors Kwan Yi and Sujin Kim offered advice on the sections regarding IR, and Professor Yi had helpful suggestions for the chapters on scripting and XML. Several individuals were willing to proofread substantial portions of this text, including Professor Rebecca Miller Banner of SLIS and Rob Aken of the University of Kentucky libraries, along with graduate assistants Helen Morrison and Sara Chatfield who offered a valuable student perspective as well. I also wish to acknowledge my editor Sue Easun, author contact Sue Stewart, assistant manager Emma Bailey, and Apex CoVantage project manager Mary Cotofan as well as all those at Libraries Unlimited who guided me through this project and brought it to fruition. I am indebted to these friends and colleagues for all they did to make this a better book; for all their advice and assistance, I offer my sincere appreciation while also absolving them of responsibility for any remaining errors.

Obviously, most of this book does not reflect original research, and I have, as they say, stood on the shoulders of others who are the inventors, programmers, engineers, designers, and experts whose efforts I have tried to summarize into an instructional narrative. I cannot thank all these individuals personally, but they appear in the many sources referenced in this book. On a personal note, I would like to thank those who have influenced and shaped my career by sharing their time, knowledge, and advice. They are too numerous to list here, but there are several I would like to acknowledge who were instrumental to my career in LIS and provided opportunities that directed its subsequent path. Professor Stan Hannah, formerly of SLIS, and Professor Emeritus Thomas Waldhart both encouraged and mentored me, and I am deeply grateful for their support and friendship. Finally, saving the best for last, I want to express my heartfelt thanks to my wife, Susan, not only for her help with this project but for inspiring me to pursue a second career in library science and for a lifetime of support, without which I would not be where I am today.

Joseph B. Miller, MSLS
School of Library and Information Science
University of Kentucky

Part 1

Internet Technologies

Part 1 is focused on Internet technologies, including chapters on general information technology issues, networks, connectivity options and technologies, TCP/IP and higher-level Internet protocols, and security issues for Internet-connected PCs.

Chapter 1

Introduction

The popularity of the Internet is the most important single development in the world of computing since the IBM PC was introduced in 1981.

—Bill Gates (1995)

THE INTERNET HAS CHANGED EVERYTHING!

The Internet is widely perceived as one of the most transformative technological innovations of the twentieth century. This text is devoted to developing a practical and technical understanding of what it is, how it works, how it is managed, and where it is going since the first ARPANET packets were sent and received in 1969. Packets, the way datagrams are formed on computer networks, are discussed in later chapters. Such a broad agenda is quite ambitious and no single book can cover all these topics in depth. A reasonable starting point is to formally define the Internet, examine its history as well as the people who made critical contributions, and describe a few examples of the far-reaching impact it has had—and continues to have—on society and the broader information environment. The Internet has influenced and driven major developments and trends in the broad areas of computer technology, bandwidth creation, software development, and commerce. Many of these topics depend on a sound understanding of essential information technology (IT) basics such as the use of binary numbers and binary addressing schemes, digital data representation, and Boolean logic. The appendix provides a review of these essential fundamentals.

The quote at the start of this chapter by Microsoft's Bill Gates in 1995 has been reaffirmed many times and by many experts and writers over the last decade. In his best selling book *The World is Flat,* Friedman (2005) identifies

10 "flatteners" in the global economy that are changing the lives and work of billions of people, and the emergence of the Internet is central to most all of them. The impact of the Internet on library and other information-related professions has been dramatic, changing not only daily activities, services, and the professional preparation of librarians, but the very notion of the library. Indeed, no information provision business has remained unaffected by the Internet and the related technologies that have developed within and around it. It is reasonable to assert that *the Internet has changed everything.*

How dramatic these changes seem depends in large measure on whether you are of the "BW" (Before Web) or "AW" (After Web) generation. Those who came of age in the Web-less world are much more amazed by the changes it has wrought; those who grew up "post-Web" take it for granted as much as electricity or running water. This is to be expected—current generations are typically unimpressed with the technological marvels that preceded them. The fact that by the late twentieth century most people in the United States could pick up a telephone and have voice communication with almost anyone in the world certainly seemed much more magical to those who grew up in an era of telegrams compared to those who grew up in today's world of ubiquitous mobile phones and Internet access. But even though we live in an ever flattening world where universal Internet access, wireless networks, mobile phones, and recreational devices such as 80 gigabyte (GB) iPods are taken for granted by many, it is still informative to step back and examine how the Internet has changed so much for so many so quickly.

THE INTERNET DEFINED

The term *Internet* occurs throughout this text, so it is important to begin by defining it. In a generic sense, the term *internet* refers to any group of interconnected networks. However, in this text, *Internet* refers to the global network of computer networks utilizing the Transmission Control Protocol/Internet Protocol) (TCP/IP) standard, which includes the family of supporting services and protocols examined in detail in other chapters.

HISTORY OF THE INTERNET

The modern Internet began with the formation of the ARPANET in 1969 by the Advanced Research Project Agency within the Department of Defense. Although earlier network and computer technologies were essential to development of the Internet, most people identify the ARPANET as the seminal event in its history. The ARPANET initiative resulted in the first packet switching computer network connecting a computer at UCLA with one at Stanford University, thereby creating a two-node network. It was from this modest beginning that the modern Internet emerged. ARPANET in part was a response to national defense concerns and a desire to build a decentralized communication network potentially capable of surviving the loss of a major hub in a nuclear strike. ARPANET interconnections utilized dedicated processors called Interface Message Processors (IMPs; Leiner et al., 1997).

While the origins of the Internet go back to the 1969 ARPANET test bed, because TCP/IP is so integral to a definition of the Internet, one could argue that the Internet of today really began with the adoption of TCP/IP by ARPANET on January 1, 1983. This foundation protocol suite is the subject of Chapter 4. Zakon (2006) provides a complete timeline using Hobbes' Internet Timeline; an abbreviated list of selected significant events since TCP/IP was defined is given here.

- 1980: TCP/IP standards are defined. The modern Internet (as well as numerous private intranets) is built on this family of protocols and services.
- 1983: TCP/IP protocols are implemented by ARPANET.
- 1986: The National Science Foundation (NSF) connects the five new supercomputer centers with the NSFNET. These supercomputers were very expensive and in high demand, and the NSFNET was created to facilitate access to these centers across the country. This network used the same foundations and infrastructure of the then ARPANET. The NSF had strict guidelines for what constituted appropriate uses of this network. It prohibited commercial activities, which gave rise to a culture that still influences the Internet community even though it is clearly now highly commercialized. For instance, the open source software movement has some of its roots in the noncommercial culture of the Internet.
- 1990: The overlapping infrastructure and uses of the NSFNET and ARPANET result in the ARPANET disappearing as a separate entity, being supplanted by the NSFNET.
- 1991: The High Performance Computing Act is approved by Congress. This legislation, introduced by Senator Al Gore of Tennessee, authorizes the National Research and Education Network (NREN). Al Gore's involvement with this legislation gave rise to the "Al Gore invented the Internet" mythology. Actually, Gore never made that claim, and he can take some legitimate credit for being an early and prominent national voice regarding the potential of the Internet for research and education. Although NREN was legislatively approved, it did not become a separate networking entity; it did influence thinking and policy decisions about the role of government in supporting Internet access for educational and research purposes.
- 1991: The World Wide Web (WWW, aka the Web) is developed by Tim Berners-Lee at CERN (an acronym derived from Conseil Européen pour la Recherche Nucléaire). The Web really provided the first glimpse of the Internet to many. Berners-Lee, a consulting programmer, initially focused on the problem of document sharing within a specialized community, namely the physicists at CERN. As he explored a hypertext solution to this problem, he recognized it could have far broader implications for information sharing via the Internet. With the support of CERN, he went on to develop many of the protocols of the Web as well as the markup language needed to create Web content. The rest, as they say, is history (Berners-Lee, 1999).

- 1993: The MOSAIC browser is created and released by a team of programmers working at the National Center for Supercomputing Applications (NCSA) at the University of Illinois, Urbana-Champaign. The team included Marc Andreesen who would go on to form and lead Netscape Corporation. The development of this user-friendly, graphical browser brings the Internet and the emerging Web to a mass audience.
- 1995: The original NSFNET has evolved into an ever more commercialized Internet, so NSFNET reverts to its research roots and becomes a very high–speed network, again devoted to education and research. It will give rise to the Internet2 initiative.
- 1997: Internet2 is developed as a nonprofit consortium of over 170 U.S. universities and institutions. Its purpose is to support research and be a test-bed for new networking technologies.
- 1998: ICANN (Internet Corporation for Assigned Names and Numbers) is formed as a nonprofit private corporation with responsibility to coordinate the stable operation of the Internet in four key areas: the Domain Name System (DNS); the allocation of IP address space; the management of the root server system; and the coordination of protocol number assignment. ICANN reports to the U.S. Department of Commerce, but international pressures are building to reformulate this organization under an international umbrella such as the United Nations.

ADMINISTRATION OF THE INTERNET

The Internet is a complex information system heavily dependent on strict adherence to standards. It is global in reach, crossing all political and geographical boundaries, yet amazingly, there is no centralized governing authority in charge of its overall administration. It is somehow fitting that an entity that has resulted in a flattened, interconnected, and collaborative world is itself managed in a similarly decentralized and cooperative fashion. Internet administration involves interaction among international standards organizations, the private sector, and government agencies. The Internet Society (http://www.isoc.org) is an umbrella organization of hundreds of groups and thousands of individuals engaged in developing technologies and standards to maintain the viability and global scaling of the Internet. Examples of groups within the umbrella include standards groups such as the IETF (Internet Engineering Task Force) and IAB (Internet Architecture Board). A progression of different entities has been responsible for the critical area of domain space control. The first was the Network Information Centers (NIC), the official provider of Internet Domain Name Registration Services to the world for registration of domain names in the .COM, .NET and .ORG top-level domains (this is now an ICANN affiliate). InterNic (http://www.internic.net) provided the public with information regarding Internet domain name registration under the auspices of the U.S. Department of Commerce. Internet Assigned Numbers Authority (IANA) provided central control for domains, addresses, and protocols. Currently, the Internet Corporation for Assigned Names and Numbers (ICANN; http://www.icann.org), a nonprofit corporation, has taken over the role of naming and address space management from IANA. Another important body is the World Wide Web Consortium (W3C), which is responsible for developing and maintaining Web standards such as Hypertext Markup Language (HTML) and Extensible Markup Language (XML).

It is not hard to imagine that the various players involved in Internet policy and oversight have differing agendas that sometimes require government intervention to resolve. One example of the intersection of government regulation, policy groups, and market forces is the issue of *net neutrality*. This is primarily a policy issue, and the involved parties hold differing views. With net neutrality, all packets are equal; no packets are given "priority" status on the Internet over others. The controversy is whether this should remain the case or if there should be packet level discrimination for some services. There are those who believe that in order to maintain quality service for new applications such as Voice over Internet Protocol (VoIP), video streaming, or interactive games, high-speed Internet "lanes" should be available at the expense of net neutrality. Much of the pressure for this position comes from the telecommunications and cable companies. On the other hand, many search engines and software companies favor the current status quo of de facto net neutrality. The argument is also philosophical; some maintain mandating "net neutrality" would increase undesired government intervention with Internet bandwidth, while others believe abandoning net neutrality could result in less technical innovation. There is some precedent for supporting the premise of net neutrality within the umbrella of telecommunication law and previous government common carrier regulation. It will be interesting to watch how this policy debate develops over time.

IT FOUNDATIONS

In this text, a basic understanding of the computing technologies the Internet depends on is assumed; however, it may be necessary to review these topics in other sources depending on your existing knowledge of IT. The following is an overview of the topics that should be part of the working knowledgebase needed to understand this text.

Computers: The Binary Machine

Computer technology is the core engine of all IT. The modern computer is an electronic, digital device that can transform inputs into outputs under the control of a stored program. Throughout this book, the terms *computer* and *personal computer* (PC) are used somewhat interchangeably. Obviously, many types of computers exist, and the PC is a relative newcomer to the computer world. In addition, while the term *PC* is most often assumed to refer to Wintel systems, it can refer to any type of personal computer (Windows or Apple). The term *PC* is used generically in this book, but all the specific examples are PCs that are based on the Wintel platform (i.e., an Intel architecture running a version of Microsoft Windows).

There were early attempts to build nonelectronic computers or electronic analog ones. As early as the 1830s, Charles Babbage was designing and attempting to build mechanical computers, and Vannevar Bush of Memex fame worked on electronic analog computers in the 1920s.[1] However, the modern computer is a digital machine. The processors that are the "brains" of the computer on a very basic level are just extremely fast switching devices with millions of transistors. Although there is still interest in analog computers or digital–analog hybrids, digital technologies are far more prevalent, making it worthwhile to examine the distinctions between analog and digital technologies.

Throughout the twentieth century, the "electronics revolution" was an analog one and included the modern marvels of the telephone, phonograph, radio, and television. These analog technologies depend on electromagnetic waves as carriers of information. Waveforms have both amplitude and frequency; *amplitude* is a measure of the height of the waveform, and *frequency* is a measure of the number of cycles per second of a waveform. Wavelength is the distance from one peak to another and is inversely proportional to frequency; that is, shorter wavelengths have a greater number of cycles per second, as shown in Figure 1.1.

Information can be added to the carrier signal through signal modulation. For instance, AM radio depends on *amplitude modulation* where the information is added by varying the wave amplitude, shown in Figure 1.2. FM radio depends on *frequency modulation* where the wave frequency is varied, as shown in Figure 1.3. Phase modulation refers to a delay in the natural cycle of alternating current waveforms as a way to carry signal information. Another possibility is pulse code modulation (PCM) where the waveforms are interpreted to represent two states, which is an analog way to carry digital data.

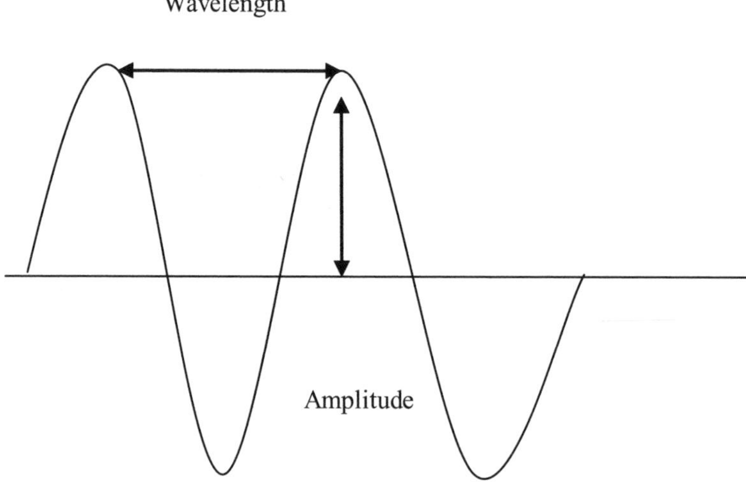

Figure 1.1 Waves have lengths and amplitude. Frequency is measured in cycles per second and is inversely proportional to wavelength.

In contrast to the continuous waveforms of analog data, digital data are represented in discrete increments. Computers and digital systems use binary numbers (0 and 1) to represent digital data. Analog to digital conversion using sampling technologies to represent the analog signal as discrete values and the sampling level determines how faithfully the analog content is captured. In the late 1940s at Bell Laboratories, mathematician Claude Shannon and others were working on the mathematics of sampling technologies. Bell Labs had a practical interest in sampling as it applies to voice communication systems.

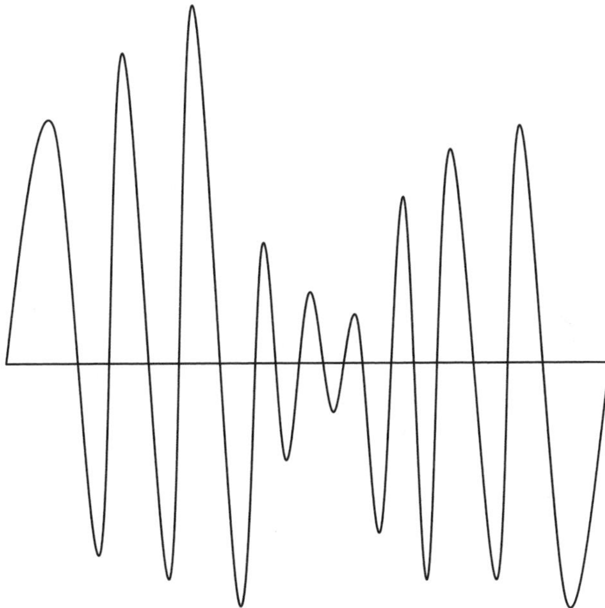

Figure 1.2 With AM, a source modulates the amplitude of a carrier wave.

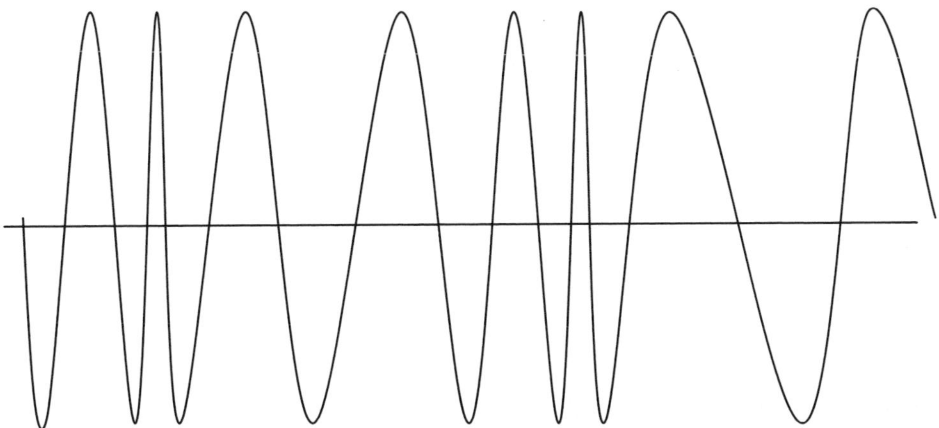

Figure 1.3 With FM, a source modulates the frequency of a carrier wave.

Analog to digital conversion requires a continuous time signal conversion to a discrete time one, which can then be used to reconstruct the original continuous signal when needed. The mathematics are complex, but the Nyquist-Shannon Sampling Theorem proved that a sampling rate equal to at least twice the bandwidth of the signal could adequately reconstitute the original by allowing the interpolation of data points between samplings during conversion (Shannon, 1949). The theorem name recognizes earlier related work by Harry Nyquist, also at Bell Labs. Inadequate sampling rates accentuate *aliasing*, which is a distortion or artifact of the sampling process. Sampling techniques are the basis of the many tools and programs developed to create digital representations that are very close to the original analog data. For instance, with commercial music CDs, a sampling rate of the original analog music of 44,100 times per second results in digital playback that is indistinguishable from the original to most human ears (Watkinson, 2000).

The modern computer is a binary, digital device. The computer is known as a binary machine for two reasons. First, computers use *binary numbers* to represent instructions and data. Second, computers are binary machines because the logic circuitry depends on a binary logic system known as *Boolean Logic*. Analog computers are possible but represent a more complex engineering problem than digital computers. Digital computers need only represent two possible states, which are then interpreted as the needed 0s and 1s. Representing two states is easier to engineer with simple switches or as the presence or absence of a magnetic charge on a disk. Within the computer, data and instructions in the form of bits move from one location to another using a *bus*, or circuit path. The number of bits moving in tandem depends on the width of this data bus, always in multiples of eight bits; it can be as narrow as 1 byte (1 byte is 8 bits) and as wide as 8 bytes in a PC. How can a digital data stream be transmitted over an analog connection like a telephone line? This is the job of a *modem*, a modulator/demodulator. This device modulates the computer's digital stream into an analog form for transmission. The demodulator in the receiving computer converts the analog signal back to a digital one. Modem technologies are an important connection technology, discussed again in Chapter 3.

Knowledge of these fundamental ideas is useful, not only as they apply to computing technology, but in a variety of other IT contexts in this text. For instance, understanding binary numbering is essential to basic topics such as how data representation codes and Internet protocols developed for text standards. Binary numbers are essential to the topics of IP addressing, subnet masks, and the encoding schemes needed to convert binary data to a text representation. (See the appendix for additional discussion of binary numbers.)

Client–Server Architecture

Another important concept is client–server architecture, an essential structure to almost every activity that takes place on the Internet. This important idea can be confusing depending on the context in which the terminology is used. Client–server architecture utilizes two pieces of software designed to work together: The client's job is to formulate a request to the corresponding server software, which in turn responds to the request. This correspondence usually takes place via a specific communication channel known as a *port.* On the Internet there are many such software pairings communicating with each other: mail clients with mail servers; telnet clients with telnet servers; FTP clients with FTP servers; Web clients with Web servers. Often each of these servers is on hardware dedicated to the server function, but it is the software that is critical to the definition of this architecture. A desktop PC could be running both client and server programs concurrently, thereby performing both roles.

THE INTERNET AND TECHNOLOGY TRENDS

The Internet has driven huge changes in how computing and IT are used, affecting the knowledgebase required by those planning to create new information services and instruct others in their use. Over the last 20 years, there have been dramatic changes in computer and storage technologies, bandwidth availability and capacity, and the use of the Internet in business and for human collaboration. The first of these core changes is how users now perceive the computer itself.

Computing to Connecting

The Internet is largely responsible for a major paradigm shift regarding computer technology that has occurred during the brief life span of the PC, a shift from "crunching" to "communicating." When computers were first developed, they were viewed primarily as computational devices able to do large scale, complex number crunching and symbol manipulation to support business and science. This was still the predominant view of computers when the PC was introduced. The first PCs were primarily marketed to small businesses and individual early adopters. These early users needed to be quite enthusiastic about the technology, as first-generation PCs were relatively expensive and not particularly user friendly. During the last several decades, the cost of computing has declined significantly, and power has increased dramatically. These trends are consistent with the expectations of Moore's Law,[2] which has been extrapolated to most everything related to computing. For instance, in 1971, an Intel 4004 had approximately 2,300 transistors and was capable of about 60,000 instructions per second. By 2005, Intel reported P4 Itanium processors with 410 million transistors performing about 10,800 MIPS or about 10.8 billion instructions per second (Friedman, 2005). The change has been equally dramatic when cost is considered. The first hard drives for the original PC were 10 megabytes (MB) and added about $1,000 to the price. Now 160 GB iPods no larger than a deck of cards have about 16,000 times the capacity for one quarter of the cost.

Even with computing power increasing and prices declining, PC sales did not really accelerate until the emergence of the Web in the early 1990s. According to the U.S. Census, the number of homes with computers grew from 15 percent in 1990 to 56 percent by 2001, and homes with Internet access in the United States went from 18 percent in 1997 to 54.3 percent in 2003 (U.S.

Census, 2006). Other factors such as lower prices and better operating systems contributed to the rapid growth in the PC market during that decade, but a major factor was the realization that computers could now connect you to information, people, and other useful services. The comparison of the Internet with previous mass-communication technologies is also compelling evidence of its success. It took radio 38 years to reach 50 million listeners and 13 years for television to reach that number of viewers. The Web reached that many users in North America in about 5 years. These numbers are not standardized for population size and economic conditions of these eras, but the learning curve associated with using the Web (such as purchasing a PC and configuring it to work with an ISP) adds to the impressiveness of its rapid acceptance by the public.

Bandwidth

An essential requirement for the computer to become an effective communication device is the availability and development of a connection infrastructure with sufficient bandwidth to support the associated activities and resulting volume of packets. *Bandwidth* is a measure of the capacity of a medium to carry a signal. Bandwidth developments have experienced the same type of self-reinforcing cycle computer technology has; namely, greater demand has resulted in more technological innovation, higher capacity, and lower cost, which creates more demand. The Internet was made possible by an existing telephone network infrastructure available throughout the developed world. Up until 1991, the original NSFNET backbone service used leased T-1 lines that could only carry 1.5 Mbps (millions of bits per second). In the "Before Web" Internet, the main backbone service of the entire Internet had less bandwidth than many home DSL or cable broadband Internet connections have today. This also means the "After Web" Internet is not just for email anymore as high-capacity bandwidth enables services such as VoIP, audio streaming, and real-time video conferencing. There continue to be huge advances in these connection technologies; for instance, fiber optic technologies are being developed to carry 1 terabit per second on a single fiber strand, which is hundreds of thousands of times the capacity of the original T1 lines. Wireless networking is also contributing to the increase in bandwidth and eliminating many of the barriers associated with a wired environment. Wireless connections and powerful portable computing devices are making Internet access possible without tethering network connections, giving rise to a seamless Internet experience more fully integrated into daily life.

Open Source Software

The *open source* software movement is an interesting trend with broad implications for many organizations, including libraries. Open source is a model of software development that provides free access to programs created and supported by developers and users themselves. The Internet has played a significant role in the success of this model by fostering a culture of open access, facilitating the virtual communities collaborating to develop and support complex applications, as well as providing a global distribution framework for the resulting programs. The notion of open source being free does not imply there are no economic costs; in fact, there are costs in terms of people or fee-based support needed to implement open source solutions. However, the programs are free in the context of source code that is available to developers to download, modify, and adapt to meet specific needs.

There are many important open source applications being used in libraries, such as the Firefox Web browser, the Apache Web server software, and the Linux operating system used for Web servers. Many libraries are also using MySQL (an open source relational database recently acquired by Sun Microsystems) for relational databases, often in conjunction with PHP scripting, another open environment. In addition to databases, general productivity applications such as Open Office provide an alternative to proprietary productivity applications. There are even open source alternatives for Library Management Systems such as Koha (http://koha.org/support/), as well as programs to support digital library initiatives such as Greenstone (http://www.greenstone.org/cgi-bin/library).

Internet-Based Collaboration

Another important trend is the use of powerful collaborative and networking tools such as blogs, news feeds and aggregators, podcasts, and collaborative content management. Really Simple Syndication (RSS) is the foundation protocol of many of these tools and is an example of XML technology. The idea of "syndication" is broadly familiar from other communication business models. For instance, a newspaper syndicate is a group of papers under the direction of a single company; in the context of RSS, it is an option to subscribe to an information source.

Blogs have become one of the hot topics of the last several years, and they are examined in more detail in the chapter on Internet content. The name is derived from the term "Web log." Blogs are a Web-published narrative of an individual or group who syndicates the content to subscribers and creates a shared and regularly updated source of commentary. The blogger frames the discussion, initiates the threads, and decides if and how comments can be added. Some blogs are very personal narratives, and others focus on a particular subject area. The software to create and manage blogs can be managed on a server the blogger controls or placed on a Web-hosting service such as Bloglines (http://www.bloglines.com/) or Blogger.com (http://www.blogger.com/start). Local reader software or a reader Web site is used for viewing the syndicated content of RSS feeds.

Another collaborative software tool is the Wiki, developed by Ward Cunningham (Bishop, 2004). The name is from the Hawaiian for "quick" and refers to software enabling anyone to add or edit Web content without having to know HTML or any details about the hosting platform. Wikis have become an important source of Internet-based reference, such as the online encyclopedia at wikipedia.com, but they also present opportunities to build and share many forms of content. Wikis are being used to create internal knowledge bases, collaboratively update committee and meeting reports, manage specialized subject pages, support online course content, and present conference programming. Wikis can also be used to further organizational goals by engaging outside constituent communities and facilitate the gathering and sharing of their input and ideas.

The Internet and Commerce

One measure of the success of the Internet is Web commerce. According to the U.S. Census (2008), Americans spent over $127 billion in 2007 on ecommerce. Networks and digital resources remove the physical constraints inherent in the economic models of the past, giving rise to new paradigms as described by Anderson in "The Long Tail" (2004). This refers to how a graph of demand for consumer items (books, music, videos, etc.) shows a large peak for the popular and a gradually declining level of demand for the less popular. In the physical world, this curve would likely go to zero, as the item would become less and less available once its sales start to decline. In a retail environment with limited space, it is logical to weed less popular items in favor of more popular ones. However, in the digital world, everything can theoretically remain available because storage space constraints are not a major concern, and the global reach of the Internet increases the likelihood that a sustainable niche market exists for these items. The power of search enables an audience to find items in the "long tail" portion of the graph. This idea is visualized in Figure 1.4.

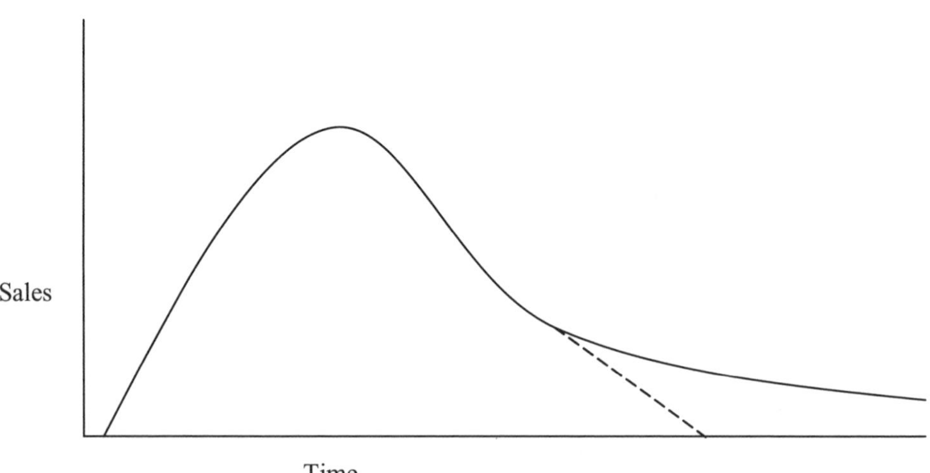

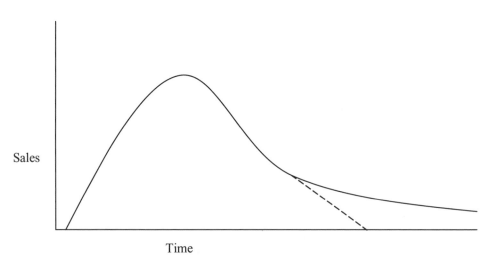

Figure 1.4 The Long Tail (after Anderson, 2004). The sales cycle of a successful consumer item will peak, but as its popularity wanes, valuable shelf space will be given to a new more popular item, and both sales and availability will decrease to zero (dashed line). However, in the digital world where the item can still be available, demand will taper off into the "long tail" portion of the graph that continues along the x-axis. This small but ongoing demand could cumulatively result in more total sales over time than that of the initial peak.

This phenomenon is being observed in many digital businesses; for instance, millions of songs are bought from iTunes each month, and the movie service Netflix passed the "billion served" mark within just a few years of operation. A concurrent decline of traditional media occurred during this period; for instance, television network market share has fallen 33 percent over the 20 years ending in 2005, and music CD sales are down 21 percent from their peak in 1999 (Nielson Media Research in Storey, 2005). Newspapers have also declined, while Internet use has gained; in the decade since 1994, overall newspaper circulation fell by 7.9 percent (Sloan, 2006). These trends all apply to the operational assumptions of libraries and other information businesses as they continue to provide access to more and more full-text materials in digital form via the Internet. The impact of these trends and technologies on libraries is explored further in Chapter 16.

SUMMARY

The Internet and the related Web technologies have changed the world, providing both new opportunities and new challenges. Looking ahead, it seems inevitable the pace of change will continue or accelerate, and the Internet will continue to drive much of this change. Although it does seem at times that the Internet has *changed everything*, a few qualifying points should be made about this sweeping generalization. First, the pre-Web Internet certainly was a change agent with the *potential* to change everything, but the post-Web Internet has driven much of the actual change that matters to most. Internet advocates in pre-Web environment sometimes used the "Field of Dreams" reference of "If you build it, they will come" to describe how they anticipated the Internet would change the world. However, much of the anticipated change did not really occur until the emergence of the Web, so it seems a more realistic statement is, "If you build it, *make it really easy to use and important to people's lives*, they will come." That said, the Internet gave birth to the Web, and Internet technologies continue to be at the center of the digital convergence emerging from the mix of cheap and powerful computers, nearly limitless bandwidth, and useful net applications. This convergence is giving rise to new generations of the Web, referred to as Web 2.0 and the predicted Web 3.0. However one views the Internet today, it definitely seems to have the applications and sufficient critical mass to remain a powerful engine of change.

Second, while emphasizing the positive impact of the opportunities the Internet has created for society and for libraries in particular, there is a dark side as well. Pornography and filtering requirements have created many administrative and ethical issues for organizations providing public Internet access. Privacy and security concerns occupy much of the daily attention of Internet users, and spam is estimated to comprise as much as 80 percent of all email (Zeller, 2005). Misconceptions about the value and usefulness of Internet resources; inappropriate materials; the long-term preservation of net-available digital resources; the potential for plagiarism; the cavalier attitude of some regarding copyright; and strategies for digital rights management that may limit fair use are just a few of the new issues that are part of the Internet story.

NOTES

1. In his 1945 article "As we may think" in the *Atlantic Monthly*, Bush described an electronic desktop capable of viewing a self-contained microfilm collection, bringing the universe of knowledge to the desktop, a scenario that has largely come to fruition with a PC connected to the Internet.
2. Moore's Law is derived from the observation in the 1960s by Intel's Gordon Moore that the number of transistors on an integrated circuit doubled every 18 months, while prices declined at a similar rate.

REFERENCES

Anderson, C. (2004, October). The long tail. *Wired Magazine, 12,* 170–177.

Berners-Lee, T. (1999). *Weaving the Web: The original design and ultimate destiny of the World Wide Web by its inventor.* New York: HarperCollins.

Bishop, T. (2004, January 26). Microsoft Notebook: Wiki pioneer planted the seed and watched it grow. Retrieved October 2007, from http://seattlepi.nwsource.com/business/158020_msftnotebook26.html.

Bush, V. (1945). As we may think. *Atlantic Monthly, 176,* 101–108.

Friedman, T. L. (2005). *The world is flat: A brief history of the twenty-first century.* New York: Farrar, Straus, and Giroux.

Leiner, B. M., Cerf, V. G., Clark, D. D., Kahn, R. E., Kleinrock, L., Lynch, D. C., et al. (1997). The past and future history of the Internet. *Communications of the ACM, 40*(2), 102–109.

Shannon, C. (1949). Communication in the presence of noise. *Proceedings of the Institute of Radio Engineers, 37*(1), 10–21.

Sloan, S. (2006, February 19). Inklings of change—inside the potential sale of Knight Ridder: Industry pressures, technology advances put print journalism and Herald-Leader at a crossroads. *Lexington Herald Leader,* p. A16.

Storey, T. (2005). The long tail and libraries. *OCLC Newsletter, 268,* 6–10.

U.S. Census. (2006). Computer and Internet use in the United States: 2003. Retrieved October 1, 2007, from http://www.census.gov/population/pop-profile/dynamic/Computers.pdf.

U.S. Census. (2008, May 15). Quarterly retail e-commerce sales. Retrieved May 22, 2008, from http://www.census.gov/mrts/www/ecomm.html.

Watkinson, J. (2000). *The art of digital audio* (3rd ed.). Oxford: Focal Press.

Zakon, R. (2006, November 1). Hobbes' Internet Timeline. Retrieved May 1, 2008, from http://www.zakon.org/robert/internet/timeline/.

Zeller, T., Jr. (2005, February 1). Law barring junk e-mail allows a flood instead. *New York Times,* p. A1.

Chapter 2

Networks

Computer networks have facilitated the transformation of the computer from a number crunching device into a communication device. The development of local computing networks presents many advantages and opportunities for resource sharing within an organization; these opportunities are even more compelling when extended to the global Internet. An understanding of basic network terminology and concepts, as well as the basic strategies and topologies networks employ, is necessary to the subsequent discussion in later chapters of how networks can be extended into a global scale through the Internet.

NETWORK BASICS

The term *networking* obviously precedes the computer revolution of the twentieth century, and it occurs in both technical and nontechnical contexts. There are radio and television networks, cable and satellite networks, telephone communication networks, and library consortium networks. So networking can be something done with computer hardware or with people at a professional meeting. In this chapter, networking is examined strictly in the technical context of connecting computers together for data communication and resource sharing.

Connecting computers and users together with networks facilitates resource sharing and has driven the "computing to communicating" paradigm shift responsible for the success of the modern PC; isolated PCs had limited usefulness to most people. Networking computers together has a cost, both in terms of hardware and human effort to manage and maintain them, but the payoff is the ability to share resources such as printers, disk space, data files, and applications across an organization. To accomplish this goal, three elements are essential, represented by the "3 Cs" of networks: *computers, connections,* and a *common language.* Each of these elements requires specialized hardware and software. The examples focus on PC networks, but all computers, from minicomputers to mainframes, are likely to be part of a network. The network now also extends to many other devices including various handheld Personal Digital Assistants (PDAs) such as the Apple iPod Touch.

Networks of limited scale and geographical coverage are Local Area Networks (LANs), and multiple LANs can be connected together in a Wide-Area Network (WAN). This hierarchy is also evident in the context of the Internet; PCs connect to LANs, which connect to WANs, which may connect to regional networks and finally to the Internet backbone service.

THE OSI NETWORK REFERENCE MODEL

To set the stage for this discussion of networks, it is helpful to examine the conceptual framework referenced in their design. The developers of all computer networks face a similar set of problems to address, and engineers have developed a reference model to formalize them. The Open System Interconnect (OSI) reference model is a framework for conceptualizing the various functions a network must handle, representing them as a series of seven layers. Tang and Scoggins (1992) provide extensive coverage of OSI. As the name implies, this is a reference model, not a plan for a specific network implementation. It is a way of identifying the various issues that real designs must consider, and actual designs might expand or compress some of these seven layers. For instance, TCP/IP combines various OSI layers to result in four layers.

Computer and network technologies utilize designs compartmentalized into layers that can communicate with adjacent layers. The standalone PC has layers at work to manage the chain of events between the user and the hardware, as shown in Figure 2.1.

People use applications, which in turn talk to the operating system (OS), which talks to the BIOS (Basic Input/Output System), which communicates with the hardware. Without these intervening layers, users would need to work directly with circuits and chips. When a PC is added to a network, the networking software creates other layers between users, applications, and the operating system. For an Internet-connected computer, there must be a TCP/IP layer above the OS, and a Winsock (for "Windows Socket") is used to plug Windows applications into the TCP/IP stack. The OSI model uses a similar

Layer:
User
Application
OS
BIOS
Hardware

Figure 2.1 System layers for a standalone PC.

type of hierarchy to identify the various functions the network must address, as shown in Figure 2.2.

KEY CONCEPTS AND TERMINOLOGY

There are a few key concepts and terms to introduce before discussing specific hardware, topologies, and protocols. Each device connected to the network is a *node.* This is very often a *computer,* the first of the 3 Cs. However, nodes can be computers, printers, hubs, or many other network devices. Networks are divided into *segments,* which are subsets of the nodes managed as a group within the larger network. Segments are bounded by devices such as routers, bridges, or hubs, which control the flow of packets (addressable chunks of digital data) to a group of nodes. Segments optimize network performance by grouping together users and devices that share data.

Nodes are connected through some medium, and the capacity of the medium to carry a signal is its *bandwidth.* In earlier applications, bandwidth was a measure of the range of frequencies possible with analog electronic communication. In the context of digital technologies, bandwidth is measured in terms of the number of bits transmitted per second. This is analogous to the idea of water moving in a pipe. The measure of bandwidth can be thought of as the "diameter of the pipe"; the larger the diameter, the more volume it can carry per unit of time. Similarly, higher network bandwidth carries higher volumes of data per unit of time. Interdevice communication takes place according to a set of rules referred to as a *protocol,* enforced via software. Internet communication takes place through a channel known as a *port,* which is assigned to the specific client–server application. Logical ports made through these client–server software assignments are not the same as physical computer communication ports such as the familiar serial, USB, or parallel connections.

The connections created among nodes may use physical wires, wireless radio signals, or a combination of the two. Wired connections may use shielded coaxial cable (thin wire) or unshielded twisted pair wiring such as that used for telephone wiring. Wired networks utilize some *topology,* which refers to the physical layout of the wired connections.

Finally, computer networks generally move data across a medium by creating *packets.* Packet switching is a process in which data are broken up into

Layer	Function
7 Application layer	What users see
6 Presentation layer	Translation formats
5 Session layer	Opening and closing of sessions
4 Transport layer	Delivery of packets
3 Network layer	Packets from data layer get addressed and routed
2 Data link layer	Packet formation and error correction
1 Physical layer	Hardware and movement of bits

Figure 2.2 OSI reference model layers.

smaller pieces, addressed according to a set of rules, and transmitted across the network.

NETWORK HARDWARE

There are many dedicated types of hardware involved in the connection between a PC and the Internet. These components include the network interface device on a local computer, which allows it to be connected to the network, and the hubs, switches, bridges, and routers that manage the various network segments and direct network traffic.

The Network Interface Card

The computers or other devices added to a network need dedicated hardware to support the connection. Connection hardware is usually present in the form of an integrated Ethernet port or is added later with the purchase of a separate Network Interface Card (NIC). As with all devices associated with a PC, an associated piece of software called a *driver* is required to mediate between the NIC and the operating system. In the PC system layers, the applications in use communicate with this driver through an Application Programming Interface (API), which allows an application to "talk" to the network.

Ethernet network or cable modem connections are common, and most PCs have an integrated port to support this type of cable connection. All NICs have a hardware address associated with them that is used by the network to identify a node. This is its Media Access Control (MAC) address; for an Ethernet port, the MAC address is specifically an Ethernet address (EA). This address may be used directly by the network to address packets, or mapped to some other type of address, such as an Internet Protocol (IP) address. The correspondence of the MAC addresses and IP addresses is explained in Chapter 4.

Packet Forwarding and Routing Hardware

How do packets coming to or from some networked PC make their journey to a network destination? For an Ethernet connected PC, the lowest level device the packets might encounter is a *hub.* A hub is an OSI physical layer device enabling multiple connections to a virtual bus or star, which are discussed in the next section. A hub only sees bit streams, not packet addresses; it connects all the devices on a particular network segment and forwards all the traffic coming to it to all those devices. With a hub, only one device can use the network at a time. If the packets need to move across different network segments or to another LAN using the same protocol, they might use another lower-level device called a *bridge.* A bridge is a device connecting two different network segments at the OSI data-link level. Bridges can filter packets based on their addresses. The packets might also encounter a "smarter than your average hub" device called a *switch.* A switch on an Ethernet network can actually use the MAC addresses associated with the frames (Ethernet packets) and filter the packet stream; it forwards the packets only to the device with the correct address. This is different from a hub, where all devices get the packets whether they are the intended destination or not; the filtering instead takes place at the destination device. Not only are switches more efficient, they allow for better security management. For instance, if a computer on a hub is infected with a worm program and is causing network problems, the network administrator may elect to cut off access to the entire hub until the problem is resolved, taking all the computers on the hub offline along with the problem machine. With a switch, control at the individual port connection level is possible, allowing the isolation of the specific MAC address associated with the individual problem host.

Finally, the packets may encounter a *router*, a device designed to forward packets between networks or segments. Routers use IP addresses, and it is their job to determine if the packets are destined for a location within the network or for some outside Internet destination. They also determine the best path for packets to get where they are going. Routers make the first determination by the application of a subnet mask. Once the packet destination is known, the best path to the destination is determined. Routers have software allowing them to "talk" to each other; they broadcast messages and use the responses to determine the networks to which they are connected. This information is used to build forwarding tables, allowing the efficient forwarding of packets. How routers apply a subnet mask and use the Address Resolution Protocol (ARP) to manage packet flow is discussed in Chapter 4.

WIRED NETWORK TOPOLOGIES

The *connections* needed for a network comprise the second "C" of the 3 Cs. They are typically a physical cable or wire, although wireless networks are becoming quite commonplace as well, as evidenced by a Pew Report Survey that found that 34 percent of all Internet users had made use of a wireless connection by the end of 2006 (Horrigan, 2007). Wireless is becoming a popular solution, but wired networks are still a common connection strategy for many businesses, schools, and libraries. Wired networks utilize a *topology* or a map of how the connections are made, much as a topological map shows the contours of the earth. The standard wiring topologies usually utilize a bus, ring, or star scheme but can utilize more complex hybrid approaches such as a *tree* combining a bus and a star, or a partial or full *mesh*, which provides many redundant data paths. Charles (1997) and Molyneux (2003) are good sources for more detailed discussions of LAN topologies.

The simplest network to create is a *peer-to-peer* (P2P) connection between two computers. In this approach, there is no central server and little needed hardware. A direct connection between the two computer Ethernet ports is made with a crossover cable, which looks identical to an Ethernet cable but has a crossed wire arrangement in the connectors at each end. The PC operating system itself handles the connection and facilitates sharing of resources on each host.

In a *bus topology*, each node comes off the connecting backbone wire in a linear series as shown in Figure 2.3. Many simple LANs used a bus topology with thin wire coaxial cable looping through each node to the next. In this topology, all nodes see all traffic.

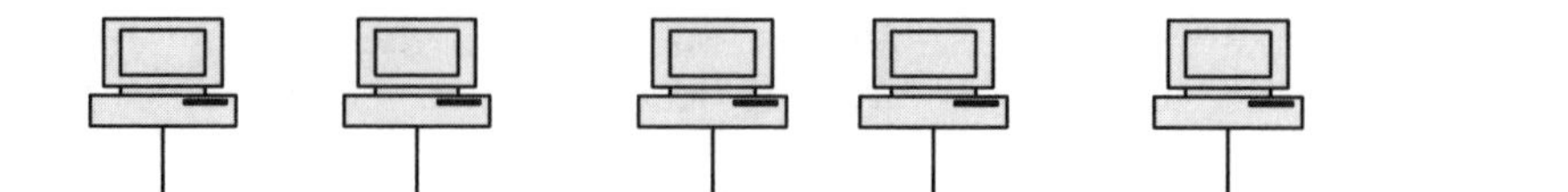

Figure 2.3 A bus topology.

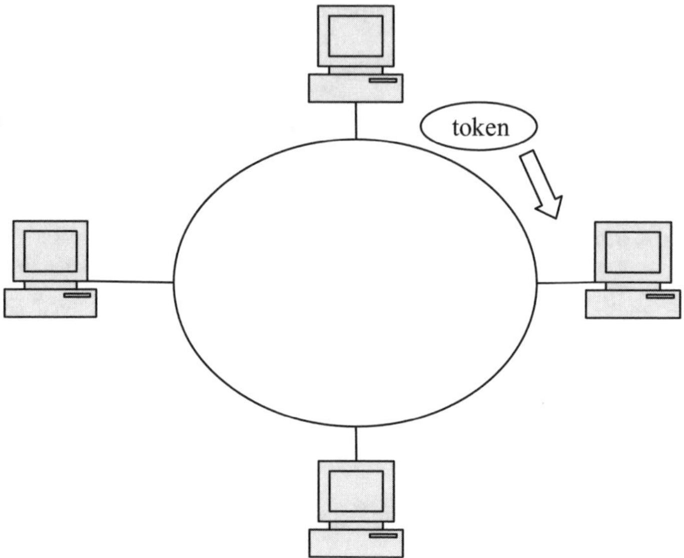

Figure 2.4 A token ring topology.

Ring networks usually utilize token passing; hence they are known as *token ring* networks. In the ring approach, computers are connected together in a circular arrangement, and a special packet, called the *token,* moves around to each node and determines what device can send data, as shown in Figure 2.4.

In a *star* configuration, wires to nodes radiate out from a central server, as shown in Figure 2.5. Many Ethernet networks use a modified star scheme to connect nodes to a central hub.

A *tree* network is a hybrid of a bus and a star, with potentially multiple stars coming off a central bus. It is also possible to combine stars and rings as a hybrid approach. Computer networks can also use a full or partial mesh. In a full mesh, every node is connected to every other node. This ensures direct communication between every pair of devices, but the wiring requirements become quite cumbersome as the number of nodes increases. Figure 2.6 shows an example of a full mesh.

Wired networks utilize twisted pair copper wire or various types of coaxial cable; fiber optic strands are a high-speed connection option. Discussion of the detailed specifications associated with the various types of wired networks is beyond the scope of this overview. The complex standards establishing the

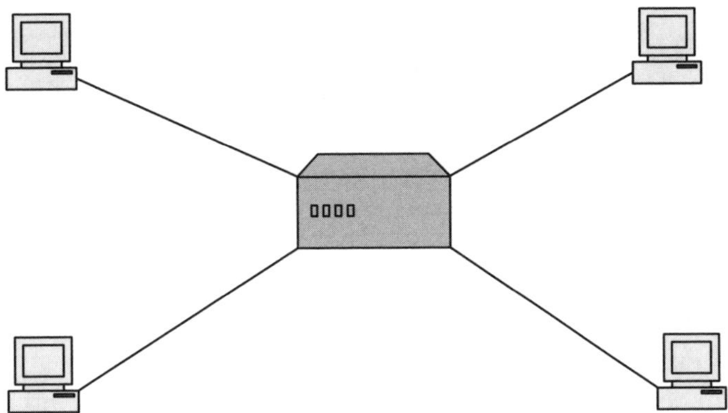

Figure 2.5 A star network topology.

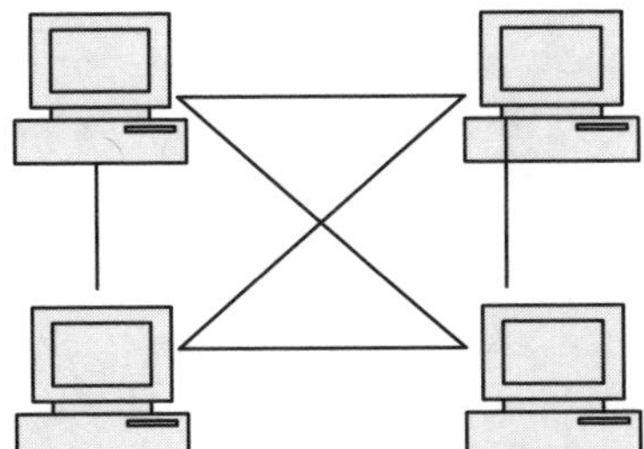

Figure 2.6 A full mesh network.

types and gauges of wiring, the distance they can cover and still maintain a reliable connection, conduit specifications, and other requirements must be thoroughly investigated in the network planning stage. Establishing a wired network in an existing older building can have significant hidden costs associated with adding the dedicated conduit needed for some networks. Some network cable is shielded; Ethernet unshielded twisted pair (UTP) wire is not. Unshielded wire is inexpensive and easier to pull through long runs, but it is susceptible to electromagnetic field (EMF) effects that can interfere with data transmission. Moving current in electrical wiring can have inductive effects on the Ethernet wire when they are in close proximity to each other. Therefore, Ethernet UTP wiring is physically isolated from electrical wiring in the runs from the hub to the node locations. Eliminating the need to add conduit is one advantage of wireless networks planned for buildings without Ethernet infrastructure in place, or where it would be prohibitively expensive to install.

PROTOCOLS: RULES FOR A COMMON LANGUAGE

The third "C" of the 3 Cs stands for a *common language.* Many different types of computers are networked together, and each uses its own OS language. How can all these different kinds of computers communicate with each other? They do so by way of network protocols that provide the needed common language. Protocol rules are implemented through software that might be part of the operating systems, such as TCP/IP with Windows, or installed later when the network is created. In addition, there may be protocols within protocols, and they may apply to different layers in the OSI model. For instance, the simple network management protocol (SNMP) is part of the TCP/IP suite designed to serve the many types of data, devices, and connectivity at the application level in various network implementations (Cisco Systems, 2008).

There are two fundamentally different approaches to how communication networks can connect nodes; one is *circuit switching,* and the other is *packet switching.* These approaches are not mutually exclusive in modern telephone or data networks; for instance, Telco service uses digital switching backbone service with analog local loop connections.

Circuit switching has a long history going back to the early telecommunication networks of the nineteenth century. The telegraph and the standard analog telephone service over copper wire are good examples of circuit-switching networks. You can visualize the idea of this technology by thinking of the old movies with telephone operators working a switchboard, where the operator made a direct circuit connection between callers. This part of the network was then unavailable to other users until they disconnected to free the connection. In contrast, computer networks generally use packet switching, which is a fundamentally different approach. The data are broken up into small, discrete packets and put into a digital "envelope" with a source and a destination address. The packets are transmitted over a network along with lots of other unrelated packets all headed toward their destination. A good physical analogy for this process is the postal service. When a letter is sent by "snail mail," the data are "encapsulated" in an envelope, which has been given a "From" and "To" address along with appropriate postage, all according to a specific set of rules (or protocols). This physical data packet is dropped into a mailbox along with lots of other unrelated packets and is forwarded to its ultimate destination by a routing process. The Internet depends on a particular packet switching technology called TCP/IP (Transmission Control Protocol/Internet Protocol), which is the subject of Chapter 4.

In packet switching communications, the network protocols control packet formation, size, header formats, addressing, and error detection. Because different kinds of networks are often part of a communication hierarchy, packets can carry packets within packets. For instance, an Ethernet packet (an Ethernet frame) can carry an IP packet as its data, which in turn carries a TCP packet. There are different types of packet technologies, each dependent on a network operating system (NOS). Novell-based LANs for instance, use a packet technology called IPX/SPX (Internetwork Packet Exchange/Sequenced Packet Exchange). When networks that use different protocols are joined together, specialized devices called gateways reside at that interface to handle the needed protocol translation.

Many networks use a central network server running a NOS as well as client software on each computer node. There have been a number of NOS software solutions from different companies over the years, and both Novell and Microsoft have a significant share of this market. Some local area implementations use the Internet protocols of TCP/IP; such LANs are *intranets.*

ETHERNET

Ethernet is a commonplace network standard used in many organizations. Although Ethernet networks often provide access to the Internet, they are not synonymous; Ethernet can be the medium by which an Internet connection is made, but Ethernet access does not in itself equate to Internet access. The Ethernet standard and TCP/IP interact with very distinct layers in the OSI reference model; Ethernet functions at the lowest OSI levels, namely the physical and data link layers. The name itself comes from this physical communication medium function; the *ether* of *Ethernet* is a reference to the pervasive ether nineteenth-century physicists erroneously postulated was a necessary medium for light waves to travel through otherwise empty space.

What follows is a brief review of Ethernet networks; Bhola (2002), Simoneau (1997), and Molyneux (2003) are good sources for additional detail on both the history and use of Ethernet networks. Robert Metcalfe developed the first Ethernet specification at Xerox Palo Alto Research Center (PARC) in 1973. This was revised in 1982 and released as Ethernet II by Digital Equipment Corp, Intel, and Xerox (this is also referred to as DIX Ethernet from the names of the companies involved). The following year, the Institute of Electrical and Electronics Engineers (IEEE) released the 802.3 standard for CSMA/CD networks; CSMA/CD is an Ethernet technology discussed later in this chapter. The number in the name refers to a working group charged in February 1980 to develop this standard; thus "802" is derived from the year and month the charge was given. The later IEEE 802.3 standard is different from the earlier Ethernet II in the structure of the address header. Both headers use 6 bytes (48 bits) for source and destination addresses, but the final two bytes of an Ethernet II header contain "Ether Type" codes for protocol type information, such as one indicating IPv4, whereas the IEEE 802.3 header has packet data length information in its header location. The 802.3 standard supports connection speeds of 1.0 Mbps, 100 Mbps, and 1,000 Mbps.

Wiring specifications are included in the Ethernet standard, and an understanding of the different wiring options is necessary because not all wiring supports all Ethernet speeds. Early versions of Ethernet used both thick and thin wire shielded coaxial cable, but most now use inexpensive and easy to work with UTP copper wiring similar to that used for telephone wiring, but with different connector jacks. Common Ethernet implementations include 10base-T and 100Base-T. The number followed by the word "base" refers to the speed possible and use of a baseband signal; the "T" is for twisted pair. For instance, 10base-T is 10 Mbps (millions of bits per second) of bandwidth with a baseband signal running on UTP wire. This standard has continued to develop, yielding ever-higher speeds with both 100 Mbps (100Base-T) and gigabit Ethernet (1000Base-T) now available. These standards each require different wiring; category 3 (Cat-3) wiring is sufficient for 10Base-T, but category-5 (Cat-5) is required for 100Base-T in order to obtain the maximum bandwidth. This problem occurred on our local network when a hub was upgraded to a newer switch.

There was some older Cat-3 wiring in place, which could not support the higher bandwidth now available. The result was the connection speed to those ports had to be reduced at the switch to a level supported by Cat-3. There are also restrictions on the distance Ethernet cables can run; the cable length is usually limited to 100 meters unless other devices repeat or boost the signal. In addition to UTP, there is a fiber cable standard for Ethernet.

Besides wiring standards, Ethernet has its own protocols to control packet formation and addressing, as well as technologies to deal with corrupted packets or packet collisions. Because packets share the same connections, collisions are possible, and computer networks need protocols to either prevent, or respond to, packet collisions. Token ring networks prevent collisions with a special packet called a token that restricts which node can send packets. This is an efficient way to prevent collisions but not a very efficient overall strategy for large networks, because any computer with data to send must wait for the token to pass through many nodes with no data to send. Ethernet uses a different approach called CSMA/CD, which stands for carrier sense, multiple access, with collision detection. The carrier signal tells all connected devices they can send data (packets); "multiple access" means many computers can send data at the same time. The protocol detects and resends packets if two computers send packets at the exact same time and they collide. Ethernet packets are frames, and like all packet schemes, there is a fair amount of overhead along with the bit stream of data. Figure 2.7 shows an Ethernet frame.

As Figure 2.7 shows, an essential part of the Ethernet frame is the six bytes set aside for source and destination addresses. These hardware addresses are called MAC addresses (or Ethernet addresses); every Ethernet frame must record both the source and destination MAC address in the locations shown in Figure 2.7. Six bytes are reserved to represent the MAC address, which means there are 48 bits used for these addresses. From this (and an understanding of binary numbers), it is deduced there are two to the 48th power (2^{48}) possible Ethernet addresses, an astronomically high number. Because people often actually have to work with these addresses for a number of network administration reasons, it is obviously not convenient to deal with 48-bit numbers in binary representation (although computers do not mind at all). To make these long numbers easier to handle, they are expressed in hexadecimal (base 16). This is because binary (base 2) converts easily to hex, and it also makes long binary numbers much more compact. For instance, four binary digits (called a "nybble" or half a byte) could be represented with two decimal digits or a single hexadecimal digit. The equivalency is: $\mathbf{1111}_{(base\ 2)} = \mathbf{15}_{(base\ 10)} = \mathbf{f}_{(base\ 16)}$.

Extending this idea, 16 binary digits can be written with four hexadecimal digits, which means the 48-bit Ethernet addresses can be written with 3 sets of 4 hexadecimal digits, such as in the hex number: **310b.11e9.f432.**

Preamble (2 bytes)	Destination (6 bytes)	Source (6 bytes)	Type (2 bytes)	Data (46–1,500 bytes)	FCS (4 bytes)

Figure 2.7 An Ethernet frame.

Because many Ethernet-connected computers are a node on the Internet, the data the Ethernet frame carries might be an IP packet. A protocol called ARP manages correspondence between these two types of addresses, as discussed in Chapter 4.

WIRELESS NETWORKS

In the previous discussion of Ethernet, the medium carrying the signals was wire, but it is possible—and often desirable—to send packets as signals moving through the air instead. There are well-established successful communication networks predating digital technologies, such as radio and broadcast television, and more recently mobile phones. Aside from the obvious advantage of eliminating the need for wiring, Wireless LANs (WLANs) have a number of other distinct advantages. They are low cost, relatively easy to set up, flexible to implement, and quite scalable. For these reasons, they are a good choice for implementations ranging from the small home network to a large business enterprise network. Wireless fidelity, or Wi-Fi, is based on the 802.11 options described later permitting connections over a distance of 150–400 feet with speeds of 5–22 Mbps (CNET Wireless Resource Center, 2008b).

As described by Bhola (2002), the roots of today's WLANs go back to a 1971-era network called AlohaNet for data connections among three Hawaiian Islands. Developed by Norman Abramson, it was the first use of radio waves to carry packet transmissions. The connection speeds were relatively slow by today's standards, but this basic idea evolved into the high-speed WLANs of today. WLAN technology began to appear as a local network solution starting in the mid-1990s using proprietary protocols that achieved connections of 1–2 Mbps. The need for a standard similar to Ethernet was apparent, and the IEEE worked with wireless vendors to develop the 802.11 WLAN standards in 1990, capable of 1.0 Mbps or 2.0 Mbps connection speeds. Rapid changes in the supporting technologies drove many extensions to the original standard, including 802.11b with speeds of 11 Mbps, and 802.11a, which uses higher frequencies permitting speeds up to 54 Mbps. Wireless networks now include the "third generation (wireless 3G) technology" allowing the integration of voice, data, and multimedia applications (CNET Wireless Resource Center, 2008a). Security is one of the concerns about WLAN connectivity. The idea that your packets are floating around in space for others to intercept certainly is a cause for concern and demands attention. The wireless device *Service Set Identifier* (SSID) can provide a minimum level of access control to a WLAN but is not highly secure because it is not encrypted and is often automatically assigned. This is a useful feature where unsecured access is needed in public spaces such as coffee shops and airports, but ease of connection comes at the expense of security. The 802.11b standard includes encryption. There are horror stories of serious lapses by organizations that have not done nearly enough to secure their wireless networks. For most organizations, especially government agencies or utility companies, ensuring high levels of network security must be a high priority. Just as Ethernet connections do not necessarily mean an Internet connection exists, WLAN technologies do not necessarily equate to Internet access. Further discussion of wireless technologies for Internet access points is in Chapter 3.

VIRTUAL PRIVATE NETWORKS

A network can be extended through a Virtual Private Network (VPN). This strategy requires a VPN client program to connect to an internal organizational network through a firewall over a public network (usually the Internet). The VPN client and firewall create a virtual, secure "tunnel" through which authentication data and private network traffic can pass, allowing a remote user to access their organization's network from the outside. Other supporting protocols and standards, such as the Point-to-Point Tunneling Protocol (PPTP), provide differing levels of security and facilitate secure connections.

SUMMARY

Networking technologies have greatly enhanced and extended the productivity of the PC. Computers would not be in almost every home and school if it were not for the resource and information-sharing capabilities networks provide. This capability comes at a cost for specialized hardware and software, local infrastructure, and network administrative personnel. The network fundamentals explored here, such as the OSI reference model and the packet technologies networks depend on, form an essential backdrop to the chapters on Internet technologies based on TCP/IP.

REFERENCES

Bhola, J. (2002). *Wireless LANs demystified.* New York: McGraw-Hill.

Charles, G. T., Jr. (1997). *LAN blueprints.* New York: McGraw-Hill.

Cisco Systems. (2008). Simple network management protocol (SNMP). In *Internetworking technology handbook.* Retrieved May 1, 2008, from http://www.cisco.com/en/US/docs/internetworking/technology/handbook/SNMP.html.

CNET Wireless Resource Center. (2008a). 3G. Retrieved October 1, 2007, from http://www.cnet.com/4520-7363-6361076-4.html?tag=wrc.ln.

CNET Wireless Resource Center. (2008b). Wi-Fi. Retrieved October 1, 2007, from http://www.cnet.com/4520-7363_1-6361076-3.html?tag=wrc.mn.

Horrigan, J. (2007, February). Wireless Internet access. *Internet and American life project.* Retrieved March 26, 2008, from http://www.pewinternet.org/pdfs/PIP_Wireless.Use.pdf.

Molyneux, R. E. (2003). *The Internet under the hood: An introduction to network technologies for information professionals.* Westport, CT: Libraries Unlimited.

Simoneau, P. (1997). *Hands-on TCP/IP.* New York: McGraw-Hill.

Tang, A., & Scoggins, S. (1992). *Open networking with OSI.* Englewood, NJ: Prentice-Hall.

Chapter 3

Accessing the Internet: Connection Technologies

Internet access requires that a connection technology be available and properly configured. Historically, access to such connection infrastructure was a major limiting factor to Internet participation. In the days when the "information superhighway" metaphor was in use, people talked about the problem of the "last mile" to reflect that the Internet was not available for every home, school, and library in many areas. Now, most areas have at least dial-up access, but broadband is not always an option, particularly in rural areas (Gilroy & Kruger, 2006). The bandwidth intensive activities of today require broadband services, and the lack of universal, affordable broadband is another facet of the digital divide that still exists for many.

During much of the early history of the Internet, direct access was not commonly available, and users often connected through an intermediary shell account on a mainframe or UNIX system. Fortunately, some form of locally available Internet access has become ubiquitous, with many thousands of Internet Service Providers (ISPs) competing to provide Internet connectivity. The common options for connecting to the Internet typically involve one of the following strategies: a dial-up connection via a computer modem and analog phone lines; a leased dedicated telephone link such as a T1 or fractional T1 line; digital telephone services such as ISDN or DSL; or broadband cable service connections. During the 1990s, the proliferation of both the connecting infrastructures and ISPs made it much easier to make a direct Internet connection through dialup, DSL, or cable. This chapter focuses on these connection technologies; how they are used to result in the assignment of an Internet address, for instance with SLIP/PPP, will be covered in Chapter 4. Before discussing these Internet communication strategies, a review of the communication hardware devices is useful. Because many of these devices are used in networked Internet connections or in other non-Internet computer applications, some of these topics overlap with content presented in the first two chapters.

MODEMS

As introduced in Chapter 1, a modem (Modulator/Demodulator) is a device that allows a computer to connect to other computers via an analog telephone line. These devices were in common use even before there was interest in connecting to the Internet; they were used to facilitate access to mainframe or UNIX hosts, to connect to online database providers, or to connect to computer bulletin board services. Modems convert analog signals to digital and digital to analog. The modem UART (Universal Asynchronous Receiver/Transmitter) chip converts the parallel data stream on a computer bus into a serial data stream for communication as shown in Figure 3.1. Modem-to-modem communication requires communication parameters, which are the number of data bits, stop bits, and parity bits used to transmit the data. Modems exchange these parameters during the initial "handshake" resulting in the "squawking" tones heard at the beginning of the session. Early modem speeds were expressed as the baud rate, which is not exactly the same as bps (bits per second). Baud rate is a measure of switching speed, equivalent to the number of frequency changes per second the modem can perform, which approximates bits per second (bps). Modern modems measure bandwidth in the more familiar bps measure. The 56 Kbps modem is standard for dialup connections, but this 56 K speed is what the device is theoretically capable of, not the actual speed of an analog data connection. The Federal Communications Commission (FCC) limits the maximum permitted speed for this connection to not more than 53 K to prevent "cross talk" (where a signal can "bleed" across a copper line and cause noise and interference). For this and other reasons, 56 K modems typically give connection speeds in the 28.8 to 45 K range ("56 K Info," 2007; Gilroy & Kruger, 2006). While this is impressive compared to the modem technologies of a decade ago, this is far less bandwidth than is possible with either DSL or cable connections.

Analog Service: POTS and PSTN

Modems were designed to work with POTS (Plain Old Telephone Service). This refers to analog signals moving on copper twisted pair wire over the Public Switched Telephone Network (PSTN). POTS was designed to carry an acoustic

Figure 3.1 The modem's UART chip converts the computer parallel bit path into a serial one for transmission. The communication parameters would typically include additional overhead such as the insertion of start and stop bits surrounding each byte. At the receiving end, the UART converts the serial bit stream back to a parallel one.

signal by converting it to an electrical signal with volume (signal amplitude) and pitch (signal frequency). Telephone networks (at the local level at least) are an example of circuit switching technology; this is the Public Switched Telephone Network (PSTN). They do use digital technology for the backbone service and trunk lines, but the connection from most homes to the local telephone company central office, referred to as the local loop, is usually analog. Although an analog connection works fine for voice communication, it is decidedly limited for transmitting digital data. Several technologies, collectively known as broadband, better accommodate both types of communication with much higher connection speeds. Broadband options include cable services, Integrated Services Digital Network (ISDN), and the many forms of Digital Subscriber Line (DSL).

BROADBAND SERVICES

Broadband is a generic term used for the various high bandwidth connection technologies. By 2005, about 43 percent of all U.S. online households were using a form of broadband, and that number is expected to grow to 80 percent by 2010 (Jupiter Media, 2005). Cable modem (CM) access has had an early lead over DSL; in 2004, cable had 75 percent of the broadband market compared to 15 percent for DSL, but DSL is expected to make gains in this area over time (Wrolstad, 2004). This expectation is based partly on the extensive infrastructure that the Telcos have compared to cable companies, especially in rural areas. However, as with many technology predictions, the accuracy of this expectation is uncertain; for instance, wireless technologies are improving and conceivably could surpass both cable and DSL. The rise of both DSL and cable connections now compete with the older but still available leased phone line options such as T1, fractional T1, or T3 lines.

Leased Telephone Lines

One of the main options for a high-speed connection to the Internet was to lease a dedicated line. AT&T developed the T1 line in the 1960s, so this technology has been available for some time. T1 lines have 24 64 Kbps channels providing 1.5 Mbps of bandwidth, about the same as a standard DSL connection. The T1 bandwidth can be subdivided and sold as a fractional T1 connection of 128 Kbps or other multiples of 64 Kbps. The T3 lines have a bandwidth of about 45 Mbps or about 30 times the capacity of a T1. The backbone service for the Internet was upgraded to T3 lines in 1992. It is interesting to note that the original NSFNET backbone service for the Internet used T1 lines until 1991, so the Internet backbone connections of that time were about the same speed as the average home DSL connection of today (National Science Foundation, 2005).

Integrated Services Digital Network

Integrated Services Digital Network (ISDN), developed in the mid-1980s, was a digital precursor to DSL. It allowed for faster connections and used multiple channels for connecting multiple devices, such as telephone, fax, and a computer. Data rates of 128 Kbps were possible along with two 64 Kbps "B" channels and a 16 Kbps "D" channel. There were often problems implementing ISDN technologies; these included inconsistent local telephone company support, the need for specialized nonanalog devices, and interoperability issues because there was no standardization of the supporting telephone company switching technologies. Although ISDN overcame some of these initial problems, various forms of DSL and cable connections have become more common for broadband access.

One advantage of ISDN was very fast call "set up" and "tear down," which refers to the "handshake" period when modems make a connection to other modems. The ISDN could accomplish this in milliseconds, allowing for very rapid connects and disconnects to and from the Internet. This was an advantage because early ISP cost models often charged by the minute for online time, and it was therefore desirable to minimize connect time. An ongoing connection is not needed once the content such as a Web page or email message has been received; it can be read offline. Being able to seamlessly connect, disconnect, and then quickly reconnect with no noticeable delay was possible with ISDN.

The per-minute charge model is not common today and thus negates this advantage of ISDN. Most service providers provide unlimited access for a set fee. However, as more users download movies and other large entertainment files, some major service providers are reevaluating this access model. Service providers Comcast and ATT recently announced that they intend to initiate "Internet metering" that charges heavy use customers a surcharge when a set bandwidth limit is exceeded. These variable surcharges could create consumer anxiety about the cost of their Internet activities, and Vint Cerf, the developer of many Internet technologies and now with Google, believes this change would hamper innovation and application development (Stelter, 2008). It will be interesting to see if such a metered approach becomes the norm for Internet access.

Digital Subscriber Line

Digital Subscriber Line (DSL) technology has become more pervasive; it has most of the advantages of ISDN for lower cost and faster speeds. DSL is one viable solution to the "last mile" problem alluded to earlier because it provides high-speed, local loop connections over existing copper wire infrastructure (Sheldon, 2001). DSL dedicates part of the available bandwidth to support an analog voice signal, which allows simultaneous computer and voice connection. Initially, DSL appealed primarily to small businesses as an attractive and affordable Internet access alternative to the more expensive T1 or fractional T1 line option. As prices have declined, DSL connections have become competitive with cable TV broadband connections for individual home use.

DSL is a generic term for a large variety of specific standards that fall into one of two basic types: symmetric, where the upstream and downstream speeds are the same, and asymmetric, where they are different. There are a

DSL Type and Description	Bandwidth	Distance Limits
DSL Lite "Splitterless" DSL: ADSL that trades off speed for not requiring a splitter at the point of service	1.544 Mbps to 6 Mbps downstream speed	18,000 feet on 24-gauge wire
HDSL High bit-rate Digital Subscriber Line: T1/E1 service for home or within a company WAN, LAN, server access	1.544 Mbps duplex on two twisted-pair lines; 2.048 Mbps duplex on three twisted-pair lines	12,000 feet on 24-gauge wire
SDSL Symmetric DSL: Same as HDSL but requiring only one line of twisted-pair	1.544 Mbps duplex (U.S. and Canada); 2.048 Mbps (Europe) on a single duplex line downstream and upstream	12,000 feet on 24-gauge wire
ADSL Asymmetric Digital Subscriber Line: For Internet and Web access, remote LAN access	1.544 to 6.1 Mbps downstream; 16 to 640 Kbps upstream	1.544 Mbps at 18,000 feet; 2.048 Mbps at 16,000 feet; 6.312 Mbps at 12,000 feet; 8.448 Mbps at 9,000 feet
VDSL Very high Digital Subscriber Line: For ATM networks or fiber to the neighborhood	12.9 to 52.8 Mbps downstream; 1.5 to 2.3 Mbps upstream; 1.6 Mbps to 2.3 Mbps downstream	4,500 feet at 12.96 Mbps; 3,000 feet at 25.82 Mbps; 1,000 feet at 51.84 Mbps

Figure 3.2 DSL types; adapted from Bytepile.com (2002).

huge number of different specifications for DSL (BytePile.com, 2002); a few of these are shown in Figure 3.2.

Because DSL is a dedicated point-to-point connection, no dial-up has to take place. This results in an ongoing Internet connection; this is convenient, but it has possible security implications for the user. Many home connections make use of some form of Asymmetric Digital Subscriber Line (ADSL). As noted previously, *asymmetric* refers to the difference in bandwidth between the "upstream" and "downstream" connection. Most users of the Internet care more about the speed of the connection coming to the computer than the connection going away. This makes sense in the context of Hypertext Transfer Protocol (HTTP), where the request header generated by the client software is quite small but results in the delivery of a number of large files to the client. With an asymmetric connection, you might have from 2.5 to 10 Mbps of bandwidth to your computer, but only 768 Kbps from it. There are many levels of bandwidth combinations available depending on the service provider and your budget. Availability of DSL is in part constrained by the distance to a phone switching facility; there is a maximum 3.4 mile (5.5 km) distance limit, and beyond that distance there is the added cost of a repeater to boost the signal.

Cable Broadband

Television cable systems have also become important providers of broadband Internet connections. The cable infrastructure is in place in most cities, and the number of people using cable services is high. Cable broadband connections require a specialized interface device (a cable modem) and a computer Ethernet port for the connection. Internet access through cable service has its own set of trade offs. The cost is generally competitive with DSL, but availability can be an issue. Connection speeds are comparable, but cable was not designed to do two-way traffic, so as with ADSL, the bandwidth is also asymmetric with downstream rates of 10–20 Mbps vs. upstream rates of about 300 Kbps. As with DSL, this is not a significant issue for most Internet users unless they are running a server or other service (such as VoIP) that may require more upstream bandwidth. Another issue for cable modem users is that the nodes in an area or neighborhood share the available bandwidth, so connection speeds can degrade with additional subscribers. Like DSL, cable connections result in a computer constantly connected to the Internet, making Internet use convenient but raising security issues as well.

Both DSL and cable technologies provide affordable and fast connections to the Internet, and they are each gaining wide acceptance (Wrolstad, 2004). There are predictions that DSL may become the more common solution, but for most users, the decision about which to choose often comes down to local availability, pricing, and other package options (Jupiter Media, 2005).

Wireless Broadband Technologies

Organizations and individuals interested in accessing the Internet within a local area are increasingly turning to wireless technologies. The Yankee Group, a technology consulting company, estimates worldwide wireless will grow to 58 million users by 2012 (Wong, 2008). One standard is Wi-Fi, which stands for *wireless fidelity*, an IEEE standard for wireless connectivity by way of a broadcast signal using Wireless Application Protocol (WAP). The various versions of this technology are derived from the IEEE 802.11 standard (other variants of this standard are covered in Chapter 2). Wi-Fi can provide access over a distance of 150 to 400 feet with connection speeds from 5 Mbps to 22 Mbps (CNET Wireless Resource Center, 2008). Wireless technologies are very viable solutions for areas where wiring is problematic or undesirable, such as older buildings, homes, and coffee shops. Wi-Fi requires an access device or router connected to a broadband source, which provides access to any device with a wireless network adapter. Security has been a concern with wireless Internet access because it is possible to intercept these signals or break into the network. Wireless security was initially addressed with Wired Equivalent Privacy (WEP), an early standard now being displaced by Wi-Fi Protected Access (WPA) for higher levels of security.

A new wireless technology that has received press attention is WiMax, developed by Sprint Nextel (Wong, 2008). WiMax stands for Worldwide Interoperability for Microwave Access. WiMax will use a licensed channel on the radio spectrum, as opposed to the free frequencies of Wi-Fi, and will provide a five-fold increase in connection speed that provides a stronger, cleaner, and more secure signal less susceptible to interference. If WiMax performs as described and is reasonably priced, it should become a popular option that will greatly extend wireless Internet access beyond Wi-Fi's limited hotspot range.

ROUTERS AND PROXY SERVERS

These network devices, introduced in Chapter 2, will come up again in Chapter 4. They appear in this discussion because they also represent an important connection option for computers on a real or virtual network. Home broadband connections use the same ports and cabling that are used in offices with direct Ethernet connections. While home and office connections look and behave in a similar manner, most enterprise networks connect individual computers or LANs to the Internet directly through a hub or router. As described in other parts of this text, routers play an essential role in the management of Internet traffic by determining the destination of packets using their IP addresses to make an appropriate routing decision.

Proxy servers can also make the connection between a LAN or host to the Internet. Proxy servers can serve as a firewall to prevent the outside world from directly interacting with any host on the LAN. By using the Network Address Translation (NAT) protocol, proxy servers can expand an IP address class by managing the correspondence between private IP address space and a single public IP for packets destined to the outside world. Proxy servers are also used to present an authorized IP address to some service that requires authentication of users accessing restricted resources. Libraries frequently manage access to certain resources by defining an authorized IP address space in a domain. Users accessing the services from within this defined address space, such as on-campus users of an academic library, automatically have access. Off-site users must first authenticate themselves to a proxy server that then presents the appropriate IP address when the request is forwarded to the service. These devices and strategies are discussed in detail in Chapter 4.

SUMMARY

The strategies and technologies supporting Internet connections still vary considerably and depend, in part, on whether you are connecting a personal computer or a LAN to the Internet. Early on, direct connections to the Internet were rare, and sessions were often initiated via a shell account on some Internet host such as a University mainframe or UNIX system. With the emergence of TCP/IP enabled PCs and competing ISPs, direct Internet access became possible using standard analog dial-up connections and with various broadband technologies such as ISDN, DSL, cable, or direct Ethernet connections. Wireless access is becoming quite commonplace in many public spaces and a primary network strategy for organizations.

Internet connection technologies include analog and digital telephone lines, cable company broadband, Ethernet, and Wi-Fi. Each option has its own set of advantages and disadvantages; the final choice is determined in the context of the local network options, availability and price of the various broadband services, and bandwidth requirements of the activities planned.

REFERENCES

56 K Info. (2007). Technical support. Retrieved May 1, 2008, from http://home.core.com/web/technicalsupport/library/56kinfo.html.

BytePile.com. (2002, October 19). DSL categories. Retrieved October 1, 2007, from http://www.bytepile.com/dsl_categories.php.

CNET Wireless Resource Center. (2008). Wi-Fi. Retrieved October 1, 2007, from http://www.cnet.com/4520-7363_1-6361076-3.html?tag=wrc.mn.

Gilroy, A. A., & Kruger, L. G. (2006). Broadband Internet regulation and access: Background and issues. Retrieved October 1, 2007, from http://usinfo.state.gov/infousa/economy/technology/docs/60574.pdf.

Jupiter Media. (2005). Jupiterresearch forecasts broadband's rise to dominance, increasing from 32 million U.S. households in 2004 to 69 million in 2010. Retrieved October, 2007, from http://www.jupitermedia.com/corporate/releases/05.06.02-newjupresearch.html.

National Science Foundation. (2005, September 28). The launch of NSFNET. Retrieved October 1, 2007, from http://www.nsf.gov/about/history/nsf0050/internet/launch.htm.

Sheldon, T. (2001). DSL (Digital Subscriber Line). *Tom Sheldon's Linktionary*. Retrieved January 27, 2006, from http://www.linktionary.com/d/dsl.html.

Stelter, B. (2008, June 15). Internet providers clamp down on users' time online. *Lexington Herald-Leader*, p. A7.

Wong, Q. (2008, May 1). WiMax to widen Net access: New device more powerful, secure than Wi-Fi. *Lexington Herald-Leader*, p. A3.

Wrolstad, J. (2004, September 10). FCC: Broadband usage has tripled. Retrieved May, 2007, from http://www.newsfactor.com/story.xhtml?story_title=FCC—Broadband-Usage-Has-Tripled&story_id=26876.

Chapter 4

Internet Technologies: TCP/IP

The core technology of the Internet is packet switching, implemented through the TCP/IP data communication protocols. Because all the higher-level protocols and many information services depend on this foundation, a detailed understanding of TCP/IP is a major goal of this text. Packet formation, packet addressing, MAC addresses, routing issues, subnet masks, address classes, IP address assignment, and the DNS lookups are all essential parts of TCP/IP. There are a number of excellent books devoted entirely to TCP/IP including Kozierok (2005) and the two-volume set by Comer and Stevens (1991a, 1991b). Other excellent sources are listed with the Additional Reading at the end of this chapter.

PACKET SWITCHING AND TCP/IP

The ARPANET was the first packet switching computer network, and the modern Internet developed from that simple beginning. Packet switching, introduced in Chapter 2, is the foundation of computer data communication; Leonard Kleinrock's early work on data communications with packet switching made ARPANET, as well as the Internet of today, possible (Kleinrock, 1996). Packet switching is the process by which data are broken up into discreet "chunks," encapsulated in a digital envelope, and sent out over a network for delivery according to the rules of some addressing scheme (Krol, 1994). Transmission Control Protocol/Internet Protocol (TCP/IP) is the foundation protocol of the Internet, and all the higher-level Internet protocols are included in the TCP/IP family of services.

Vinton Cerf and Robert Kahn were among the group that was instrumental in designing the original ARPANET; they went on to develop the TCP/IP network standards in 1980 (Leiner et al., 1997). ARPANET adopted the TCP/IP protocol in 1983, establishing the Internet of today (Zakon, 2006). In simple terms, these two communication protocols are responsible for breaking up all the data that move on the Internet into small packets, encapsulating it into electronic envelopes, and applying a standardized source and destination address to facilitate its movement across the globe. Understanding how TCP/IP works is central to understanding all Internet technologies and services.

TCP/IP represents two companion protocols working together. The IP part is responsible for the application of the source and destination address to all packets; each IP packet typically holds a TCP or, sometimes, a User Datagram Protocol (UDP, described later) packet. The TCP part is the process that takes the large piece of data and breaks it up into many small pieces, usually from 1 to about 500 bytes each. All data are first encapsulated into TCP or UDP packets, which in turn are encapsulated into IP packets, which are the packets that are routed on the Internet. The successful delivery of all the packets depends on locating the host with the destination IP address. The IP packets are delivered to the Internet host, and then the TCP takes over to reassemble the information into a coherent whole.

Krol (1994) explains packet switching with the analogy of how letters move through the U.S. mail. When a letter is sent via the postal service, the information is put into an envelope with a "To" and "From" address, as well as postage, all applied according to standardized rules. Then this packet is put into a mailbox with lots of other, unrelated packets. The successful delivery of the letter is analogous to the IP part. The IP is "unreliable and connectionless"; it is "unreliable" because there is no guarantee of packet delivery nor is there any acknowledgement of receipt. It is "connectionless" because there is no ongoing connection between the source and destination hosts. Figure 4.1 represents an IP packet.

To extend the U.S. Mail analogy to TCP, assume an additional rule is imposed; namely that each envelope can only carry a single sheet of standard letter paper. To send a 10-page letter, the pages would need to be numbered and put into separate envelopes, each of which is then addressed and mailed. The delivery of each "letter" is the job of IP. However, the receiver of the multiple letters must now open each and reassemble the pages in the intended order, which is analogous to the job of TCP. In addition, TCP packets carry a port assignment to designate which client program they are destined for at that host. Again using the mail analogy, consider mail to an apartment building; a street address needs to be refined with the unit number. The job of IP is to get the packets to the right host; TCP uses port assignments to ensure they get to the right client program on that host. Figure 4.2 represents the idea of how these two protocols work together.

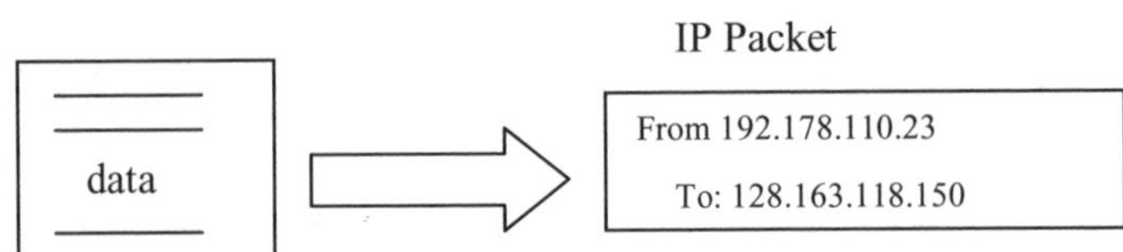

Figure 4.1 A simplified representation of an IP packet.

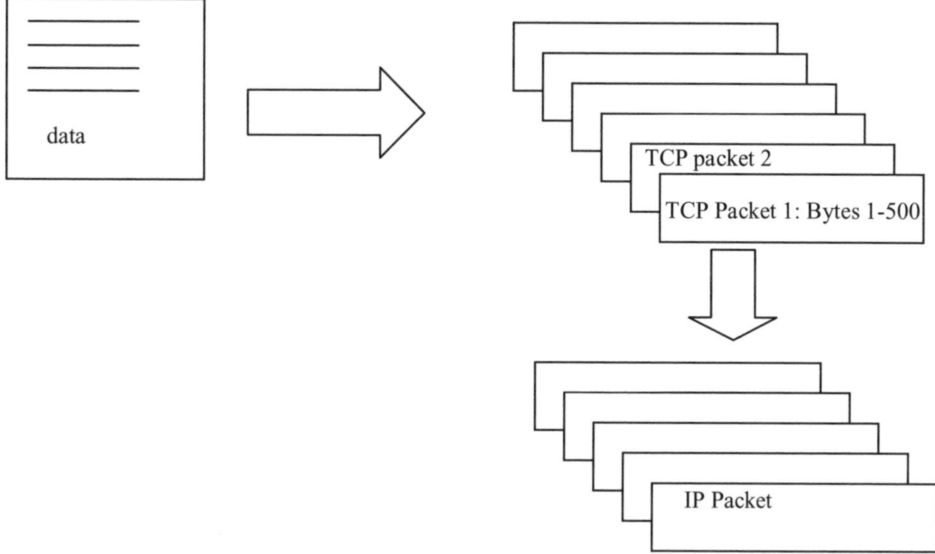

Figure 4.2 A representation of how TCP is combined with IP. Data is broken up into multiple TCP packets, each of which is placed in an IP packet and sent over the network.

IP PACKET ADDRESS HEADERS

This packet technology has significant overhead; that is, a significant portion of the packet itself is not data, but instead information needed to identify and move the data. The kind of overhead that is present in network packets has some similarities to the overhead in another standard that libraries are familiar with—the MARC record. The MARC record was designed to facilitate the transmission of "machine readable cataloging" (i.e., bibliographic data in electronic form). This record format has a leader and directory containing meta-information useful to the reliable transmission of the cataloging record. Similarly, the fields in the IP and TCP packet address headers contain the meta-information needed to get the packets to the correct destination and check for possible errors. The structure of the IP address header is shown in Figure 4.3.

The packet header identifies the IP version (IPv4 is the most common standard), the header length, the length of the packet itself, and the service type, which associates differing levels of service priorities for packets using a unique packet identifier. The fields that are labeled **flags, fragment offset, header checksum,** and **options** determine how this packet fits into a larger fragmented message (fragment offset), perform header error checking (checksum), or provide information about routing (options). The **TTL** field is the "time to live" and specifies the finite lifetime of an IP packet; without this, undeliverable packets could be clogging the Internet forever. The most critical fields are those for **source address, destination address,** and **data.** The header fields for the addresses are 32 bits long. The data field is typically a TCP or UDP packet. An IP packet carrying a TCP packet is an example of *packet*

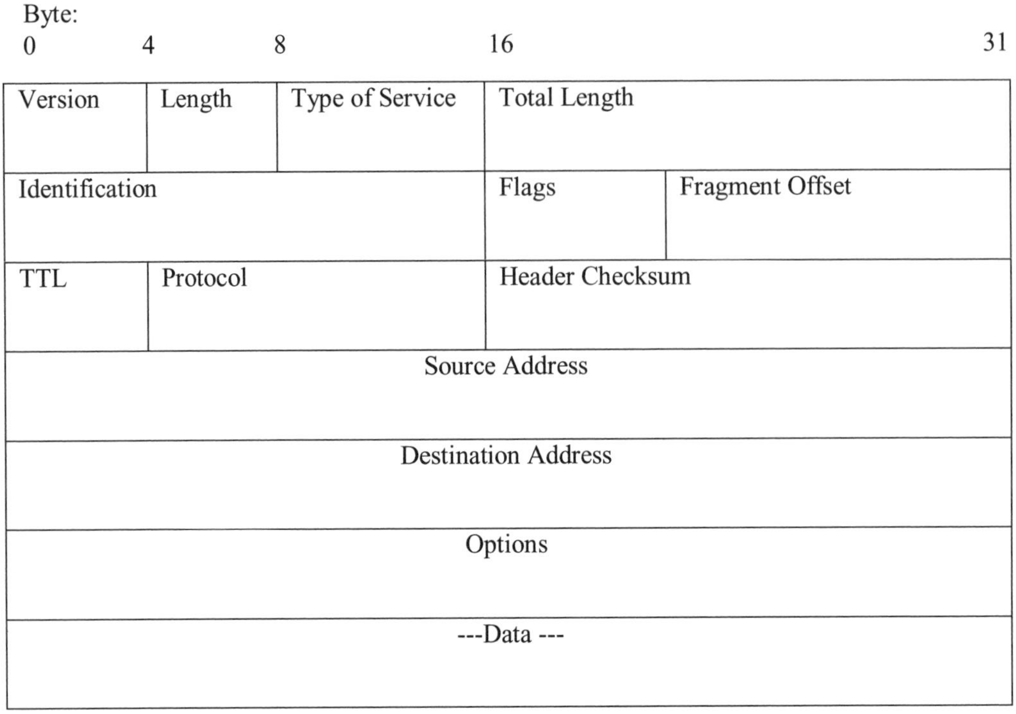

Byte:

0	4	8	16		31
Version	Length	Type of Service	Total Length		
Identification			Flags	Fragment Offset	
TTL	Protocol		Header Checksum		
Source Address					
Destination Address					
Options					
---Data ---					

Figure 4.3 The IPv4 address header.

encapsulation. Encapsulation can also involve higher levels of nesting, for instance when the data portion of an Ethernet frame is an IP packet, which in turn carries a TCP packet.

TCP, UDP, AND ICMP

TCP is a reliable protocol designed to ensure all the "chunks" of data are delivered and reconstituted into a coherent whole. There is significant overhead associated with TCP headers, as shown in Figure 4.4.

It is not necessary to this discussion to examine the details of each field in this header, but a few important points about TCP header information are worth a closer look. First, there are 16 bits reserved for port assignments. Ports, described in Chapter 2, are a communication channel for network data communications. All the various higher-level Internet protocols such as telnet and HTTP have default port assignments. Because TCP/IP uses 16 bits to identify a *port,* there are 65,534 (2^{16} – 2) possible ports (2 is subtracted from this total because binary addresses that are all zero or all ones are not permitted as port numbers). Other key header components include the sequence number, which allows the "chunks" of data to be reassembled, and the acknowledgement field, which confirms the receipt of the data and makes

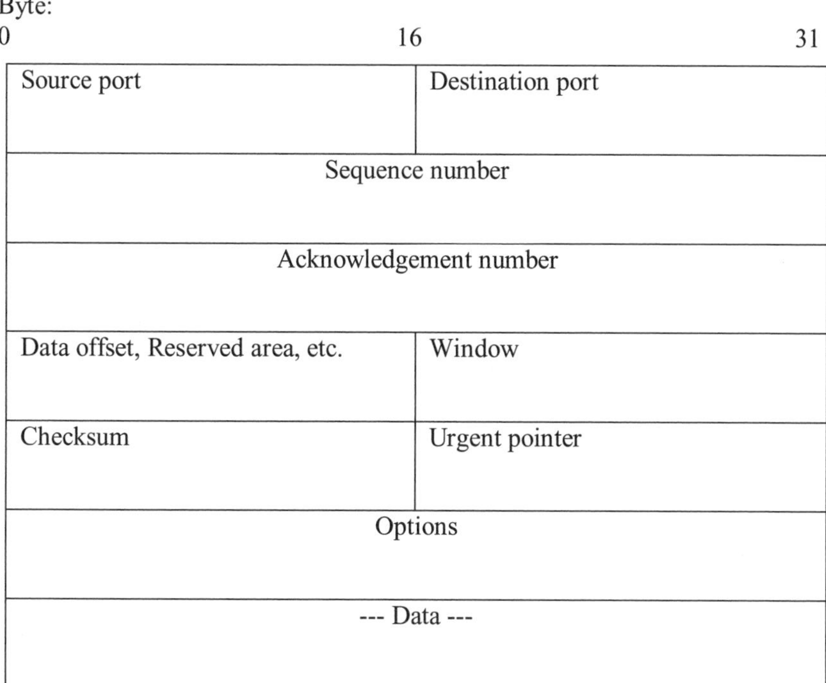

Figure 4.4 The TCP address header.

this a "reliable" protocol. Missing packets are re-requested, so TCP does care about the connection between the hosts, at least as far as confirming packet delivery.

User Datagram Protocol (UDP), referred to earlier, is an alternate protocol to TCP. As described previously, TCP has significant built-in error checking to ensure the integrity of the delivered data and to create a connection aware environment until the successful delivery of all needed data. However, there are times when added reliability is not needed and just adds unnecessary overhead. For instance, audio and video streaming use UDP. With streaming, a player connects to a server, determines the bandwidth of the connection, and starts to play as soon as the incoming packet stream can keep up with the output of the music or video. These applications give priority to the speed of packet formation and delivery, and the acknowledgement features of TCP would just slow the process down. UDP, shown in Figure 4.5, has less overhead than TCP, and it is better suited to streaming technologies because by the time a missing packet could be resent, the stream would already be past the place where it was needed.

The Internet Control Message Protocol (ICMP) is used for error checking between gateways and hosts and between different hosts at the Internet layer. It handles error reporting and plays a role in routing decisions. ICMP is another type of datagram carried in an IP packet just as UDP or TCP packets are.

Byte:

0	31
Source Port	Destination Port
Length	Checksum
--- Data ---	

Figure 4.5. The UDP packet header.

There are helpful utilities used for network testing and troubleshooting that are based on ICMP.

Everything that takes place via the Internet, whether it is sending or receiving email, using VoIP, browsing the Web, listening to music, or watching a video, depends on these packet technologies. The next time you are impatient with a slowly loading Web page, consider all the packets that must be created, addressed, delivered, and reassembled to present the content you see.

IP ADDRESSING

IP addressing is the foundation for all Internet technologies. Network management depends on a thorough understanding of IPv4 address structure, IP address classes, and the strategies employed to administer and assign IP addresses within an organization. Many information services use IP addresses or an IP proxy as a mechanism to manage licensing agreements that require user authentication.

Computers depend on binary numbers and do not share the human bias for base 10 numbering. Success with this section depends on familiarity with numbering systems, specifically base 2 or binary numbers, hexadecimal numbers (base 16), and the familiar decimal numbers (base 10). IPv4 uses 32-bit numbers for the source and destination address. These addresses all are in the form of 32-bit binary numbers; a series of 32 zeros and ones are used to represent the pool of unique addresses. Assuming all these addresses are available, there are at most 2^{32} possible IP addresses, or approximately 4.3 billion. However, there are restrictions that reduce this potential pool of addresses associated with each address class. This pool of IP addresses seemed more than adequate in 1980 when TCP/IP was developed; after all, in 1981, there were only about 200 hosts on the Internet. However, the demand for IP addresses has stretched this original scheme, as more devices need IP assignments. Users may need multiple IP addresses to support many devices such as a desktop computer, a laptop, mobile phone, or a handheld PDA. It is conceivable that soon household appliances or cars will need IP addresses, too.

Class A	N	H	H	H
Class B	N	N	H	H
Class C	N	N	N	H

Figure 4.6 The three most common IPv4 address classes.

Organizations have become increasingly Internet connected; for instance, universities no longer just connect offices, but computer labs, dorm rooms, libraries, and public areas with ports for laptop connections. The high demand for IP connectivity has strained the existing addressing system. There are a number of workarounds for this problem such as using VPNs to extend the address space. Migration to IPv6, a newer version of IP that uses 128-bit numbers for addressing, is another solution. The address pool for IPv6 is 2^{128}—a very big number. Other differences between IPv4 and IPv6 are discussed later.

The 32-bit numbers of IPv4 are expressed as a set of four octets. Computers use these in binary form, but when written for humans they are shown in decimal notation, each separated by a period and referred to as a "dotted quad." Because each part of this is an octet of binary numbers, the possible decimal values are between 0 and 255 because $2^8 = 256$ possible values, starting with 0. An example of a dotted quad could look like this: 128.163.188.75.

The set of possible addresses is divided into classes for administrative purposes, cleverly named Class A, Class B, Class C, Class D, and Class E. This discussion focuses on Classes A–C; Classes D and E do not really factor into this analysis. Class D is used for special nodes and multicast groups, and Class E is reserved for future use. There are two facets to understanding this addressing scheme: First, classes assign different octets for the identification of the network and hosts on that network; and second, there are restrictions on the values for the first octet of the network identifier. For Class A networks, one octet is reserved for network ID, and three octets for hosts; for Class B, two octets are reserved for network ID, and two octets for hosts; and for Class C, three octets are reserved for network ID, and one octet for hosts as shown in Figure 4.6.

It is apparent from this structure that there cannot be very many Class A networks, but each one can theoretically have a large number of hosts: 2^{24} or 256 x 256 x 256 or about 16 million. Because values of all zeros or all ones are not permitted in either the network or host portions of the address this would really be $2^{24} - 2$. A Class B network could only accommodate $2^{16} - 2$ or 65,534 hosts; Class C, only $2^8 - 2$ or 254 hosts.

The added address constraints relate to permitted values for the first octet and the fact that the host portion cannot be all zeros or all ones in any class. The first octet restrictions are: Class A, the high-order bit (the bit on the far left of the eight digit binary number), must be 0; for Class B, the high-order bits must be 1 and 0, and for Class C, the high-order bits must be 1, 1, and 0. The permitted decimal values and how they are obtained is shown in Figure 4.7.

Class	Maximum Binary Value of First Octet	Decimal Equivalent
A	0 1 1 1 1 1 1 1	127
B	1 0 1 1 1 1 1 1	191
C	1 1 0 1 1 1 1 1	223

Figure 4.7 Constraints on the first octet for Classes A, B, and C.

Class	# Networks	# hosts
A	126	16,777,214
B	16,256	65,534
C	2,064,512	254

Figure 4.8 Number of networks and hosts for Class A, B, and C.

Therefore, Class A addresses can have a first octet value from 1–126 (the 127 value, while it appears to be available, is reserved for special purposes), Class B networks can have a first octet value from 128–191, and Class C networks must begin with a number in the range of 192–223.

A local network based on TCP/IP is an *intranet.* Intranets can use any of the class addresses allowed in TCP/IP. However, when an intranet connects to the Internet it must use the appropriate class designation assigned to it from the domain registration. As can be seen from how these classes are structured, the type and size of the organization determines the appropriate class assignment. Figure 4.8 summarizes the networks and hosts possible within each class.

A useful special address is 127.0.0.1, known as the *loopback address.* This diagnostic address redirects packets back to the originating host thereby testing the TCP/IP installation on the host machine.

Private IP Addresses and NAT

One way for organizations to extend their IP address space utilizes private, internal IP addresses assigned to a single public IP. The address ranges reserved for this function within each IP class are shown in Figure 4.9.

The Network Address Translation (NAT) protocol manages the correspondence between the public and private addresses. This works much like a proxy server by serving as an intermediary for the packet streams. Packets going outside the network get a public IP assigned to them that is associated with this proxy device but use the private IP address when staying within the internal network, expanding the address space available to organizations and ISPs. For instance, all nodes in a campus dormitory usually use private

IP Class	Private IP address ranges
Class A	10.0.0.0 –10.255.255.255
Class B	172.16.0.0 – 172.16.255.255
Class C	192.168.0.0 – 192.168.255.255

Figure 4.9 Internal IP address ranges for each IP class.

network addresses. Most ISPs handle the IP assigned to customers in this fashion as well.

Proxy Servers

Proxy servers were introduced in Chapter 3 and are relevant to this discussion as well. Proxy servers have many uses with TCP/IP networks: They serve as firewalls, to authenticate users to a service, and to restrict or filter Internet access. The term *proxy* is quite literal; it stands in as your proxy for Internet activities. Proxy servers allow for higher security, and K–12 schools often use them to centralize control of filtering activities. Many libraries provide services requiring authentication of the user before access to the service or database is granted. Often such authentication is transparent to the user through IP authentication. Here at the University of Kentucky, most IP addresses begin with the Class B domain assignment of 128.163. License-restricted resources are accessed without a separate login through automatic authentication based on the presence of a known domain address (or perhaps a specific address range within the domain) in the IP header of the request. For remote users, a proxy server acts as the intermediary between the end user and the licensed resource. The user is authenticated to the proxy server via a library or student identification number, and subsequent requests for service are forwarded from the proxy server with the approved IP. Users on the network are automatically authenticated by virtue of their source IP address, but off-network users must use either a proxy server or a VPN to present an approved IP address to the service.

IPv6

Even though an IP address space can be extended with private network addresses as described previously, IPv4 is reaching its limits. By the early 1990s, proposals for the Next Generation IP (IPng) were developed. IPv6 was derived from one proposal known as Simple Internet Protocol Plus (SIPP) presented in RFC 1710, an Internet Engineering Task Force "Request for Comments" white paper (Simoneau, 1997). One goal of IPv6 is to solve the IP address space shortage, but it is also an opportunity to simplify the IP header and enhance the privacy and security of data transmission. IPv6 abandons the address "class" structure of IPv4 and instead identifies three types of addresses: unicast, multicast, and anycast. For instance, a multicast sends packets from a single host to multiple addresses simultaneously (Loshin, 1999).

The acceptance of IPv6 is dependent on strategies ensuring backward compatibility with existing IPv4 networks. Two approaches exist to allow its implementation in what is still an IPv4 world. One is to provide dual support for IPv4 and IPv6 in all hosts and routers, and the other is to permit the "tunneling" of IPv6 packets within IPv4 headers (Loshin, 1999; Simoneau, 1997). While IPv6 does offer advantages, there has been little deployment within many organizations. Many campus network administrators do not feel much urgency to fix a problem that does not yet seem critical and that is expected to have significant costs (Kiernan, 2005); most seem to be taking a "wait and see" stance.

Managing IP Address Assignments

For a host to be on the Internet, it must be assigned an IP address. There are different strategies for the management of this assignment. In the early days of Internet use, most users connected via a shell account, that is, an account on a large-scale computer such as a mainframe that is host connected to the Internet. This required that a non-Internet dial up connection first be established between the PC and the mainframe host; the mainframe then served as the jumping off point to the Internet. Early ISPs such as CompuServ and America Online offered direct Internet access via Serial Line Internet Protocol/Point-to-Point Protocol (SLIP/PPP), making the local PC an Internet host. Internet Service Providers provide a variety of connection choices in almost all locations. Another option for businesses is direct connections to the Internet via an Ethernet network. These different approaches are shown in figures 4.10a, 4.10b, and 4.10c.

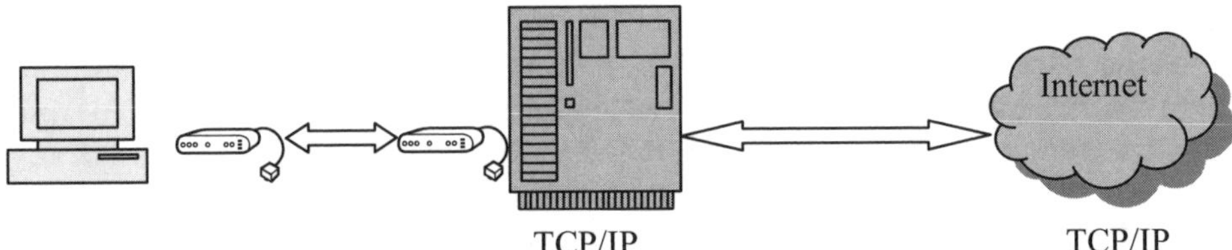

Figure 4.10a Shell account. A PC modem connects to mainframe modem pool, which connects to the Internet. Note that TCP/IP is on the mainframe, so both the client software used and the data received are there.

Figure 4.10b Internet connection via an ISP assigns an IP address to the PC. TCP/IP and the desired client software are also on the PC.

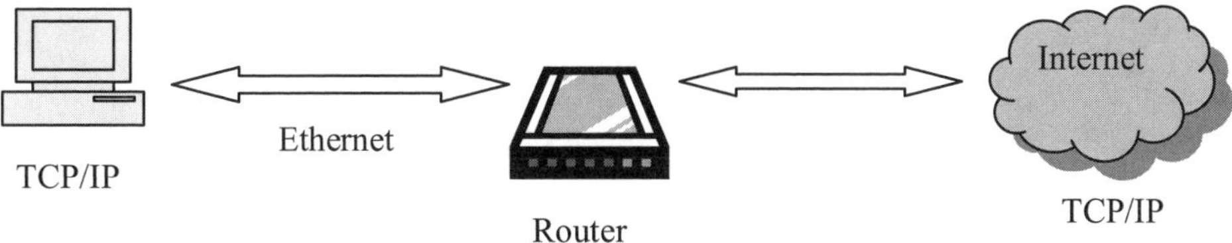

Figure 4.10c A direct Ethernet connection to the Internet via a router.

The shell account scenario was very common throughout the 1980s and into the 1990s. There are several obvious disadvantages to this approach. To begin with, for those not connected to a university or other large organization, getting an account on a mainframe was not always possible. There were examples of cooperative ventures that resulted in access for the public, such as the Cleveland Free-Net and the WELL in San Francisco, but these did not reach a mass audience. In addition, TCP/IP and the supporting client software were mostly UNIX or mainframe-based. This was not a very user-friendly environment, and it resulted in the retrieved Internet data staying on that host; a second non-Internet-based download had to take place to get the information to the desktop.

Several events in the 1990s made it much easier to get direct access to the Internet. With the introduction of Windows 95, TCP/IP became part of the operating system. This was a huge leap forward because earlier versions of client software for Windows required a separate WINSOCK (Windows sockets) installation to direct the TCP/IP packet stream to Windows client applications. Integrating this function into the OS eliminated the problem of incompatible, multiple WINSOCK versions. The proliferation of ISPs using SLIP/PPP provided IP addresses assigned directly to the desktop host. SLIP, the Serial Line Internet Protocol was the initial approach for these dial-up connections, but SLIP was not really a standard. The improved and more efficient Point-to-Point Protocol (PPP) standard had better error checking and compression technology and soon replaced SLIP.

The direct Ethernet-based connection shown in Figure 4.9c is typical for Internet access within larger organizations and companies. In this scenario, an appropriate IP address is assigned to the corresponding EA address making it an Internet host. Strategies for handling this IP assignment included manually hard coding an IP address in the PC setup, the Reverse Address Resolution Protocol (RARP), the Bootstrap Protocol (BOOTP), and the Dynamic Host Configuration Protocol (DHCP).

Entering the desired IP address manually sounds like the simplest way to make this assignment, but this is problematic for most large networks. In Windows, the TCP/IP properties are available through the control panel Network Connections icon. Figure 4.11 shows these options in Windows XP.

To set the IP manually, select that radio button and enter the assigned IP address, the subnet mask value, and the DNS server addresses (the latter two topics are discussed in the following sections). However, this approach enhances the chance of duplicating an address in use by another host on the network, and such a conflict prevents a successful Internet connection. It also makes updating the address space difficult because individual machines have to be reconfigured manually if needed. Network administrators therefore do not typically use or allow this approach. It can, however, be useful for diagnostic testing of a system that is failing to connect by substituting another address known to be functioning.

RARP, BOOTP, and DHCP are ways to manage and possibly automate the assignment of IP addresses. The hardware address for the Ethernet port, known as the MAC address (also referred to as the physical address or Ethernet address), is hard-coded with the hardware. However, IP addresses are logical addresses and come from different classes depending on the type of the organization. The assigned address space comes from the domain registration process. Once assigned, it is up to the local administrators to manage the address space. There are protocols designed to exchange Ethernet and IP address information; they are ARP (Address Resolution Protocol) and RARP. ARP allows routers to request that the host with a certain IP address respond with the associated MAC address. Why this is done is discussed in the section on

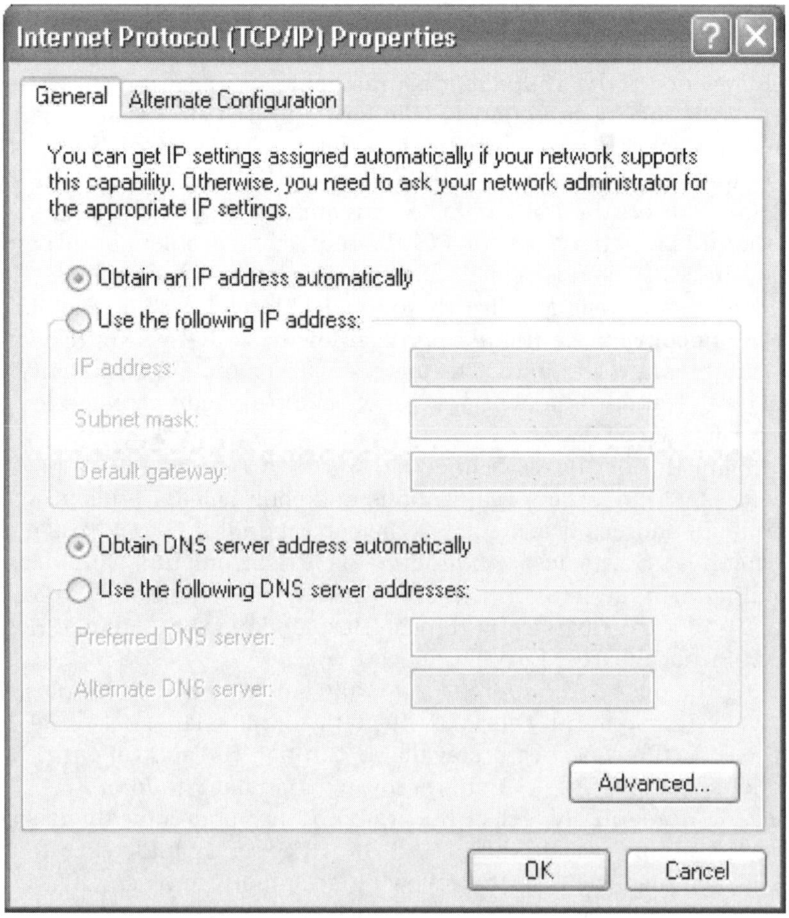

Figure 4.11 Windows XP TCP/IP properties display.

routing. RARP does the opposite; that is, it requests the IP address associated with some known MAC address. This simple protocol can be used to request an IP address for a MAC address on a network. However, RARP by itself has some limitations; for instance, it does not allow the use of subnet masks.

The BOOTP approach is similar but has been refined to include other parameters such as the subnet mask as well as the IP address. In BOOTP, the computer booting up on the network broadcasts a request message with its MAC address. The BOOTP server receives the message and responds with the IP address as well as other network configuration information as shown in Figure 4.12. Network administrators maintain a database of registered MAC addresses and associated IPs on the BOOTP server. This usually results in the same IP address assignment for that host each time it boots on the network. Separate from assigning the IP, the database also helps with network administration by tracking the computer hostname, location, and the contact information of the user. Registration of new equipment on the network is required for IP assignment.

The other possible approach is DHCP, the Dynamic Host Configuration Protocol. DHCP looks very similar to BOOTP, and it too depends on the exchange of broadcast messages between the host and some server. However, there are some key differences with BOOTP. With DHCP, there is a pool of available IP addresses, and one of these is dynamically assigned to the host for that session (see Figure 4.13). The IP address is "leased" for a period by that host, but

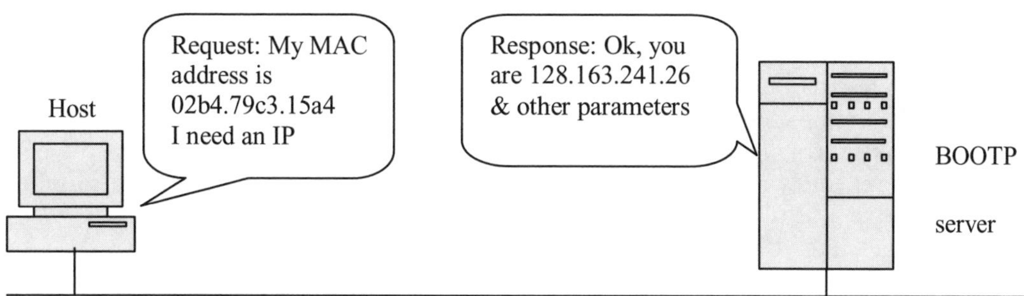

Figure 4.12 BOOTP address assignment.

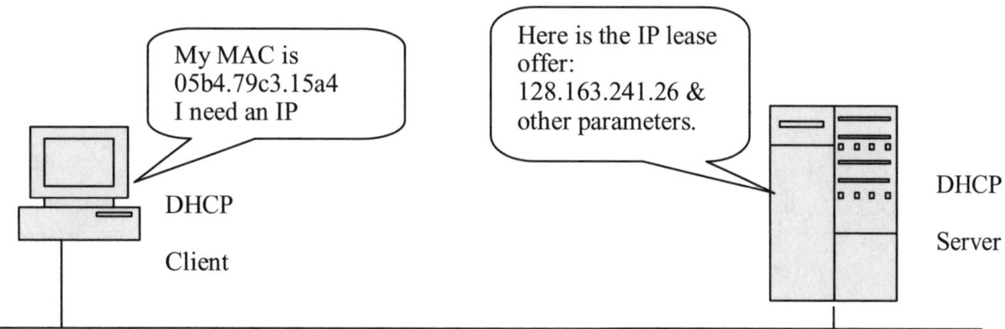

Figure 4.13 DHCP request and lease offer.

once it expires or is released, a different address might be assigned for future sessions. Having a pool of dynamic addresses available is useful for a number of reasons. Users or guests can connect a laptop or a new desktop computer to the network and immediately gain Internet access without being previously registered on the network. DHCP can therefore support library visitors wanting to connect their laptop or can provide temporary access to new users on the network so they can then register for subsequent BOOTP address assignment. However, one possible complication of dynamic addressing is that the IP assigned is not always the same, so it cannot be used for computers running a service such as a Web server that requires an unchanging IP assignment to associate with the server name.

ROUTING AND SUBNET MASKS

Routers are essential devices for the movement of all Internet packets and determine the appropriate path packets should take. Routers use IP addresses, and they "talk" to the devices that are connected to it to learn their IP addresses. The addresses of all the devices attached to the router are then stored in the router table. The initial routing decision is based on the answer to a simple question: Is the packet destined for a host on the router subnet or to a host in the outside world? To make this determination, the router applies the *subnet mask.* A mask refers to the idea of hiding something to isolate one element of interest (think of "masking" tape used when painting windows).

The management of an IP address space often utilizes *subnets,* which are created by "borrowing" some of the bits reserved for host ID to extend the network ID portion. Although it is possible to "borrow" any number of bits from the host octets, the simplest example is when a full octet is used for this purpose; this is then a *byte boundary* subnet mask. Subnets are used when different network protocols connect at a router. They also perform a number of other useful functions:

- Subnets keep the pool of network addresses smaller and therefore easier to manage and troubleshoot.
- They reduce overall network traffic because packets are often destined for hosts on the same subnet.
- They make routing tables smaller and more efficient.
- They allow for geographical association of network addresses within buildings or areas.
- They make network security easier to manage.

Each IP address class has a default subnet mask. For a Class A, it is 255.0.0.0; for Class B, 255.255.0.0; and for Class C, 255.255.255.0. For example, consider a Class B byte boundary mask. There are two octets associated with the host ID, which means there can be 65,534 (2^{16}–2) possible hosts to manage on such a network; two is subtracted because addresses that are all 0s or all 1s are not permitted. Having all these addresses together as one network is more difficult to manage and results in less efficient packet routing because each router must maintain a very large routing table with all these addresses. For a Class B network, the byte boundary mask functionally results in three octets associated with the network part of the address; the two octets assigned to all Class B addresses by default, along with the first octet of the host portion of the address. This third octet becomes the subnet assignment; making it possible to have 254 (2^8–2, again removing the two addresses with all 0s and all 1s) subnets, each of which can have 254 (2^8–2) hosts. This partitions the network.

As mentioned previously, the number of borrowed bits can be less than a full byte. The number of bits borrowed is determined by the number of subnets needed and the number of nodes expected on each subnet. The general formula for calculating subnets is $(2^n)-2$ = the number of subnets or hosts, where "n" is equal to the number of bits in the mask. So, if the number of bits in the mask is 3, then $2^3-2 = 8-2 = 6$ subnets.

All IP address classes can utilize this strategy and borrow differing numbers of host bits to accomplish the needed configuration. Simoneau (1997) describes the subnet tables for Class A, B, and C networks. Note that for a Class C network, borrowing a full byte is not an option, as that leaves no bits for host addressing. The process of creating a partial byte subnet mask and the resulting number of subnets and hosts is illustrated in the Class C subnet table in Figure 4.14.

The application of a default or modified subnet mask provides a simple process to separate the network part of the address from the host part so routers can determine if packets are to stay within the local network or go outside of it. To illustrate the application of a subnet mask, the default mask for a Class B network is given to reveal how it enables a router to make the routing decision.

Assume a Class B network has the domain address 128.163 and a default subnet mask of 255.255.0.0. If a packet is sent between two machines on the same network the network portions of the packet addresses are the same; for example, assume Machine A has the address 128.163.118.27 and Machine B the address 128.163.118.25. (Remember these addresses are shown in decimal notation for our convenience, but the machine addressing is in binary.)

Subnet Bits	Subnet Mask Value	Last Octet in Binary	Number of Subnets	Hosts
0	255.255.255.0	0000 0000	0	254
2	255.255.255.192	1100 0000	2	62
3	255.255.255.224	1110 0000	6	30
4	255.255.255.240	1111 0000	14	14
5	255.255.255.248	1111 1000	30	6
6	255.255255.252	1111 1100	62	2

Figure 4.14. Class C subnet mask table—the number of subnets or hosts is based on formula 2^n = total, where n equals the number of bits associated with mask or host.

The router sees the source and destination addresses in the IP packet header. If the network portion of both addresses is the same, the packet is destined for a host on this network. To determine this, the router applies the subnet mask and performs a Boolean AND with the IP address associated with the packet source, as shown in Figure 4.15. (Note: Boolean logic is discussed in other areas of this text; for the purposes of this discussion, all the reader needs to know is that with AND, the only time the result is 1 is when both operands are also 1).

To determine the network part of the ID for the destination IP address, the same operation occurs for address B, as shown in Figure 4.16.

The network part of the ID is preserved for both addresses; this is the only possible outcome of a Boolean AND performed when the mask values are 1s. The first two octets are the same for both addresses so the router determines the packet is destined for a machine on the same network.

Subnet masks permit routers to isolate the host portion of the address when needed by first inverting the value of the mask and again performing a Boolean AND with the addresses. This is shown for address A and the inverted subnet mask in Figure 4.17.

This process preserves the host part of the ID when the router needs the host portion. The overall result is that routers use this simple Boolean approach with the subnet mask value to make a routing decision. If the network parts of the "from" and "to" address are the same, the packet is destined for a host on the same network. If this is the case, the router lets the Ethernet frame carry the traffic directly to that host. However, routers only see IP addresses, and Ethernet needs a MAC address, so the router gets the needed

Machine A:	10000000.10100011.01110110.00011011
AND	
Mask:	11111111.11111111.00000000.00000000
Result:	10000000.10100011.00000000.00000000

Figure 4.15 Boolean AND with address A and subnet mask.

Machine B:	10000000.10100011.01110110.00011001
AND	
Mask:	11111111.11111111.00000000.00000000
Result:	10000000.10100011.00000000.00000000

Figure 4.16 Boolean AND with address B and subnet mask.

MAC address by way of ARP. The router broadcasts a message on the network asking for the machine with the IP address in question to respond with its corresponding MAC address; this MAC address is then used to move the data to the destination by way of the Ethernet.

If the application of the subnet mask determines the network portions of the addresses are different, the packet is therefore destined for a host on a different network. Getting the packet on its journey to the outside host is the job of the default gateway machine. The default gateway is ARPed, the data are sent there as an Ethernet frame, and then the default gateway determines where the IP packet should go next in the outside world.

THE DOMAIN NAME SYSTEM

Throughout this discussion, the emphasis has been on the numeric IP addresses used by TCP/IP and routers to move data. However, people do not typically use these numeric addresses when using the Internet; people prefer names. The domain name system facilitates both the registration of domain names and the assignment of names to numbers. This information is then stored in servers to create a mechanism to automate the lookups that happen with each Web client request to go to a site. These functions all are part of the Domain Name System (DNS).

Domain Name Registration

The Network Information Centers (NIC) and the Network Service Centers (NSC), originally part of the NSFNet, were the official providers of Internet domain name registration services to the world, offering registration of domain names in the .COM, .NET and .ORG top-level domains. InterNic (http://www.internic.net) operated under the umbrella of the U.S. Department of Commerce and provided the public information regarding Internet domain name registration services. Then Internet Assigned Numbers Authority (IANA) took over central control for domains, addresses, and protocols. All this now falls to the Internet Corporation for Assigned Names and Numbers (ICANN, http://www.icann.org), a nonprofit corporation operating under the U.S. Department of Commerce.

Domain names use a high-order suffix to identify either the type of organization or the country of the site. The common Internet domain suffixes include

Machine A:	10000000.10100011.01110110.00011011
AND	
Mask:	00000000.00000000.11111111.11111111
Result:	00000000.00000000.01110110.00011011

Figure 4.17 Boolean AND with address A and an inverted subnet mask.

com, for commercial organizations; **edu** for educational organizations; **gov** for government entities; **mil** for military sites; **org** for other organizations; and **net** for network resources. In the late 1990s, ICANN added seven new domain names to join this list of generic Top-Level Domains (gTLDs) on the root server: **biz** and **info** for general purpose; **name** for personal; and four that are restricted to specific communities of sites: **museum, aero, coop**, and **pro.** In addition, two-letter country codes are available as well. Examples of country codes include **us** for the United States; **au** for Australia; **fr** for France; **uk** for the United Kingdom; and **ie** for Ireland.

For a time, buying and selling domain names was big business. In 1992, there were only about 5,000 registered domain names, but by the late 1990s, there were that many requested every day. By mid-2000, estimates had grown to 15–17 million registered names (Arnold, 2008). Domain name speculation was common; in the early days of the dot com bubble, some names were auctioned for millions of dollars. Examples include the sale of Business.com for $7.5 million, Loans.com for $3 million, Autos.com for $2.2 million, and Bingo.com for $1.1 million (White, 2000).

The process of registering a domain is quite straightforward and begins with determining if the name you want is already in use. Registration information is stored in a database that can be queried by individuals using **whois** command utility or at the InterNIC Website. Alternatively, there are many commercial domain registration services; Google, Yahoo, and many other companies can provide these services. The registration process is shown in Figure 4.18. Each top-level domain (TLD) has an associated registry that feeds into a TLD server, as shown in Figure 4.19.

Each domain has dedicated servers to handle services for the registrants. The name associated with a machine at a domain is a Fully Qualified Domain Name (FQDN). For example, the University of Kentucky is assigned the **uky.edu** domain name. There are a number of named servers at that domain, such as www.uky.edu (the main campus Web server) and sweb.uky.edu (the student Web server). When a Web client is used, the location entered is a FQDN with a filename, but TCP/IP needs the assigned IP address. The correspondence between the numeric IP and the registered name is managed by a *DNS lookup.*

DNS Lookups

The essential job of a DNS lookup is to convert the names people prefer for Internet domains and URLs into the number the protocol actually uses. When a URL is submitted or a link followed, a request header is formulated by the client software, which is sent to the appropriate server. The server responds with a response header along with the content of the requested page. However, before the client request header is sent to the server, a lookup must happen to translate the URL into the IP number needed to address the packets of the request. If the URL **http://www.uky.edu/welcome.html** is entered in the location bar of a browser, the client formulates a request header to send to the server via TCP/IP. However, the packets of the request need the numeric IP address for that server. The Domain Name System is a hierarchical system of servers maintaining a database of names and addresses providing these

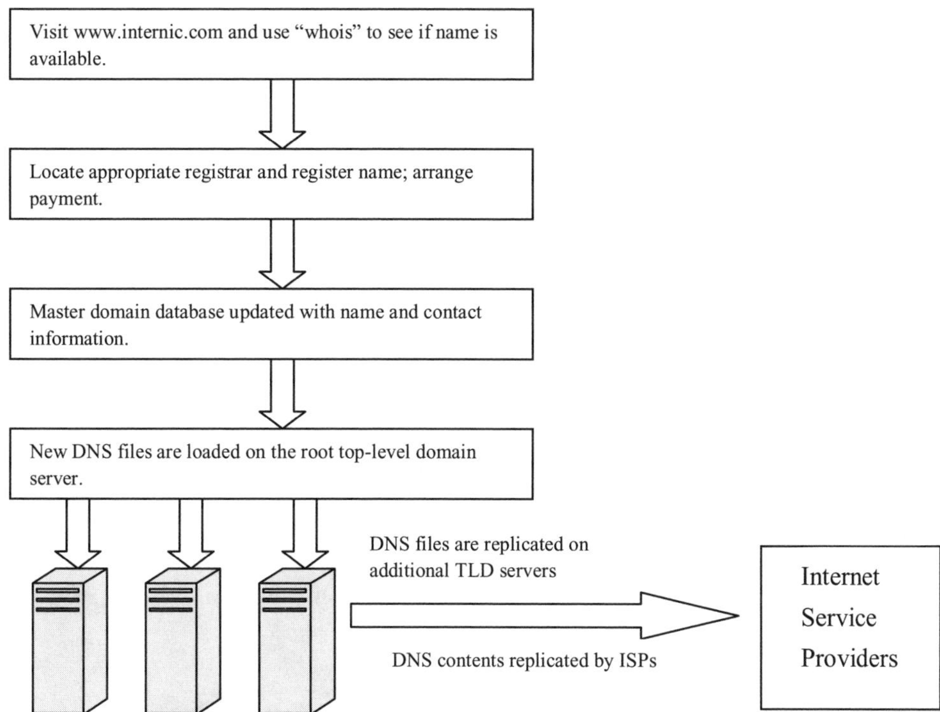

Figure 4.18 Registering a domain.

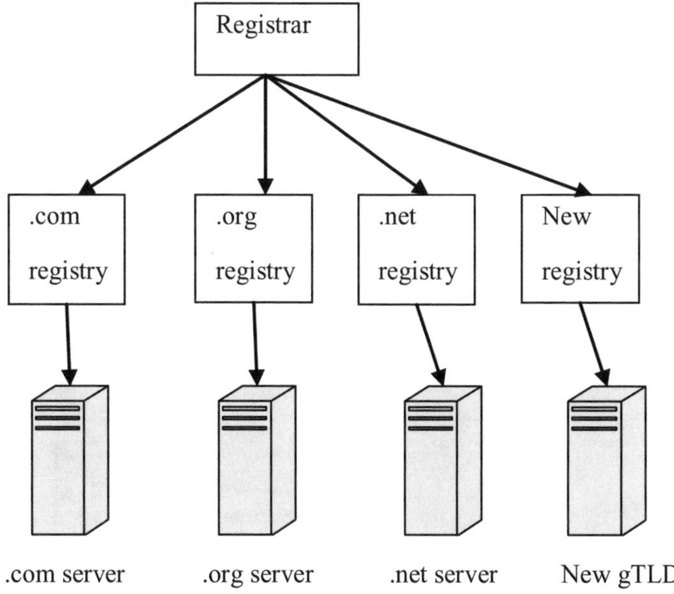

Figure 4.19 Registration information goes from the registrar to the registry for that TLD to the root server.

lookup services; this is how IP addresses are associated with a URL. Figure 4.20 shows an overview of this process.

A demand for DNS lookups could become a significant bottleneck for Internet activities so both caching and a tiered approach are employed to make the process more efficient. The simplified lookup described previously actually takes place by querying a cache or a database at multiple levels as shown in Figure 4.21. In each instance, the request is passed up the chain until the needed lookup is found.

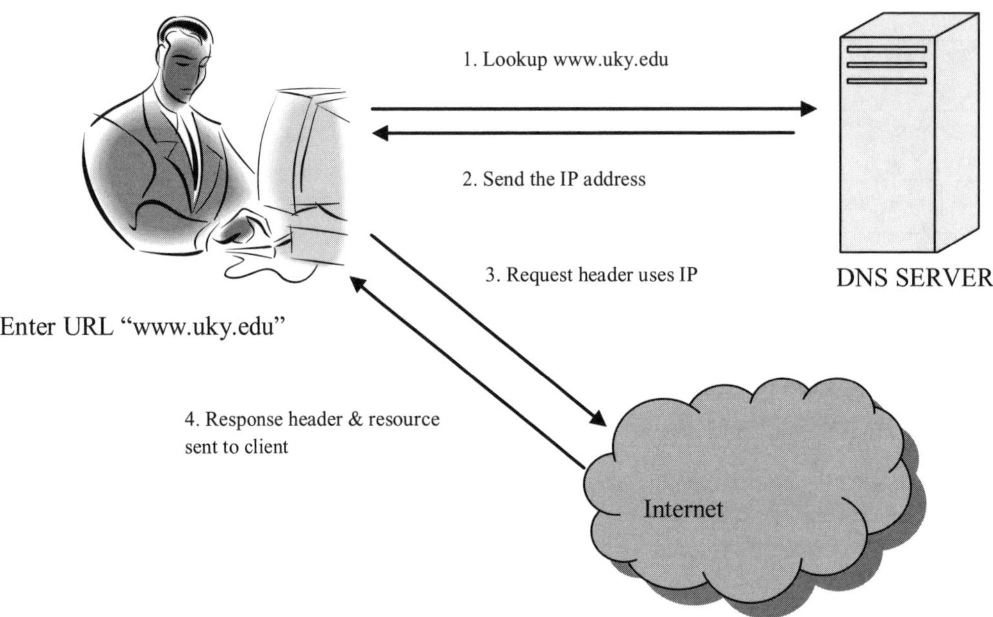

Figure 4.20 A simplified DNS lookup.

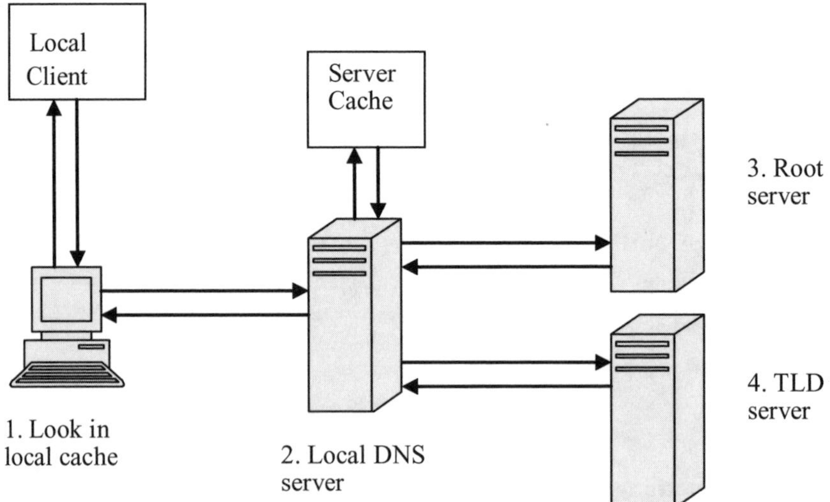

Figure 4.21 DNS lookups take place in a hierarchical fashion starting with the local cache, then to the local DNS server and cache, then to the root or other TLD server.

TCP/IP, SYSTEM LAYERS, AND OSI

TCP/IP uses system layers according to the functionalities outlined in the OSI Network Reference Model. Figure 4.22 is a view of the system layers for a computer connecting to the Internet with PPP. When an Internet client application runs, it plugs into TCP/IP via a port assignment; TCP/IP plugs into PPP, which plugs into the OS via a windows socket; and the OS uses drivers to connect to the BIOS and the hardware.

The expanded TCP/IP layers are mapped to the OSI model as shown in Figure 4.23. In the implementation of TCP/IP, some OSI Model layers are combined, resulting in four layers instead of the seven of OSI. This is not

Layer
User
Application
TCP/IP
PPP
OS
BIOS
Hardware

Figure 4.22 System layers on an Internet-connected PC.

OSI Layer	Function	TCP/IP Layers
7 Application layer	What users see	4. Application
6 Presentation layer	Translation formats	
5 Session layer	Opening and closing of sessions	3. Host-to-Host
4 Transport layer	Delivery of packets	
3 Network layer	Packets from data layer get addressed and routed	2. Internet Layer
2 Data link layer	Packet formation and error correction	1. Network Layer
1 Physical layer	Hardware and movement of bits	

Figure 4.23 OSI layers mapped to TCP/IP.

<table>
<tr><th>TCP/IP Layer:</th><th colspan="5">Protocols Associated with Layer</th></tr>
<tr><td rowspan="2">Application</td><td>SNMP</td><td>SMTP</td><td>NNTP</td><td>TFTP</td><td>FTP</td></tr>
<tr><td>HTTP</td><td>telnet</td><td>BOOTP</td><td>DHCP</td><td>DNS</td></tr>
<tr><td>Host-to-Host</td><td colspan="2">TCP</td><td colspan="3">UDP</td></tr>
<tr><td rowspan="2">Internet</td><td colspan="2">IGMP</td><td rowspan="2">IP</td><td colspan="2">ARP</td></tr>
<tr><td colspan="2">ICMP</td><td colspan="2">RARP</td></tr>
<tr><td>Network</td><td colspan="5">Just sees bits</td></tr>
</table>

Figure 4.24 Overview of TCP/IP layers and Common Protocols.

surprising because the OSI Model is just a reference model that is adapted to many specific network implementations. The TCP/IP suite can be further expanded to include the common higher-level protocols as shown in Figure 4.24, many of which are discussed further in Chapter 5.

COMMAND UTILITIES FOR TCP/IP

Ping is a utility run from a command prompt on Internet-connected hosts. A ping forms a message based on an ICMP echo request directed to a host so see if it is "alive." If the host is available and not prevented from responding by a firewall, it bounces the message back (hence the name; *ping* is also a sonar term based on the reflection of sound waves by an object in water). There is a loopback ping address (127.0.0.1) that can test the TCP/IP status of your local host computer. Two ping examples are shown in the command window in Figure 4.25.

Another frequently used command is **ipconfig** along with the "**all**" modifier (written either as "/all" or "-all") used in Windows. Older Windows95 systems used the similar **winipcfg** command. There are graphical options to reveal the IP configuration in the control panel, but the command version gives all the essential information in one screen of output, as shown in Figure 4.26. Another command is the **tracert** (or **traceroute** depending on the OS) command showing the path test packets take to a destination along with the number of "hops" (routers) needed. The **netstat** command gives the status of the ports in use. The **arp** command with the "-a" modifier reveals the physical addresses stored in the ARP table.

SUMMARY

The foundation of the Internet is TCP/IP. A knowledge of this technology is essential to understanding how all the higher-level protocols work and how many information services are delivered via the Internet. TCP/IP depends on the key technologies of packet switching, IP addressing schemes, the use of

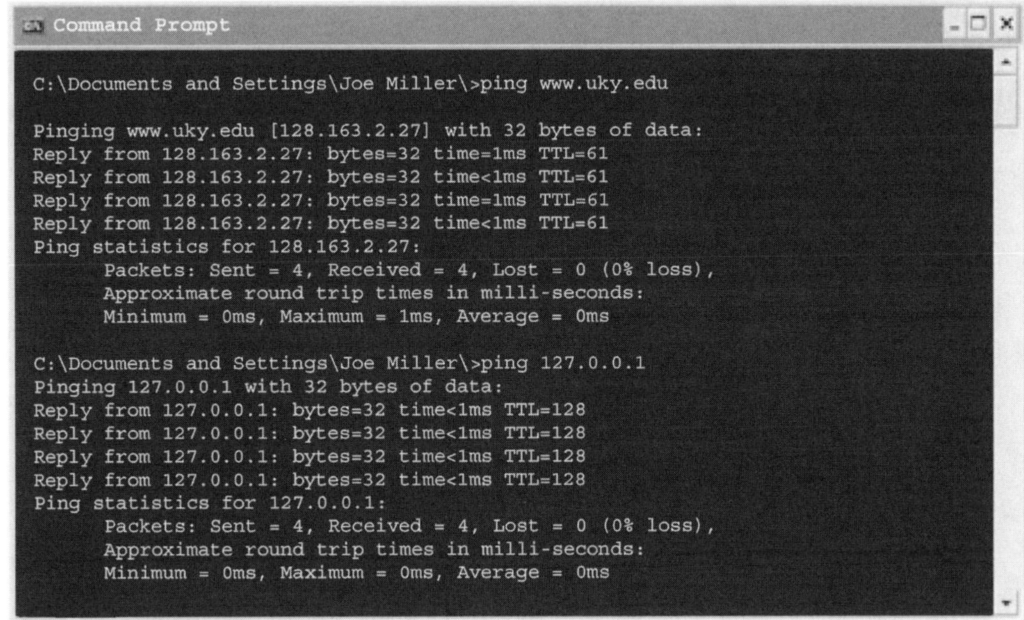

Command Prompt
Primary Dns Suffix Node Type Hybrid
IP Routing Enabled No
WINS Proxy Enabled No
DNS Suffix Search List gws.uky.edu
Ethernet adapter Local Area Connection: Connection-specific
DNS Suffix gws.uky.edu
Description Intel(R) 82566DM-2 Gigabit Network Connection
C:\Documents and Settings\Joe Miller\>ping www.uky.edu
Pinging www.uky.edu [128.163.2.27] with 32 bytes of data:
Reply from 128.163.2.27: bytes=32 time=1ms TTL=61
Reply from 128.163.2.27: bytes=32 time<1ms TTL=61
Reply from 128.163.2.27: bytes=32 time=1ms TTL=61
Reply from 128.163.2.27: bytes=32 time<1ms TTL=61
Ping statistics for 128.163.2.27:
Packets: Sent = 4, Received = 4, Lost = 0 (0% loss),
Approximate round trip times in milli-seconds:
Minimum = 0ms, Maximum = 1ms, Average = 0ms
C:\Documents and Settings\Joe Miller\>ping 127.0.0.1
Pinging 127.0.0.1 with 32 bytes of data:
Reply from 127.0.0.1: bytes=32 time<1ms TTL=128
Reply from 127.0.0.1: bytes=32 time<1ms TTL=128
Reply from 127.0.0.1: bytes=32 time<1ms TTL=128
Reply from 127.0.0.1: bytes=32 time<1ms TTL=128
Ping statistics for 127.0.0.1:
Packets: Sent = 4, Received = 4, Lost = 0 (0% loss),
Approximate round trip times in milli-seconds:
Minimum = 0ms, Maximum = 0ms, Average = 0ms

Figure 4.25 Two ping commands; ping a known host and the loopback ping. The first informs us that the host is "alive" (note that the IP address of the host is also returned). The second tells us that TCP/IP appears to be working on this local computer.

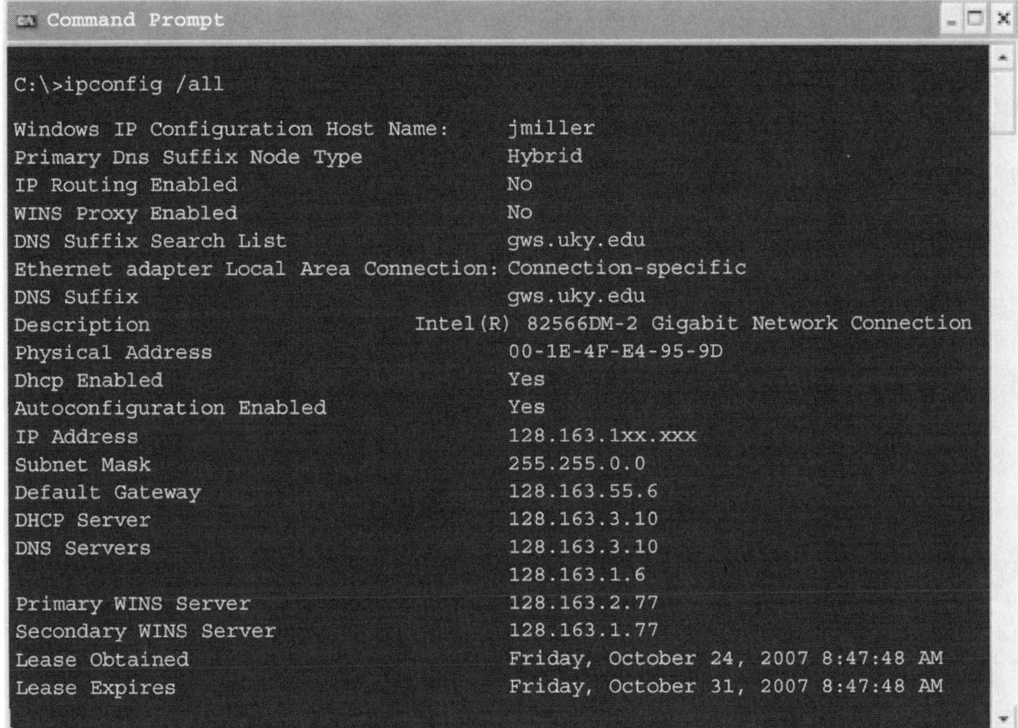

Dhcp Enabled Yes

IP Address 128.163.1xx.xxx

Default Gateway 128.163.55.6
DHCP Server 128.163.3.10
DNS Servers 128.163.3.10
128.163.1.6
Primary WINS Server 128.163.2.77
Secondary WINS Server 128.163.1.77
Lease Obtained Friday, October 24, 2007 8:47:48 AM
Lease Expires Friday, October 31, 2007 8:47:48 AM

Figure 4.26 Sample ipconfig command output with the /all modifier (the actual IP address for this machine has been partially removed in this output).

subnet masks and subnet administration, and the DNS system. In addition, VPNs and proxy servers are used to extend IP address spaces or serve as an intermediary between a user and the Internet. Various command utilities are available to assist with configuring and troubleshooting TCP/IP Internet connections. All these foundations are referenced in the next chapter on the higher-order protocols associated with the TCP/IP suite.

REFERENCES

Arnold, B. (2008). Sizing the web: Domains, sites, hosts. Retrieved May 1, 2008, from http://www.caslon.com.au/metricsguide1.htm#domains.

Comer, D. E., & Stephens, D. L. (1991a). *Internetworking with TCP/IP Volume I: Principles, protocols, and architecture* (2nd ed.). Englewood Cliffs, NJ: Prentice Hall.

Comer, D. E., & Stevens, D. L. (1991b). *Internetworking with TCP/IP Vol II: Design, implementation, and internals.* Englewood Cliffs, NJ: Prentice Hall.

Kiernan, V. (2005). Missing the boat, or penny-wise caution? *The Chronicle of Higher Education, 51*(27), A33–35.

Kleinrock, L. (1996, August 27). *The birth of the Internet.* Retrieved October 1, 2007, from http://www.lk.cs.ucla.edu/LK/Inet/birth.html.

Kozierok, C. M. (2005). *The TCP/IP guide.* Retrieved June 1, 2006 from http://www.tcpipguide.com/index.htm.

Krol, E. (1994). *The whole Internet: Users guide and catalog.* Sebastopol, CA: O'Reilly and Associates.

Leiner, B. M., Cerf, V. G., Clark, D. D., Kahn, R. E., Kleinrock, L., Lynch, D. C., et al. (1997). The past and future history of the Internet. *Communications of the ACM, 40*(2), 102–109.

Loshin, P. (1999). *IPv6 clearly explained.* San Francisco: Academic Press.

Simoneau, P. (1997). *Hands-on TCP/IP.* New York: McGraw-Hill.

White, M. (2000, February 2). Loans.com latest web name to make millionaire of seller. *Herald-Leader,* p. C2.

Zakon, R. (2006, November 1). Hobbes' Internet timeline. Retrieved May 1, 2008, from http://www.zakon.org/robert/internet/timeline/Additionalreading.

ADDITIONAL READING

Arick, M. R. (1993). *The TCP/IP companion: A guide for the common user.* Boston: QED Publishing Group.

Hofstetter, F. (2005). *Internet technologies at work.* Burr Ridge, IL: McGraw-Hill.

Leiden, C., & Wilensky, M. (2000). *TCP/IP for dummies* (4th ed.). Foster City, CA: IDG Books Worldwide Inc.

Molyneux, R. E. (2003). *The Internet under the hood: An introduction to network technologies for information professionals.* Westport, CT: Libraries Unlimited.

Young, M. L. (2002). *Internet: The complete reference* (2nd ed.). Berkeley, CA: McGraw-Hill Osborne.

Chapter 5

Higher-Level Internet Protocols: Making the Internet Work

The higher-level protocols defined within the TCP/IP standard enable users to do activities such as email, chat, FTP files, Web browsing, or VoIP. These higher-level protocols support the utility of the Internet and allow access to services and content, presenting a new array of acronyms to define, such as SMTP, FTP, and HTTP. The higher-order Internet protocols depend on the packet technology associated with TCP/IP, and they rely on client–server applications designed to utilize them; a good overview of these advanced Internet protocols is by Black (1999).

As discussed in earlier chapters, client–server architecture utilizes two pieces of software that are associated with the protocol working in tandem; the client software designed to formulate a request to the corresponding server, and the server software designed to reply to the request. All of this client–server activity happens through the formation and movement of packets (or datagrams) destined for some Internet host, and all are created and routed according to the rules of TCP/IP covered in Chapter 4. However, there might be a number of client applications running on a host, and getting the packets to the correct application is the function of the port assignments in TCP, discussed in the previous chapter. In that discussion, IP was introduced using the analogy of how the U.S. mail system moves physical packets using a standardized addressing scheme. The analogy was extended to TCP by considering how mail delivered to an apartment building needs additional information to ensure delivery to the correct apartment. This is analogous to port assignments associated with higher-level protocols for Internet packets; TCP ensures packets get to the right client application. Figure 5.1 shows the standard default port assignments for some common protocols.

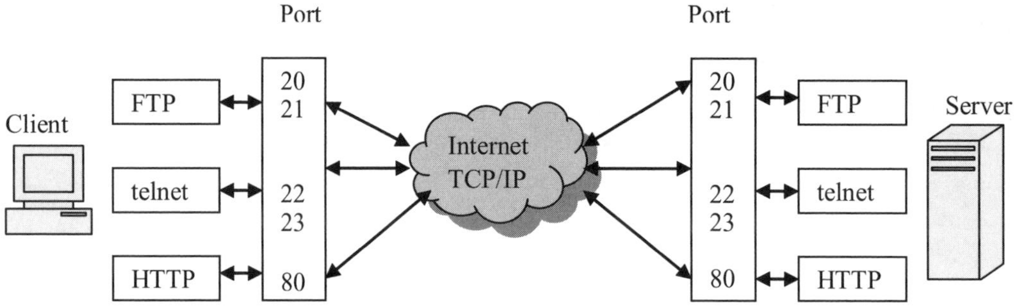

Figure 5.1 Common client–server TCP port assignments.

EMAIL: SMTP, POP, IMAP

Even though it has lost ground to Internet search, email has been, and still is, one of the most popular Internet applications (Rainie, 2005). The Simple Mail Transfer Protocol (SMTP) makes Internet email possible. Email has been a popular application since the days of BITNET, which was a precursor to the Internet at many institutions. In fact, the incredible success of email has earned it the title of the original "killer app" of the Internet. It is somewhat ironic that something that was so high tech not long ago is now becoming passé to many of the millennial generation, who complain it is too slow and not as instantaneous as cell phone texting, computer instant messaging (IM), or other forms of computer chat. However, even with its predicted demise, traffic analysis reveals the majority of the packet volume of the Internet is still email (Rainie, 2005). Even with more immediate communication options such as text messaging and the growing spam problem, overall email use continues to grow. A survey of business executives found 71 percent identified email as their preferred medium compared to 27 percent in 2001 (OfficeTeam, 2006). In 2006, there were an estimated 6 trillion nonspam emails sent or about 25 billion messages per day (Ferris Research, 2008). Unfortunately, much email is spam, the generic term for unwanted and unsolicited mail. A little spam trivia: The term is from the classic Monty Python restaurant skit where all the breakfast options included varying amounts of the processed meat known as SPAM™, whether the customer wanted it or not. Spam is an ever-increasing and costly problem. A 2005 *New York Times* report estimated almost 80 percent of the email sent that year fit this category; a 2006 estimate put spam at 75 percent of all email (Ferris Research, 2008). Spam is difficult to control or regulate because so much of it is from foreign sources; China is currently the country of origin for the majority of U.S. spam (Talbot, 2008).

Early access to electronic mail was often through a shell account on a mainframe or other large-scale computer, which was not a very user-friendly environment. All ISPs now offer email service, and it is available for those on the "have not" side of the digital divide through free Web-based services such as Hotmail, Yahoo mail, and Google mail, which are freely available and can be used from public access computers in many libraries. The alternative to Web-based mail is to use a specialized mail client such as Microsoft Outlook or the Eudora mail client program. These programs generally have more features for improved filtering and handling of email compared to Web browser mail systems, but they require separate software configurations for each user.

Mail servers handle the large traffic associated with email systems by using one or more protocols to implement SMTP. Two common strategies for mail services are Post Office Protocol (POP) and Internet Message Access Pool (IMAP) server approaches. Another mail solution is the Microsoft Exchange Server option. All allow users to view their mail using a mail client or through a Web browser interface; user preference determines whether the mail remains on the server account or is downloaded to a local computer.

SMTP was designed to transmit ASCII text data, and encoding schemes are needed to allow for the attachment of binary files. Examples of such schemes include Multipurpose Internet Mail Extensions (MIME) and UUENCODE. Both schemes convert a binary file into an ASCII representation for transmission and then convert it back to binary on the receiving end. This feature is both "good news and bad news" as binary attachments allow users to exchange data in all formats, but it also allows easy dissemination of viruses, Worms and Trojan Horse programs, which are explored in Chapter 6. These encoding actions require that both sender and receiver have the encoding technology as part of their mail program. Styled mail with much more formatting than simple text is now possible by the insertion of HTML markup into the message to enhance presentation in the mail client. Because HTML is all just ASCII text, this approach works fine within the text-only constraints of SMTP as long as the recipient email program can render HTML.

Email represents an essential communication channel for students, teachers, businesses, and the public. Librarians were early adopters of this technology and found it applicable to many work situations. Email provides options for reference service, interlibrary loan requests, and professional development. Electronic discussion lists were an early application of email that allowed subscribers to join a community of people interested in sharing ideas, questions, and answers with each other. They are still widely used, although blogs and social networking sites are more popular and are displacing these email applications. Discussion lists may be moderated and strictly controlled, or very open and unregulated. Most discussion lists are run by programs such as the LISTSERV or MajorDomo at some hosting site. Because a program is managing the subscription process and options, list participants must learn how the program expects to receive instructions for list management activities; this is done either through email commands or through a Web interface. Those new to lists need to learn the culture of the list and the proper "netiquette" for such email communication in the context of established boundaries of acceptable activities for the list in use. Professional discussion lists expect participants to behave in a professional manner. This includes considering how the message is styled (such as not writing notes in all capital letters), the tone of the content ("flaming" other members of the group is not considered professional behavior), and understanding the list reply settings to avoid replying to all when intending to reach an individual.

Usenet groups still exist and at one time were a popular, albeit primitive, form of a virtual community made possible by the availability of email. Groups developed around most every conceivable topic, and instead of having messages "pushed" to each member as in a discussion list, users posted messages to a common area where others could read them and respond. These groups are similar to the older "computer bulletin boards" that were quite common in the pre-Web era. The interest in Usenet groups has declined as other options such as blogs and social networking sites have become more common.

The blog, or the personal Web log, may feel somewhat familiar to those who participated in Usenet, but blogs are reaching a newer and much wider audience; Pew estimated in 2006 that 1 in 10 U.S. adult Internet users have a blog (Lenhart & Fox, 2006). Blogs are no longer simply a personal journal for many individuals but a media source that has become increasingly important to information professionals. Blogs are made possible by the XML-based RSS (for Really Simple Syndication, also Rich Site Summary, or RDF Site Summary) protocol. Discussion lists, Usenet archives, and now the blogosphere all reflect significant content channels available on the Internet; these content sources and Web 2.0 technologies are discussed further in Chapters 13 and 16.

REAL-TIME INTERNET CONNECTIONS

Several Internet protocols accommodate "real-time" connections enabling a "conversation" between client and server. The earliest is the telnet protocol allowing remote users to send commands to a host and see the command output. Although many today have never used telnet, they may use newer "real time" activities such as voice over IP that are made possible by broadband connections.

Telnet and TN3270

The telnet protocol facilitates a real-time connection between two Internet hosts. This was an essential tool needed to meet one of the early goals of the Internet; namely, to connect remote researchers to some powerful host such as a NSF supercomputer. The telnet protocol was important to libraries as a way to provide access to OPACs (Online Public Access Catalogs) in the pre-Web Internet, and many libraries provided this access. Libraries also used telnet connections with the Library of Congress catalog or the Online Computer Library Center (OCLC) as a way to import cataloging records for local use and to connect to fee-based services such as DIALOG. Most of these library telnet servers are no longer available and have been replaced with Web services.

There are several versions of telnet used for connections to the different types of Internet host, most commonly these were either IBM mainframe computers or UNIX systems. IBM mainframes are screen-mode machines; that is, they paint an entire screen of output at a time. UNIX hosts are line-mode, showing output one line at a time. These differences in real-time output required separate versions of telnet; TN3270 for connections to IBM mainframes (3270 refers to a terminal emulation type) and standard telnet for line-mode

UNIX systems. In addition, "secure shell" telnet is available to provide the enhanced security required by many hosts for such a connection.

Telnet takes care of the connection to the remote host, but once connected, the user is required to login to an account on the host. Some connections to publicly available resources did not require a login or accepted a generic one such as an email address; this was useful for access to public services such as library catalogs. In either case, once connected to the remote host, you had to know enough about the remote operating environment to make effective use of it.

RTP and IRC

The increase in broadband connections has stimulated interest in Internet-based delivery of live video feeds, video and music recordings, instant messaging, podcasts, and Voice over IP (VoIP). Initially, multimedia delivered via the Web required the client to completely download the resource before playback could begin. This combined with the limited bandwidth of dial-up connections made delivery of this type of content problematic. Multimedia delivery now uses *streaming* technologies. A connection is made to a streaming server, which then assesses the available bandwidth and calculates how much data has to be "buffered" on the client. This ensures that once playback begins, the incoming data stream will keep up with the media output. The Internet protocol used for streaming is the transport level Real-Time Transport Protocol (RTP) and it utilizes User Datagram Protocol (UDP) in place of TCP. UDP has less packet overhead and prioritizes speed of delivery over error checking; streaming does not require reliable delivery because by the time packets could be re-sent, the player is usually past their location in the stream. There are additional standards working in conjunction with RTP, such as the Real-Time Streaming Protocol (RTSP), a standard for controlling streaming data on the Web, and Session Initialization Protocol (SIP) for VoIP. Internet Relay Chat (IRC) is another form of instant communication over a client–server Internet connection. Unlike the RTP protocol, IRC uses TCP packets. IRC enables a communication channel over which an online conversation can take place.

All these technologies had broad applications in libraries in their time, and some are becoming more popular. Although telnet as a way to access public information has been replaced by Web access, it is still used to interact with servers in a command mode to modify UNIX file permissions or change a password. Newer technologies such as instant messaging and IRC are an option for reference and other real-time help, and podcasts and audio/video streaming are being used to support library instruction and tours.

Another real-time connection is Voice over IP (VoIP); IP-based telephone now competes with the traditional Telco voice services. Some services simply enable a TCP/IP connection, which allows one computer host to "call" another, as with the Skype service. Many ISPs offer VoIP, providing the same service experience of standard analog telephone with the added benefit of eliminating long-distance fees. Many companies and individuals now elect to combine both their voice and data services using TCP/IP technologies.

INTERNET FILE MANAGEMENT WITH FTP

The File Transfer Protocol (FTP) allows the uploading or downloading of files between a FTP client and server. FTP servers accessed with FTP clients provided a way to access and share updated software drivers, programs, and data in the pre-Web environment. Files available on various FTP servers were accessed by using a known URL or by searching the Archie index discussed in Chapter 15. Early FTP sessions were launched from a shell account, and the user needed to know how to work in a command environment. Success depended on knowing how to use the FTP client to issue GET or PUT commands and also the commands to inform the protocol whether the requested file was ASCII or binary. Modern graphical FTP clients make this process much more intuitive with a "drag and drop" interface that automatically detects the file type. Another feature of most FTP clients is an option for the manipulation of UNIX file permissions. As this protocol is frequently used to upload content to a Web server, being able to modify permissions is often desired.

GOPHER INFORMATION SERVICES

Gopher began as a local campus-wide information system developed at the University of Minnesota in the early 1990s. It used a system of hierarchically structured menus linked to resources. The development team was lead by Mark McCahill, and as with the emerging Web, the developers of this service almost immediately recognized its applicability to all types of Internet resources and locations. Gopher was released in 1991 and became an immediate success; many libraries, universities, and government agencies created Gopher services to provide Internet access to their documents. Yet, by the mid-to-late 1990s, Gopher had all but disappeared, supplanted by the Web. Obviously, the emergence of the Web had a huge influence on the decline of Gopher services; and its demise was helped along by the University of Minnesota's 1993 decision to charge licensing fees. In addition, the Gopher client software could not view the newly emerging HTML Web content, but Web browsers could view existing Gopher resources, adding to the obsolescence of the Gopher client.

During its short heyday, Gopher servers were setup at most institutions of higher learning and many companies. Menu systems were created, and these were then registered with the "mother gopher" at Minnesota. Gopher client applications became freely available for most platforms, and users could browse the list of all the Gopher servers, select one of interest, and then browse the hierarchical menus at the site. As with the Web, the number of servers and resources grew quickly and made browsing inefficient. Steve Foster and Fred Barrie at the University of Nevada developed the searchable VERONICA index, which enabled keyword searching of Gopher menu terms (Vidmar & Anderson, 2002). Supposedly an acronym for the "very easy rodent-oriented net-wide index to computer archives," it was a companion service to the already present Archie index of FTP servers, so the choice of the name also was a humorous reference to the characters from the Archie and Jughead comics. The VERONICA index was a precursor to the search engines of today, but it had several limitations. First, there were only a few mirror sites of this index, and it was consequently difficult to access as demand grew; second, the intellectual access to the resources was limited to an index built using only terms from the menus themselves, not the full text of the resource. Gopher's day in the sun was short-lived, but it represented the first real attempt to organize Internet content into a more useable and user-friendly information retrieval system.

THE WORLD WIDE WEB

The Web has become equivalent to the Internet in the minds of many users, but they are not synonymous terms. The entire Web is part of the Internet, but not everything on the entire Internet is part of the Web. The Web uses the Hypertext Transfer Protocol (HTTP) and links to form a hypertext database. Because the Web was such an important Internet development, some background on its history is of interest here. A brief discussion of developments associated with Web 2.0 and beyond is at the end of this section, but further discussion of Web 2.0 and its implications for libraries is in Chapter 16.

The Development of the Web

In the late 1980s, a British programmer named Tim Berners-Lee was working on a system at CERN in Switzerland to enable scientists to share and interlink documents. Early in this process it became apparent that, as with Gopher, the technological solution he was developing as a local information-sharing problem could be extended to the global Internet. To their credit, the people at CERN encouraged Berners-Lee in this broader vision. Berners-Lee's early work led to the establishment of all the key elements of the Web as it used today: the URI, a Universal Resource Identifier, changed to the URL (Uniform Resource Locator) by the Internet Engineering Task Force (IETF) in 1992; HTTP, the hypertext transfer protocol; and the hypertext markup language (HTML), which is the markup language used for creating and linking Web content. Of course, this new information system needed a name, and Berners-Lee considered several. One early candidate name was TIM (for "The Information Mine"), but Berners-Lee decided this sounded a little too egocentric (Berners-Lee, 1999). The idea of interlinked resources naturally suggested a "Web," and it was also now viewed as a global possibility, so it became the World Wide Web, also known as WWW or simply, the Web.

As with many great ideas, earlier visionaries, programmers, and engineers influenced it. The modern idea of creating a technological system bringing the knowledge of the world to a desktop goes back at least to 1945 and the Memex proposed by Vannevar Bush (1945) in his seminal article "As We May Think." The Memex as described was a great idea but the wrong technology. The idea of hypertext had also been around for some time; most attribute the term to writer and Xanadu project originator Ted Nelson, who coined it in 1965 (Wolf, 1995). Digital hypertext databases became common by the mid-1980s in the form of CDROM databases and encyclopedias. However, it was Berners-Lee who extended these ideas to develop a global Web of information by combining the Internet with hypertext. He also developed all the essential elements needed to make it a reality, including a transmission protocol, a resource identifier scheme, and a simple markup language, which made it possible to use simple ASCII text programs to create sharable, interlinked content across the globe. The Web was first publicly demonstrated during the Hypertext '91 Conference in San Antonio Texas, and the Internet has not been the same since (Berners-Lee, 1999).

The first view of the Web required a direct telnet connection to CERN. There were just three Websites available on this embryonic Web, so the idea of browsing to find content was a reasonable retrieval strategy. The first personal Web browser clients were text-only and designed for the UNIX platform, such as the Lynx browser developed at the University of Kansas. Anyone with a shell account on a UNIX system where this browser had been installed could view Web content. However, the release of the Mosaic browser brought the Web into the public consciousness. Mosaic was developed by a team led by Marc Andreessen at the National Center for Supercomputing Applications (NCSA) at the University of Illinois Urbana-Champaign. Andreessen went on to form Netscape Corporation, which became the dominant browser client through much of the 1990s until Microsoft entered the browser market with full force. The Internet Explorer (IE) browser gained a dominant market share, but the strategy of bundling it with the Windows OS resulted in an unfair practices court challenge. When the dust settled, the browser wars ended with IE still in a dominant position, but other browsers such as Netscape, Opera, Firefox, and Safari have a significant market share, and Google Chrome is expected to further shake up the browser market.

The Uniform Resource Locator

The key elements to the development of the Web included an Internet protocol to specify the client–server interaction, a way to identify the location of a resource, and a way to create content not dependent on a proprietary format, which was the HTML format.

Initially, Berners-Lee (1999) proposed a URI, a Uniform Resource Identifier, as the way to identify a resource, but the IETF standards body changed this to the now familiar URL, the *Uniform Resource Locator.* URLs have a standard syntax: They begin with a protocol followed by a colon and a double forward slash, followed by a Fully Qualified Domain Name (FQDN; i.e., a host at some domain), followed by the directory path to a resource ending with the full file name. Figure 5.2 shows the structure of a sample standard URL.

Besides the usual HTTP, URLs can begin with other Internet protocols as well, for instance a URL could designate "gopher" or "TN3270" as the protocol. Also note filenames are not always required because several default names are sought by a server when the path ends with a machine or directory name; "**welcome.html**" or "**index.html**" are sought without being specified. URLs typically point to resources on Web servers running on UNIX machines, making case-sensitivity a potential issue; most browsers have a "smart browsing" feature to overcome this problem. In addition, URLs can be shortened with the creation of an alias name and a subsequent HTTP redirect; for instance, in the

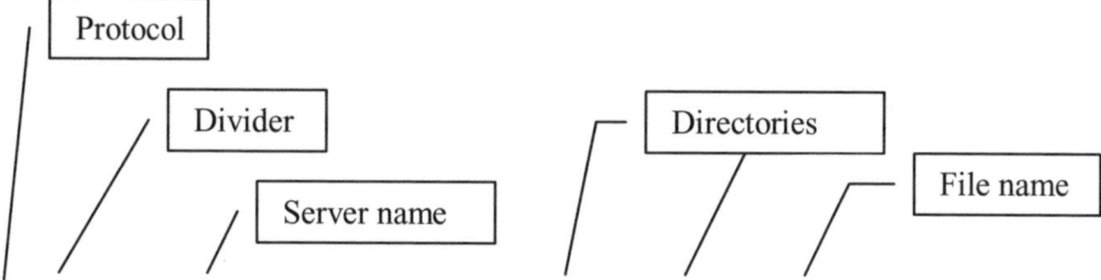

http://www.uky.edu/CommInfoStudies/SLIS/welcome.html

Figure 5.2 A sample URL; note that the protocol designation can be any standard Internet protocol, but http is the default for Web resources.

URL shown in Figure 5.2, the **CommInfoStudies** portion can also be replaced with the abbreviation "**CIS.**" However, as discussed in Chapter 9, when URLs appear in HTML the match must be exact; a link reference in HTML that did not use the mixed case in **CommInfoStudies** portion of the reference would result in a "page not found" error. The strategies to shorten URLs for easier access to a site involves a link resolver; several options to accomplish this are described in Chapter 7.

HTTP

The hypertext transfer protocol controls the interaction between client and server for Web resources and is available in two versions. These are HTTP 1.0, which is still widely used, and HTTP 1.1, which has a persistent connection feature. There are eight different methods defined for HTTP; these are GET, POST, HEAD, PUT, DELETE, TRACE, OPTIONS, and CONNECT, briefly defined in Figure 5.3.

In a standard client–server transaction, the Web client formulates the request header sent to the Web server via TCP/IP. This request has information about the resource, the method of the request, and information about the browser version. The Web server responds with a formal message followed by the requested content; the formal message is a standard response header preceding the requested file content. This standardized "conversation" takes place between client and server. The three methods for HTTP examined in detail here are POST, where data are posted to a program; GET, where something is requested from the server; or HEAD, where only the relevant response headers from the server are sent and not the full content of the referenced object. The HEAD method retrieves information about a transaction but not the actual resource itself. This method could be used to determine if a document or program expected to handle data is even actually present on the server, or it could get metadata about a resource such as the MIME type or the date last modified without requesting the resource itself.

As with all Internet protocols, HTTP is based on the transmission of ASCII text, and all communication between client and server takes place as a stream of 8-bit characters. As mentioned previously, there are two versions of HTTP;

GET—Requests a representation of the specified resource. By far the most common method used on the Web today.
HEAD—Asks for the response identical to the one that would correspond to a GET request, but without the response body. This is useful for retrieving meta-information written in response headers, without having to transport the entire content.
POST—Submits user data (e.g., from an HTML form) to the identified resource. The data is included in the body of the request.
PUT—Uploads a representation of the specified resource.
DELETE—Deletes the specified resource (rarely implemented).
TRACE—Echoes back the received request, so that a client can see what intermediate servers are adding or changing in the request.
OPTIONS—Returns the HTTP methods that the server supports. This can be used to check the functionality of a Web server.
CONNECT—For use with a proxy that can change to become a SSL tunnel.

Figure 5.3 Summary of HTTP methods.

each is discussed separately starting with HTTP version 1.0. Version 1.0 manages four discrete stages in the client–server interaction; these stages are (1) a connection is opened via the default or other specified port; (2) the client sends a request; (3) the server responds; and (4) the connection is closed.

Stage 1 begins as with all Internet client–server interactions: A connection is made via a specific port; the default assignment for the protocol is assumed or if it is different, it must be specified by the user with the URL. HTTP uses port 80 as the default (note that HTTPS, discussed later, uses a different default port), but other ports can be designated in the server setup. If a nonstandard port assignment is used, it must be appended to the end of the URL string with a colon followed by the port assignment. The second stage is the client request, which is a structured message sent to the server. The message sent from the client requests service by sending request headers identifying the method, the client capabilities to receive different types of data, and in the case of forms, the data posted with the form. For example, assume someone is looking at a page called **students.htm** found at the URL **http://www.uky.edu/CommIn foStudies/SLIS/students.htm**. Assume that page has a link to another page called **lisso.htm** that the user follows. In response to that action, the client software formulates a request header to send to the server. Figure 5.4 shows such a hypothetical client request header sent to a server.

The request begins with the specification of the method followed by the name of the requested resource. In this case, the server is directed to locate the file **lisso.htm**. The "body" of the message begins with a list of the various file types this client can accept; the ***/*** designation means it will accept any file type—it then is up to the local client to activate helper applications

```
GET /students/lisso.htm HTTP/1.0

Accept: text/plain

.

.

Accept: */*

If Modified-Since: Mon, 13 Oct 2003 15:00 GMT

Referrer: http://www.uky.edu/CommInfoStudies/SLIS/students.htm

User-Agent: Mozilla/4.0

        [a blank line, containing only CRLF]
```

Figure 5.4 A client request header as sent to a Web server using method GET.

if the browser itself cannot handle the format. The **if modified** information instructs the server to send the resource only if the date/time stamp on the requested file is newer than that of a previously requested version of the file the client has in its local cache. The **referrer** information gives the location of the page with the link that initiated the process, and it is how the server determines where the requested file is in relation to the referring page. In this case, the server is directed to the file sought by removing the **/students.htm** part of the referring URL and replacing it with the string **/students/lisso.htm**, thereby building the absolute reference needed to locate the requested page.

The third stage is the server response to the request, which begins with the response header containing information about the transaction followed by the actual data. Server responses include locating a file requested in a GET, sending an appropriate error message if necessary, or accessing a server-side script to post data to for further processing if necessary. If the requested object is really at the location specified, the server responds with header information followed by the actual HTML resource as shown in Figure 5.5. The server response begins with the "HTTP 1.0 200 OK" and provides HTTP version status information as well as a numeric code (200) indicating a successful transaction. Status codes for normal responses are between 200 and 299; codes 400–599 are error codes such as the infamous "404—file not found" server response. The response includes date/time and server name/version information, as well as metadata about the resource, which includes the length of the file in bytes and the file type, in this example, **text/html**. A blank line with an ASCII CRLF (carriage return/line feed) separates the header from the stream of bytes making up the requested file content. The fourth and final stage is to close the connection.

```
HTTP/1.0  200 OK

Date: Thu, 16 Oct 2003 15:25 GMT

Server: NCSA/1.4.2

MIME-version: 1.0

Context-type: text/html

Last-Modified: Mon, 01 Oct 2003

Content-Length: 345

        [a blank line, containing only CRLF]
<html>
<head>
<title>L.I.S.S.O.</title>
</head>
<body>
<center>
<img alt="LISSO" src="banner.jpg" height="100" width="550">
<br>...
</html>
```

Figure 5.5 Data from a server responding to the GET. The three dots after the <br> are just a placeholder in this figure for what would be the remaining content of this file.

THE STATELESSNESS OF THE WEB

From this discussion, it is apparent that in this version of HTTP everything that happens on the Web consists of these short communication events between client and server ending with the closing of the connection, *at which time the server forgets everything that has just transpired.* There is no record of the transaction kept by the server; this condition is responsible for the *statelessness* of the Web. There is just one transaction per connection, and multiple connections are needed for even a simple Web page with a graphic. If there are six image tags referencing six separate images in the **lisso.htm** page, there must be seven trips to the server for each separate transaction between client and server; one for the initial HTML file, followed by six others to get each separate image file. One analogy highlighting the problems inherent in this approach for transactions is to imagine how a telephone conversation might proceed using the same rules. I would call up a friend (make a connection), ask if someone is there (make request), the person answering could say yes (response), and then hang up (close connection). I would have to call back, and proceed with the next cycle of request and response. This analogy is somewhat flawed in that it is at least likely a friend will remember who just called; this is not the case with a machine. This lack of connection memory is a problem for any kind of transactional activity such as online shopping or interactive searching where maintaining or mimicking a stateful connection is necessary.

Several solutions exist to overcome or compensate for the problem of statelessness. One is the use of cookies, which are "client-side persistent information." Why is it called a cookie? According to Netscape, where the technology was developed, the state object is called a cookie "for no compelling reason." A *cookie* is a small chunk of textual information produced by a server and stored in a cookie file on the client computer; the cookie can contain information about the status of a transaction or a profile you have given to a site. A few basic rules relate to cookie use: First, it is your prerogative to enable cookies; you can set the browser to refuse them. However, doing so can be problematic because cookies are used extensively by many sites. Second, these are just text files, and they can be located, viewed, or deleted. Some browsers create a file called "cookie.txt," but different browsers handle cookie information in different ways. However, viewing the file contents is not very informative because it is information intended for the server program requesting it and uses codes intended for the server. Third, only the server that sets the cookie with your client can subsequently request it, so theoretically, other servers cannot extract information about a transaction you had with another. You can view a cookie by entering a JavaScript command in the URL location bar as you visit a page; Figure 5.6 shows the cookie set when visiting Amazon.com.

Some users are suspicious of cookies and believe they present a privacy issue. However, they are widely and safely used by many servers for online transactions. In addition to cookies, hidden input tags represent another method to pass transaction information back and forth between client and server. These tags are discussed in Chapter 9.

As mentioned previously, HTTP 1.1 specifically addresses the issue of statelessness by the addition of the "keep alive" feature, which enables client and

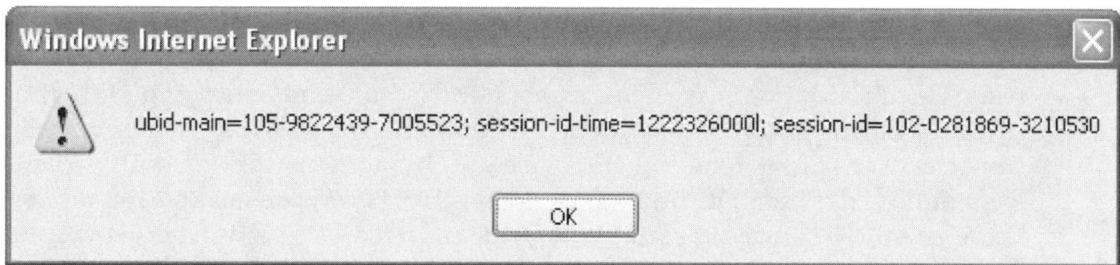

Figure 5.6 A view of the cookie set by Amazon when visiting that site, viewable by entering the line "javascript:alert(document.cookie);" in the URL location bar.

server to maintain a TCP port connection for multiple transactions. Another advantage of HTTP 1.1 is it permits multiple requests to be processed simultaneously (a process known as *pipelining*). However, even with HTTP 1.1, the TCP connection can be lost or terminated for a variety of reasons, so cookies continue to be used in many Web transactions.

HTTP can take place via Secure Sockets Layer (SSL), indicated with URLs beginning with **HTTPS** instead of **HTTP**. These URLs are for HTTP connections over TCP port 443 instead of the default port 80 and have higher packet security due to the addition of an authentication/encryption layer. The addition of the letter "s" to the standard "http" is sometimes overlooked when addresses are shared or linked, resulting in pages that either do not load or behave as expected.

WEB 2.0

The term *Web 2.0* coined by Tim O'Reilly of O'Reilly Publishing has come into general use to describe a transition from the initial Web, consisting primarily of content housed in static HTML pages residing on isolated servers (i.e., Web 1.0), to a more dynamic and interactive computing platform supported by a number of new technologies and protocols. Web 2.0 is characterized by applications used for collaboration (wikis), interactivity (blogs), social networking (MySpace, Facebook, LinkedIn, etc.), and mashups (various forms of Web application hybridization resulting in new functionalities). Protocols and technologies supporting or enabling Web 2.0 include RSS, Simple Object Access Protocol (SOAP), and Representational State Transfer (REST), as well as Cascading Style Sheets (CSS) and scripting for database-driven dynamic content. Web 2.0, the future of the Web, and its uses in libraries is discussed further in Chapter 16.

SUMMARY

The various client–server applications utilizing the higher-level protocols included within the TCP/IP family represent the programs people use for Internet communication or information seeking. Some of these protocols, such as Gopher, are no longer in use, or represent specialized activities, such as uploading files with FTP or command interactions with a UNIX host via telnet, which most nonexperts rarely need. Other protocols, such as SMTP and HTTP, represent the major activities of Internet users. Client programs simply and transparently handle the protocols, making their role less obvious to the user. Information professionals benefit from an understanding of the full range of all the Internet protocols that support the various programs used to perform tasks such as uploading new Web pages or working with a UNIX system hosting them. An understanding of the HTTP protocol and the related issue of statelessness in data communications is critical to the delivery of transactional services. The Web 2.0 view of the Internet depends on adapting TCP/IP protocols and applications to the development of new services for users.

REFERENCES

Berners-Lee, T. (1999). *Weaving the Web: The original design and ultimate destiny of the World Wide Web by its inventor.* New York: HarperCollins.

Black, U. (1999). *Advanced Internet technologies.* Upper Saddle River, NJ: Prentice Hall.

Bush, V. (1945, July). As we may think. *Atlantic Monthly, 176,* 101–108.

Ferris Research. (2008). Industry statistics. Retrieved May 1, 2008, from http://www.ferris.com/research-library/industry-statistics.

Lenhart, A., & Fox, S. (2006, July 19). Bloggers: A portrait of the Internet's new storytellers. Retrieved October 1, 2007, from http://www.pewinternet.org/pdfs/PIP%20Bloggers%20Report%20July%2019%202006.pdf.

OfficeTeam. (2006, January). We never talk anymore. Retrieved October 1, 2007, from http://www.officeteam.com/portal/site/ot-us/template.PAGE/menuitem.f641a8b96a6cc83772201cb202f3dfa0/?javax.portlet.tpst=2bc7e8a27266257872201cb202f3dfa0&javax.portlet.prp_2bc7e8a27266257872201cb202f3dfa0_releaseId=1601&javax.portlet.prp_2bc7e8a27266257872201cb202f3dfa0_request_type=RenderPressRelease&javax.portlet.begCacheTok=com.vignette.cachetoken&javax.portlet.endCacheTok=com.vignette.cachetoken.

Rainie, L. (2005, November 20). Search engine use shoots up in the past year and edges towards email as the primary internet application. *Internet and American Life.* Retrieved May 1, 2008, from http://www.pewinternet.org/PPF/r/167/report_display.asp.

Talbot, D. (2008, May/June). Where spam is born. *Technology Review, 111,* 28.

Vidmar, D., & Anderson, C. (2002). History of Internet search tools. In A. Kent & C. Hall (Eds.), *Encyclopedia of library and information science* (vol. 71, pp. 146–162). New York: Marcel Dekker, Inc.

Wolf, G. (1995, June). The curse of Xanadu. *Wired, 3,* 137–202.

Chapter 6

Internet-Connected Computers and Security

Computer and network security is a broad topic with many facets, and Internet connections add significant new security issues for computer users. General security topics go beyond just dealing with malware. They include preventing intrusions into server and client computers, maintaining secure Web transactions, protecting individual and organizational privacy, and securely administering servers. There are a number of related technical, ethical, and legal topics such as encryption and cryptography, respect for intellectual property, and the role of law enforcement agencies, especially in the context of expanding governmental initiatives and mandates. This overview explores only a few of these security topics, emphasizing how Internet connections create new risks and highlighting risk reduction strategies. Norton and Nielsen (1992) and Cohen (1994) provide comprehensive coverage on how viruses work, and various authors, including Rubin, Gerr, and Ranum (1997), explore a number of Web security issues.

Internet connections create TCP/IP port issues that can be exploited in attacks; some specific examples of Internet-related threats are discussed. Security threats and solutions are platform specific, and this chapter focuses exclusively on Windows-based PCs for most of the examples discussed. This is not to imply there are not similar issues for Apple or UNIX systems, but it is simply a reflection of the dominance of Wintel in the world market. Many workplaces, including libraries, have personnel dedicated to identifying and solving Internet security problems, but sometimes much of this responsibility falls to individuals who are not necessarily network or computer security experts. This overview is for the nonexpert who must become more knowledgeable about computer security issues.

Security has been a major concern throughout the history of computing, and computer viruses targeting the PC have been a problem for users from the beginning. While most people are familiar with the term *virus* in the context of computing, not all threats are true virus programs. *Malware* is a generic term used to describe any of the programs designed to annoy, damage, or otherwise invade your computer and includes viruses, worms, and Trojan horses as well as various types of spyware and adware. In addition to malware, social engineering threats such as phishing schemes also pose security problems.

Transmission of early virus programs depended on mechanisms requiring that users physically share infected disks. However, with the transformation of the personal computer from an isolated word processor and number cruncher into an Internet-connected communications device, many new avenues for transmission are possible. The networked Internet environment has created a more urgent interest in malware transmitted via networks, also known as Malicious Mobile Code (MMC). This broader term encompasses any program that moves from computer to computer via a network that is intentionally designed to modify a computer system without the user's consent (Grimes, 2001). There has been an explosion in various forms of malware; one estimate reports 5 million new variants were released in 2007, an increase of 4 million over 2006 (Heise Security, 2008); the Kaspersky Lab (2008) predicts a 10-fold increase in malware in 2008.

The emergence of the Web, the expansion of broadband connectivity, and new versions of the Windows operating system make it possible to share information and files around the world with the click of a mouse. While it is easier than ever to connect to any host on the Internet to share information or to set up your own Internet-based information services, it is also easier for *others* to find and connect to your machine as well. Many users have become painfully aware of this new reality with the arrival of a cheerful note from their network security officer informing them there are rogue servers or worms operating on their networked computer. It is important to understand how such attacks can happen and how to deal with them. An increased awareness of the external threats to the networked PC is the first step for detecting and deterring them.

SECURITY ISSUES FOR WINDOWS SYSTEMS

The first widespread PC computer virus was the Elk Cloner virus written by a ninth grader in 1982. Given the flip response by some who suggest the solution to the well-publicized Windows vulnerabilities is to "get a Mac," it is somewhat ironic that this first virus targeted the Apple II. Although there are differing approaches and unique security issues for each of the PC platforms, the focus of this chapter on Windows systems is not intended to imply either inferiority or superiority of Wintel PCs, but instead simply reflect how ubiquitous this platform is. Since that first primitive virus, there have been a long succession of new threats and corresponding responses, and the ongoing struggle continues between those who use programming to attack or annoy and those who produce programs to prevent or eradicate these problems.

The Windows operating environment allows for multiple users with differing levels of authority to access to the system. The most powerful access level is an account with administrative privileges. Administrators can set up other accounts, install programs and Internet services, and access, delete, or modify any file on the system. The TCP/IP standard is the foundation of the Internet, and it is part of the Windows operating system. The Microsoft IIS (Internet Information Services), a suite of programs now part of Windows, allows any desktop machine to easily function as a server supporting various Internet protocols such as telnet, file transfer (FTP), chat (IRC), and Web (HTTP).

Any operating system has potential security gaps, and it may seem that Windows has a disproportionately large number of such security problems. However, there are two mitigating factors to consider: First, it is a priority of its developers to make advanced features accessible to nonexperts, and this goal is sometimes at odds with security. Second, the huge world-wide base of Windows systems makes them attractive targets for hackers for both practical and philosophical reasons. Because these powerful platforms are so ubiquitous and sometimes quite vulnerable, there are large numbers of hackers and virus programmers who exclusively target Windows-based systems trying to exploit any weaknesses. Hackers usually have at least one of many malicious goals, including data or identify theft, system vandalism, or rogue server operation.

OS AND OFFICE APPLICATION UPDATES

Microsoft provides service packs and patches on a regular basis to respond to security issues as they are identified. Updating the operating system with the latest patches is essential and it is one of the easiest security measures to implement. Service Packs refer to major updates to the OS with a large number of bundled updates and fixes. There is a steady stream of specific patches to fix immediate problems. You should also update Microsoft applications as well; Outlook, Internet Explorer, and Office all have security issues to monitor. Users can go into Internet Explorer under the "Tools" menu option and select "Windows Update." This connects to a Microsoft Website that scans a system, identifies critical updates, and downloads them for installation. The best strategy is to automate this process; in the "Control Panel," there is an option for "Automatic Updates" where one can schedule a periodic check of a system; once a week is reasonable unless there is a specific threat announcement. However, note that administrative access to the system is needed to schedule this or to do major OS updates. In addition, remember Microsoft never sends out broadcast email messages with patches attached; emails purportedly delivering patches are fake and are just a clever attempt to distribute malicious code. Keeping up with OS security is like dealing with a leaky roof; if it is raining all the time, vigilance is called for. Not only must the damage be minimized when a leak is discovered, but preventative patches can address potential problem areas before they are exploited.

INTERNET CLIENT PROGRAMS AND SECURITY

All Internet activities depend on client programs tailored to specific activities. The list of these various client–server combinations is fairly long and covered in other part of this text, but for most users the vast majority of daily Internet activities involve either a Web browser or an email client. Client-side program security options in these programs are extensive, but their success in large measure depends on the knowledge and subsequent choices of the person using them. There is no question that the simple acts of surfing the Web and receiving email can cause security problems; for instance, Websites can deliver pages with embedded scripts or applets resulting in spyware installations, and email messages can be used for phishing and to distribute malware attachments. There are a number of client-side technologies that can be used for nefarious purposes including embedded Java applets, JavaScript, Active X controls, and Visual Basic scripts. Newer technologies such as Asynchronous JavaScript and XML (AJAX) are used to create Web widgets, which is the term given to mini-applications popular in a variety of Web 2.0 tools. The use of AJAX technology is a new source of concern because these widget applications can enable cross-site scripting attacks (Yaneza et al., 2008). Web developers frequently use these technologies for legitimate purposes to enhance the Web experience, so globally turning them off for all Web sessions is not a very practical option. Vigilance is called for, and some more specific and less draconian suggestions are offered in the following sections.

Spam mail is a huge annoyance for email users; some estimates suggest 75 percent of all email is spam (Ferris Research, 2008). Not all spam is a direct security threat, but some types of spam, such as phishing mail messages, are worrisome. Phishing is a form of "social engineering," which refers to any technique designed to trick individuals into revealing personal or other information. These are fake emails with address spoofing to trick users into believing the source is legitimate, enticing them to volunteer personal information. Everyone is familiar with the infamous "Nigerian email money offer," which offers to share in a large sum of money in exchange for the victim's bank account information, supposedly needed for the transaction. An example of this type of phishing offer is in Figure 6.1.

Most users are aware of these well-known frauds, but there are approaches that are more devious and are more of a risk. One survey reports losses of $3.2 billion to phishing schemes in 2007. The same survey found 3.3 percent of Internet users reported losing money to phishing in 2007 compared to 2.6 percent in 2006 (McCall, 2007). Phishing emails may purport to be from PayPal, your local bank, or your organization's helpdesk asking you to verify or update your account information. These can look quite authentic, using details such as a spoofed "From" address header that uses legitimate addresses, real logos or trademarks, and appropriate URLs. However, "hovering" over the link in such a phishing message often reveals a completely different URL that the spoof address redirects to, often a numeric IP address pointing to a script. Figure 6.2 shows examples of these more devious types of phishing with notes claiming to be from the IRS (left) and a local helpdesk (right).

A reasonable response is to develop both a healthy suspicion of any email solicitation and to utilize the spam settings available on the mail server and/or the client software to prevent them. Many mail servers allow users to customize the spam settings at the server level in addition to using the capabilities of client-side software. Aside from software settings, there are a few commonsense practical behaviors to follow. Do not respond to suspicious unsolicited messages; responding to spam with pleas to stop sending you mail just results in more spam. The "auto-reply" mail option often used by people away from their office is a courtesy to those expecting a reply, but it also automatically

Important read carefully
I am Mr. xxxxxx and I represent Mr. Mikhail Khordokovsky the former C.E.O of Yukos Oil Company in Russia. I have a very sensitive and confidential brief from this top (oligarch) to ask for your partnership in re-profiling funds US$446 Million. I will give the details, but in summary, the funds are coming via Bank in Europe. This is a legitimate transaction.
You will be paid 20% as your commission/compensation for your active efforts and contribution to the success of this transaction. You can catch more of the story on this website below or you can watch more of CCN or BBC to get more news about my boss.

http://www.mbktrial.com/
http://news.bbc.co.uk/1/hi/business/3213505.stm
http://www.themoscowtimes.com/stories/2005/04/11/041.html
If you are interested, please do indicate by providing me with the Following.

Your Full Name:
Your Complete Address:
Date of Birth:
Confidential telephone number:
Fax number:
Your Occupation:
Sex:

I will provide further details and instructions.
Please keep this confidential, as we cannot afford more political problems.
Please do send me your response's soon as possible via my personal email: xxxxx look forward to hearing from you.
Regards,
xxxxx

Figure 6.1 A classic phishing scheme email.

replies to spam mail, which can result in even higher levels of future spam. Do not open attachments or URLs accompanying suspicious messages. Since spam is often the result of email address harvesters crawling the Web, many users try to hide their email addresses from these programs by inserting an image for the "@" in the address; programs cannot interpret an address with such an image. Browser software should be set to prevent, or at least warn, of any attempt to install add-ons; for Internet Explorer, zone settings should be set as high as can be tolerated, at least to the "medium" setting, and third-party cookies should be refused.

The balance between higher security and convenience involves constant trade-offs. For instance, adjusting spam filters to their maximum levels can flag legitimate mail as spam, requiring added effort to identify and retrieve it. Browser security settings may cause interruptions with dialog boxes asking for explicit permission to perform some action or run an applet. Antivirus programs can interfere with legitimate software installations and need regular updating. For now, there are no perfect solutions.

Tax Notification **Internal Revenue Service (IRS)** United States Department of the Treasury After the last annual calculations of your fiscal activity we have determined that you are eligible to receive a tax refund of **$184.80.** Please submit the tax refund request and allow us 6-9 days in order to process it. A refund can be delayed for a variety of reasons. For example submitting invalid records or applying after the deadline. To access the form for your tax refund, click here. Regards, Internal Revenue Service Document Reference: (92054568).	CONFIRM YOUR EMAIL IDENTITY BELOW Sent: Wed 4/16/2008 5:13 PM To: customer@customeronlinehelpdesk.com Dear Edu Email Account Owner, This message is from edu messaging center to all edu email account owners. We are currently upgrading our data base and e-mail account center. We are deleting all unused edu email accounts to create more space for new accounts. To prevent your account from being closed, you will have to update it below so that we will know that it's a present used account. CONFIRM YOUR EMAIL IDENTITY BELOW Email Username : .... EMAIL Password : .... Date of Birth : .... Country or Territory : .... Warning!!! Account owner that refuses to update his or her account within Seven days of receiving this warning will lose his or her account permanently. Warning Code:VX2G99AAJ Thank you for using edu.

Figure 6.2 Two phishing emails that appear genuine seeking personal information.

INTERNET SERVER SECURITY

The focus of this chapter is on client-side security; Web server administration requires significant expertise with the platform in use because the consequences of a server security failure are very serious. An infected or compromised desktop computer misbehaving on a network can simply be unplugged from the network until the problem is resolved, but taking a server offline means lost productivity affecting many users. Many Web servers run on UNIX (or LINUX) machines, and the system administrator controls them. Security on these hosts begins with UNIX administration; a practical workbook on this topic is by Kaplenk (1999). Most of these server issues go well beyond the scope of this overview but a few general comments are included here.

Web server software runs on a computer that could be performing other concurrent server functions. It is generally considered better to have dedicated computers for different major functions, so the administrator does not have to be concerned with securing many concurrent programs on the same server. Using strong password protection for server access is essential, and protecting access to the system "superuser" or "root" privilege account is critical. Default passwords are sometimes associated with new server installations; these always should be reset to new highly secure ones. Services not requiring authentication by users such as anonymous FTP servers can be exploited by hackers and therefore should be set up by those who understand the risks and know how to minimize them. In addition, other server-side add-ons that are installed or enabled to run with the Web server may introduce security issues. For example, earlier versions of the PHP engine used for script processing had the "register_globals" setting set "on" by default, creating security issues. This setting default changed to "off" starting with version 4.2.0 to enhance security of server script processing, but that change created some problems for older PHP scripts designed around the previous assumption. Another area of server-side security concern is the use of Common Gateway Interface (CGI) scripts because these server scripts can be accessed by, and accept parameters from, a URL submitted by a browser. Firewalls and VPNs are one strategy to protect servers from outside incursions. Many Web services require a high degree of transactional security to protect personal or financial data exchange between client and server. Protecting transactional data usually involves encryption and authentication at the network or application level. Clearly, the topic of Web server security for large organizations is extensive and best left to the expert.

COMMON THREATS: VIRUSES, WORMS, AND TROJANS

Computer viruses, worms, and Trojans are common threats that can result in simple annoyance or a disaster by seriously compromising a system. There are four main types of problem files afflicting the Internet-connected PC, all of which fall under the general label of malicious mobile code. *Viruses* are executable code that act as either a file infector or a boot sector infector. The virus code runs whenever the infected program runs or when an infected disk is shared. One common early transmission strategy was the boot sector virus. All DOS/Windows disks have a boot sector outside of the data area that is not visible when the disk contents are viewed. A virus placed there was functionally invisible to the user, but when the disk was used on another computer, the virus was transferred to the hard drive boot sector and then copied to all subsequent disks used on the infected machine. Such an etiology is somewhat primitive by today's standards, but nonetheless, many PCs were infected in this manner. There are also *macro viruses* that can infect and spread via certain data files. These are written within the Visual Basic macro capabilities found in Office applications, thus making data files a possible security threat. One of the first macro viruses was the Concept virus, named because it proved the "concept" that formerly harmless data files could spread a virus. The Concept virus infected the Microsoft Word template file **normal.dot** with the result that all new documents created and shared by the user contained the virus.

Worms and Trojan horse programs do not act in the same manner as classic viruses. They may cause any number of problems; they can turn computers into "zombie" spambots, cause thousands of replicated copies of itself to be sent out over a network, take part in "denial of service" attacks, or cause the afflicted host to lose data or crash (Trend Micro, 2008). The first widespread Internet worm program was the Morris worm, written by a Cornell graduate student in 1988. Since that time, there have been many other examples of Internet-based malicious mobile code. The Melissa virus of 1999 was one of the first to spread by email attachment; it would launch when opened and then send itself to the people listed in the user's address book. In 2002, David Smith was convicted and imprisoned for writing and releasing this worm (Sophos,

Inc., 2002). The Love Bug, Code Red, Nimda, Blaster, and Sassar are other well-known examples of worms that were widely disseminated.

Worms use host systems to replicate and spread, often without the user being aware of this action, and the Morris worm quickly infected over 6,000 university and government computers on the Internet. Worms and Trojans are often lumped together, but they are somewhat different in action. As the name implies, Trojan horse programs are imposters; they claim to be something good but are, in fact, malicious. They depend on misleading the user to run them, and this misrepresentation is their defining characteristic. Unlike worms, they are nonreplicating, and unlike viruses, they do not infect other files. Nevertheless, if they succeed in tricking the user to run them, they can serve as an entry point for a future attack. The TROJ_PROXY malware program is a recent example; it propagates either as a zipped email attachment or through a Website visit. When run, it establishes itself as a startup service that connects to other malware sites for further programs or instructions. The result could be programs engaging in DoS (Denial of Service) attacks, initiating a spam blast, or stealing data (Yaneza et al., 2008).

The first line of defense for individual users against all types of virus attacks is up-to-date antivirus protection. However, because most antivirus software depends on file recognition based on a definition file, one is always at risk of attack by a new virus or a variant the antivirus program has not seen before. An alternate solution is to run added software that blocks any nonauthorized program from running. The downside of that approach is it can interfere with the running of legitimate programs that have not been added to the list of permitted software, which means you must know if it is wise to override the protection software whenever a program asks permission to run.

Further complicating our computing life, many virus threats turn out to be hoaxes. The JDBGMGR hoax is a prime example, propagated by well-intended but uninformed users tricked into believing they have sent you a virus after receiving the hoax email stating they have. The cycle begins with receipt of an email from an email address you recognize warning you that they been infected by a virus and that you have likely gotten it from them. It goes on to claim that you can tell if you've been infected by looking for a specific file called JDBGMGR.EXE, and that if you find it, you should delete it because it means you have the W32/Bugbear worm. The message goes on to ask that if you discover you have this file, you should follow the advice in the message stating "IF YOU FIND THE VIRUS IN ALL OF YOUR SYSTEMS SEND THIS MESSAGE TO ALL OF YOUR CONTACTS LOCATED IN YOUR ADDRESS BOOK BEFORE IT CAN CAUSE ANY DAMAGE." It turns out users always find this executable file because JDBGMGR is a legitimate Windows program (the Java debugger), and the warning you send to others starts the cycle anew (Sophos, Inc., 2008).

Another source of confusion comes from programs such as the KLEZ Worm, which is spread by an email attachment of an executable file randomly assigned the **PIF, SCR, EXE** or **BAT** extension. It infects program files on the machine and makes changes to the registry. It then uses addresses found on the infected system to create "spoofed" email messages (i.e., messages where the TO and FROM addresses are randomly generated from addresses found on the machine by the virus) that are then sent out with the virus attached. Because the address in the mail message FROM line is random and mailers often reject the message because of the attached virus, they "bounce" it to the address of the apparent sender. Receiving such a "postmaster bounce message" indicating that an infected email was sent from your account causes much unneeded alarm because in most cases, your system was not the true origin of the message. This problem was also an issue with the Sobig.F worm (Nahorney & Gudmundsson, 2003).

Other examples include Nimda, Code Red, and Blaster programs, all of which were potentially quite dangerous. Nimda spread in two ways: either as an attached file called **README.EXE** or by infecting certain Web pages with malicious JavaScript code on computers running the Microsoft IIS Web server (Chien, 2001). Nimda also attacked servers by using holes left behind by a previous Troj/CodeRed-II attack. Nimda attempted to create additional security holes by granting administrator rights to the "guest" account, giving a hacker full access to the system. The Code Red virus put a copy of the program **explorer.exe** in the root of drive C: and made changes to the registry allowing a hacker to issue commands and run programs on the infected machine. Once such control was gained, rogue servers could be set up. Infection by the Blaster worm resulted in the downloading of a program (**msblast.exe**) to a system directory where it executes. This program caused system crashes as well, allowing further attacks through the creation of a hidden command shell that could be exploited remotely. The worm distributed itself by scanning for IP addresses that have an available TCP port 135 and then attacking those systems.

Many of these programs, such as the Swen worm, are downright sneaky; it arrives as an attachment to a message apparently from Microsoft that says it is a Windows patch. This is highly suspicious; in general, it is safe to assume Bill Gates does not have time to email you, and besides, Microsoft does not distribute patches in this way. If you started this program, a phishing attack begins with a dialog box asking you to provide personal login and password information as shown in Figure 6.3; the program runs whether you respond with "yes" or "no" in the dialog box (Canavan, 2007).

TCP/IP AND PORTS

Many virus programs are spread through an Internet connection using an available port. As discussed in earlier chapters, ports are an essential component of TCP/IP as all the Internet protocols depend on client–server interactions operating on a designated port. These Internet protocols use client–server architecture, and any given computer can run both client and server programs. The TCP/IP specification uses 16-bit numbers for ports; hence, there are over 65,000 ports theoretically possible. The port assignment is responsible for directing the separate streams of TCP/IP packets destined for the various client or server programs running a particular host. The common protocols have default port assignments, such as port 80 for HTTP; this assignment results in a Web server "listening" at port 80 for client requests. Processes running in the background waiting to respond to an event are generically referred to as daemons; a Web server listening at an assigned port is referred to as the HTTPd.

TCP/IP specifies a large number of unused communication ports that are potentially available for hackers and worm programs to exploit as a communication channel. In addition to TCP/IP ports, NETBIOS (Network Basic

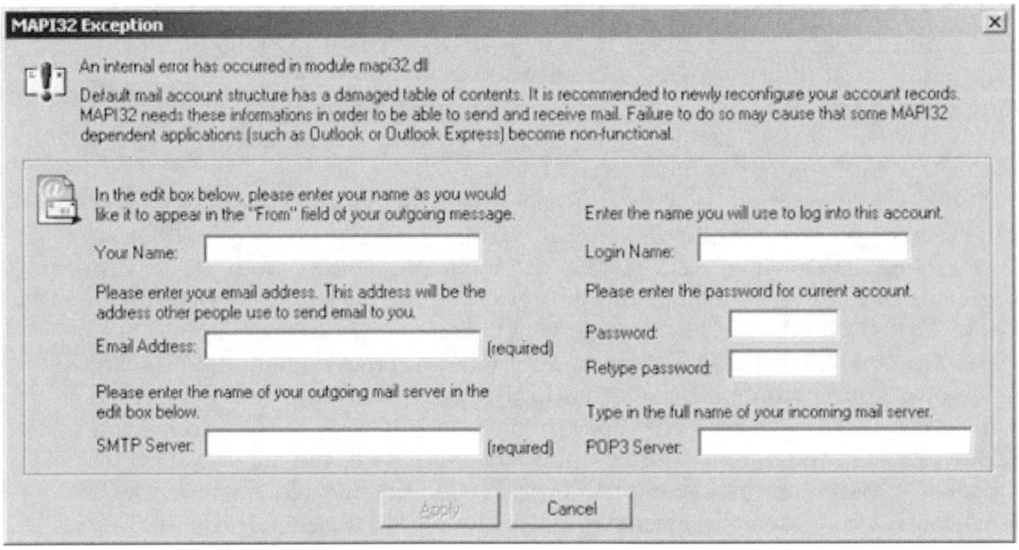

MAPI32 Exception

An internal error has occurred in module mapi32.dll

Default mail account structure has a damaged table of contents. It is recommended to newly reconfigure your account records. MAPI32 needs these informations in order to be able to send and receive mail. Failure to do so may cause that some MAPI32 dependent applications (such as Outlook or Outlook Express) become non-functional.

In the edit box below, please enter your name as you would like it to appear in the "From" field of your outgoing message.

Your Name:

Please enter your email address. This address will be the address other people use to send email to you.

Email Address: (required)

Please enter the name of your outgoing mail server in the edit box below.

SMTP Server: (required)

Enter the name you will use to log into this account.

Login Name:

Please enter the password for current account.

Password:

Retype password:

Type in the full name of your incoming mail server.

POP3 Server:

Apply Cancel

Figure 6.3 A screen shot of a spoofed Windows error message generated by the Swen worm.

Input/Output System) Ports that are used by Windows network for file and print sharing functions can create security concerns. Even though many systems do not need these services, many Windows systems enable NETBIOS through TCP/IP. These ports can become a security issue by providing a conduit used by hackers and worm programs to extract information about your computer. The NETBIOS Ports 137, 138, and 139 are referred to as "scanner bait" because hackers and worm programs scan for their availability to utilize them in their attacks. One academic institution reported during a single day over 18,000 different sources were probing campus IP addresses on port 137. About half of these reflected more than 100 attempts by the remote probing software for a given port; a single IP address in Taiwan accounted for over 20,000 such attempts to access campus computers via port 137 (Caltech Information Technology Services, 2003). Unfortunately, these troubling results are common, and it is no wonder many technology departments block these ports at their firewalls. These ports have legitimate functions in Microsoft networks, but they carry security vulnerabilities if they are enabled over TCP/IP on computers that do not need them for legitimate uses.

The sequence often goes something like this. First, a vulnerable machine is located either via a virus attack or with port scanning programs. A hacker may gain administrative access, either by cracking or stealing passwords, or by using programs to upgrade privileges for another account. A hacker can then setup server functions using the Microsoft IIS suite. These rogue server programs often are assigned an unusual TCP/IP port, given legitimate sounding names (sometimes by renaming a legitimate Windows system file), or can be hidden away in some system directory where they are not easily noticed. Your computer is now the base of operation for the remote user or is acting as a zombie machine generating spam or worse.

COMPUTERS UNDER ATTACK

There are two different, but interrelated, types of attack. The completely automated attack is from malware introduced through email or a Website visit. In this case, the damage is solely from the invading program. However, this type of attack is frequently the precursor to a direct attack by hackers who want to use the computer for their own purposes. Hackers can get control of a networked PC through several approaches involving local or remote techniques. Local issues relate primarily to the level of system access possessed by someone on a computer designated for use in a public area. Administrators achieve protection of these computers by effectively "locking down" the computer with strong passwords and rights policy management. In addition, computers in public areas are often managed by ghosting programs that reconstitute the drive each day, or even multiple times each day, to ensure it retains preferred settings with a clean start. The guest settings influence the prospects for a remote attack, but there are TCP/IP-related vulnerabilities that can sometimes escape attention. Because of this, there could be many computers in physically secure environments such as offices or homes that users naively believe are not at significant risk. However, there is a possibility of a remote attack on such a machine, perhaps by someone halfway across the world.

How can hackers identify a vulnerable machine? It is surprising how much information can be obtained from a networked computer to programs that just ask for it, often for legitimate reasons. The IP address and a list of the available TCP/IP ports are two critical types of information easily obtained. Once a machine has been identified as vulnerable, the next step is to gain administrative access either through guessing weak or nonexistent passwords, through the use of hacking programs such as CRACK (a password decoding program), or with other programs designed to exploit security holes. For instance, programs exist that can upgrade privileges of the built-in guest account to give it administrator rights or that can record passwords and send them to a remote user. Trojan horse programs, Internet worms, and other viruses can play a role in this process. An attack might begin with exposure to malware that both identifies a potential host and provides the entry point for a hacker or program. With administrative access, the remote user can do just about anything they want; one goal might be to set up one or more Internet services to support chat with IRC (Internet Relay Chat) or FTP (File Transfer Protocol) sites for music or other materials. Such rogue servers can operate in stealth mode for some time before detection and final shut down. The security breakdowns allowing this to happen usually relate to security failures in one of three critical areas: OS and application maintenance, antivirus program currency, and TCP/IP port security.

WARNING SIGNS OF A PROBLEM

If a scan with your antivirus software detects a virus on your computer, the best strategy is to go to "red alert." One must immediately begin dealing with the problem by doing whatever is required to remove the virus and correct any changes it made to the registry or other system components. Infection by

Trojan horse or worm type viruses can be a prelude to a hacker gaining full access to your computer and should not be taken lightly. A few general "red flags" might be:

- Unusual activity on your machine (but be sure you know what's "unusual"). This includes the sudden disappearance of free disk space; the appearance of new user accounts or folders; or a sudden, dramatic change in how long it takes a system to start up or shut down.
- Services "listening" at unusual ports can indicate a problem, as can the appearance of new services such as FTP or IRC. Unusual packet volume associated with the system, if monitored, is also a red flag.

Of these warning signs, one of the most important, but one of the hardest to interpret, is unusual port activity. For most users, the easiest way to check out a system is to go to one of the various Web-based security scanning sites (the Symantec software site provides such a service). These sites scan your system and identify vulnerabilities such as high-risk ports accessible to the outside world. For those comfortable examining their systems in more detail and interpreting the results, the Windows **NETSTAT** command or some separate port scanning program such as the Active Ports freeware program are useful tools for examining ports in use.

To use the **NETSTAT** command, go to a command prompt, enter "**netstat –ano**" and press enter. The"**-ano**" portion of this command identifies a set of three specific command modifiers (to see all these modifiers and their use, enter "**netstat –?**"). These modifiers provide added information, including the Windows process identifier, called a PID. This command identifies all ports "listening" for services. If ports appear to reflect services you have not installed, you can then look up the Windows process associated with them. Not all strange ports are indicators of problems; legitimate programs such as mail clients use some unusual port assignments. To see what program is using such a port, you can go to the Windows Task Manager and lookup the PID to reveal with what program the port is associated. Although NETBIOS ports can be exploited, just seeing they are in use is not always a sign of trouble. However, finding new services such as telnet, FTP, or IRC servers assigned to nonstandard ports is a strong indication the computer has been compromised, and appropriate remedial action is called for.

RESPONDING TO ATTACKS

First, take the suspect system off the network. Then confirm the exact nature of the problem. Many sites such as **snopes.com** help distinguish hoaxes from real threats. If a problem is confirmed, the remedy may just involve applying an appropriate security update or using a specific malicious software removal tool. However, if the system has actually been hacked, it may be best to wipe the system clean and start over. Such radical treatment may be called for because just applying patches or removal tools does not guarantee the elimination of the threat. The use of ghosting software alluded to earlier makes it easy to reconstitute the original state of a compromised computer. If it must be done manually, back up all data files, reformat the system, and install a clean version of the operating system. After reinstalling the OS, immediately update it with all appropriate service packs and patches. Get good antivirus protection and update it. Consider the added protection of a firewall at the machine level. Firewall protection is built into Windows, and other third-party products are available as well. However, with local firewalls, be aware some settings can cause unexpected problems for computers on organizational networks. For instance, the default firewall settings may not allow the host to respond to a **ping** request (these are test packets sent to a destination address to see if it responds). On some networks, periodically responding to a ping may be required for the computer to retain the IP address assigned to it, so denying this response could result in the loss of the IP assignment. It is best to check with network administrators before implementing a firewall restricting ICMP activities such as ping.

The networked world gives people almost unlimited access to information, but the access comes with a cost. One cost is the need for constant vigilance and proactively protecting the security of your personal and workplace computers. The old adage of "an ounce of prevention being worth a pound of cure" is especially true in the world of the networked PC.

PC SECURITY "TOP-TEN LIST"

The following Top-Ten list of easy-to-do activities reflects a good starting point for the security-conscious Windows user.

1. Use secure passwords for administrative access to the computer.
2. Implement the principle of "least privilege"—consider not logging in routinely as administrator. Disable the guest account if it is not needed.
3. Know your machine! Have an idea of how much disk space you have available, how many user accounts are on it, who has administrative access, as well as what programs and services are installed.
4. Keep the Windows OS up-to-date with the latest patches and fixes.
5. Keep Internet Explorer and Office patches up-to-date.
6. Use antivirus software, and keep it current.
7. Consider a local firewall if it will not interfere with legitimate network functions.
8. Investigate disabling NetBIOS ports over TCP/IP, and turn off the Microsoft file and print sharing features if they are not needed.
9. Learn how to check or monitor port activity with the "netstat" command, some port scanning software, or a Web-based security scan service.
10. Be informed! Know about problematic email attachments and what file extensions indicate high-risk files. Use important resources such as CERT to learn about common Internet hoaxes and real threats.

SUMMARY

Computer security has many facets, and this overview just touches on a few of the security issues encountered by Window systems connected to the Internet. Understanding security begins with a proactive stance and commitment to ongoing vigilance. Some of the best advice is just common sense, but as threats become more sophisticated and pervasive, a higher level of attention is warranted, especially for those with broader organizational responsibilities for IT.

REFERENCES

CalTech Information Technology Services. (2003, January 6). NetBIOS blocked at campus border. Retrieved August 1, 2003, from http://www.its.caltech.edu/its/security/policies/netbios-block.shtml.

Canavan, J. (2007, February 13). W32.Swen.A@mm. Retrieved May 1, 2008, from http://www.symantec.com/security_response/writeup.jsp?docid=2003-091812-2709-99&tabid=2.

Chien, E. (2001). Nimda mass mailing worm. Retrieved August 1, 2003, from http://www.symantec.com/security_response/writeup.jsp?docid=2001-091816-3508-99.

Cohen, F. B. (1994). *A short course on computer viruses* (2nd ed.). New York: John Wiley & Sons.

Ferris Research. (2008). Industry statistics. Retrieved May 1, 2008, from http://www.ferris.com/research-library/industry-statistics.

Grimes, R. A. (2001). *Malicious mobile code.* Cambridge, MA: O'Reilly and Associates.

Heise Security. (2008, January 15). Quantity of malware booms. Retrieved May 1, 2008, from http://www.heise-online.co.uk/security/Quantity-of-malware-booms—/news/101764.

Kaplenk, J. (1999). *UNIX system administrator's interactive workbook.* Upper Saddle River, NJ: Prentice-Hall.

Kaspersky Lab. (2008, April). Kaspersky Lab forecasts ten-fold increase in new malware for 2008. Retrieved May 1, 2008, from http://www.kaspersky.com/news?id=207575629.

McCall, T. (2007, December 17). Gartner survey shows phishing attacks escalated in 2007; More than $3 billion lost to these attacks. Retrieved May 1, 2008, from http://www.gartner.com/it/page.jsp?id=565125.

Nahorney, B., & Gudmundsson, A. (2003). Symantec corporation security updates Sobig page. Retrieved August 2, 2003, from http://www.symantec.com/security_response/writeup.jsp?docid=2003-081909-2118-99&tabid=2.

Norton, P., & Nielson, P. (1992). *Inside the Norton antivirus.* New York: Brady.

Rubin, A. D., Gerr, D., & Ranum, M. J. (1997). *Web security sourcebook.* New York: John Wiley and Sons, Inc.

Sophos, Inc. (2002, May 1). Melissa worm author sentenced to 20 months. Retrieved May 1, 2008, from http://www.sophos.com/pressoffice/news/articles/2002/05/pr_uk_20020501smith.html.

Sophos, Inc. (2008). JDBGMGR hoax. Retrieved May 1, 2008, from http://www.sophos.com/security/hoaxes/jdbgmgr.html.

Trend Micro. (2008, January). Malware today and mail server security. *A Trend Micro white paper.* Retrieved May 1, 2008, from http://www.emediausa.com/FM/GetFile.aspx?id=8541.

Yaneza, J. L., Thiemann, T., Drake, C., Oliver, J., Sancho, D., Hacquebord, F., et al. (2008). 2007 threat report and 2008 threat and technology forecast. Retrieved May 1, 2008, from http://us.trendmicro.com/imperia/md/content/us/pdf/threats/securitylibrary/tre_threat_report.pdf.

Part 2

Web Publishing

Part 2 focuses on the technology of Web content production and includes chapters on general principles of Web design, graphic formats for the Web, HTML, the use of CSS for presentation control, and the applications of scripting to creating more dynamic and interactive sites. The section concludes with an introduction to XML and related technologies.

Chapter 7

Web Design

Any discussion of the topic of Web design must acknowledge and appreciate that there are both aesthetic and technological considerations and that the skills and talents needed for each are quite different. Web designers must not only have the requisite artistic talents and abilities, but they must also implement their designs within the framework of HTML and related Web technologies. Therefore, designers need an understanding of the limitations of this markup language as well as knowledge of how CSS and scripting can expand or limit design possibilities. In addition, the results of Web design efforts are potentially affected both by the server that hosts the site and by the viewing software of the user. The browser, the type of display device, the OS of the host, and the specific hardware configurations in use all potentially impact design choices and results.

On the surface, Web design can seem straightforward and somewhat formulaic. An overview of the design process could be summarized in the following "10 step plan":

1. Decide what the mission of the site is and identify the audience it is to serve;
2. Examine other Websites to develop an appreciation and understanding of the design approaches of similar organizations;
3. Develop an initial site plan and get the needed organizational "buy in" from those in a position to approve or veto the site;
4. Explore the site hosting environment to determine technology options and preferences;
5. Develop and/or evaluate the content the site is to present;
6. Create a schematic or "story board" that shows the planned structure of the site and the interconnections among the different main pages;

7. Develop a visual metaphor or concept for the branding and rapid identification of all pages as being part of an intellectual whole;
8. Create or acquire the needed graphics;
9. Create a prototype, test for accessibility, and modify based on user feedback or focus groups;
10. Launch and monitor the site for scalability, usability, and actual use.

Although each step might seem straightforward, the reality is that each step presents a host of issues and details to address, and each step requires different kinds of expertise. For instance, designers interested in a dynamic, database driven site must work closely with the technical experts to determine the server-side add-ons it would require as well as to produce the scripts that draw content from the database. However, successful designs require an understanding of not just the content presented and the technologies of the Web but also knowledge of visual arts. Because the intention of many Websites is to inform an audience, knowledge of the pedagogy of online learning environments also contributes to successful design. Web design employs many different techniques and requires a vast array of knowledge, skills, and talents, which is why large-scale organizational Web development is not typically a single person enterprise but instead often delegated to a design team.

DESIGN TEAMS FOR WEBSITE DEVELOPMENT

When the Web first burst on the Internet scene, many organizations responded by either outsourcing their design needs to professional designers or by looking for in-house expertise to handle their Web development. Limited resources, coupled with the newness of the Web, often led organizations to seek to manage development internally with existing personnel. It was not uncommon for a single person, often someone in IT, to be designated as the Webmaster with full responsibility for the launch of the Website. Typically, these individuals were already involved with other Internet technologies such as running FTP or gopher services. Their expertise was often in UNIX server administration and programming, not necessarily graphic design. Consequently, much of the early Web tended to be graphically unsophisticated, utilizing textual designs on the browser's default gray background. Today, the Webmaster designation might still refer to the individual who administers the server, but that person is not usually the sole designer and proprietor of the Website. The desirability of including graphic artists, designers, and content experts, coupled with the use of Web authoring and content management programs, has reduced the need for the technical expert to handle all aspects of Web design and implementation.

The design team has many advantages over a single person. Not only is it difficult to find a single individual with all the needed skills and talents, but a team approach offers differing perspectives on what makes an effective design. The design team clearly still needs the technical expert, not only to deal with issues related to the hosting environment but also to assist with the Web programming needed for scripting dynamic and interactive Web designs. The server operating system, the directory structure employed, and the other server-side programs available are also the responsibility of the technical expert. For instance, a design plan based on Microsoft's Active Server Page (ASP) technology requires additional server-side programs to function, which may or may not be available. In addition, the IT administrator can arrange FTP access to the server for those who need that access to upload content.

Content expertise is necessary to create and evaluate the material presented. This expertise could come from a single person or committee, but content management systems make it possible to distribute content control and facilitate collaboration across a larger group within the organization. The content experts develop new materials, evaluate them, and make selection decisions about digitization of existing materials and prepare them for Web delivery. Designers must also make content format decisions; for instance, the choice of HTML, PDF, or other proprietary formats such as Microsoft Word or Excel significantly affects subsequent access to Web content.

The graphic artist/designer is a key player on the team. Almost anyone can learn HTML, but the creative side of Web design requires the unique training and talents of design experts. A full exploration of the graphic arts is outside the scope of this text. Just as learning the rules of a game does not make everyone expert players, learning about design principles certainly does not make everyone an artist. However, a discussion of graphic design guiding principles may at least lead to a conceptual understanding of these issues and an appreciation of the critical role of text fonts, color, and visual layout in successful designs.

The Web team might also include someone with legal expertise to address questions about intellectual property rights, develop or vet consent forms for images, and comment on accessibility compliance. Engagement of higher management is also important to ensure that the site is developing appropriately within the mission of the organization and is consistent with organizational policies. Management should designate who has the authority to make final decisions about the implementation of the design.

SITE MISSION AND AUDIENCE

In many ways, a Web development project is similar to planning a database. Large database projects usually begin with systems analysis to address fundamental questions and create system models. This process includes the distinct steps of needs analysis, data dictionary development, and system modeling using dataflow diagrams and/or entity-relationship (ER) diagrams. As in database design, where the first step is to identify what kinds of questions the database is expected to answer, the Web designer begins similarly by seeking answers to the questions of who is expected to use the site and why: Who is the intended primary audience? Is the site primarily for an internal audience or more for public relations (PR) and directed to potential external constituents? Is the site attempting to sell something, or is it mostly informational?

These questions often do not have a single or simple answer, and the various answers result in potentially conflicting design imperatives. For instance, the goals of a public relations department may prioritize branding at the expense of usability. Consider the example of a large academic library Website. It is part of a larger organization that may impose design mandates. The audience is diverse and includes undergraduates, graduate students, faculty, staff, and often the public. Each of these groups brings very distinct needs, expectations, and levels of experience to their use of a library Website. The audience has expectations not only regarding what information is available but also regarding ease of use; the search engine Google has dramatically influenced user expectations in both areas. One "Google effect" is that many users accustomed to the simplicity of its interface become frustrated by the more complex information environment presented by library Websites. However, complexity is not always just the result of the interface design but is a direct result of the many functions library Websites must perform as well as the huge array of databases and services they present. Library Websites are expected to be a marketing and public relations tool; a way to provide information about the system hours, locations, services, and staff listings; and to serve as a gateway to the myriad databases, indexes, and catalogs that are available. Library site designs are complicated further by the fact that the databases they offer are heterogeneous information "islands," each with its own separate interface. There is interest in applying federated search or metasearch approaches to address this problem, but these single search solutions are not yet perfected. Given the diversity of both the audience and the various content sources libraries must manage, it is not surprising that a design for such a site involves many tradeoffs that rarely satisfy all users.

The ability to see a site from each of these different users' perspectives is imperative. In library sites, the content expert team members are generally the librarians themselves. Assuming that library users are the main audience of their efforts, designers do need to be careful about specific jargon. Many terms and acronyms instantly recognizable to librarians as efficiently naming a service or product may not serve as meaningful labels to others; for instance, terms such as OPAC, WorldCat, JSTOR, or EBSCOhost all would require further explanatory text or alternate labels.

Library Web designers often find themselves engaged in the same debates that have gone on for some time about their roles, such as the goal of providing what the public *wants* versus a professional assessment of what *should be* in a collection, or the conflicting roles of teacher versus mediator. The library Website is not only a gateway to information, but also a teaching tool, providing opportunities to inform users and enhance their level of information literacy. Related to these differing missions, another design debate has emerged between those who see the simplicity of the Google search interface as a boon to end users worthy of emulation or, conversely, a "dumbing down" of search systems that does not serve end users well. As the Website is an extension of the library itself, it is not surprising that these debates find their way into Web design, and they will not go away once the site is complete.

In the initial design stages, it can be very informative to ask the various constituencies to evaluate the designs of similar organizations. This process can be made more rigorous with an evaluative matrix that allows numeric ratings of various design elements such as visual appeal, color schemes, layout, navigation, and content organization. Such a process will highlight the often-conflicting assessments of different user groups. Such data collection can reveal trends regarding what elements most users find effective and attractive as well as which elements are not, resulting in a design that incorporates the "best practices" of many similarly focused sites.

GENERAL DESIGN GUIDELINES

Much of Web design literature is directed to a business audience, but the general principles described are applicable to all types of Web development, including that done by libraries. One cautionary note about general design guidelines is that they can be contradictory and are constantly evolving to accommodate new technology and new thinking. For instance, two suggestions are "make links predictable" and "make screens as simple as possible." However, in order to make links predictable, you need to add extra explanatory text, which violates the "make it simple" rule. Another guideline is to require a consistent look and feel to every page on a site; yet, there may be instances where more idiosyncratic designs for a particular page better serves a specific function or niche audience. Ultimately, final design choices reflect the trade-offs inherent in resolving the difficulties of presenting complex information environments while attempting simultaneously to keep things simple. Guidelines provide best practices, not fixed rules, and it is with this caveat these principles of Web design are considered.

Key Elements of Web Design

First, just as you were likely always told, first impressions matter. The site home page, sometimes referred to as a "splash page," is the entry point for most users, and it is the initial hook (McClelland, Eismann, & Stone, 2000). Regardless of the wealth of content within the site, the entry page must engage users and help them understand both where they are and why they should stay and look around; it shapes the user impression and experience with the site. If the main page is too busy, has poor navigation, or does not make clear the nature of the organization that it represents, it will not be successful. Frustrated users will likely abandon a poorly designed site and seek an alternate path to the information they are seeking.

A successful entry page needs to accomplish multiple goals. It should (1) "brand" the site with a meaningful visual metaphor, (2) clearly present its content and information about the organization it represents, (3) orient users to where they are, (4) provide excellent navigation, and (5) be stylistically and holistically consistent. Specific features expected in all designs include a search-within-the-site option, the date last modified, and contact information. This last item is unfortunately frequently missing; it is surprising that many Websites do not include basic contact information or telephone numbers in a convenient, easy-to-find location for those who are simply using the site to find a contact person.

To grab the visitor's attention, designers are often tempted to try to impress users with the latest "cool" technique. This can be very striking, but it is important to consider what value is added by the special effect, especially if there is potential for some to find it annoying as opposed to cool. For instance, when Flash animations first became popular, many designers created elaborate animations that, when fully loaded, resulted in a single "enter my site" link. Although these effects can be memorable and visually appealing, they lose their charm after multiple visits. Because many users are interested in getting directly to the site content, an option to skip any introductory animation should always be available.

Another consideration is, as they say in real estate, "location, location, location," which on the Web is the Uniform Resource Locator (URL) itself. The URL is not only used by the browser and bookmarked by the user, but it also appears in many documents such as letterhead, business cards, and brochures. A very long URL can be problematic for these publications and for the user who must enter it from a printed source. URLs that result from database-driven Websites are particularly challenging; they are potentially long and do not end with a meaningful file name. One simple way to shorten a URL is simply to uses one of the default entry page names of **welcome** or **index** with the **htm** or **html** extension. When these names are used, they can be omitted from the URL. But if the designer has control of the URL, keeping it short and meaningful is ideal. The URL assigned is usually predetermined by the organization, but there are strategies that allow it to be shortened or modified if needed. These usually involve some type of link resolver or the use of a name alias that performs a redirect to the site. For instance, the School of Library and Information Science (SLIS) at the University of Kentucky has the assigned URL http://www.uky.edu/CommInfoStudies/SLIS (**welcome.html** is the assumed file name). This reflects that SLIS is part of the College of Communications and Information Studies at the University of Kentucky. Although it logically reflects our place in the organizational structure of the University, it results in a long URL. An alias has been assigned that shortens the college portion of the URL to "CIS" resulting in http://www.uky.edu/CIS/SLIS. This is easier to remember and better for printed materials. Another approach is to use a link resolver service such as TinyURL (http://tinyurl.com/). A long URL is submitted to the service that maps the true URL to a shortened one of the form http://service.com/name. However, such an alias hides the true location of the site, which raises branding issues for organizations or can result in abuses such as creating innocuous appearing links to shock sites (sites intended to shock or offend).

A related issue is that URLs that are very similar to yours can create confusion for the user or result in a potentially embarrassing situation. The URL "whitehouse.com," formerly a pornography site and now a "people search" site, was often confused with the official "whitehouse.gov" site. Purchasing and holding unused but similar URLs is a common strategy to prevent this situation; when initially registering their domain name, organizations can register all the variants of the URL that are still available.

A key design concept is site consistency; each interrelated page should have the same look and feel. Text styles should be consistent and navigation, search features, and logos consistently placed within the page. The look and feel of the site comes back to the idea of branding mentioned earlier. Branding is a key design element that helps users always know what organization the site represents, no matter what page they come to in a search. Developing this visual metaphor for the site allows users immediately to recognize your brand identity by the logos, color schemes, and textual cues. The use of templates and style sheets can greatly assist in creating and maintaining visual consistency throughout a site.

A common goal for many business sites, especially those using the site to sell a product or earn income through ads, is the creation of a "sticky" site; that is, one that retains a user for some time each session. This is not a universal goal; the click-through business model does not expect users to dwell on that site but instead use it as a means to find some other location. Search engines recognize that most users are destined for other sites and do not expect them to linger on their site for long, but as much of their income comes from advertising, they do have an interest in retaining users long enough to present advertising and sponsored links. However, for many business models "stickiness" is a goal: The longer a user is on the site, the better the chance is that they will find something of interest that might lead to a sale. As search engines expand their services to become Web portals, they care more about extending the time a user stays on their site. Many search engines have become full-fledged portals; that is, a site defined as your starting point for all subsequent Web activities. Such full service portals seek to keep users by offering search along with email, Web hosting, shopping, messaging, or other services. The idea of stickiness, however, has both positive and negative aspects. On the positive side, it can mean that a site is so visually interesting and useful that users tend to stay on the site for an extended time. However, sites can achieve stickiness through techniques that do not embody good design, such as not allowing back button navigation and continually reloading themselves into the same or a new browser window, or deploying multiple popup windows before allowing the user to move on. A well-designed, informative site that retains users not because they cannot escape but instead because they find worthwhile content or services is the main goal of the best designs.

A number of guidelines qualify as design myths, or at least overstatements. Heuristics such as "The Rule of Seven" or "The 3 Click Rule" may be well entrenched but are worth revisiting. The rule of seven suggested people can best handle at most seven categories of information; the three-click rule requires all points of content should be available within three mouse clicks. Wisniewski (2008) suggests that neither matters as long as categories are appropriate to the content and the clicks to the content have feedback to show users they are on the right path. This later idea has been called the "information scent" that provides cues to the user that the trail they are on is leading to the desired location (Nielsen, 2003).

The notion that people always want more selection is often embedded in Web design thinking. A counter trend in design is to enforce the "KISS" rule—keep it simple. This view is predicated on the belief that too many choices can be confusing, so it is better to emphasize simplicity. This view appears in other contexts—for consumers in the marketplace, it is described as the "tyranny of choice" (Schwartz, 2005). Schwartz examines the paradox of a consumer-driven society where choice is highly valued juxtaposed with the evidence that too many choices can make even simple decisions overwhelmingly complex. Applied to Web design, the thinking is that pages with too many choices results in a design that does not present any of them very well and that needlessly confuses the user with endless options. Designs that try to do everything for everybody are "Swiss Army knife" designs. It may sound great to have one tool that is not just a knife but also a can opener, bottle opener, corkscrew, file, screwdriver, toothpick, and saw, until you actually try to use it for these diverse functions. Applied to design, the implication is that a site that tries to perform many functions for a diverse audience is inherently problematic. The problem is that this is exactly what libraries must accomplish in their designs. In addition, there are exemplars of sites that handle site complexity well; Amazon is a multifocus site that presents many diverse products and services. Large-scale library Websites must accomplish a similarly wide breadth of sources and services, offering many choices out of necessity. These sites benefit from strong organizational thinking to compartmentalize the diverse choices in way that effectively leads the user through the maze of possibilities. It seems that the KISS rule, like all broad generalizations, has been overstated; its application depends on the mission of the site. Simplicity is easier to prioritize in designs focused on a more specialized audience or functional niche.

Studies of user preferences can inform design practice. A report of the User Interface Engineering Task Force offers some rather counter-intuitive findings that highlight the difference between print and Web publishing. For instance, it reports that the use of white space, which is generally important in print designs, can hurt Web usability. However, recent design trends that encourage simplicity and use of whitespace would take exception with that finding. The Task Force also found that users are more successful with information seeking when following longer, more descriptive links compared to shorter, less informative ones. This is further evidence that explanatory text can be helpful. It also concluded that users do not really hate having to go below the "fold" at the bottom of the screen, so requiring some vertical scrolling to see additional content is not a design flaw. However, it does seem that users do dislike horizontal scrolling, and designs should avoid that necessity.

As noted at the beginning of this section, the design field is evolving as both the nature of the Web and user preferences continue to change, and some designers and information architects are challenging accepted design assumptions. Peter Morville (2005) summarizes three key "mantras" that should guide modern Web design (p. 104):

1. "You are not the user." He emphasizes the need to understand the user experience through using data-driven approaches such as field studies and search log analysis.
2. "The experience is the brand." He suggests a shift from a preoccupation with site image to the site experience itself; this implies that attractive sites cannot compensate for a negative user experience.
3. "You can't control the experience." Simply stated, users do not always engage the site in the ways you have anticipated, and your expectations often are not aligned with the user experience.

Web 2.0 and Design

Web 2.0 thinking has definitely influenced Web design. There is even some speculation that Web 2.0 tools may eliminate Web design as an autonomous, stand-alone process performed separately from simple content management. Even with more user-friendly tools such as Dreamweaver, creating and managing a Website and keeping it current is a labor-intensive activity. Web 2.0 technologies provide an alternate avenue to traditional Web publishing for content delivery and promotion. Instead of a traditional Website, blogs are available with free accounts on WordPress.com or Blogger.com. Images or video can be pulled into the blog content from Flickr or YouTube, and an RSS subscribe option can be added through a service such as FeedBurner.com. These combined activities result in a Web-delivered, targeted content stream that is easy to update with little of the fuss of a full design implementation. This is clearly appealing to many who do not have the resources to manage a full Web presence. Although some larger organizations are utilizing similar strategies, most still utilize traditional Web design techniques as described in this chapter. One hybrid solution is to maintain a site by distributing the content update function throughout the organization with a content management program. Although expertise with design, HTML, CSS, and scripting is still needed within the organization, those without these skills can still participate in revising content.

Content management systems are Web 2.0 technologies that provide access to a Web delivered WYSIWYG editor for content updates. The Web editor allows source code manipulation if needed; however, HTML knowledge is not required. Often the edited updates are actually posted to a database table; the Web page with the new content is delivered through styled templates and scripts that pull the new content from the database. One such system used by some libraries is the open-source FCKeditor (2008) found at http://www.fckeditor.net. Another open source CMS that is becoming quite popular is Drupal (http://drupal.org/), a feature-rich platform that utilizes PHP and MySQL technologies to build powerful and flexible Websites.

Web 2.0 thinking has influenced design by reinforcing the mantra to "keep it as simple as possible." As discussed in the previous section, simplicity may result in fewer site features but with the benefit of ease of use and less user frustration. The Google search page is an exemplar of this "less is more" design paradigm. However, as Wisniewski (2008) notes, Google has the advantage of focusing primarily on one function—search. It does not attempt to present everything it does in the main page. Norman (2007) argues that complexity in design is not inherently bad; people often accept the tradeoff of more complexity for the benefit of added useful features. It seems the bottom line is that while the KISS view should be considered in design, it must be adapted to, and balanced with, the mission of the site.

In addition to visual simplicity and a centered design with a good deal of whitespace, Kroski (2007) highlights other important characteristics of Web 2.0 design, such as more interactivity; interface development utilizing XML and scripting technologies; the use of overlays with maps and other "mashup" approaches; and more collaborative, socialized designs. Socialization of the site includes opportunities for user commentary and reviews, RSS feeds and subscriptions, and "send-to-friend" options for site content. Another interactive feature is the use of links that result in pull-down text boxes or callouts instead of loading a new page. While all these features extend the design possibilities, designer Jakob Nielsen adds a note of caution, warning that although Web 2.0 is the "latest fashion," designers should still heed established principles of good design that emphasize usability more than trendiness (BBC News, 2007).

SITE SCHEMATICS

After the basic questions about the nature of the site are addressed and the initial content decisions made, it is helpful to create a schematic of the anticipated site structure. There are many techniques employed for this design phase, ranging from a simple sketch on paper to more formal "storyboarding," a technique used in the visual and dramatic arts to understand the story to be told by creating scene posters. Film storyboarding is a very involved process that visualizes the scenes and characters as well as the order in which they will appear. Web schematics are functionally similar to database modeling techniques that utilize dataflow diagrams to identify processes and/or entity-relationship (ER) diagrams. Similarly, Web schematics help the designer identify what the site is about and how the elements are interrelated. Initial views might emphasize just the main pages and their relationships, but other more detailed maps might show the full site hierarchy. This initial drawing or blueprint is a rough sketch done using the "butcher paper method" of design (Tittel, Price, & Stewart, 1997). This leads to a more formal representation of any site hierarchies. Figures 7.1 and 7.2 are examples of a rough "butcher paper" sketch drawing and a more formal site map.

LAYOUT

Cultural influences play a role in layout preferences. Westerners read from left to right and from top to bottom, so our eyes tend to gravitate initially to the upper left. Eye tracking studies of people viewing Web pages support this general tendency. A study by the Nielsen Norman Group found that users specifically view a page in an F-shaped pattern; a horizontal glance across the top, followed by a second horizontal glance at about the middle of the screen, and finally a vertical glance down the left side (Nielsen, 2006). These findings reveal that (1) users do not read a page thoroughly and that (2) essential content should be placed in one of these specific optimal areas on the screen.

In addition, layout is influenced by the viewing medium, which for the Web typically is a screen and not a printed page. Layout is complicated further by the variety and unpredictability of the various types of devices used to view the site as well as the various screen sizes and resolutions in use. The desktop computer browser has been the main way people look at Web content, but more mobile and handheld devices are being used to access the Web via other user agents than the standard browser. Such devices often require alternate views of the content that do not utilize style sheets or scripts. Anticipating these parameters is a design challenge, and although the designer can attempt

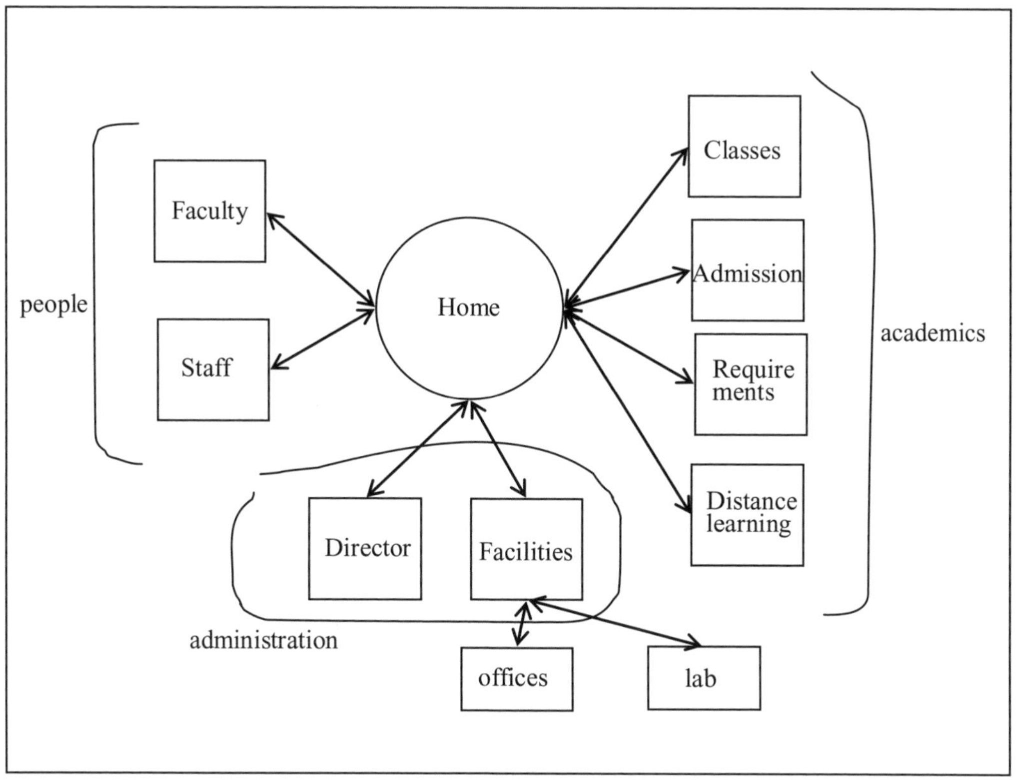

Figure 7.1 A butcher paper sketch of the main pages in a design.

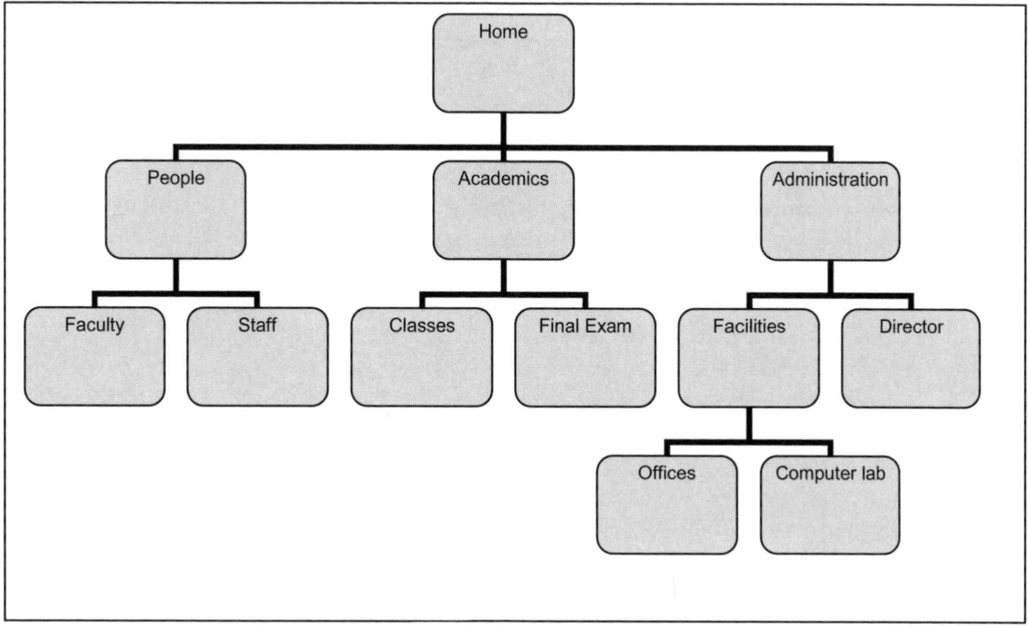

Figure 7.2 A formal site map showing the site hierarchy.

to match a page version to the viewing device, some design decisions reflect a best guess about the "typical" viewing environment of most users.

Many designs use a multifaceted "container" view of the document. Such a design might begin with a layout template that specifies four distinct areas within the page as shown in Figure 7.3. Note that there are many possible templates, and each has potential issues to consider. The style coding details used to achieve these different "boxes" are discussed in the section on CSS, but as an aside, note that the CSS float declaration, which determines the box location, is not handled in the same fashion by all browsers. In addition, having a footer appear at the bottom of the *page* is not the same as making it appear at the bottom of the *screen*. If the content box above is full, the footer appears at the bottom of the page, but controlling the location of the footer is problematic if the content area is less than a full screen.

In many earlier Web designs, templates often used HTML tables or framesets to accomplish this layout. Framesets present problems that make them inappropriate for most designs, and tables should be limited to presenting tabular data and not used to control layout. Using tables for layout creates accessibility problems, and in addition, there are better layout options available in CSS. The use of frameset and tables for layout control has been largely abandoned, but because of browser version issues with CSS, tables sometimes still are part of a layout solution.

HYPERTEXT

Content has driven the success of the Web, but it is the power of hypertext, the ability to create links within a narrative to other parts of the document or to

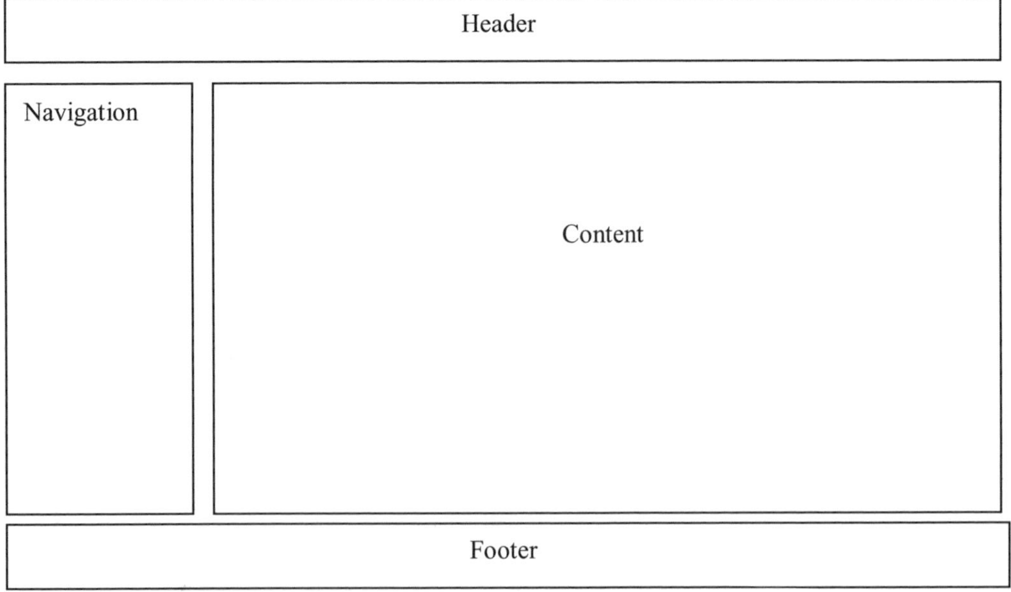

Figure 7.3 A design template specifying functional areas.

other related information sources, that uniquely defines it compared to other content delivery technologies. All Web designs are (or should be) created to take advantage of the power of hypertext. The Web as a whole is nonhierarchical and nonlinear in use. It empowers users to create their own paths through a knowledgebase that is largely unconstrained by the narrative order imposed by the content creator. Hypertext, coupled with the fact that the viewing medium is typically a screen and not paper, significantly influences the publishing process for the Web author. A large textual document can be presented in a continuous flow that the viewer can scroll through, but large blocks of text are usually broken up into discrete but interlinking pages that are graphically enhanced. Because the content may be divided among many separate files, each of which can be indexed by search engines, the Web author must assume that users do not always enter the narrative from a logical starting point. This means that good navigation is paramount to enable users to see how the pages they have found fit into a broader intellectual framework. The selection and creation of meaningful hyperlinks within a work, as well as related external content, add value to the Web publication. In addition, the link structure and its associated anchor text is used by some search engines to assess page relevance, which is another reason why creating meaningful links associated with appropriate text is truly a "value-added" activity.

Links to other places in the same document are *local* and are references to named anchors within that same document. Links to outside sources (i.e., to different files or sites) are *external*. The default browser rendering of a link is to show it in blue text with underlining; this default can be changed, or styles can be applied to links that alter the appearance of a link when hovered over or followed. One consequence of the common use of the default rendering for links is that other text styles are not always recognized as hyperlinks, and conversely, other uses of underlining or blue text for nonlink text can be confusing because most users assume such text represents a link.

SITE ORGANIZATION

Site navigation and site organization go hand in hand. Both of these interrelated topics are reflected in the site model documented in the site schematic. The overarching goal of site organization and navigation is to maximize information access and minimize the number of clicks needed to get to the desired information. Design heuristics refer to a "three-click" rule, which suggests that everything someone needs should be within three clicks. This is not always realistic for large-scale sites, requiring too much navigational overhead in each page. Nonetheless, it is worthwhile to consider how much effort users have to expend to get to the content they need. Although organization and navigation are clearly interrelated, site organization is considered first, as these organizational decisions largely determine the internal navigational strategies for the site.

In the world of the printed book, content is thematically related and the author imposes the narrative order. Navigation is then straightforward because the expectation is that topics are encountered sequentially; chapter numbers and page numbers along with an index to provide nonlinear access to content. However, Websites represent many "stories" that are not presented in a linear fashion. Website designers often confront information organization problems similar to those building Internet subject directories. Making links to *everything* from the home page is rarely possible. Designers therefore consider creating navigational aids such as branching structures that fan out from the home page, menu-based hierarchies to organize the site, a site index available from each page, a visual site map, layers of pages within a screen with "tabs" to select multiple page options within a single screen, a "site search" appliance, or various combinations thereof. Each solution entails tradeoffs, and no solution is perfect.

Site hierarchies and drop down or pull out menus are two popular strategies but present design issues to weigh. Menu systems that depend on JavaScript for submenus have ADA accessibility issues and can be problematic mobile devices. Hierarchies require the formation of categories and have the advantage of organizing knowledge according to some predetermined scheme. However, this approach assumes a high degree of match between the categories and terms used by the creator and user. In addition, hierarchy navigation can be inefficient; if users are uncertain about the correct entry point, they must drill down in a branch to discover if they are on the right track. The addition of a search function can circumvent this problem. Often a design uses multiple approaches to provide alternate organizational structures for a site. Figure 7.4 shows a library system page at the University of Kentucky that utilizes multiple strategies to present various navigational options in a limited amount of screen real estate.

NAVIGATION

The hypertext, nonlinear nature of Web content makes good, consistent navigational tools essential, and hypertext is both part of the problem and the solution. Hyperlinks within the context of a narrative empower users to create their own narrative and path through the content, but they can also be a detriment as users can lose focus and lose their way. Navigational aids allow users to return to their initial path while exploring new information avenues. Such navigational aids can be textual, image-based, or both. The key is that the navigational links be consistent in location and function on every page. The need for such good navigational aids is heightened by the way search engine results can land a user in a page that is quite distant from the initial home page; users should be able to quickly and easily see how to navigate from any site entry point to the main page of the site.

Navigation links with simple words such as "top" are informative enough, but words such as "back" are not very meaningful. It is more helpful to have less ambiguous and more descriptive navigation links. As an aside, a page script may force a reload of the same page, effectively disabling the use of the "back" button; although site navigation should not depend on browser functionalities alone, it is not good practice to force a page reload unless there is a compelling need to prevent back navigation. The application of styles or scripts can make textual navigation links more visually animated and noticeable. Navigation can be associated with images by using either the whole image or using selected image areas to provide multiple links by creating an image map.

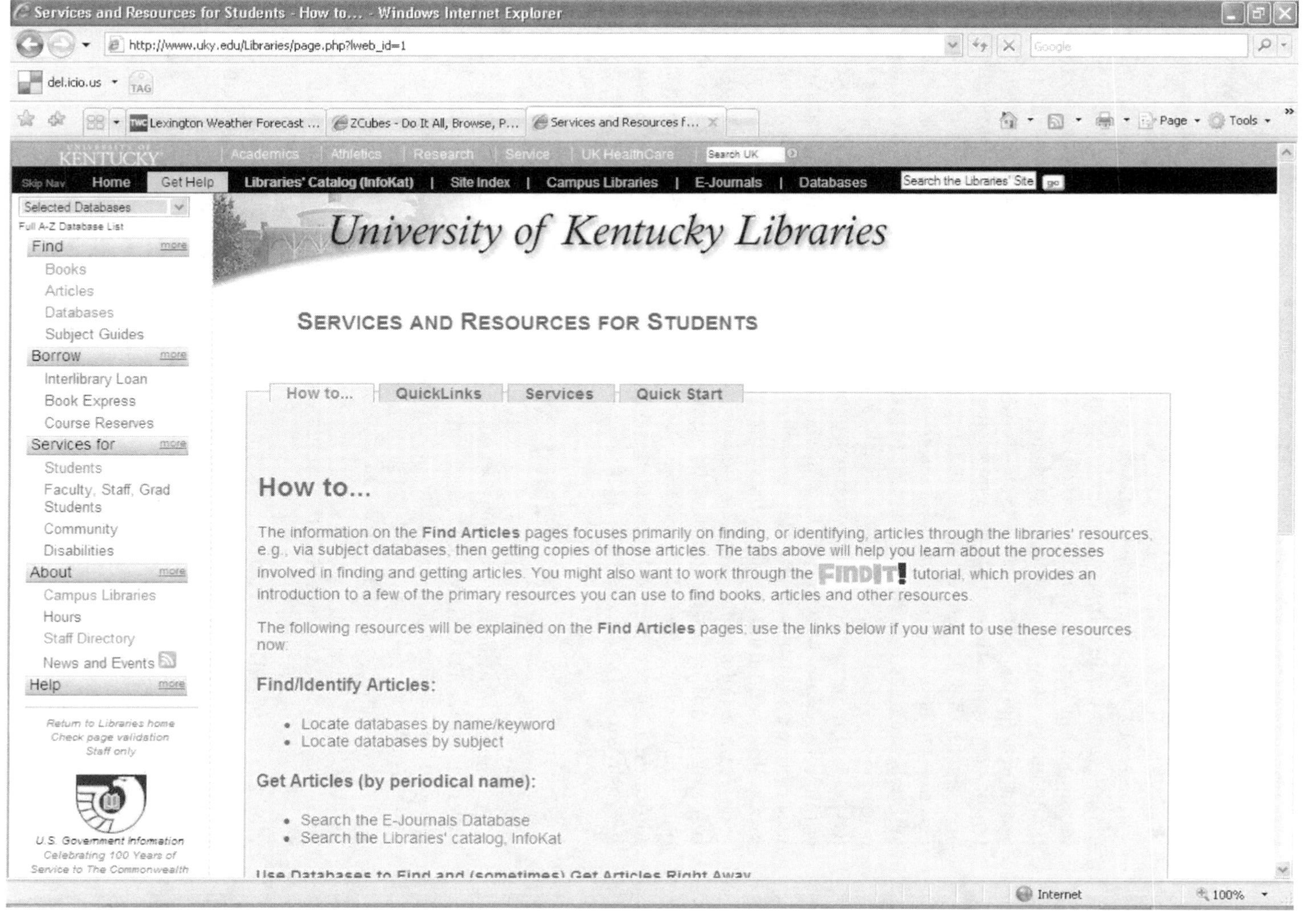

Figure 7.4 A library page with multiple navigational strategies to present many options in limited space.

Rollover scripts that change in appearance when hovered over or clicked can also activate image links, but CSS approaches that make use of styled lists of links are largely displacing these image-based navigation techniques.

IMAGE SYMBOLISM

Images can represent ideas and content in many ways and, whether used for navigation or to supplement and enhance the content, are part of the ongoing appeal of Web publishing compared to earlier text-only Internet services. Some image uses are examples of iconography, which is an attempt to represent the shape or features of an object; a stick figure drawing of a person may not be very sophisticated but is nonetheless instantly recognizable. Ideographs are images that are not as literal but represent an abstract concept, such as the use of the skull and crossbones to indicate danger or death. Mnemonic symbols are ones that have a learned meaning; for instance, a hypertext link is a learned symbol. Much of the success of computer graphical user interfaces (GUIs) is due to the preference of most people for icons to pictorially represent commands. Many images used for navigation are simple buttons that contain descriptive text within them. Hover-over and on-click changes further animate image links and indicate their function. Navigation images without explanatory text are potentially problematic because iconic representations may not be recognizable by all; in addition, recognition of ideograph or mnemonic symbols is culturally dependent and therefore may not be universally understood. Alternate text provides additional description for image-based links and is necessary for ADA accessibility.

Image Maps

An image map allows for different parts of an image to be associated with different URLs. (The HTML coding for image maps is discussed in Chapter 9.) Image maps can serve as a site map or as a navigation bar that appears on every page. There are two classes of image maps: server-side and client-side. Both treat a two-dimensional image as an x-y coordinate plane; different shapes are defined in the image by identifying their geometric coordinates. Each shape can then in turn be associated with a unique URL, complete with alternate text. These coordinates and URLs are stored in the map tag instructions located in a map file or the HTML file itself. As the names imply, server-side maps require a program on the server that can read the map instructions; client-side maps are handled exclusively by the browser. The HTML code associated with a server-side map is shown in Figure 7.5; the code for a client-side image map is shown next in Figure 7.6.

TYPOGRAPHY AND FONTS

The varied Internet protocols accommodate the transmission of textual information. Text formats are those where every byte value is associated with a character in the ASCII text-encoding scheme. HTML files are a special form

```
<a href="/htbin/cgi-bin/maps/search" <img src="graphics/search.gif' ISMAP></a>
```

Figure 7.5 The HTML code for a server-side image map; note the ISMAP attribute.

```
<img src=."./graphics/sitenav.gif" border="0" usemap="#sitenav">
.
.
.
<map name="sitenav">
<area shape="rect" alt="here's our form" coords="195,45,267,167"
href=."http://www.uky.edu/CIS/SLIS" alt="link to our School">
<area shape="circle" alt="link to the  University library" coords="64,104,52"
href="http://www.uky.edu/Libraries">
<area shape="default" nohref>
</map>
```

Figure 7.6 The HTML code for a client-side image map. The map tag is within the HTML file along with the image tag; note the USEMAP attribute.

of simple text file where certain characters are reserved for markup; a huge amount of the content available on the Web is in this form.

Text files are just containers of character data, but how these characters appear when printed on a page or screen is their *typography*. Typography is expressed as different fonts and sizes. Although related, typography and font are not synonymous; typography refers to a typeface and may include a whole family of fonts, whereas a font defines a specific style. In addition, the text appearance conveys or adds meaning to the message. Fonts have "personality" and can be formal or informal, serious or frivolous. Fonts can use bold or all caps for emphasis, italics for highlighting, and light or heavy weights. And just as text decoration reveals something about the nature of the text to the reader, search engines can also make use of text decoration in determining term weight in an index.

There is some jargon related to typography that identifies important attributes essential to the control of font properties in style sheets. Fonts have a style, identified by the name of the typeface. Font size is measured in points or pixels. A point is a printer's measure that is about 1/72nd of an inch. A larger unit, the pica, measures 12 points. Pixel designation can also be used to specify size for screen display but will produce variable sizes depending on the resolution setting of the display. Given the common resolutions in use on standard desktop screens, 10, 12, or 14-point fonts are often best, and anything smaller than 10-point is not recommended for Web pages. Fonts rest on a baseline, and the amount of space between two adjacent baselines is the *leading;* increasing the leading gives more white space between lines and can improve screen readability.

Font styles can be serif or sans serif. Serif font verticals end with a right-angled stroke that gives a "flourish" to the stroke. Sans serif fonts lack these right angle finishes to the vertical. Examples of each type of font are compared in Figure 7.7. Serif fonts have definite appeal in printed materials, but sans serif are generally preferred for display on a monitor. Web readability studies at the Software Usability Research Laboratory (SURL) find that while there are not significant readability differences in serif compared to sans serif fonts at the same resolution, there are differences among font types (Bernard, Mills, Peterson, & Storrer, 2001). They found that Arial is much preferred for screen reading when compared to Times New Roman; they also found that as a group, older adults prefer sans serif fonts.

Font alignment on a page requires controlling margins (top, bottom, left, and right) as well as text justification, which can be left, right, or full. These distances can be specified in styles as absolutes or in a relative fashion. Font alignment is particularly important in navigation areas, and many sites use styled lists as navigation menus. Designer Jakob Nielsen reports that right-aligned menu lists impede readability; a ragged left edge to the text interferes with a quick scan of the menu (Nielsen, 2008). Font positioning and other font properties are discussed as part of typographical control in CSS style sheets.

COLOR IN DESIGN

The Web has become much more visually attractive and more graphically animated since the early days of text-intensive pages that used black text on default gray backgrounds. Certainly, aspects of color selection are personal, and preferences are quite subjective. However, color choice is more than a personal choice; the emotional and/or cultural influence of color should be considered in those choices. HTML allows for the use of hexadecimal codes to specify colors based on the varying amounts of red, green, and blue. The amount of each is represented with an 8-bit number and can be expressed either as a 3-digit base 10 number (0–255) or a 2-digit hexadecimal one (0–ff). A number that is all zeros indicates the absence of color (black) while a maximum level of each is white (the full spectrum of white light). Color codes appear as an attribute in many HTML tags and style rules.

A few general guidelines about color are useful in this discussion of design principles. Borrowing from the Hippocratic Oath, the designer's first priority should be to do no harm. Dramatic and busy-body background colors can

Serif font (Times New Roman)	Sans serif font (Verdana)
T H Y I P i l p H T P I Y i l p	T H Y I P i l p H T P I Y i l p

Figure 7.7 Serif font Times Roman on left is compared to sans serif font Verdana on the right.

be visually stimulating but also reduce contrast with the text, resulting in difficult-to-read pages; the same goes for background images that appear as a watermark. The priority should always be readability. Color choices should also be tempered with an understanding of how long visitors are expected to stay. A splash welcome page with minimal text may utilize bold colors that might be less appropriate on a page requiring more reading of text where bold color choices become more visually fatiguing. One technique to troubleshoot color issues is to change the site pages to a grayscale background. By removing the color and replacing it with varying degrees of gray, you can test for contrast and identify colors that may interfere with readability.

Psychologists know that color can evoke an emotional response, and its use in Web design establishes a "mood." Some color combinations are dissonant, and too many colors can create visual chaos. Graphic artists recommend choosing a dominant color first, and secondary colors later, where the role of the secondary color is to lessen or accentuate the dominant color choice. This is where the aesthetic sense and expertise of the graphic designer is important to the design team.

There is a cultural component to color responses; for instance, in the United States, red and blue have a patriotic connotation. There are many such examples from many cultures; for instance, the color yellow is associated with cowardice in the United States but happiness in Egypt, success in India, grace in Japan, and wealth or power in China. Table 7.1 shows some examples of this cultural effect on the meaning of color (Russo & Boor, 1993). Awareness of the symbolic power of color is needed when designing for a culturally diverse audience.

Color choice also becomes an accessibility issue as it relates to readability, especially because it is estimated that about 1 in 20 people have color

TABLE 7.1 Cultural Associations with Color

Culture	**Red**	**Blue**	**Green**	**Yellow**	**White**
United States	Danger	Masculinity	Safety	Cowardice	Purity
France	Aristocracy	Freedom/ Peace	Criminality	Temporary	Neutrality
Egypt	Death	Virtue/ Faith/ Truth	Fertility/ Strength	Happiness/ Prosperity	Joy
India	Life/ Creativity		Prosperity/ Fertility	Success	Death/ Purity
Japan	Anger/ Danger	Villainy	Future/ Youth/ Energy	Grace/ Nobility	Death
China	Happiness	Heavens/ Clouds	Ming Dynasty/ Heavens/ Clouds	Birth/ Wealth/ Power	Death/ Purity

From Russo & Boor (1993).

perception disabilities. Various forms and degrees of color blindness can make it difficult to distinguish between, for example, red and green. Color contrast issues make some text almost invisible against certain background colors and could make sections of an image map difficult to use. Graphics and color choices should therefore be tested on one of the many sites designed to reveal potential color use problems.

GRAPHIC FORMATS FOR WEB DESIGN

Graphics and graphic file formats are discussed in Chapter 8 but are discussed briefly here in the context of design. The graphic format chosen must be one that a browser can display; the common formats that most browsers handle are GIF, JPG, and PNG. The recent Scalable Vector Graphic (SVG) format is not supported in all browsers, so it has not gained wide acceptance as of this time. However, these are not appropriate formats for retaining all the advanced features possible within sophisticated graphics programs. For all features to be available for future edits, the image must be saved in the proprietary format first; a second "save as" in the appropriate format creates a version for the Web.

From a design point of view, there are questions that should be asked about each image used:

- Does the image add value to the site?
- Is the image aesthetically pleasing?
- Given the limitations of the viewing medium, is the image file resolution appropriate?
- Is the image appropriately sized and proportional to the rest of the visual space?
- Is the image well balanced with the adjacent text?
- Is the image a file size that results in an acceptable download time?

The answers to the first two questions are subjective, but the others are less so and best practices guidelines are available. Most graphics programs create new graphics at default resolutions settings higher than required for Web-based monitor display; this is especially true for images with large blocks of uniform color, for example, as with simple banner graphics. For such an image, any resolution higher than 72–96 DPI (dots per inch) rarely looks better on the screen and only results in much larger file sizes. Scanned photographs may need to be resized or cropped to achieve images that are appropriately sized for the Web page. Alternatively, images can be resized by adjusting the height and width attributes in the image tag itself, but if not done in a proportional manner, the image will be distorted. Finally, file size should be taken into account. If high-resolution photographs or images are made available, they should not be displayed in high-resolution on the initial page but instead in a low-resolution version or as a thumbnail that is linked to the larger file for those who need the higher-resolution version.

ACCESSIBILITY

Web designs are expected to meet accessibility standards, so an awareness of accessibility issues and their resolution should be part of all design plans. There is a huge amount of content currently published on the Web without considering accessibility; in fact, some describe the efforts to address this backlog of noncompliant pages as the next "Y2K" for many organizations.[1] Although it may not have the same disruptive potential, correcting these older pages does involve a potentially significant cost.

The mandate for accessibility is not just good design and ethical imperative—it is a legal issue as well. The Americans with Disabilities Act (ADA), passed in 1990, protected the access rights of the disabled and raised the level of general awareness of accessibility issues. The Rehabilitation Act Amendments of 1998, particularly Section 508, applied accessibility requirements to federal government electronic information and information technology. Although this legislation was concerned primarily with access to federal information systems, recipients of funds under the Assistive Technology Act (AT Act) are expected to comply with section 508. The WWW Consortium Web Accessibility Initiative (http://www.w3.org/WAI/) documents accessibility issues and best practices for Web design.

The numbers of people affected by disabilities is significant, and Web designs should accommodate their needs. The U.S. Census summary data for disabilities reported that as of 2002, 51.2 million people (18.1 percent of the population) had some level of disability and 32.5 million (11.5 percent of the population) had a severe disability.

- About 10.7 million people aged 6 and over needed personal assistance with one or more activities of daily living (ADL) or instrumental activities of daily living (IADL).
- Approximately 7.9 million people 15 and older had difficulty seeing words and letters in ordinary newspaper print, including 1.8 million people who reported being unable to see.
- An estimated 7.8 million people 15 and older had difficulty hearing a normal conversation, including approximately 1 million who reported being unable to hear. (U.S. Census, 2002)

In addition to physical disabilities, census data reveals that 14.3 million people (about 6.4% of the population) have some cognitive, mental, or emotional condition that interferes with their daily activities, representing everything from severe mental illness to various levels of learning disabilities.

What is the impact of accessibility on design? Specifically, the designer must consider both what can be done as well as what should be done to accommodate the disabled in the design. First, accessibility awareness should be integrated into all stages of Web design and site implementation. One way to enhance accessibility is to utilize designs that incorporate multiple formats for content delivery. Some solutions are purely technical and involve some level of tradeoff between the goal of compliance and the desired functionalities of the site. Easy technical solutions include avoiding unlabeled graphics, poor use of tables (including tables without summary information), framesets without alternate viewing options, image maps as the only means of navigation, and menus options exclusively dependent on JavaScript. Screen reading programs, necessary for those with visual or mobility disabilities, have difficulty with pages using noncompliant designs. These programs read across the page and have problems interpreting tabular data or columns, resulting in a nonsensical reading of the page. In addition, they cannot provide meaningful information about graphics or image maps without the availability of descriptive alternate text.

Another accessibility issue occurs with dynamic Web content that is dependent on DHTML and various types of scripting. The Accessible Rich Internet Application (WAI-ARIA) is part of the Web Accessibility Initiative; it addresses how to make advanced site features more accessible by "providing information about user interface controls—such as expanding navigation bars—to assistive technology" (W3C, slide 24).

The use of a screen-reading program or a Website that simulates one is an informative test for all Web designs. A related topic is the use of audio content without captioning or an alternate textual view of the content for those with hearing disabilities. The inclusion of navigation that is not exclusively dependent on the ability to use a mouse and an awareness of various assistive technologies can further assist those with mobility disabilities. Cognitive disabilities are exacerbated by the lack of clear navigation, overly complex presentations, the lack of illustrative nontextual materials, and the lack of descriptive links. Jargon that is not well described is even more of a potential issue for those with cognitive disabilities. Flickering or blinking text should be avoided as not just annoying but potentially dangerous to those susceptible to seizures.

All design prototypes should be tested for accessibility using one of the available Web-based services that examine the HTML of a submitted URL and generate a report identifying potential problems. There are times when the value of a desired design feature might be balanced against the ideal of complete accessibility and result in its inclusion, but all such judgments should at least be an informed and conscious decision based on tradeoffs among site needs, best practices, and available technologies.

DESIGN AND THE LOWEST COMMON DENOMINATOR

A concluding topic is to again consider the question of *who* the design is for. This discussion of design began by emphasizing the need to identify the audience, focusing primarily on site content. However, this question should also be considered from the perspective of the intended groups' expected hardware and software preferences. Consideration of the likely viewing technologies in use influences whether the design should be aimed at the "lowest common denominator" of the various technologies. Obviously, the designer would not expect many users to be using Netscape 1.0, but that said, there are many different browsers and browser versions in use. Differences in display hardware can be especially problematic; although 15" monitors set to 256 colors with

640 x 480 resolution are no longer common, that combination is nonetheless a possibility. There are also differences between the Apple and Wintel computers that represent the main PC platforms in use, and non-PC mobile devices such as the iPhone, iTouch, and other devices are becoming commonplace. In addition, Web browsers allow for a high level of user control of presentation and security settings, resulting in a viewing environment that is neither homogenous nor easy to anticipate. This means that it is incumbent on the designer to (1) try to accommodate these potential device differences in the design and (2) to test the results with multiple platforms, devices, browsers, and display settings. This situation highlights the importance of CSS techniques that enable different versions of the site to be presented to various display environments, but in the end, there are always design tradeoffs that require implementations not ideal for all viewing hardware or user agents.

USABILITY AND FINDABILITY

The discussion of design throughout this chapter emphasizes the creation of highly usable Websites. Much of the design literature focuses on the issues surrounding how to make a site highly functional and usable to visitors who start engaging the site with the home page. However, as noted in other parts of this book, searching has become one of the main activities of the Web, and users typically find content outside of the exploration of a single site through a search that leads directly to a particular page. This adds a new dimension to the design process; not only do designers care about how well the site performs when it is used, but they must also consider the *findability* of the site. This does not mean the various principles of good design covered here are irrelevant; usability is still a priority, and the attention it has received has improved the quality of most Websites over time. However, ensuring a site will appear within a set of pages retrieved by a search creates a new, additional design imperative.

There are companies that offer search engine optimization services, but Peter Morville (2005) describes a number of "findability hacks" the designer could consider. A primary strategy is determining the most common keywords those in your target audience use when searching for sites like yours and including them in your content as well as in metadata tags and in image alternate text. HTML framesets, JavaScript for menus, and dynamic HTML, however, all reduce the visibility of a site to search engines. Appropriate use of hypertext links also contributes to page placement within a ranked retrieval set by search engines that utilize link analysis.

SUMMARY

Websites were initially designed by IT personnel, but most designers now are graphic artists, whose talent and visual sensibility are critical to developing an attractive, functional site. However, content development and technical functionality require a number of other expert skills. Because of the diverse knowledge and skills needed, a team approach with content experts working closely with graphic artists and technical experts is desirable. Even though not everyone may have a great deal of artistic talent, an understanding of general principles and design guidelines is attainable by all Web publishers. Similarly, although many artists may not be technical experts, an appreciation of the limitations and enhancements possible with HTML and Web programming can inform their designs.

The initial phases of a typical design process include both content development and the creation of site schematics to envision site layout, organization, and navigation. Site appearance and readability issues require consideration of appropriate fonts, colors, and supporting graphics. Finally, accessibility considerations and testing on multiple platforms with different display settings and browsers will reveal possible problems with the design.

NOTE

1. The Y2K problem was the anticipated disruption of many computer systems using a two-digit year date when the year 2000 came. Most organizations spent considerable time and effort to address this problem.

REFERENCES

BBC News. (2007, May 14). Web 2.0 "neglecting good design." Retrieved October 1, 2007, from http://news.bbc.co.uk/2/hi/technology/6653119.stm.

Bernard, M., Mills, M., Peterson, M., & Storrer, K. (2001). A comparison of popular online fonts: Which is best and when? *Useability News, 3*(2).

FCKeditor. (2008). The text editor for the Internet. Retrieved October 1, 2007, from http://www.fckeditor.net.

Kroski, E. (2007, April 2). Information design for the new Web. Retrieved October 1, 2007, from http://infotangle.blogsome.com/2007/04/02/information-design-for-the-new-web.

McClelland, D., Eismann, K., & Stone, T. (2000). *Web design studio secrets* (2nd ed.). Foster City, CA: IDG Books.

Morville, P. (2005). *Ambient findability.* Sebastpol, CA: O'Reilly Media, Inc.

Nielsen, J. (2003, June 30). Information foraging: Why Google makes people leave your site faster. Retrieved October 1, 2007, from http://www.useit.com/alertbox/20030630.html.

Nielsen, J. (2006, April 17). F-shaped pattern for reading Web content. Retrieved May 1, 2008, from http://www.useit.com/alertbox/reading_pattern.html.

Nielsen, J. (2008, April 28). Right-justified navigation menus impede scannability. Retrieved May 1, 2008, from http://www.useit.com/alertbox/navigation-menu-alignment.html.

Norman, D. (2007). Simplicity is highly overrated. Retrieved October 1, 2007, from http://www.jnd.org/dn.mss/simplicity_is_highly.html.

Russo, P., & Boor, S. (1993, April 24–29). *How fluent is your interface? Designing for international users.* Paper presented at the INTERCHI '93, Amsterdam, The Netherlands.

Schwartz, B. (2005). *The paradox of choice: Why more is less.* New York: Harper Perennial.

Tittel, E., Price, S., & Stewart, J. M. (1997). *Web graphics sourcebook.* New York: Wiley & Sons, Inc.

U.S. Census. (2002). Census data on disabilities. Retrieved September 30, 2007, from http://www.census.gov/hhes/www/disability/sipp/disab02/awd02.html.

W3C. (2007, July). WCAG 2.0 Web content accessibility guidelines update. Retrieved May 1, 2008, from http://www.w3.org/WAI/EO/Drafts/wcag20pres/wcag2intro20070725.doc.

Wisniewski, J. (2008). The new rules of Web design. *Online, 32*(2), 55–57.

ADDITIONAL READING

Fahey, M. J., & Brown, J. W. (1995). *Web publisher's design guide for Windows.* Scottsdale, AZ: Coriolis Group.

Holzschlag, M. E. (1998). *Web by design: The complete guide.* San Francisco: Sybex.

Leary, M., Hale, D., & Devigal, A. (1997). *Web designer's guide to typography.* Indianapolis, IN: Hayden Books.

DESIGN WEBSITES OF INTEREST

Accessibility analysis at http://Webxact.watchfire.com.

Annoying design at http://www.netmechanic.com/news/vol3/design_no14.htm.

Best practices at http://developer.apple.com/internet/Webcontent/bestWebdev.html.

Color blindness check at http://www.vischeck.com/vischeck.

Libraries and design at http://www.firstmonday.org/issues/issue3_5/sowards/index.html.

Markup validation at http://validator.w3.org/ and http://www.w3.org/WAI.

Screen reader simulation at http://www.Webaim.org/simulations/screenreader.

Chapter 8

Graphics Primer

The capability of the Web to deliver and display images within a page greatly enhances the richness of Internet content. Successful Web publishers must master enough of this complex topic to understand and use the various models for graphic formats and color schemes, to know what formats are best for what application, and to understand the trade-offs between resolution choices and reasonable file size for optimal display. Graphic formats also directly connect to Web design; both Holzschlag (1998) and Tittel, Price, and Stewart (1997) have good coverage of this intersection of graphics with design. This chapter focuses on the technical side of graphics as opposed to the more artistic and creative aspects of image creation and use; these topics are best left to those with the requisite training and artistic talent and are not explored here. McClelland, Eismann, and Stone (2000) provide a number of practical tips for working with graphics.

HARDWARE ISSUES

The acquisition of graphic images has become much easier with the development of the vast array of relatively inexpensive digital devices for capturing images. Early in the development of PCs, scanners were expensive, slow, and cumbersome to configure and use; now there are many types of scanners available with fast USB 2 or FireWire connections. Digital cameras enable the easy capture of images and video for subsequent Web distribution. Large high-resolution flat screen displays and high-resolution color printers allow high-quality output for online viewing or hard copy production. Because the hardware determines the quality of the input and output of graphics, a review of some basic hardware concepts and terminology precedes the discussion of graphics.

Most Web images are viewed on a screen, which is comprised of *pixels*, a contraction of the terms *picture* and *element*. A pixel is a single point of color on the screen; the resolution setting and the dot pitch of the monitor determine pixel size. The resolution setting of a display refers to two different measures: the vertical resolution is the number of rows of pixels on the screen, and the horizontal resolution is the number of intensity changes permitted across each row of pixels. Therefore, the vertical resolution is the number of pixels in a screen column, and the horizontal is the number of pixels in a row across the screen. The dot pitch refers to the distance between pixels measured in millimeters. The higher the resolution, the more pixels there are per square inch. For instance, a 15" monitor set to VGA (640 x 480) has about 53 pixels per linear inch; 53–100 pixels per inch is common on most displays. Many people prefer higher resolution settings, but there is always a trade-off between the resolution setting and object size on the display: the higher the resolution, the smaller the object becomes.

For graphics intended to be viewed exclusively online, using very high resolutions is often a waste of effort because they are not rendered that sharply on the screen. Manipulating and displaying graphics also requires significant computer memory resources. High-end computers for graphics may have standalone graphics processors such as those from Nvidia. Video adapters use dedicated memory or portions of RAM memory via an accelerated graphics port (AGP). Even at the very lowest resolution setting of 640 x 480, there are 307,200 pixels displayed on the screen. If the color depth setting requires 3 bytes per pixel, about 1 MB of data must be delivered to refresh the screen. This was a challenge for the limited memory of the early PC, which was one of the reasons additional memory was added to video cards. Screen output resolution is controlled by the video controller settings in the OS, and many resolution and color depth settings are possible. When different resolution settings are selected, the correlation between image resolution and image size becomes apparent; as resolution increases, image size always decreases, and conversely, as resolution decreases, image size increases.

ANALOG TO DIGITAL

Converting analog data to digital requires the smooth curves of the analog data be approximated in digital form through data sampling. This idea was introduced in Chapter 1 in the context of sampling rates used to convert analog music to digital form based on Nyquist-Shannon Sampling Theorem (Shannon, 1949). Sampling issues also apply to the digitization of images. Sampling techniques are analogous to approximating the area under a curve by summing the area of rectangles drawn within it. The larger the number of rectangles used, the better the approximation of the area and the smoother the curve they form appears. For instance, a better approximation of the area under a curve results if 24 rectangles are used compared to when eight rectangles are used. Figure 8.1 shows the curve with just eight rectangles used under the curve; Figure 8.2 shows the area estimated with 24 rectangles under the curve. For both examples, a consequence of this approach is that the edges of the curves appear "jagged" when the shape is approximated in this fashion.

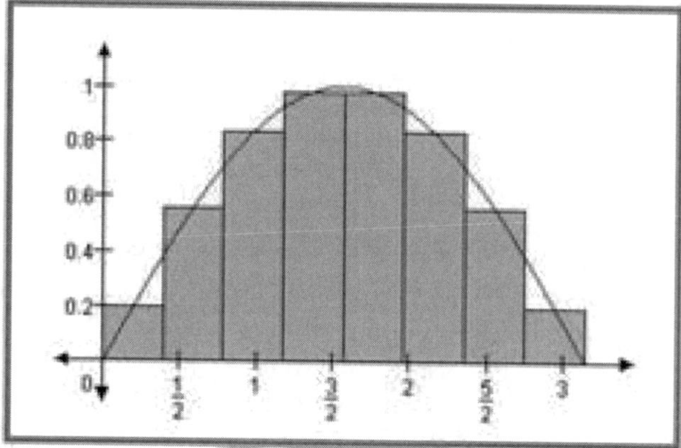

Figure 8.1 The area under a curve can be approximated by summing the areas of rectangles that can be drawn under it. Here eight rectangles are used.

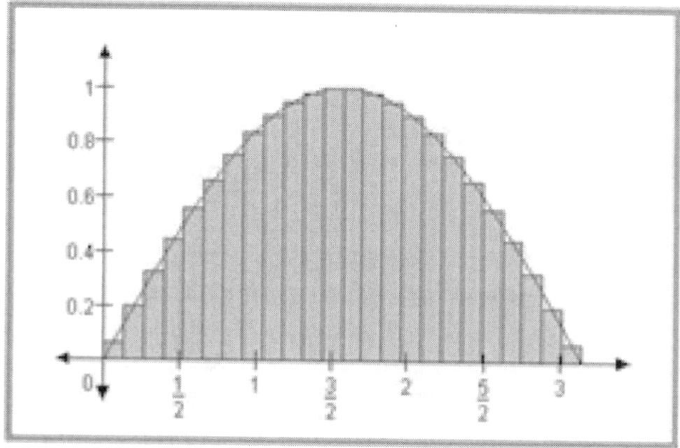

Figure 8.2 The area under the curve is more accurately estimated with 24 rectangles compared to the previous example.

This relates to the aliasing effect, introduced in Chapter 1 and discussed again with raster images.

GRAPHIC TYPES

The two main types of images created by graphics programs are *vector graphics* and *raster graphics*. In a raster graphic (or a *bitmap*) the shapes are approximated by filling in squares within a grid much like the example of using rectangles to determine an area under a curve. The grid is an x-y coordinate plane, and the more boxes in the grid, the better the appearance of the desired shape. However, whenever this type of image is magnified, the grid itself is also expanded, and the jagged edges are revealed; it does not take much zoom magnification for an image to appear "pixilated." The curved line shown in Figure 8.3 could be represented by superimposing it on a fine grid and filling in squares to approximate this curve. The creation of raster graphics always results in the edges of shapes having these slightly jagged edges. This effect is known as *aliasing*, which is a general phenomenon associated with the conversion of analog data to a digital representation. In Figure 8.3 this aliasing effect will be more visually pronounced in the parts of the curve with steeper slope than in the flatter parts of the line.

People are accustomed to seeing textual fonts rendered quite smoothly in most printed materials, so this phenomenon is especially noticeable when text is placed in raster images for use on the Web. Graphics programs compensate for this effect with an *anti-aliasing* feature. When anti-aliasing is enabled the program attempts to "smooth out" the jagged edges. This results in a slight fuzziness to the edges, making them appear smoother but also not quite as sharp. Figures 8.4 and 8.5 show this effect by magnifying the letter "e" created in a graphics program with and without anti-aliasing enabled.

The other main image type is the *vector image*. In a vector image the shapes are mathematically defined by formulas to create shapes. For instance, a circle is defined in the formula pi(r^2); to make a circle shape larger or smaller, the program simply adjusts the value for the radius (r). This action therefore does not alter the quality of the final image as the new shape is created from the new calculation. Both types of images have two essential properties: color depth and resolution. Resolution refers to the number of pixels used to create the image; color depth is the amount of digital data associated with each pixel to represent color.

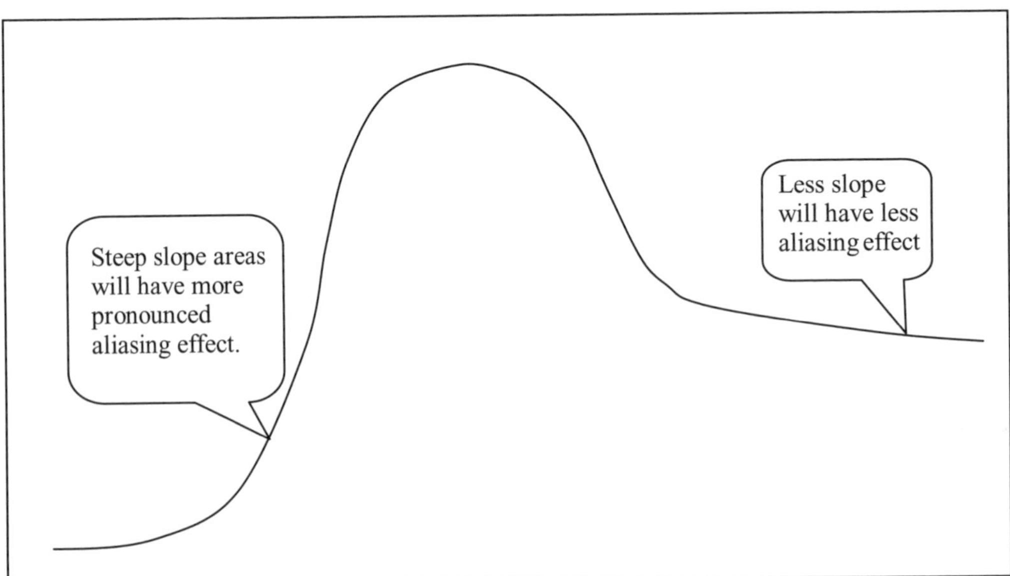

Figure 8.3 This curved line can be represented by filling in squares in a superimposed grid.

Figure 8.4 The magnified letter “e” created with anti-aliasing on.

Figure 8.5 The magnified letter “e” created with no anti-aliasing.

COLOR SCHEMES

Graphics may be line drawings, bilevel images, or continuous tone images such as color photographs. Computer programs handle color images in different ways for different types of output; the three important color models available in most graphics programs are the RGB, HSL, and CMYK models.

All the colors of the spectrum can be represented by specifying the amounts of red, green, and blue mixed together. This is the RGB model, and it is based on the way the human eye works to see a spectrum of color. White light is a mix of all these primary colors; this spectrum appears when light passes through a prism. In this model, the color black is represented as the absence of color and the color white with the maximum amounts of all three components. Computers use binary numbers for data representation, and the size of the number determines the number of unique "things" that can be represented; color depth relates to the amount of data associated with color representation. If 8 bits (8-bit color) are used to represent the array of possible colors, there are consequently only 256 colors in the palette ($2^8 = 256$). This was the color standard for VGA displays common with the early PC. If the system uses 16-bit color, 65,536 colors are possible; 24-bit color makes more than 16 million colors available (2^{24} or 256 x 256 x 256). The RGB model is a 24-bit color model that uses 8 bits for the level of red, 8 bits for blue, and 8 bits for green, giving 24 bits total. This model is used in HTML and CSS to express color values for backgrounds, fonts, and other elements. The computer sees these as 24-bit binary numbers, but the numbers are represented in decimal or hexadecimal notation by graphics programs and HTML authoring programs. In decimal, these are expressed as three numbers that range from 0–255; in hex, they range from 0–ff (ff in hex is 255 in decimal because 15 x 16 + 15 x 1 = 255). Note that whenever all three color values are equal, a shade of gray results. When all three values are 0 the result is black (the absence of color); when they are all 255 (or ff) the result is white (the full value of each component of white light). By varying the amounts of each of these primary additive colors, any color in the spectrum can be represented.

There are constraints on how colors are rendered other than the number of colors theoretically possible in an image. For instance, graphics programs can utilize millions of colors, but if the computer display supports only 256 colors, that is what the user sees. Some graphic formats for the Web, such as **GIF**, use 8-bit color, so the file format selection determines the final color depth. A topic related to color depth issues is the "Web safe" palette, which goes back to the display standards when the Web first emerged. Because most PC displays at that time used the VGA standard with 256 colors, and the Apple computer of that era also had color restrictions, a palette of 216 "safe" colors that were common to both the Mac and Windows platforms was adopted. The first browsers and Web graphics programs were designed to work with this smaller standard set of colors. When developers varied from this standard palette, a problem known as *dithering* could result; this happens when a nonsupported color is specified in an image but unavailable to a browser. The browser would substitute a similar available color, often with poor results. Dithering compensated for the limited Web palette, but it could result in graphics with a blotchy appearance, especially in images with large color blocks of substituted color. Graphics programs usually have optimization features to control the effects of dithering, and most programs still include the smaller Web-safe palette option for simple Web graphics.

Another color model important to graphic artists is the HSL Model, which stands for Hue, Saturation, and Lightness. People see hues of color, not mixes of the three additive primary colors described in the RGB model. Hue refers to the color's place on the spectrum, represented on a scale of 0–255. Saturation values refer to the clarity of degrees of hue; lightness refers to how light or dark the color appears. Graphics programs can provide representations for any color using either RGB or HSL, as shown in the screen shot of the color selector in Jasc's PaintShop Pro Version 9. Clark (1999) summarizes the use of this program, as well as a number of other graphics issues related to its use.

The final color model is the CMYK Model, which creates colors by mixing various amounts of cyan, magenta, yellow, and black inks. This is the foundation for inkjet printing of color images; often the printer has separate ink tanks for these colors.

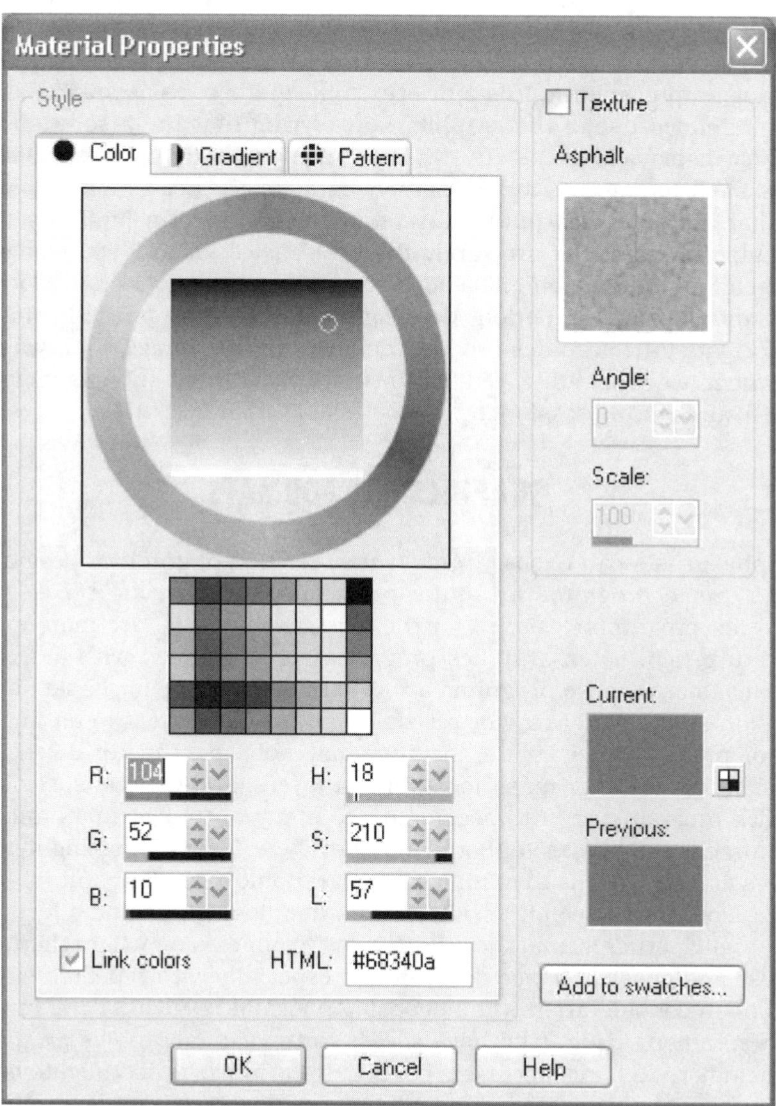

Figure 8.6 The color sector tool in Paint Shop Pro showing various color model representations.

RESOLUTION ISSUES

Generally, references to image resolution refer to the number of pixels per inch it contains. As noted previously, for images displayed on a computer screen, the size of each pixel depends on the dot pitch of the monitor itself. However, the term *resolution* comes up in multiple, differing contexts. *Bit resolution* refers to the number of bits per pixel; *monitor resolution* is the number of image pixels on a screen, and *output resolution* refers to the DPI of printed output. There are three key relationships to keep in mind regarding image resolution: (1) changing the image size always changes the resolution; (2) conversely, changing the image resolution always changes its size; and (3) increasing resolution can dramatically increase final file size.

In the context of Web publishing, there are a few heuristics to keep in mind regarding graphics. First, it is a priority to keep file sizes as small as possible for the intended use of the graphic. Considering that the resolution of most computer displays is in the 70–120 DPI range, many images, especially block images such as banners or navigation bars, rarely need higher resolutions than that. Second, Web publishing requires the use of a limited set of Web compatible formats that are rarely the best choice for archival copies of images. In addition, the Web image formats are generally poor choices for future image editing or manipulation. Keeping a version of the image in the proprietary format of the graphics program ensures highest image quality as well as subsequent access to advanced features of the program, such as image layering, in future editing sessions.

GRAPHICS FILE FORMATS

Graphic artists can choose from a wide selection of graphics programs and formats. Some programs are quite basic and available as free downloads, while other programs designed for the true graphic artist are more expensive and feature-rich. Often graphics programs come bundled with a scanner or a digital camera. These programs are generally adequate for basic image manipulation such as cropping or resizing images, adding text to an image, and selecting areas for new colors, but they may not have the advanced features such as magic wand or mask tools, filters, layers, and various special effects. Graphics programs need to accommodate many output formats and have a large number of "save as" options. Many of these formats use highly efficient compression algorithms to minimize file size. Some formats result in "lossless" compression; that is, compression without data loss that could affect the final image quality; other formats result in "lossy" compression where there is some data loss and possible image degradation, especially with repeated saves.

The main consideration when choosing a format is whether the image is to be shared among users who have access to the same graphics program or if some common exchange format is needed. If the image is destined to be part of a Web publication it must be a format supported by Web browsers. The proprietary formats that are the default save format for each graphics program have the advantage of being highly efficient file containers retaining access to all the special features of the program. Therefore, it is always useful to keep a copy of the image in the proprietary format. If the image is to be shared among users of different graphics programs, the TIFF (Aldus Tagged Image) format is considered as a reasonable exchange format. TIFF is a high-quality format option available in almost all graphics programs. If the image is to be part of a Web publication, the most common formats are GIF, PNG, and JPG, each of which is discussed later. The XML-based SVG (Scalable Vector Graphic) format is receiving attention, but it is not yet widely supported by all browsers (SVG Working Group, 2003). In addition to these, the SWF Flash format is a common format for animated graphic content (Adobe.com, 2008). Many sources cover the details of the formats summarized here (Kientzle, 1995; Tittel et al., 1997; Holzschlag, 1998).

GIF (pronounced "jiff") is the Graphics Interchange Format and was originally developed by CompuServ for banner and other block color images. Although it was a proprietary format, it was so commonly appropriated by Web developers it became a de facto standard early in the history of the Web. The format uses LZW compression, which stands for Lempel-Ziv-Welch, the names of its developers. However, the patent for this compression technology was held by Unisys, so GIF use required licensing agreements to be arranged (Fahey & Brown, 1995). The Unisys patent for LZW has expired, so the GIF format is no longer restricted by it (Unisys, 2008). LZW is a lossless compression technology of the same form as zip-file compression. This algorithm associates longer bit strings with shorter codes stored in a "code book," and this code can then substitute for other occurrences of the longer string in the file. This file format is available to Web publishers through almost all graphics programs (who licensed the right to make it available). There are several versions of GIF, including 87a and 89a; the later allows for animated GIFs. Animated GIFs save multiple still frames together in a single file container and then play them as a simple animation. Adobe Flash has become more common now for Web animations. GIF files are very compact and use only 8 bits per pixel. This keeps the file size small, but 8-bit color provides only a 256-color palette. GIF images display in interlaced data order, so images appear in full form on the screen and get gradually sharper. Transparent GIFS are also possible, which makes the background color of the page the background color of the image placed there.

PNG (pronounced "ping") is the Portable Network Graphic, a newer standard specifically designed to be better adapted to the needs of Web publishing. It was intended to be a patent-free replacement for the GIF format that would have no ownership or licensing issues. As with GIF, it uses lossless compression and supports interlacing while supporting better transparency capabilities and even smaller file sizes; files are often 10–30 percent smaller than a similar GIF.

JPG or **JPEG** (pronounced "jay-peg") is the Joint Photographic Experts Group format, a standard for continuous tone images such as photographs. The actual file container is the **JFIF** format (JPG File Interchange Format). JPG uses a lossy compression algorithm and is not suitable for many types of graphics such as line drawings. The lossy nature of this format means successive saves of the same image to JPG can result in degradation of image quality, so it is desirable to keep a copy of a photographic image in a proprietary format (or a lossless format such as TIFF) for future edits.

SWF, or Shockwave Flash file, is a proprietary format developed by Macromedia, Inc. which is now owned by Adobe, Inc. This format, which uses vector objects for images, was developed for delivery of simple multimedia animations on the Web. It requires the installation of a free browser plug-in for display, but most users have, or can easily get, the Adobe Flash player. Flash has become an important format for content delivery. For instance, for my online course content, I use the Camtasia Studio program to convert PowerPoint slide shows with accompanying audio to the Flash format. The resulting package is very compact—a 30-minute, audio-enhanced PowerPoint lecture output as Flash results in a group of files that total only about 5–12 MB, depending on the number of added graphical elements. This is a very compact package that is smaller than the native PowerPoint file with added audio. In addition to taking up less space on a server and faster downloads for students, the Flash viewer is both free and easy to install. Note that there are other programs and techniques available for converting PowerPoint to Flash.

GRAPHICS AND HTML

Images are incorporated into HTML documents with the image tag. The image tag is an example of an empty element, that is, one that does not mark up any content. Its function is to designate the place where an image is to appear and identify the location and name of the image. It performs the later role with the source attribute that provides location and name information. Another image tag attribute is used to provide alternate text; this is required for accessibility because screen-reading programs depend on it to provide a description of the image. The alternate text is displayed when the cursor hovers over it, providing useful descriptive information to the user. The height and width attributes inform the browser how much screen area is needed for the incoming image so text can flow around it even as the image is downloading. Images can be resized in the display using these tag attributes, but attempting to modify image size by changing the height and width in HTML without using the appropriate aspect ratio can distort the image proportions. HTML codes for color are a feature most graphics programs can provide; a selection made in a color wheel or palette shows the numeric values for the color. This is useful because, as noted in the section about the RGB color model, hexadecimal codes for color are commonly referenced in HTML and in CSS style sheets.

SUMMARY

A basic understanding of graphics and the appropriate formats for them is needed for successful Web design and publishing. Graphic creation requires both technical and artistic skills, and even those with artistic training find graphics programs have a substantial learning curve. Most large-scale Web projects engage one or more graphic artists to ensure the graphics used suitably enhance the site and create an appropriate balance of graphical and textual elements. Even if you are not the primary graphic designer, an understanding of the format options available as well as the tradeoffs inherent with decisions about resolution, color depth, file formats, and resulting file size is important to all members of the Web project team.

REFERENCES

Adobe.com. (2008). SWF technology center. Retrieved May 1, 2008, from http://www.adobe.com/devnet/swf.

Clark, T. M. (1999). *Teach yourself Paint Shop Pro 5 in 24 hours.* Indianapolis: SAMS.

Fahey, M. J., & Brown, J. W. (1995). *Web publisher's design guide for Windows.* Scottsdale, AZ: Coriolis Group.

Holzschlag, M. E. (1998). *Web by design: The complete guide.* San Francisco: Sybex.

Kientzle, T. (1995). *Internet file formats.* Scottsdale, AZ: Coriolis Group.

McClelland, D., Eismann, K., & Stone, T. (2000). *Web design studio secrets* (2nd ed.). Foster City, CA: IDG Books.

Shannon, C. (1949). Communication in the presence of noise. *Proceedings of the Institute of Radio Engineers, 37*(1), 10–21.

SVG Working Group. (2003, January 14). Scalable vector graphics (SVG) 1.1 specification: W3C Recommendation. Retrieved May 1, 2008, from http://www.w3.org/TR/SVG.

Tittel, E., Price, S., & Stewart, J. M. (1997). *Web graphics sourcebook.* New York: Wiley & Sons, Inc.

Unisys. (2008). LZW patent information. Retrieved September 19, 2008, from http://www.unisys.com/about_unisys/lzw.

Chapter 9

Web Publishing with the Hypertext Markup Language

The rapid acceptance and overall success of the Web has been driven by the vast amount of useful content found there that is increasing every day. The proliferation of Web pages is largely due to the minimal software and technical requirements of working with the Hypertext Markup Language (HTML). Although Internet content exists in many formats, the vast majority of the resources accessed through browsing and Internet searching are made up of static, autonomous HTML documents. The Web and HTML are closely intertwined technologies with a codependent relationship.

An understanding of HTML is essential to most Web publishing ventures; even content that is dynamically generated from a database is typically presented in the form of an HTML document created "on the fly." Many early Web pages were written with nothing more than a simple text editor and knowledge of the HTML language. Today, many sophisticated authoring programs provide a WYSIWYG (What-You-See-Is-What-You-Get) view of the page, but a knowledge of the HTML language is still often required for various forms of problem solving and other direct code interventions. Even the users of Content Management Systems (CMS) benefit from some familiarity with HTML coding. In learning the HTML language, the operative word is *language,* and as with any language, learning both the vocabulary and syntax is necessary to understand its structure, uses, and limitations.

This overview of HTML includes many of the commonly used markup tags used to structure and present documents, but it is not intended to be a comprehensive treatment of this extensive standard. There are many such comprehensive sources: Graham (1996) and Lemay (1997) both cover HTML, and Powell (2003) includes coverage of XHTML as well as CSS and scripting. The goal of this chapter is to provide a general understanding of the structure of HTML along with specific uses of many common tags; it is assumed you will consult one of the many printed or Web-based reference sources to become more fully conversant with HTML as needed. Note that all the examples in this chapter are based on HTML version 4.01, but there is a working draft of the proposed HTML version 5.0 available for review at the W3C site (http://www.w3.org/html/wg/html5/). There is a brief discussion of the evolution of the HTML standard to an Extensible Markup Language (XML) compliant form known as XHTML. The chapter ends with discussion of a few of the issues that can arise on UNIX servers and their implications for content producers.

MARKUP LANGUAGES

The idea of "mark up" has been around as long as publishing itself. In the earlier, pre-Web context, markup referred to using margin notes to instruct printers and typesetters regarding fonts, point sizes, and styles associated with various structural parts of the document such as chapter headings. In a broad sense, markup is everything in a document that is not content. Markup standards for digital documents were developed early in the history of computing and predate the Web. Documents have structural and other semantic elements that can be described independently of how the elements should be displayed. A markup language is a way of describing what the content means or how it appears by way of embedded instructions to a displaying program. Digital documents with markup are portable and adaptable to other media because some program can interpret the meaning of the markup instructions according to its lexicon and nesting rules.

There are two general approaches to markup for digital content. *Procedural* markup refers to the unique codes that various programs use to control a single way of presenting a document; for instance, the selection of 12-point, Times Roman font for a block of text. *Descriptive* (or generic markup) is a way to describe the purpose of the text rather than just the appearance. In this approach, content is separated from a specific style; for instance, certain text might be designated as a section heading, but the exact formatting of that type of text may vary in different renderings of the document. Procedural approaches are common but have several disadvantages: The author must invest significant effort and time on simply controlling the appearance of the content, global changes are harder to manage, software changes may mandate document style translation, and document interchange and consistency is limited.

The first standard for digital markup, developed by IBM in 1969, was General Markup Language (GML). Standard Generalized Markup Language (SGML) was developed as an ANSI standard in 1983 and became an ISO standard in 1986. As the foundation of both a specific markup language of interest (HTML) and an important meta-language (XML), SGML is important to our introduction to markup.

SGML is a standard for creating and describing a markup language; as such, it is important to recognize that it is not a specific document language itself but is instead a meta-language. A DTD (a Document Type Definition) is a specific markup language definition developed according to the rules of SGML. The DTD defines what the markup codes are and how they are to be processed. A DTD begins with a document type declaration and then defines the vocabulary and grammar of the new language by defining the permitted elements, their attributes, and the nesting rules for them. Specifically, the DTD describes the structure of the document in much the same way a database schema describes the types of information and the relationships among database fields; it provides a framework for document elements and serves as a document model. A document created according to the rules of some DTD is called an *instance document.* Documents are processed by some DTD reader, which is sometimes referred to as the SGML compiler. The DTD can be a separate file from the document or be integrated into the document file itself. By including the DTD with the document, any device with the appropriate reader can reference the DTD to print or display the document. A more detailed examination of the topic of DTDs is in Chapter 12, where it is examined in some detail and contrasted to the XML Schema Description Language as an alternate way to define a markup language. The key points about the relationship between SGML and HTML are:

- HTML is derived from SGML.
- HTML uses DTDs to define the elements and their uses.
- There are three variations on the HTML DTD: strict, which does not include deprecated tags (tags that have been deemed unacceptable); transitional, which includes deprecated tags; and frameset, which includes everything from the transitional DTD plus support for framesets.
- The browser is the DTD parser; the DTD is "built in" to that client software.
- Everything we can do with HTML tags, their permitted attributes, comments, and character entities, is defined in some HTML DTD.

HTML—THE HYPERTEXT MARKUP LANGUAGE

When Tim Berners-Lee developed the WWW at CERN, he needed a document format that met a number of specific criteria. He chose to develop a text-based standard derived from SGML, where markup controls the document structure, its presentation, and the linking that adds the power of hypertext. The HTML standard he developed is documented and maintained by the World Wide Web Consortium (http://www.w3c.org). The HTML standard continues to evolve, and different versions and DTDs exist. Web documents might include various nonstandard proprietary tags added over the years by both Microsoft and Netscape during the browser wars of the 1990s. HTML files represent a subset of the world of text files; that is, they are text files where the format control codes are themselves simple ASCII text. HTML documents are therefore simply ASCII text files that have been "marked up" with special tags that control how the document appears when viewed by certain programs. Basing HTML on the ASCII text standard enhances the simplicity and portability of these documents. It also meant that no special programs were required to create the documents because almost all computer systems have access to a text editor, which, along with knowledge of HTML, is all one needs to begin creating Web content.

In HTML, certain text characters are reserved for the control functions that identify instructions. These instructions are called tags, and they are themselves simple text. Tags are identified by the less than (<) and greater than (>) symbols. Note that this is fundamentally different from most proprietary approaches to document structure and presentation. The old WordPerfect "reveal codes" feature that showed text that was marked as bold or italic looked somewhat similar to HTML, but those WordPerfect codes were binary control codes that only that program could interpret. Because HTML reserves some characters that might also occasionally need to appear as text content, the DTD defines character entities for this purpose. For instance, if the < (less than) symbol is needed as content and not a tag identifier, a special name is referenced for it (a character entity). HTML uses tags to specify both the formatting and the logical organization of a document.

While the creation and modification of basic HTML files can be accomplished in any text editor, many programs exist that can format content as HTML. Word processing programs and dedicated Web authoring programs provide a WYSIWYG view that does not require knowledge of the underlying source code. However, even with such programs, knowledge of source code is required for many kinds of troubleshooting, and source code knowledge is also needed for certain tasks, even in these user-friendly authoring programs. Because learning this language is an important objective, you should use HTML authoring programs that permit direct interaction with source code. Many HTML editors have built-in tools to facilitate the insertion of appropriate HTML code, so it is not necessary to manually type in tags. Two examples of such editing software are Chami's HTMLKit (http://www.chami.com/) and NVU (http://www.nvu.com/), both of which have versions available for download and use.

There are ample examples of tags and coding provided in this overview of HTML, but experience is the best teacher, and as in learning any language, practice is required to become truly proficient. Some excellent Websites with interactive tutorials allowing hands-on practice with HTML are listed in the resources section of this chapter.

THE HTML SPECIFICATION

The HTML specification is an established standard maintained by the World Wide Web Consortium (W3C). A few of the main items in the HTML specification are:

- The document type declaration: This statement, with the version, language, and the DTD specification comes at the very beginning of every document. However, it is not actually part of the HTML document itself because it occurs outside of the root element (i.e., the HTML tag pair).
- Comments: Markup languages and scripting always allow for comment notes; an example is **<!--this is a comment to you-->**. The string <! introduces the *comment declaration*, and it can contain more than one comment. The comment itself is surrounded by double dashes.

- Character entities: These are special names or ASCII code number references associated with characters that may occur as content but are also reserved to identify markup codes (such as the "less than" symbol) or that require special display (such as diacritics, the tilde, accent marks). Character entities are referenced with the ampersand character (&) followed by either the named entity (such as "gt" for the > symbol) or a # combined with an ASCII character reference number. Both forms are closed with a semicolon (;) character.
- Elements and attributes: Elements in HTML are defined by tags; attributes refine tags and are expressed as a property with some assigned value such as a source file designation in an image tag (**src = "somefile.ext"**).
- Empty elements: These elements do not markup any content. Most tags are containers of textual content, but some simply designate the insertion of an object such as an image or a horizontal rule.

In addition to defining the tags, the DTD also dictates the nesting rules. Figure 9.1 shows the basic structure of an empty HTML container (that is, one with just markup and no content).

The first line, which begins with **<!DOCTYPE. . .>**, is really outside of the HTML container; it is the Document Type Declaration (not to be confused with the Document Type Definition). It provides information about which of the three HTML DTDs are being referenced with this instance document. This sample document was created according to the rules of HTML version 4.01 as referenced in the Transitional DTD maintained by the W3C consortium. As mentioned earlier, there are other HTML DTD versions: the Strict DTD and the Frameset DTD. The **<html> </html>** tag pair serves as the container for the entire document; because all other elements must be within this tag pair, it is referred to in the DTD as the *root element*. Like a directory tree, there is a hierarchy within the HTML structure: Elements can have parent, sibling, and child elements. The root element (in this case the HTML tag pair) by definition is the only element that has no parent (just as the "root" directory has no parent directory). The HTML document has two main structural parts: the <head> area, which is reserved for metadata elements (such as the title tag shown), and scripting and style functions, discussed later. The <body> area is where all the document content must go. Note that nothing should be placed in the "no man's land" between the end of the head area and the start of the body. The

```
<!DOCTYPE HTML PUBLIC "-//W3C//DTD HTML 4.01 Transitional//EN">
<html>
        <head>
            <title>Our Web page</title>
        </head>
        <body>
        </body>
</html>
```

Figure 9.1 A basic HTML container.

body area is where all the remaining nested tag pairs that mark up the content appear. By definition, in HTML anything that is not markup is content.

The structured nature of HTML also dictates the rules that apply to nesting order. Tags cannot overlap each other; they must be completely contained within other tag pairs. In addition, some tag nesting does not make sense. For instance, a heading level two should not occur within a heading level one; although it is not a nesting violation, the following example is not logical:

<h1><h2> This tag nesting is not logical</h2></h1>

An example of inappropriate tag overlapping would be the following markup, which attempts to present content as a heading level two with italicized text:

<i><h2> This is inappropriate nesting; the tags overlap.</i></h2>

If the italic tag is used with a heading, it should occur within the heading level two tag pair.

PHYSICAL VS. LOGICAL MARKUP

Even before the Web, documents formatted with word processing programs gave us the choice between controlling documents at the physical level (a procedural approach) or at a logical (or descriptive) level. In addition to the many font types and sizes that exist for text they have other properties such as bold or italics. Different structural parts of a document, such as a chapter heading or paragraph text, are usually visually distinguished from each other by applying different text decoration features to each. These properties could be physically controlled for each separate occurrence of these different uses of text throughout the document. However, this approach has a number of limitations and inefficiencies when compared to the descriptive approach of defining and applying styles. Not only is procedural control more labor intensive, but style inconsistencies are more likely, and style changes are more difficult to implement. It is more efficient to designate what the text is structurally and then let the program handle the application of an appropriate style formatting for that class of text.

The same is true when controlling documents in HTML; the markup employed can be either procedural or descriptive. HTML has both forms of markup, also referred to as *physical* vs. *logical* markup. Physical markup attempts to control the physical appearance of a document, such as inserting the code that causes specific text to appear with italics. Another approach would be *logical* markup, which uses a tag such as with the emphasis tag pair **<em> </em>** that informs the browser that the text is to be emphasized but leaves it to the displaying software to determine exactly how it should appear. The markup options that favor logical over physical markup are another distinction of the Strict DTD as opposed to the looser Transitional DTD.

ELEMENTS, TAGS, AND ATTRIBUTES

Elements are parts of the logical structure of a document, including headers, paragraphs, tables, lists, and images. In HTML, tags mark an element and identify it to the browser. Parsing programs recognize tags by the surrounding less than (<) and greater than (>) signs, which delimit them. Generally, HTML tags always occur in pairs with a starting tag and ending tag. Empty elements that do not always require an ending tag are discussed later. The ending tag is distinguished from the starting tag by the presence of a forward slash in front of the tag text. Document content appears between the beginning and ending tags; the tag pair can be thought of as a container of the content. An example of a tag pair that marks up heading level 1 content is:

<h1>This is a header</h1>

Tags identify elements and may have *attributes*. An attribute is a property, characteristic, or modifier of the element. Attributes are expected for some elements, but more often, they are optional. When an attribute is used, a *value* for it must be provided, and the value should be set within quotation marks. One important attribute used in HTML is NAME, which permits the element to be associated with an identifier. Note that in XHTML, the "ID" attribute is replacing the use of "NAME." Throughout this discussion, the older HTML convention of using NAME for an element identifier is used, but these are functionally equivalent. In later discussions of CSS and XML, the newer approach of using ID for NAME is used.

The previous heading example could be modified by adding the align attribute as shown here:

<h1 align = "center">This is a header that is centered</h1>

HTML permits both tag and attribute names to be in either upper or lowercase (but this is not the case in XHTML, as discussed later). Although HTML allows for some exceptions, generally the value string for an attribute must appear within quotation marks. The exceptions have to do with whether the values are literal strings or name tokens. Name tokens are assigned when an attribute can only have a limited and defined set of permitted values; for instance, the align attribute only allows values of left, center, or right. These name tokens therefore do not have to appear within quotation marks (although it is good practice to use them in HTML, and they are required with XHTML). When the attribute value is unpredictable and can be any literal string (a file name for instance), it must always appear within quotation marks.

HTML also defines certain *empty elements;* they are by definition elements that do not "markup" any content and are therefore empty. Examples include the **
** tag, which forces a line break; the **<hr />** tag, which results in a horizontal rule; and the **<img />** tag, which points to some image file to be placed in the page. Note that all these empty element examples do not markup any content; they also do not appear to have traditional ending tags. However, more rigorous approaches to HTML markup demand end tags for every element, so these tags are typically ended by placing the forward slash character before the closing greater than sign (>) as shown in the preceding examples.

The *Document Object Model* (DOM) treats a document as a collection of objects that give a structured and uniform programmatic interface for HTML, and elements represent specific objects. The DOM model is discussed further in the chapters on CSS, scripting, and XML.

Deprecated Tags and Attributes

Some older HTML tags or attributes are designated as *deprecated;* that is, although still supported by most browsers, they are being phased out because there are better ways to accomplish what the tag or attribute was intended to do. Examples of deprecated tags and attributes are the center, basefont, and underline tags. These tags have been mostly supplanted by the use of style sheets. In addition, there are tags that, while not deprecated, their usage in certain contexts is discouraged: for example, the use of the table tag to control page layout as opposed to presenting tabular data.

Inline and Block-Level Elements

HTML specifies both *inline* and *block-level* elements. Inline elements are ones that appear without creating a new line break. Block-level elements always appear on a new line. Inline tags are rendered on the same line by a browser, and they can contain only text or other inline elements. Examples include the anchor, image, and font tags. Block-level elements can contain either inline elements or other block-level ones. This category includes tags such as those for heading levels, forms, tables, lists, and the frequently used division container. However, the browser default display of these elements can be overridden with style directives; for instance, list items that are normally presented as block-level can be forced to display as inline elements if desired. The DIV tag is the generic block-level container, which is frequently used as a way to identify a named section of a document that can then be referenced in style rules.

USING HTML: COMMON TAGS

As with learning any language, the necessary starting point is to learn basic vocabulary and grammar; so to learn HTML, you must begin with some basic tags and their uses. A partial list of tags needed to start exploring HTML follows. There are many excellent resources on HTML, so recreating a complete HTML reference will not be attempted. (See the list of HTML resources for more information on the use of these and other tags.)

<html> </html> The root element that identifies an HTML document container.

<head> </head> The tag that identifies the head area; generally contains metadata as well as style and scripting functions.

<title> </title> The title tag within the head area that represents the minimum requirement for metadata.

<meta> Meta tags, also in the head area, contain generic or structured metadata.

<body> </body> Identifies the content area of the document.

<h1> </h1> A level one header, the structural element that indicates a section heading. Each subsequent level in the hierarchy is given a numeric value (h2, h3, etc.).

<p> </p> The tag that indicates a paragraph container. The ending tag is not strictly required except in XHTML.

 The tag that creates a line break (an empty element).

<div> </div> A generic block level container.

<span> </span> A generic inline container.

<img /> An image tag; an empty element that references an image to be displayed in the document.

<a > </a> The anchor tag; the tag needed to create anchored hypertext references and as named anchors.

<table> </table> The table container; tables contain <tr> </tr> tags for rows and rows contain <td> </td> for table data.

<ul> </ul> An unordered list.

<ol> </ol> An ordered list.

<li> </li> A list item.

<dl> </dl> Definition list that contains the tags <dt> </dt> definition term and <dd> </dd> for definition.

Preformatted text: <pre> </pre> Tells the browser to maintain the text layout as it would appear in a text editor view.

<hr /> A horizontal rule that creates a lined division across the page.

Images and HTML

HTML files are just a special type of simple text file. How can a text format accommodate a binary image object? The simple answer is that it cannot; it can just point to where such an image resides on a server, and it must be sent to the client in a subsequent transaction. The markup informs the browser to display the separate image file at the specified location in the document. This is fundamentally different from how most word processing programs incorporate images, which use proprietary binary formats. When an acceptable image type is placed in such a document, that binary object becomes a part of the code that makes up the document file itself, resulting in a single file container that has both the text and the image available to the displaying program. This is very efficient but also requires that those using the file have the same word processing program to view it.

HTML is a text format and therefore can only use a text directive (the image tag and source attribute) that points to some external image file that resides outside of the HTML file container on the server. When the browser requests an HTML file, the server sends that file. The browser then must make separate requests for the image files referenced in the image tags. The image tag is one of a small set of empty elements (no content is "marked up" by it). The image tag has a required attribute for the source file and another expected attribute for alternate text, which is useful for all displaying programs and essential for accessibility compliance, as in the following example:

```
<img src = "cat.jpg" alt = "This is my cat">
```

The source attribute is shown with the **src = "string,"** which specifies the name of the required image file. If the image file is not in the same directory location as the HTML file, the path to the appropriate location must be specified along with the filename. The **alt = "string"** gives the alternate text that displays when the curser hovers over the image in most browser views. Attribute values should appear in quotation marks and, if that value is a filename, it must be an exact match with the actual name. This is complicated further by the use of mixed case for filenames. The hosting platform is often a UNIX host, which is a case sensitive OS. Case sensitivity is a source of potential problems because Windows is not case sensitive and tends to apply uppercase letters for file extensions with many programs. Most authoring programs let you add an image to HTML by "browsing" to the image on a local drive and selecting it. When the source code is actually examined, the filename may be in upper or mixed case, which means that often the source code must be edited or the referenced file renamed to ensure the HTML reference and actual name match exactly. For this reason, it is a good practice to enforce a consistent naming convention for all files and directories created for a Website.

The Hypertext Reference

Much of the power of the Web is due to its hypertext capabilities, and the successful creation of meaningful hypertext references is an essential role of the Web publisher. The anchor tag has several important attributes that alter its function, but when used to create the standard link, the hypertext reference (**HREF**) attribute is specified. The content that appears between the beginning and ending anchor tag is by browser default rendered as the blue underlined text universally recognized as a link. Style applications can change this default formatting, but the conventional blue underlined style is so ingrained that users often do not recognize alternate link formats as links. An example of an anchored hypertext reference is shown here:

<a href = "minutes.htm">Meeting minutes</a>

The browser default is to display the link text "Meeting minutes" in blue with underlining, and when the text is clicked, the file "**minutes.htm**" is requested from the server. From the information in the HREF value string, the file "**minutes.htm**" must be in the same directory as the file that contains this source code because no other path information is provided. The various ways to make these references are discussed in the section on absolute vs. relative references.

In addition to simply making a link to a file, which loads the file starting at the beginning of the file, it is sometimes desirable to point to a specific place in that file. To do this, a type of "bookmark" is created in that file that can then be referenced in the link HREF string. Assume that the "**minutes.htm**" file is quite long and that a reference that goes to a specific section of that file that begins with a heading called "Proposals" is desired. The first step is to create a named anchor in the file "**minutes.htm**" at the appropriate place, as shown here:

```
<a name = "propose"><h2>Proposals</h2></a>
```

To do this, the anchor tag attribute "**NAME**" is specified instead of the "**HREF**" attribute. In addition, while the example anchor tag pair shown encloses the H2 tag pair, it does not have to "contain" any text because the tag just acts as an "invisible" placeholder that can be referenced later in a link. Finally, note that the string used as the value for the "**NAME**" attribute can be anything; the name could be "xyz" or just a number. Any anchor name is permitted as long as it does not have any spaces in the string and is referenced correctly in the link that will use it. Once a named anchor is created, a link can be made to that particular place in the file, as opposed to simply displaying the document from the beginning. To do so, the link needs to reflect not just the filename but also the named anchor within that file, as shown here:

```
<a href = "minutes.htm#propose">Meeting minutes—proposals</a>
```

The pound sign (#) separates the filename from the named anchor. This technique can create links to other places within the same file providing quick access to various parts of a long document by beginning with a table of contents with links to various document sections. In the case where the link and the named anchor are in the same file, the **HREF** value does not need to include the filename, as shown in the following code:

```
<a href = "#propose">Proposals</a>
```

The named anchor is assumed to be in the same file container as the file that contains this link because the HREF contains no filename.

Relative vs. Absolute References

Whether you are pointing to some image source file or making a link with the anchored hypertext reference, it is critical that the location of the external file is accurately reflected in the reference. There are two ways to specify any external file. The reference can be *absolute,* which provides a complete URL that unambiguously defines where the resource is on the Web. Alternatively, the reference can be *relative,* which provides directions as to its location in relation to the location of the HTML file that is pointing to it. When an external resource is on the same server, it is very common to use relative references. This might be as simple as just providing the name of a file located in the same directory. However, because it is also common to create subdirectories (i.e., folders) to organize the many files that might comprise the site and to colocate similar types of content or formats, it is useful to know how to reference other locations in the directory tree. Making most references relative simplifies the source code, facilitates testing of links locally, and makes site maintenance easier and more efficient. For instance, a server administrator may relocate a group of folders to another place in the directory tree, but as long as the relationship among the adjacent directories stays the same, the links and image references still work after the move. As an aside, another way to handle this issue of directory tree relocation is with the use of the **<base>** tag, which allows for a base URL to be set that is independent of the referring page location. This is possible because a server never actually sees relative URLs. As described in the discussion of HTTP, when a user selects a link constructed in a relative fashion, the server appends the relative location information to the truncated URL of the referring page also in the browser request header to construct the full URL path.

A conceptual model or map of the hierarchical directory tree structure is required in order to make valid relative references. Many Web servers are UNIX-based, and these systems have elaborate directory structures. The root directory is the starting point on such a system and is the one directory that by definition has no parent directory. Directories below the root are "level one" directories and have the root as the parent; subdirectories below a level one directory are level two directories, and so on. All directories then (except the root) have a parent that is one level above them in the tree; subdirectories are referred to as child directories and would be one level further down in the tree; and directories at the same level in the tree share a common parent and are therefore sibling or parallel directories.

In addition to the machine tree structure, the Web server program is configured to establish a type of "virtual root" that the program uses when seeking Web documents; this location is typically named **HTDOCS.** Unless directed otherwise, the Web server looks "down" in the tree from some current location, which is defined simply as the directory that contains the HTML file with the link code. Therefore, to reference a file in a child directory, the path requires just the name of the child directory along with the filename. To reference a parent directory, the "two dot (..)" convention is used; a "single dot (.)" explic-

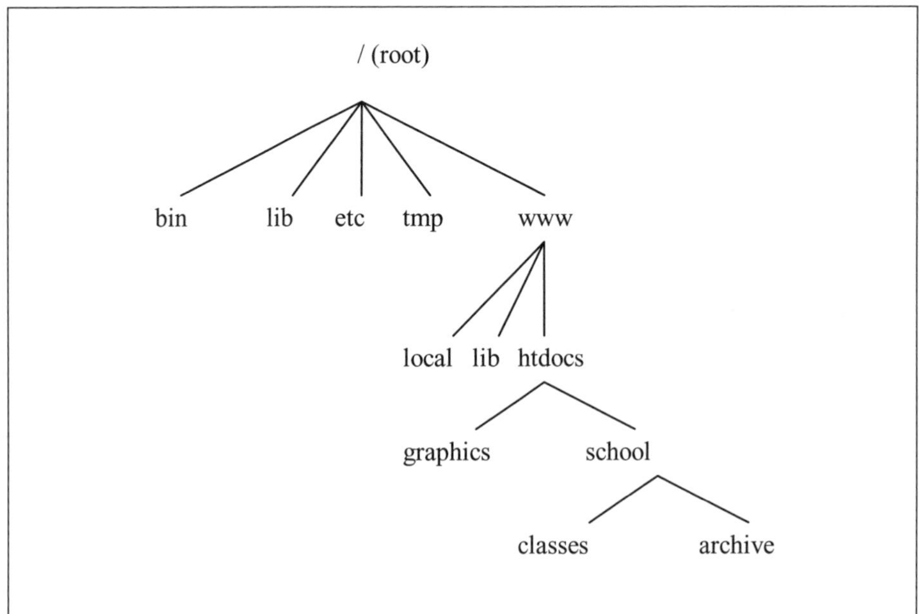

Figure 9.2 A hypothetical directory tree.

itly references the current directory. A hypothetical directory tree is shown in Figure 9.2.

In this directory tree, assume that a file called welcome.html is stored in the directory called school, which is a subdirectory of **htdocs,** which is a subdirectory of **www,** which is below the root. The directory called **graphics** is a parallel (sibling) directory to the directory **school.** If there is an image called "**banner.gif**" that is to appear in a Web file "**welcome.html**" that is stored in the directory called **graphics,** there are two ways to make the source reference in the image tag: an absolute reference or a relative reference.

First, consider the construction of an absolute reference. As noted, Web servers are set up to start the search path to Web resources at some location other than the true system "root" directory. Assuming that the location **htdocs** in Figure 9.2 acts as a "virtual root" for the server, the absolute reference would be, **<img src = "http://servername.com/graphics/banner.gif">**.

Alternatively, this could be done as a relative reference. This approach simply provides the path that describes where the image file is in relation to the location of the referring HTML file. Because "**welcome.html**" is in a sibling directory of that location, the path to it must specify first to go up one level in the tree (to the parent directory) using the dot-dot (..) convention. From there, the path continues down into the graphics location where the requested image file is located. Relative references could be thought of as similar to a "mall map" that shows how to get to other stores from your current location. Such a map visually places you in a current location with a "You are here" marker and then shows how to get to other locations from that place. On the server, the "You are here" location is the current directory where the file with the HTML code is stored. The relative reference for the image would be, for example, **<img src = "../graphics/banner.gif">**.

The same idea applies to anchored hypertext references. Assume a link is needed from "**welcome.html**" to a file called "**LIS600.html**," which is stored in the directory called "**classes**" in Figure 9.2. Again, there are two ways to make this reference.

As before, an absolute reference could be made. Remember that the location of **htdocs** is like a "virtual root" for the Web server and is not explicitly specified in the path. The full URL in the absolute reference completely and unambiguously defines this file as a point of content on the Web, as shown here:

<a href = "http://servername.com/school/classes/LIS600.html">

As before, a relative reference also works. This simply supplies the path to locate the image file from the location of the referring file. Because the location of "**LIS600.html**" is in a child directory of the current location, to get from where the referring file *is* to the *directory location of the resource referenced* the only required information is the child directory name along with the filename. This reference could include the explicit notation for the current directory (a single dot) at the beginning of the **HREF** string, but it is not required. The relative reference is shown here:

<a href = "classes/LIS600.html">

The relative reference is not only simpler, it also still works if the **school** portion of the directory tree with these subfolders is relocated on the server. The ability to write relative and absolute references is an extremely useful HTML authoring skill. A few common technical errors consistently crop up in making these references, including:

1. Not using a consistent file-naming scheme and directory structure. Because many hosting servers are UNIX based, they are case sensitive. Names such as "**Banner.GIF**" and "**banner.gif**" are treated as completely different names.
2. Confusing the two slash angle variations. Windows use a backslash (\) to designate the root and to separate directory and filenames from each other. UNIX-based systems use a forward slash (/).
3. Failure to specify protocols in URLs. For absolute URLs, HTML code requires that the protocol be included. A HREF value of "www.uky.edu" needs the beginning protocol designator, as in "http://www.uky.edu."

HTML Tables

Tables have been used and abused in HTML. In addition to simply presenting tabular data, borderless tables without visible gridlines are often employed as a strategy to control layout and formatting of HTML documents. However, this use of tables is discouraged because CSS is the recommended way to control presentation; in addition, this use of tables causes accessibility problems as well. As in word processing, HTML tables are for presenting tabular data. The markup for tables is straightforward but detailed because they require that each row and data cell be specified. A simple HTML table container is in Figure 9.3.

Tables may have a border surrounding them or no border, depending on the border attribute. Tables may cause problems for display programs, especially with screen reading programs used by the visually disabled, but the inclusion of the summary attribute at least provides descriptive information about the tabular content to those programs. Table headers use the **<th> </th>** tag pair. Table rows are created with the **<tr> </tr>** tag pair, and table columns are determined by the creation of table data cells with the **<td> </td>** tag. The colspan and rowspan attributes allow the spanning of columns and rows as needed. Finally, cell spacing and cell padding controls can be added as table attributes to further modify the appearance of the table.

```
<table summary="">
<tr>
        <td></td>
</tr>
</table>
```

Figure 9.3 HTML code for a simple table.

Forms

HTML forms have many important applications on the Web. They are used to create the interface for search queries with engines and library databases as well as deliver user feedback or questions, for example, for reference questions, surveys, interlibrary loan requests, and orders, to name just a few. The use of feedback forms is a more user-friendly method of soliciting users' questions or comments compared to simple "mailto" links that depend on the availability of a local mail client program. **Mailto** links are created with an anchor tag where the HREF value uses "mailto" in place of a protocol assignment and an email address in place of a URL. However, **Mailto** links often do not work as expected because they depend on the computer configuration and the mail software of the end user. For instance, even if a mail client program has not been setup on the user's machine, a "mailto" link nevertheless often launches a mail client such as Outlook Express anyway, leaving users confused, or worse, giving them the impression that a message has been sent when it really might be just queued up in the outbox and never actually sent. The proper use of HTML forms also requires an understanding of how data is posted to server-side scripts; this aspect of form use comes up in the context of the discussion of HTTP protocol methods.

The tag coding needed to begin a form, not surprisingly, is the <form> </form> tag pair. The form tag has two essential attributes: **action** and **method**. Generally, forms send data to a script identified in the value of the action attribute. The method in the form is determined by how the script was written; often the script expects the HTTP method *post*. The input tag determines the options for data entry sent to the script. Some commonly used form tags:

- **<form action = "some_script " method = "some_method"> </form>** Identifies a form container along with the script it interacts with and the method for the interaction.
- **<input> </input>** Form input elements usually always have the **type** and **name** attributes defined. Sometimes a specific data *value* is also specified if the value to be sent to the script is predefined.
- **<select> </select>** Creates a select list of options to choose from.
- **<textarea> </textarea>** Creates a textbox where comments can be placed.

Figure 9.4 shows the HTML code for a simple form; Figure 9.5 shows how a browser would render that code.

The form code begins with a form tag to identify the form container, as shown here:

```
<form action = "http://www.uky.edu/AnyFormTurbo/AnyForm.php"
   method = "POST">
```

The action attribute specifies a php script called AnyForm that resides in a specific location on a Web server. This particular script has a relatively simple job: to accept the data from the form of variable name/value pairs in the script and use them to create and send an email message. (Note: this script does

```
<html>
<head><title>SLIS Info Request Form</title></head>
<body>
<h1>Request for Class Information</h1>
Please use the following form to request an information packet.
<br>

<form action="http://www.uky.edu/AnyFormTurbo/AnyForm.php" method="POST">

<input type="hidden" name="AnyFormMode" value="mail" />
<input type="hidden" name="AnyFormDisplay" value="Standard" />
<input type="hidden" name="AnyFormTo" value="jbmiller@uky.edu" />
<input type="hidden" name="AnyFormFrom" value="class Web page form" />
<input type="hidden" name="AnyFormSubject" value="Class Information" />

<p>Place your cursor in the first box, then use TAB to move to the next box. </p>
Please enter your name: <input type="text" name="nm" size="30"><br />
Your Street Address: <input type="text" name="street" size="30" /> Apt # <input type="text"
name="apt" size="4" /><br/>
Your City: <input type="text" name="city" size="20" /> State <input type="text"
name="st" size="2" /> Zipcode: <input type="text" name="zip" size="5" /><br />
<br />
Please rate your computing skills:
        <Select name="Self Rating">
        <option>Newbie</option>
        <option>Middle</option>
        <option>expert</option>
        </select>
<br />
Are you Male <input type="radio" name="gender" value="male" /> or
Female <input type="radio" name="gender" value="female" />
<br />
Your email address if you have one:
<input type="text" name="email" size="30" />
<br />
Enter any comments or questions here:<br />
<textarea name="comment" rows=6 cols=40></textarea>
<p>
Thank you for your interest.
</p>
<input type="submit" value="Send Info" /> to the instructor.
<input type="reset" />
</form>
<hr />
</body>
</html>
```

Figure 9.4 HTML code for a form.

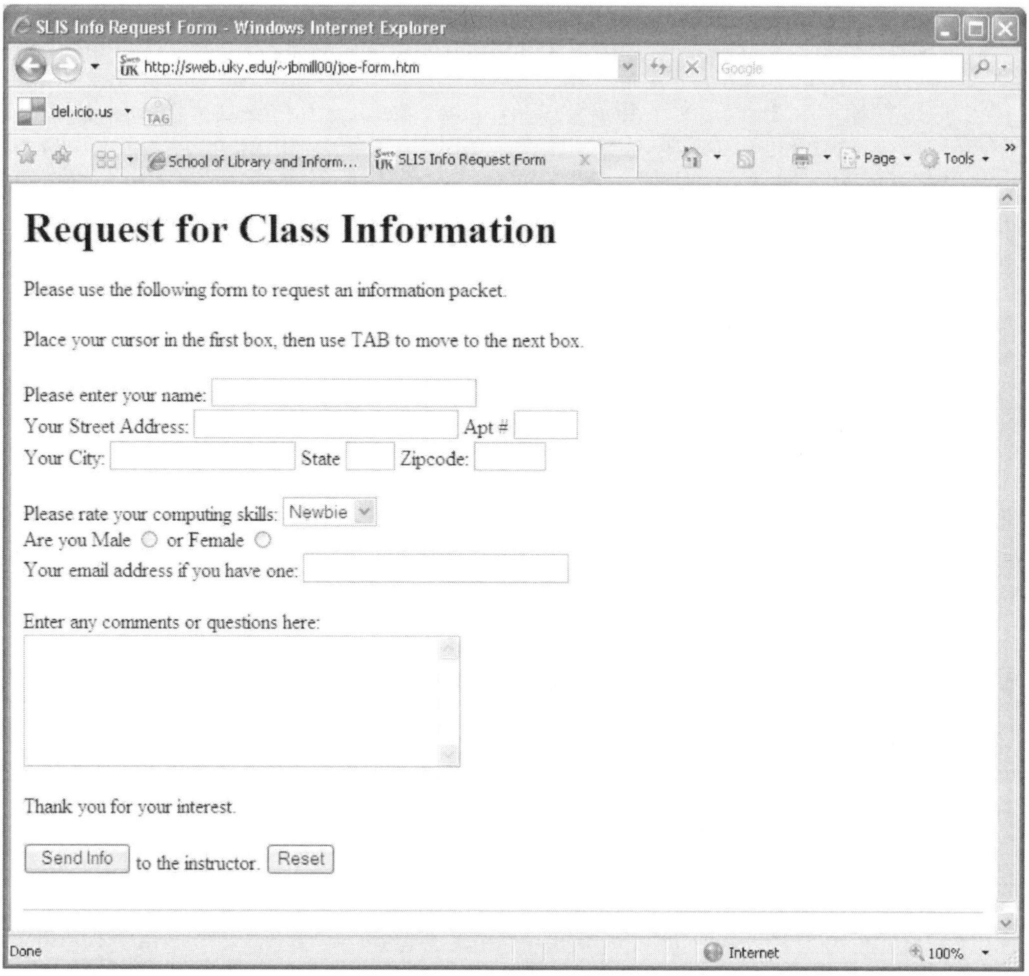

Figure 9.5 A browser view of the form code.

not accept requests from outside this network, so if you want to try this out, you'll need to locate or create a different script!) The following tags are types of input tags:

```
<input type = “hidden” name = “AnyFormMode” value = “mail” />
<input type = “hidden” name = “AnyFormDisplay” value =
   “Standard” />
<input type = “hidden” name = “AnyFormTo” value = “jbmiller@uky.
   edu” />
<input type = “hidden” name = “AnyFormFrom” value = “class Web
   page form” />
<input type = “hidden” name = “AnyFormSubject” value = “Class
   Information” />
```

As the "input" label implies, these tags accept input to send to the script. Note that they are also "empty elements" that do not markup any content. They do not require an end tag, but it is good practice (and an XHTML mandate) that they all have an ending forward slash before the greater than symbol to serve as the end tag notation. These input tags have three defined attributes:

- The type = "hidden" attribute means that these tags do not result in any display in the browser; they are used as a way to pass data to the script without interaction with the user.
- The name = "string" attribute creates a variable name that is associated with some value.
- The value = "some_value" attribute pre-assigns the desired value to the variable name.

Hidden input tags send the variable name/value pairs that the script uses to format and address the email message that is created when the form is used. A variety of input tags intermixed with descriptive content and formatting HTML follows:

**Place your cursor in the first box, then use TAB to move to the next box.
**

Please enter your name: <input type = "text" name = "nm" size = "30" />

Street Address: <input type = "text" name = "street" size = "30" /> Apt # **<input type = "text" name = "apt" size = "4" />**

Your City: <input type = "text" name = "city" size = "20" /> State **<input type = "text" name = "st" size = "2" />** Zipcode: **<input type = "text" name = "zip" size = "5" />
**

The section above has four input tags of **type = "text."** These tags result in text boxes of the size specified in the size attribute. The name attribute creates four new variable names, each of which is associated with whatever data the user puts into the text box displayed in the browser window. The next section creates a select list:

<Select name = "Self Rating">

<option>Newbie</option>

<option>Middle</option>

<option>expert</option>

</select>

The select tag results in a new variable name called "self rating" and a click down list of options. The options tags create the available choices. The next section creates a variable called "gender" and displays radio button choices:

Are you Male **<input type = "radio" name = "gender" value = "male" />** or

Female **<input type = "radio" name = "gender" value = "female" />**

A value is pre-assigned with each choice in these **type = "radio"** tags; because the same variable name is used, the choices become mutually exclusive (that is, only one choice is permitted; selecting one radio button deselects the other). Next is another **input type = "text"** and an open ended text area for comments:

Your email address if you have one:

<input type = "text" name = "email" size = "30">

<p>

Enter any comments or questions here:

<textarea name = "comment" rows = 6 cols = 40></textarea>

The final input tags in the form result in the creation of buttons for "submit" and "reset," followed by the ending form tag, shown here:

<input type = "submit" value = "Send Info" /> to the instructor.

<input type = "reset" />

</form>

If student Mary Smith filled in this form, as shown, the variable name/value pairs shown on the left in Figure 9.6 are sent to the script, and the email message generated is shown in Figure 9.7.

Image Maps

Image maps, also referred to as "clickable images," provide a mechanism to associate areas of an image with different URLs. Separate from mapping, any entire image can be made into a single link simply by enclosing the image tag within an anchored hypertext tag pair, as opposed to using some string of text for the link. However, it is sometimes desirable to make a series of "hotspots" within a single image that enable more than one hypertext reference to be associated with it; such an image is useful as a navigational graphic or site map image. There are ways to accomplish this effect with scripting, but image maps are a viable option. The image area to be associated with a URL is defined in terms of pixel areas within an X-Y coordinate scheme. The X-axis is the horizontal grid line and starts with pixel 0 at the extreme left; the Y-axis is the vertical grid line, starting with pixel 0 at the top. A map file or map tag container holds the coordinates that define the shape and associate the link with the defined image area. Originally, image maps were all *server-side;* that is, the map file had to be stored and processed on the server. However, browser clients can now process these instructions, so it is more common for the map instructions to be embedded in the HTML code. The client in the later case does all the processing; hence the name *client-side* image maps. Although you could create such a set of map instructions manually, there are specialized programs that facilitate this process; in addition, this functionality is often available in various Web authoring and graphics programs.

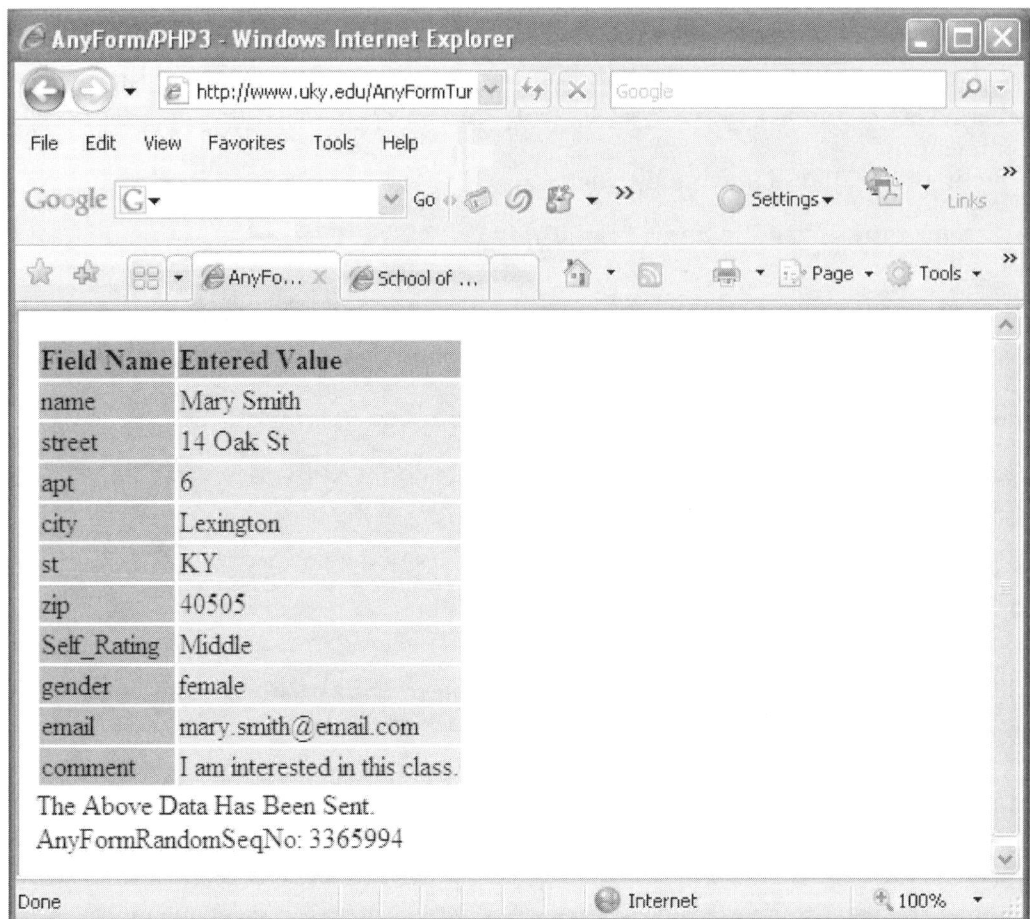

Field Name	Entered Value
name	Mary Smith
street	14 Oak St
apt	6
city	Lexington
st	KY
zip	40505
Self_Rating	Middle
gender	female
email	mary.smith@email.com
comment	I am interested in this class.

The Above Data Has Been Sent.
AnyFormRandomSeqNo: 3365994

Figure 9.6 The variable name/value pairs sent to the script when a hypothetical student fills in and sends the form.

Both server-side and client-side approaches require that an image be available with which URL hotspots can be associated. One of two different attributes of the image tag identifies the image map type. Server-side mapping is associated with the **ismap** attribute, which means the image is an active image. This requires the image tag be enclosed within an anchor tag that specifies the URL of the server map file. The cursor location data is then sent to the server when the hotspot is clicked on.

The client-side approach uses the **usemap** attribute in the image tag. The name value for the **usemap** attribute must match the name associated with the map tag container. The map tag instructions are usually located in the same HTML file as the image tag. With the client-side map, the coordinates are specified in the HTML source code and interpreted by the browser. Figure 9.8 shows an example of the code for a server-side map, Figure 9.9 shows the code for a client-side one.

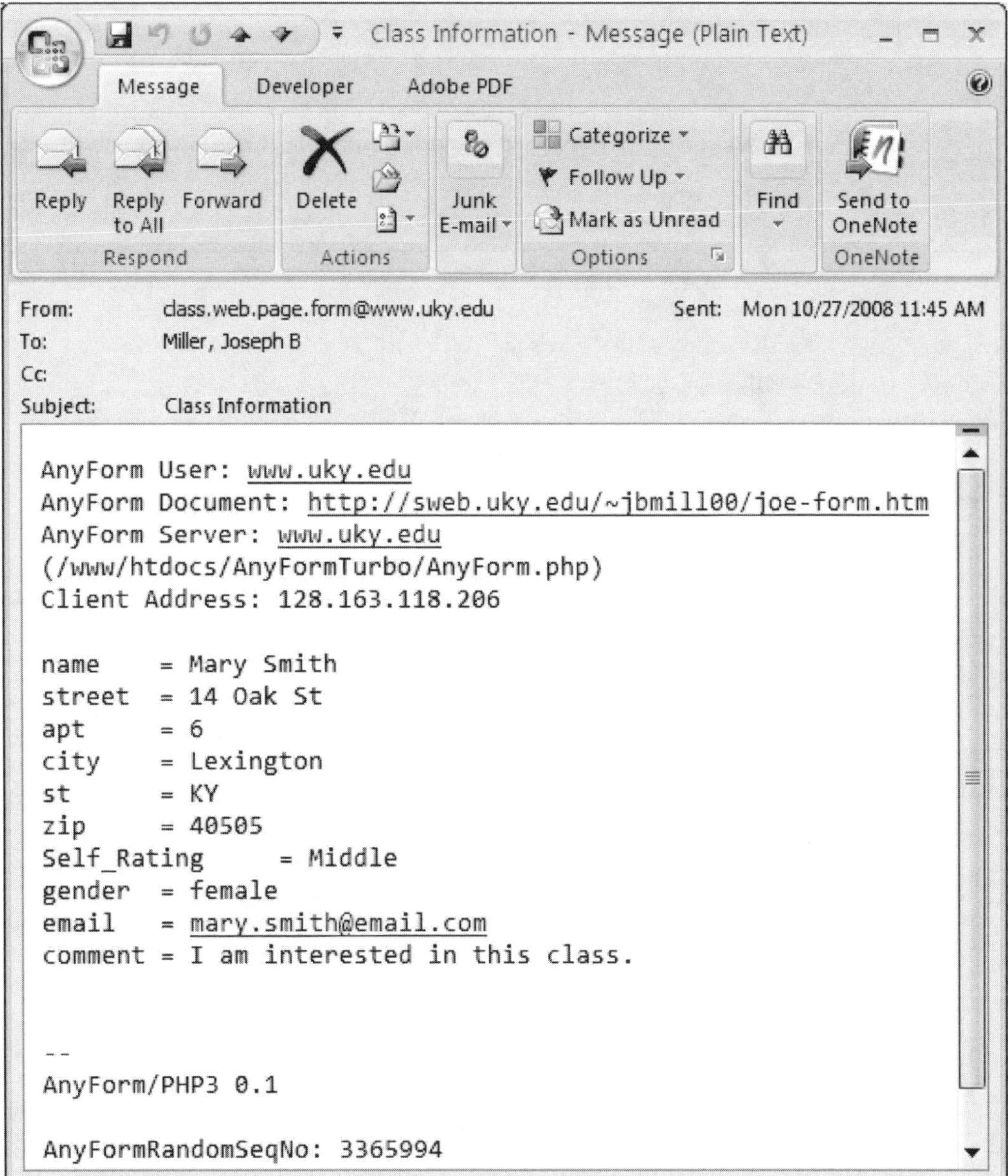

Figure 9.7 The resulting email message sent by the script action.

Framesets, Frames, and Iframes

Framesets provide a way to divide the screen up into different windows and fill each window with a separate file. A common use of frameset designs was to provide an index file of site links that remain visible on the left side of the screen while displaying the selected document content on the right. Although the frameset tag is not officially deprecated, the use of framesets has generally fallen out of favor for a number of reasons. One issue is the problem of

```
<a href="/htbin/htimage/search.map"><img src="graphics/search.gif" ismap></a>
```

Figure 9.8 HTML code for a server-side image map; note the ISMAP attribute.

```
<img src="king.gif" border="0" usemap="map.htm#king">
```

```
<map name="king">
<area shape="rect" alt="here's the sWeb host" coords="195,45,267,167"
href="http://sWeb.uky.edu">
<area shape="circle" alt="here's the UK Web server" coords="64,104,52"
href="http://www.uky.edu">
<area shape="default" nohref>
</map>
```

Figure 9.9 Client-side map example. Image tag with usemap attribute in the top row; map tags with matching name attribute in the lower row.

how search engines find and index the files and content; when framesets are used search results often lead users to content outside their intended context. There are also issues about how links display in framesets as well as serious accessibility issues. There are better alternatives to create this layout effect that use CSS. However, there are still occasions where framesets may be useful or where you may have to deal with their use whether they are your design choice or not; for instance, some course management systems display content within a frame environment. Separate from design considerations, an examination of how to control where linked pages display in framesets demonstrates useful tags and attributes with which you should be familiar. Therefore, although framesets are not recommended for most designs, it is still useful to understand how they work, if for no other reason than to be aware of their limitations and problems.

Framesets are codified in HTML Frameset DTD. Framesets always consist of multiple files that work together to present the screen layout and content. The rule of thumb is that the number of files needed to create a frameset environment equals the number of windows on the screen plus one. Usually, one file is the frameset file with separate HTML files filling each window it creates on the screen. The function of the frameset file is to create the screen layout and provide pointers to each of the HTML files that fill each window it creates. The frameset file typically does not contain any content, and a unique feature of this DTD is that there is no body tag in the frameset file. The content of a typical frameset file is shown in Figure 9.10; Figure 9.11 shows how a browser would render this code.

The DTD referenced in this document is the frameset DTD. There is a head area that can contain metadata, but no body tag. Placing the frameset tag within a body element can cause some browsers to ignore the frameset directive. The first tag after the ending head tag should be the frameset tag, shown next:

```
<!DOCTYPE HTML PUBLIC "-//W3C//DTD HTML 4.01 Frameset//EN"
"http://www.w3.org/TR/html4/frameset.dtd">
<HTML>
<HEAD>
<TITLE>A frameset document that includes the NOFRAMES option</TITLE>
</HEAD>
<FRAMESET cols="25%, 75%">
<FRAME src="index.html">
<FRAME src="main.html">
<NOFRAMES>
<P>Here is the <A href="main.html"> non-frame based version of the document.</A>
</NOFRAMES>
</FRAMESET>
</HTML>
```

Figure 9.10 A frameset file that will divide the screen vertically and fill each window with two separate files. The noframes option provides content to a browser that cannot handle framesets.

<FRAMESET cols = "25%, 75%">

This tag declares a frameset; the **cols** attribute divides the screen into two vertical spaces. The values that size the screen windows can be expressed absolutely in pixels or relatively as percentages, as shown in the previous tag. As the designer cannot know the screen size or resolution of the end user, defining numbers of pixels is problematic, so it is best to define the space with percentages. If three screen windows are needed, then a third value is listed for this attribute. If the desired screen layout is horizontal instead of vertical, use the rows attribute in the frameset tag. There are other permitted attributes for this tag that control the presentation of the windows, such as **frameborder** and **framespacing**. The next two tags are the frame tags, which identify the source files for each window created.

<FRAME src = "index.html" />

<FRAME src = "main.html" />

The general rule is that one frame tag is needed for each window defined in the frameset tag. The essential attribute and value provide the source file information that supplies the content displayed in the frame window. These separate, autonomous files can be displayed independently of the frameset environment if desired. As mentioned previously, this is one of the problems with framesets because a search engine crawler can index the content from each of the source files (in this case, **index.html** and **main.html**) independently of the frameset of which they are a part. Such access to one of the files outside of the frameset is then missing its essential navigational context. More elaborate framesets can be created; for instance, it is possible (but

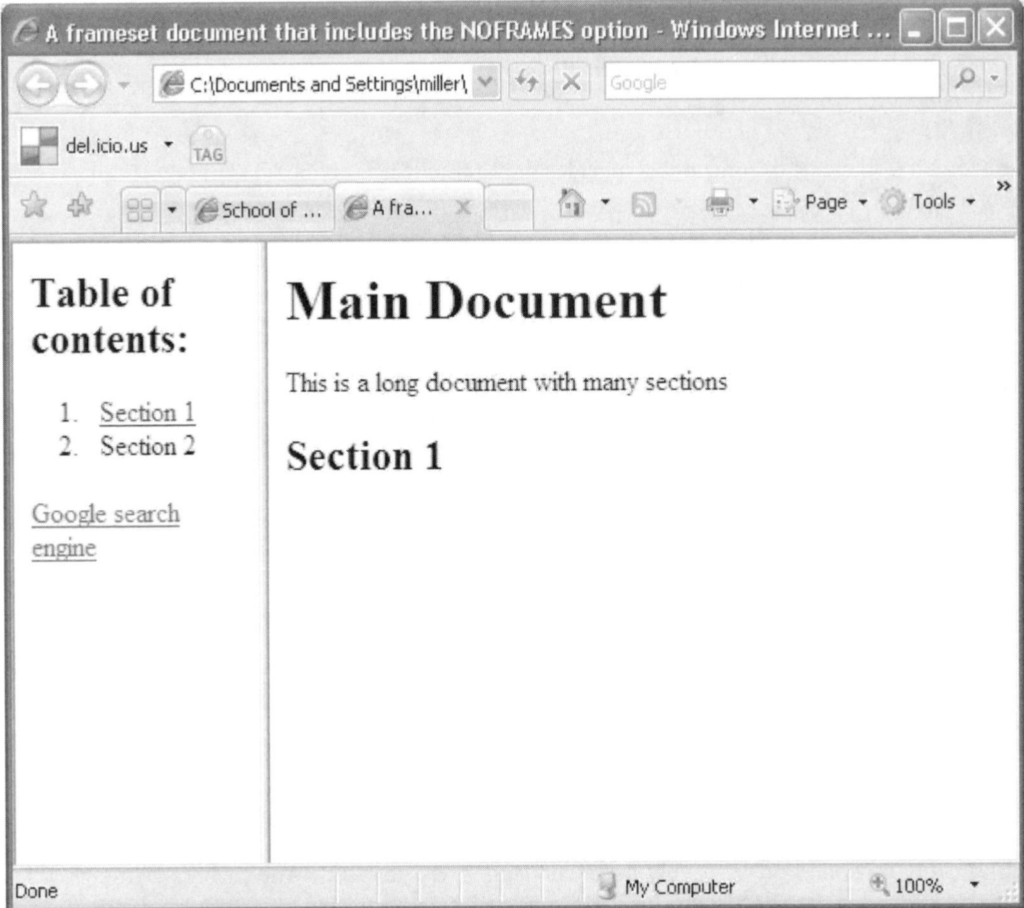

Figure 9.11 The browser rendering of the frameset file code in Figure 9.10. Note that the content shown in each window is dependent on the content of the index.html and main. html files, respectively.

not necessarily recommended) to nest framesets within framesets. One of the frame source files could itself be another frameset file.

Other attributes of the frame tag include controls for appearance and presentation. The "**noresize**" option determines whether the user is allowed to resize the frame window in the browser, and scrolling options can be turned on or off. The "**name**" attribute assigns each window a unique identifier, which, when referenced as the target for links, allows the page to load in a window other than the window that contains the link. Finally, the "**noframes**" tag is used to provide an alternate view of the site content for a user agent that cannot process the frameset environment.

Hypertext Links and Framesets

A common use of framesets was to create an environment where a navigational aid to a long document is always available by presenting a "table of contents" in the left frame with links to different sections to be presented on the right (a CSS approach to this is discussed in Chapter 10). The index file links often reference a set of named anchors embedded in the longer document displayed in the adjacent window. However, the default display for a link is for the resulting page to appear in the *same window* that contains the link unless there are instructions that direct the link to appear in a different window location. This means that if a link available in the left window is followed, it will by default appear in the same window on the left. This is not usually the desired outcome. Instead of the new content displacing the navigation index, the usual intended use of the frameset design is to keep the contents of that left window the same and display link-to content in the window on the right. To accomplish this end requires several additional tag attributes. First, a **name** attribute in the frame tags assigns a name value to each frame window, as shown here:

```
<FRAME src = "index.html" name = "left" />
<FRAME src = "main.html" name = "right" />
```

The specific choice of a value for the name attribute (in this case, left and right, respectively) is unimportant; it simply serves as an identifier that is referenced later in links. The use of **name** as an attribute is being replaced by the attribute **id** in XHTML, so you may also encounter that convention. These window names can now be used in links as a way to determine where the linked content appears. The content of the two HTML files index.html and main.html is shown in Figures 9.12 and 9.13.

To control which window a link will appear in, the **target** attribute is added to the anchored hypertext reference, as in the code here:

```
<a href = "main.html#s1" target = "right">Section 1</a>
```

Several things occur when this link is clicked: First, the page "**main.html**" is retrieved, and the page loads beginning at the point where the named anchor "**s1**" is located. Second, the **target** attribute designation forces the linked resource to appear in the desired window named "**right**" instead of the window that contains the link, which would otherwise be the default.

There is also a link to the Google search engine in this page, which is set to appear in a special target called "_blank." Another frameset issue is the implied "ownership" of content presented within a frameset. It is considered bad form to present external content within a frameset environment. To allow the Google link to appear in a new window outside the frameset, a "magic target" called "_blank" is used. This is one of four "magic targets." They all begin with an underscore character and are listed here:

1. "_blank" launches the linked resource in a new window;
2. "_self" loads the resource in the same window in which the link appears;
3. "_top" loads the resource in the full body of the window;
4. "_parent" loads the resource in the immediate frameset parent.

```
<!DOCTYPE HTML PUBLIC "-//W3C//DTD HTML 4.01 Transitional//EN">
<html>
<head>
<title>Table of contents</title>
</head>
<body>
<h2>Table of contents:</h2>
<ol>
<li><a href="main.html#s1" target="right">Section 1</a></li>
<li>Section 2</li>
</ol>
<a href="http://www.google.com" target="_blank">Google search engine</a>
</body>
</html>
```

Figure 9.12 HTML code for index.html.

```
<!DOCTYPE HTML PUBLIC "-//W3C//DTD HTML 4.01 Transitional//EN">

<html>
<head>
<title>Main document</title>
</head>
<body>
<h1>Main Document</h1>
<p>This is a long document with many sections</p>
<h2>Section 1</h2><a name="s1"></a>
</body>
</html>
```

Figure 9.13 HTML code for main.html.

The Base Tag

Another tag useful in the discussion of framesets is the **<base />** tag. Assuming that most of the links in the left-side frame should appear in the window on the right, adding target information to each link is tedious and inefficient. HTML allows the setting of a **base target** that controls the window location of all links unless overridden within a particular link. The base tag, placed in the head area of the index.html file, is shown here:

<base target = "right" />

The base tag may also be used outside of the context of framesets to create a base URL for a file with the **HREF** attribute. In the earlier discussion of HTTP, a standard "Get" request header was shown to include the URL of the referring page. However, if a base tag specifies a different HREF from the actual location of the file that contains it, that new location is substituted for the actual location of the file as the referring location. This use of the base tag maintains the integrity of relative links if the referring page has been relocated to a different location in the server directory tree. Both the base tag and the use of predefined link window targets have applications beyond the frameset environment.

Inline Frames

A newer use of the frame concept is the **inline frame** or **floating frame,** which uses the **<iframe> </iframe>** tag pair. The element defines an inline frame window for the inclusion of external objects, which can also function as a target window in which linked content can appear. It is similar to the object element, which also allows for the insertion of a HTML document within another; inline frames are another way to nest a document within a document. The **<iframe>** element has many of the same attributes covered in the discussion of the frame tag. A source attribute (**src**) informs the client what file should be displayed in the object window, the **name** (or **id**) attribute identifies the window as a target location in which linked content can appear, and the standard width, height, align, scrolling, frameborder, marginwidth, and marginheight attributes control the frame window appearance. Figure 9.14 shows the code for such an iframe, followed by its appearance in a browser display, shown in Figure 9.15. The **<iframe>** tag is now a common way to embed external content sources or other Web 2.0 widgets, such as Flickr images or a shared Google calendar. The code provided by these services to accomplish the embed usually starts with an IFRAME tag to create the object window.

XHTML

XHTML is a reformulation of the HTML standard to comply with the rules of XML. HTML and the browsers that display it were designed to provide a relatively forgiving environment. Many HTML documents were (and are) created by nonexperts and consequently often have errors in the code, such as the absence of a root element, open tags, and various nesting errors. Browsers ignore most of these common mistakes, and errors do not stop the processing of the rest of the document. When the browser encounters these errors, it usually just displays what it can of the document. XML is much less forgiving of such errors; a parsing error results in the display of an error message with no other content. The reformulation or migration of HTML into XHTML is a goal of many Web publishers, and new content is usually expected to comply with XHTML. The specific requirements of XHTML that HTML does not strictly enforce are:

```
<!DOCTYPE HTML PUBLIC "-//W3C//DTD HTML 4.01 Transitional//EN">
<html>
<head>
<title>An inline frame</title>
</head>
<body>
<h1>A page with an Inline Frame</h1>
This page has an inline frame. For instance, it could be used to display additional
explanatory  text when highlighted terms are selected.

<IFRAME src="sidebar.html" width="400" height="400" scrolling="auto"
frameborder="1" align="right">
  [Your user agent does not support frames or is currently configured
  not to display frames. However, you may  visit
  <A href="sidebar.html">the related document.</A>]
  </IFRAME>

</body>
</html>
```

Figure 9.14 HTML code that creates a floating frame.

1. All documents must contain a root element.
2. All tags must be closed, even empty elements.
3. All tag and attribute names must be written in lower case.
4. All attribute values must be enclosed within quotation marks.
5. Tags must be properly nested.

Empty elements, defined as those that do not markup any content, require specific attention because most early HTML programs did not apply end tags to them. Examples of empty elements previously discussed that may commonly appear without end tags are the image tag **<img>**, the line break **
, and the horizontal rule **<hr>. A forward slash placed at the end of the tag string ends these tags, for example, as in this image tag: **<img src = "cat.jpg" />**. The use of name tokens that are predefined values for some attributes did not require quotation marks in HTML, but because quotation marks are required for all values in XHTML, it is good practice to use them consistently. Another change with XHTML also alluded to earlier is the use of the ID attribute to create an element or object identifier in place of the NAME attribute.

HOSTING ISSUES

The platform that houses the Website creates a number of potential issues for the Web author, and an awareness of the idiosyncrasies of the operating

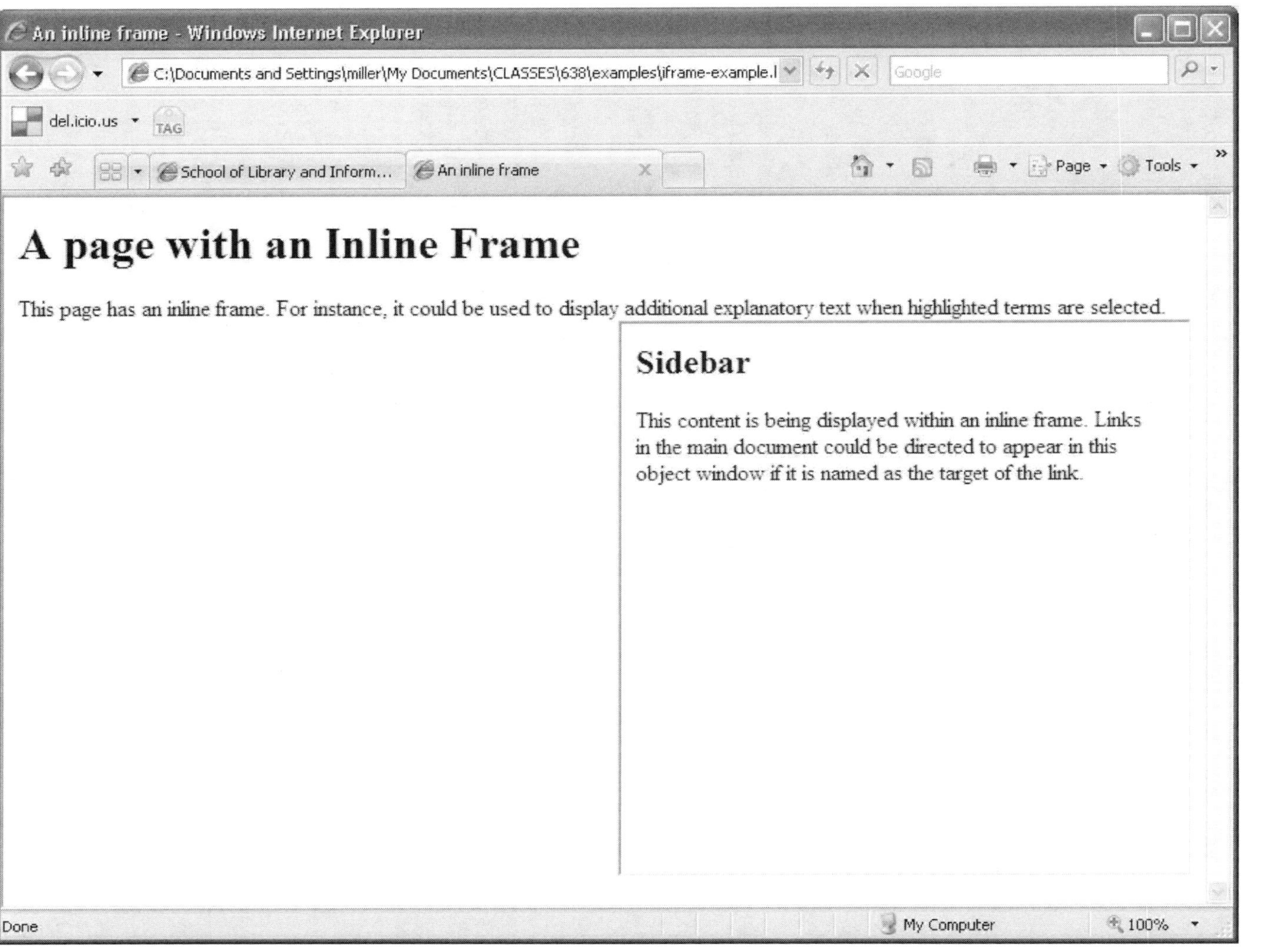

Figure 9.15 Browser rendering of the HTML code in Figure 9.14.

system in use and the availability of other server-side programs is needed in the design and implementation of a site. For example, case sensitivity may or may not be an issue on a particular host. In addition, a Website designed to utilize Microsoft's ASP technology requires the installation of the Microsoft SSI components, so it is important to know if these are available prior to committing to that approach.

UNIX Web Servers

Many large-scale Web servers are UNIX or Linux (a PC version of UNIX) systems; this is the case for a number of important reasons:

1. Historically, UNIX was the preferred OS for the high-end workstations that were available when the Web was developed.
2. UNIX was an early multiuser, multitasking operating system that could handle the large number of input/output operations such servers must perform.
3. UNIX "scales up" well to accommodate the large number of simultaneous users often accessing such a server compared to alternative operating systems.
4. UNIX can provide a reasonably secure operating environment.
5. UNIX has a large, well-defined support and developer community.

Many Web designers and authors therefore find they must work with a UNIX host as a Web server at some point in their careers, so a basic knowledge of some UNIX features as they affect Web authoring is useful. This UNIX discussion is limited to that perspective; clearly, the administrator would have many responsibilities that require greater expertise. Those needing coverage that is more detailed should consult one of the many excellent UNIX sources (Kaplenk, 1999; Martin, Prata, Waite, Wessler, & Wilson, 2000).

First, unlike Windows systems, UNIX is a case-sensitive environment; consequently, directory and file name references in HTML code must be written with this in mind. Links and image references that work fine on a local Windows PC will fail when uploaded to the UNIX host if there are case mismatches between source code and actual names. The adoption of a consistent directory and file-naming convention such as always using lowercase for all filenames and extensions can help alleviate this problem.

Another feature of UNIX is directory and file-level security. Understanding permissions and their application is necessary for the successful delivery of Web content from a UNIX host. Failure to assign the correct permission array to both the file and the directory (i.e., folder) that houses it results in the HTTP error message "FORBIDDEN—you don't have permission to view this file," or, if the permissions are incorrect for an image, the "broken image" icon appears in the browser view. Although these errors can result from other causes, directory and file permissions that are incorrect are the mostly likely reason.

UNIX Permissions

There are three permissions that can be set on or off for a directory or file; they are **read** (you can view the file), **write** (you can write to the file), and **execute** (if it is executable, you can execute it). Each of these permissions can be on or off for different users, depending on who needs access and why. If there are two states (on or off) and three permissions (r, w, and x), the number of combinations is then 2^3 or 8, ranging from all three permissions denied to all three granted. The eight combinations of possible permissions are referred to as the **octal value** for a specific permission assignment. If each of the eight combinations of permissions is assigned a number starting with 0 and ending with 7, the octal values that can be associated with each permission setting are as follows: 0 = none, 1 = execute, 2 = write, 3 = write + execute, 4 = read, 5 = read + execute, 6 = read + write, 7 = read + write + execute. These combinations are summarized in Figure 9.16.

UNIX also identifies three entities when it comes to whom permissions are granted. UNIX systems have many users, and the first entity is the **user** who has rights to the directories and files they own. Second, the entity **groups** are a reflection of the fact that multiuser systems typically allow the creation of workgroups who share certain privileges. UNIX administrators routinely create groups of users, so certain types of access can be granted to the group as a whole. Finally, there is the entity **others,** referring to the rest of the world who might access this system. Why should you care about these others, whoever they are? It is because when you wish to publish Web content, UNIX needs explicit permission to share those files out to everyone's browser. The three entities—user, groups, and others—are abbreviated in commands with the first letter of each word: **u, g,** and **o**.

To set file permissions, the system requires information about *what* permissions are granted and to *whom* they are given. The general rule of thumb is to grant both **read** and **execute** permissions to both **groups** and **others** while retaining **read, write,** and **execute** for the **user**. Execute permission is

Mode	Octal Value
---	0
--x	1
-w-	2
-wx	3
r--	4
r-x	5
rw-	6
rwx	7

Figure 9.16 Mode and octal values for permissions.

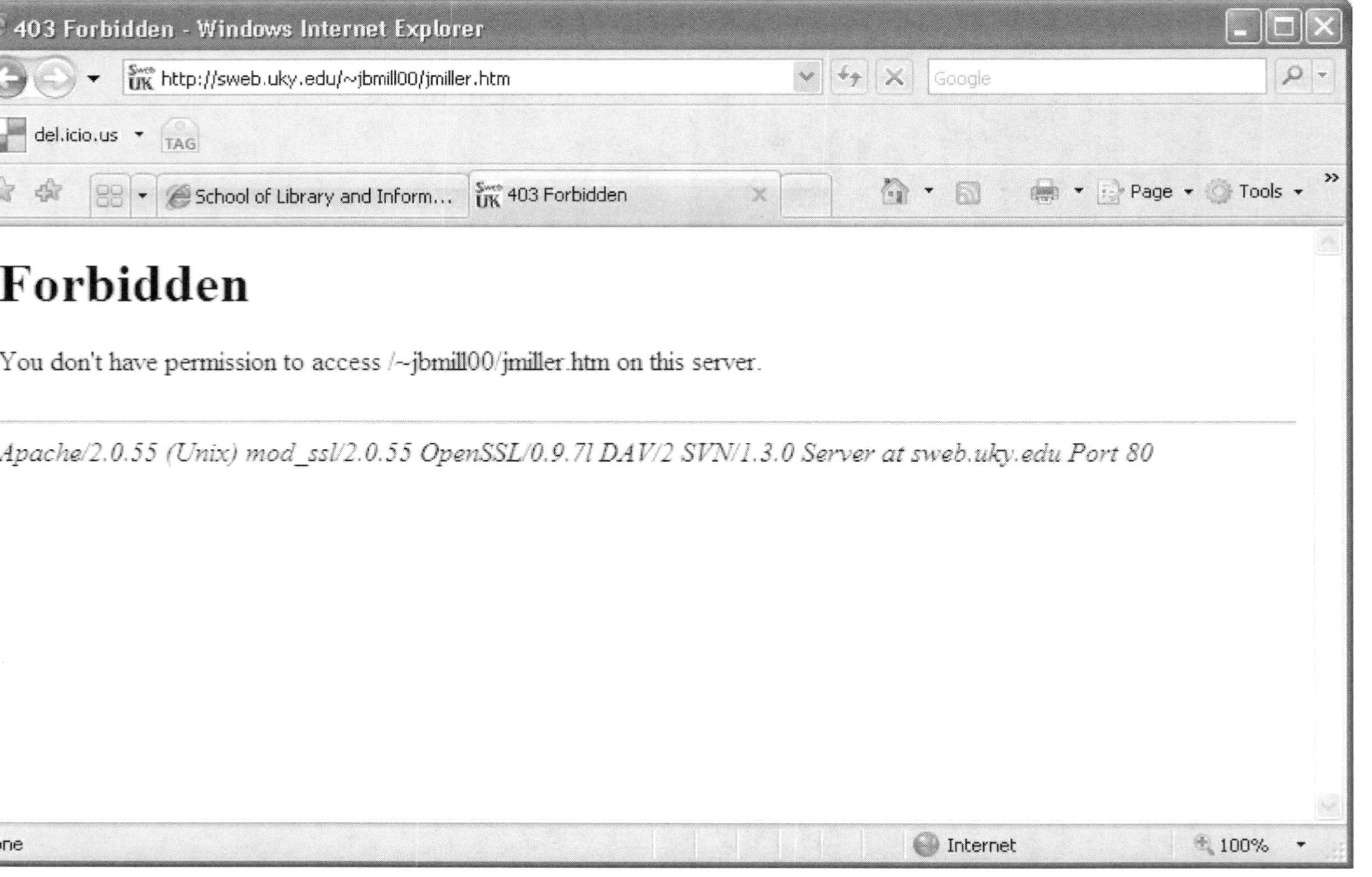

Figure 9.17 The “forbidden” message from inadequate permissions.

needed for directories but not always for files unless the page contains scripting—in that case execute permission is required. Write access is restricted to the user or perhaps to a specific group but never granted to the entity "others." If the file (or directory) permissions are not correct, the UNIX server does not send the requested file and instead responds with the "Forbidden" message as shown in Figure 9.17.

There are several ways to modify file permissions when needed. Most FTP clients have this feature, often from a menu initiated by right clicking on the file or directory. The UNIX host can also be accessed via a telnet client and the **chmod** (for "change mode") command issued. For example, if a file named "**main.html**" needs to have the permissions set, the following command syntax should be used:

chmod 755 main.html

The 755 octal values grant the user read, write, and execute (7), groups read and execute (5), and others read and execute (5). Hence, the "755" octal setting is the "mantra" of Web file permissions; it is the common default for Web directories and files.

SUMMARY

The huge success of the Web is largely due to the wide acceptance of HTML as a document format that presents graphically attractive content with useful hypertext links. This introduction to HTML described its origins, DTD, elements, tags, and structure. Examples of simple HTML files demonstrated the nesting rules and tags for linking, image references, framesets, and iframes. Some of these techniques, such as frames, are no longer commonly used; better ways to control layout with CSS are discussed in the next chapter. Nonetheless, a discussion of how they work provides a deeper understanding of link targets as well as revealing their structural limitations in the context of the discussion of search engines in Chapter 15. The need to create both absolute and relative references was emphasized with examples utilizing each approach. The successful production of a Website also depends on an understanding of the capabilities and requirements of the server platform. The fact that many Web servers are UNIX systems creates possible file-naming and permission issues that Web publishers must address when writing HTML.

REFERENCES

Graham, I. S. (1996). *The HTML sourcebook* (2nd ed.). New York: John Wiley & Sons.

Kaplenk, J. (1999). *UNIX system administrator's interactive workbook*. Upper Saddle River, NJ: Prentice-Hall.

LeMay, L. (1997). *Teach yourself Web publishing with HTML 4* (2nd ed.). Indianapolis, IN: SAMS.

Martin, D., Prata, S., Waite, M., Wessler, M., & Wilson, D. (2000). *UNIX primer plus* (3rd ed.). Indianapolis: Sams.

Powell, T. A. (2003). *HTML and XHTML: The complete reference.* Emeryville, CA: McGraw-Hill/Osborne.

ADDITIONAL READING

Lehnert, W. (2002). *The Web wizard's guide to HTML.* Boston: Addison-Wesley.
LeJune, U. A. (1996). *Netscape and HTML Explorer.* Scottsdale: Coriolis Group.

WEBSITES OF INTEREST

HTML 4.01: http://www.w3.org/TR/html401.
HTMLKit Free Editor http://www.chami.com/html-kit.
W3Schools HTML tutorials: http://www.w3schools.com/html/default.asp.
XHTML: http://www.w3.org/MarkUp.

Chapter 10

Controlling Presentation with Styles

The Hypertext Markup Language was well-suited to the initial needs of the Web, providing an exchangeable, structured, text-based file format for documents that could be enhanced with hypertext links and attractive formatting. The first views of the Web were strictly text-based as were all available browsers. Even in this text-only environment, early Web browsers such as the NeXT, Viola, and Harmony clients provided some accommodation of style languages. In 1993, the graphical Mosaic browser arrived and made the graphically enhanced Web easily accessible to the public. It also resulted in HTML pages that were more attractive than those that could be displayed with simple text-based clients; Web pages could have color, text could be styled, and images could be included and displayed. However, even this new graphical browser environment was stylistically limited; users could do little other than change display colors and fonts, and designers had limited control over the layout and appearance of their Web publications.

Controlling presentation has always been problematic in HTML. Presentation was typically dictated by the browser display defaults and the HTML publisher had to invest much time and effort in applying the procedural markup that is available in HTML to modify presentation. For example, procedural markup can be used to specify a font family, its size, and its weight, all of which has to be repeated many times throughout a document as applied to different HTML elements. The presentation problem also gave rise to a variety of "hacks" that were used to accomplish desired effects. Tables were frequently abused as a way to control placement of HTML elements, and other odd tricks were often employed to overcome HTML deficiencies. For instance, there is no "tab" HTML tag, so the indentation of the first line of a paragraph might be accomplished by the use of a small transparent gif to act as an image spacer. Such devices worked, but they were not very elegant solutions to the layout problem.

As the Web grew and attracted more serious design efforts, the limitations of HTML for controlling presentation within standard browsers became more apparent. One response by both Netscape and Microsoft to the increasing demand for better presentation control was to create new, proprietary HTML markup. Of course, the immediate problem with proprietary approaches is that those tags would not work across all browsers, making display in different environments problematic. Another approach was the development of style languages that could address presentation issues in a standardized fashion.

Just as in word processing, the creation of styles and style sheets for HTML has many obvious advantages. Style sheets allow the separation of content and presentation and represent a much more efficient way to control layout and appearance. This separation results in easier to manage Websites as multiple HTML files can be controlled by a single set of style instructions in a style file. This centralized control of styles enables site-wide presentational changes by editing style information in just one location. Procedural approaches to formatting that require style information be inserted with each structural part of a document are time consuming and hinder global changes throughout a document or site. Another advantage of styles is the ability to deliver a view of the document tailored to the viewing device or user agent (i.e., client). Without style directives, if a specified presentation is unavailable, preferred alternates in place of a default presentation are not available. So in addition to being more efficient, styles allow for multiple views of the same content. Styles languages accomplish this without modifying the HTML standard with new, proprietary tags.

Style languages were an early Web development, and the development community was considering a number of competing proposals during that time. The approach that has been widely adopted is Cascading Style Sheets (CSS). The fact that the style sheets could "cascade" recognized that for Web content the style preferences of the author and the viewer as well as the capabilities of the display device and the browser all need to be accommodated. The origins of CSS are in the 1994 "Cascading HTML style sheets" proposal by Hakon Lie to the World Wide Web Consortium (W3C); the reference to HTML was later dropped because CSS use is not limited to HTML (Lie & Bos, 1999). Since that time, Lie and others have developed CSS into a well-supported standard. There have been several iterations of CSS, and the current version is Level 2.1, with Level 3 under way. The full specifications can be viewed at the W3C site (W3C, 2008).

The success of CSS and its wide acceptance is due to its relative ease of use and the support of all major browsers. Some style approaches require a full-fledged programming language, but the straightforward, declarative nature of CSS is quite accessible and easy to learn, and many excellent tutorials are available (McClelland, Eismann, & Stone, 2000; Powell, 2003; W3Schools, 2008). As with HTML and scripting languages, learning CSS really requires a hands-on approach. When teaching about these technologies, it is always a dilemma whether to provide background first and then go to examples or to start with examples first and then discuss broader principles. I have elected the former approach here, providing an overview before analyzing examples. However, some readers may prefer to first look at the examples provided and then come back to this overview. Either approach has its merits, but if you prefer the later, you may jump ahead to the examples section and return to the overview later.

During the "browser wars" of the 1990s, both Microsoft and Netscape promoted proprietary HTML, but when Internet Explorer (IE) began to support CSS with IE version 3.0, Netscape came on board with its release of Netscape version 4.0. Although all major browsers support CSS, there are subtle differences in how each interprets and displays styled pages; these differences sometimes require special accommodation within the CSS code. Code modifications to accomplish browser specific effects are the "hacks" used to ensure consistent appearance across various browsers.

THE BOX MODEL

The Box Model is essential to understanding CSS layout control. This view of the visual space of the screen allows for the creation of a number of containers or boxes that can be arranged as desired within the page. As discussed in Chapter 7, many designs make extensive use of such an approach (see Figure 7.3 in that chapter). Each HTML container is given a unique identifier that is referenced in CSS rules, which is a mechanism to apply certain styles to just those HTML containers. Each container created has margins, borders, and padding that can be adjusted to control the positioning of the box, the location of its content, and its appearance in the page. Each box has a border that can be visible or not. Padding is the space from the border to the start of the margins around the content. Margins are already familiar to most everyone from word processing experience; they are the empty space around an area of content. Specific measurements can be set for left, right, top, and bottom spacing. In this model, boxes can be nested within boxes to achieve desired layouts. Figure 10.1 shows these various box attributes.

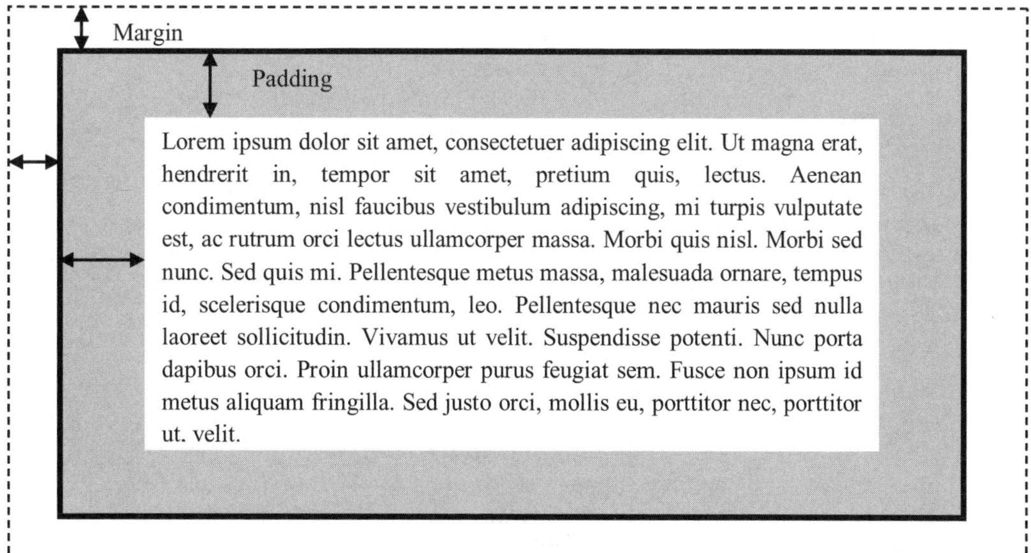

Figure 10.1 A box container with a black border. The margins surround the border and the gray area is the padding surrounding the content block, shown in white. The "Lorem ipsum . . ." paragraph is "pseudo-Latin" (some real words but used in a "jabberwocky" way); this is a common convention when "dummy text" is needed for layout purposes.

In HTML, block-level elements are always rendered on a new line, and inline elements flow across the page. Tables, lists, and forms are examples of block-level elements; images, links, and the actual content are examples of inline elements. Block-level and inline boxes are permitted in CSS. The generic block-level HTML container is the **DIV** tag; the generic inline container is the **SPAN** tag. A block-level box serves as the container for any boxes nested within it. The top-level container is the document window.

CSS POSITIONING

Boxes are positioned on the page with relative, absolute, or float directives, each with their own rules. In the absence of positioning directives, the normal flow is for block-level boxes to appear one after another vertically and for inline boxes to flow across the page from left to right, wrapping to new lines as needed. The two vertical margins are collapsed into a single margin that reflects the larger of the two values when boxes appear under other boxes.

Relative positioning starts with a box positioned with normal flow; the next box is then positioned using the offset values. Relative positioning can result in boxes overlapping other boxes and hiding content in another layer; how boxes overlap varies with different browsers. Absolute positioning forces the container to appear in a specific location on the page. Fixed positioning is a form of absolute positioning that forces the box to appear in the same place relative to the browser window; fixed locations do not change as the user scrolls through a page. This is useful when you would like to ensure that a box, such as one with a navigation menu, is always visible in the same place on the screen. The FLOAT directive controls the location of the box and aligns it either at the top left or top right of another box; the floated box appears as would any other content within the container it is placed. The inline content of the parent box then flows around the floated box. Examples of these types of positioning are provided later in the chapter.

ADDING STYLES TO HTML

There are many ways to incorporate style information into HTML. When no style information is given within the HTML, the Web page appearance is determined by the browser defaults and the user's preference settings within the browser. For Web designs using CSS, many options are available to add style information. Style information can be placed within a separate file and then referenced within the HTML document, or it can be embedded within the HTML container itself. The most common way to place style information within the HTML is with the addition of the **<style></style>** tag pair in the head area that contains the set of rules to be referenced. Within the style tag, it is possible to import style information from some external source to add rules to those written in the local file. It is also possible to add inline styles through the addition of a style attribute within an HTML element itself. How each of these approaches are different, and how rule conflicts are resolved if more than one rule is available for an element, is discussed next.

External Style Files

Putting style information into a separate file from the HTML file itself has several practical and design advantages. By completely separating style information from the content, the HTML code is kept free of added coding that clutters the content and HTML code of the page. In addition, if a style change is desired, updates made in that single file will then apply to every HTML file that references it; the alternative requires style changes be made in every individual HTML file that needs the change.

To use an external file, a text file must be created containing the rules that would have been placed within the style tag pair in the HTML file. This style file has a "**CSS**" extension and should contain nothing other than the rule set; there must not be any extraneous text or markup, nor should there be a beginning or ending **<style></style>** tag in this file. To reference such an external style file, the HTML **<link>** tag is placed in the head area as shown in the following example:

```
<link rel = "stylesheet" type = "text/css" href = "mystyle.css" />
```

The relation and type attributes identify this as a preferred style sheet created in a text format. Note that the **REL** attribute can also refer to an alternate style sheet as well. In addition, multiple **LINK** tags can be used in the head area; for instance, a separate style file might be used for the less commonly used HTML elements. The **HREF** attribute value points to the location of the file with the style rules.

The **LINK** tag also allows for an optional **MEDIA** attribute that has a defined set of possible values, some of which are shown in Table 10.1. (Note that not all browser versions handle media attributes.)

Embedded Styles

To embed styles, the **<style></style>** tag is placed in the head area and serves as a container for the rule set. Some or all the rules may be imported from the other source file with the "**@import**" statement. There are two equivalent ways to structure the **@import** statement, shown here:

@import "somestyle.css" OR **@import url("somestyle.css")**

TABLE 10.1 Link Media Attributes

Media Attribute Values	**Purpose**
Screen	Default media setting; for computer displays
Print	Optimize for a printer
Projection	For projection displays
Aural	For screen-reading programs

These **@import** statements can coexist with the specific rules that are in the head area style container. Given that there are multiple sources for CSS rules that could potentially give conflicting instructions for the presentation of the same elements, there are rules about what rules "trump" other rules; the specifics of those rules are discussed later in this chapter.

Inline Styles

Inline styles refer to style attributes added to an element itself. Control at this level requires the micromanagement of every element in the document, and it is usually only used as a technique to override a broadly applied style for a specific element where overriding an inherited style is desired. For example, the alignment of text for a specific paragraph could be set with a style attribute placed in the paragraph tag itself as in the example: **<p style = "align: right">**.

CSS SYNTAX AND RULES

Languages have vocabulary and syntax, and CSS is no exception. The vocabulary is the defined set of selectors and properties; the syntax dictates how each CSS statement is structured and the punctuation needed for successful parsing by the displaying program. CSS applies style information to HTML elements by the formulation of rules. Style languages also permit the inclusion of comments. Comments in CSS begin with a forward slash and an asterisk and end with an asterisk and a forward slash. Comments may be used to explain what the style sheet is intended to do or to provide statements of authorship or terms of shared use. In addition, it is common to use comments as a way to deactivate code without actually removing it; this is referred to as "commenting out" a code block. This use of comments is a helpful technique for troubleshooting style rules. It is also an effective learning technique that allows you to turn rules off or on by adding or removing comment designations and then observing the effects on document presentation.

CSS Rules

CSS rules have a selector and a declaration. The selector identifies one or more HTML elements that the style is applied to, for instance, in the following example the **H1** header tag is the selector. Declarations specify properties and values. The declaration can consist of one or multiple property/value pairs. The set of properties consists of the 50 or so style attributes that determine the presentation of an HTML document; the property is specified by assigning a value to it. A property is separated from its value by a colon, and multiple declarations in a single rule are separated by semicolons. CSS rules are either embedded within a style tag container in an HTML document or in a separate CSS file; an example of a simple CSS comment and rule is shown in Figure 10.2.

```
/* this is a comment; a rule is on the next line*/
H1 {color: red}
```

Figure 10.2 A style tag with a simple CSS rule. Here H1 is the *selector,* and the portion in curly brackets is the *rule.* The rule consists of a *property* (in this example "color") and a *value* (in this example, "red").

```
H1, H2, H3 {
color: red;
font-weight: bold;
font-family: helvetica;
font-variant: normal;
font-style: normal;
}
```

Figure 10.3 A rule with multiple selectors and declaration.

In this rule, **H1** is the selector, and the declaration, within the curly brackets, has a property (color) and an assigned value (red). This rule selects all the heading level 1 elements in the document and presents them in red text in the browser.

In Figure 10.3, there are three selectors: **H1, H2,** and **H3**. Multiple selectors are grouped together and separated by commas. The declaration has five property/value pairs; each pairing is separated by a colon, and each declaration is terminated with a semicolon. Wildcards can also be used as a way to apply a declaration to all possible selectors.

Rules can reference elements that are nested within other elements. Figure 10.4a shows a rule with a hierarchical selector string; the selector "**ul li a**" selects only anchor tags that are within list items within any unordered list. Figures 10.4b and 10.4c show rules with an "**id**" selector, which is indicated by a pound sign (#) either at the beginning of the selector string (10.4b) or after an initial selector (10.4c). The pound sign convention is used as a way to bind a style to a particular **<div>** container in the HTML file that has been given a matching "**id**" attribute. (Note that "**id**" name values should not begin with a number as this may not work in all browsers.)

CSS Classes

A group of declarations can be associated with a **style class.** A class can be independent of any selector, or it may be associated with a specific element selector. As with scripting, classes make use of a "dot notation." When a selector is assigned to a class, it is separated from the class name with a dot; independent classes without selectors are designated with a starting dot and followed by the name to be given to the class. Note that, as with ID names, class and pseudo-class names should not begin with numbers due to possible problems with some browsers. Figure 10.5 shows an example of a CSS rule creating a class called "new" with two declarations.

In the previous example, the class "new" is associated with the paragraph element with the "**p**" selector. To create an independent class not associated with any particular element, the selector would be dropped as shown in Figure 10.6.

Just creating a class by itself does not change any aspect of the presentation; it simply is available for possible use. To see the class in action, it must

Example	Rule	Action
a.	ul li a {color: red}	This would select anchor tags (links) within list items that are part of any unordered list.
b.	#nav ul li a {color: red}	Selects a DIV container with the id of "nav" and then applies the rule to any anchor tag that occurs as a list item within unordered lists, but only to those within that DIV container.
c.	p#first {text-indent: 2 em}	Selector is paragraph, but application of the rule is restricted only to paragraphs that have the attribute id= "first."

Figure 10.4 Three example rules and their actions.

```
p.new {
color: red;
font-family: arial;
}
```

Figure 10.5 A class associated with a selector; selector is "p" and class name is "new."

```
.new {
color: red;
font-family: arial;
}
```

Figure 10.6 A class definition without a selector.

be referenced as a class attribute added to some element. If a class is created with a selector, it is applied only to that element, whereas an independent class can be associated with any element. For instance, to apply the two classes shown in Figures 10.5 and 10.6, each could be referenced in some HTML code as shown here:

<p class = "new">

<H1 class = "new">

Note that either class definition could be applied to the paragraph element. However, only the independent class definition would work as applied to the **H1** shown previously; classes with selectors are applicable to only that designated element. Independent classes are more powerful and flexible, but classes with selectors clearly identify the intended element to be associated with the class. Both selector and nonselector classes are used in CSS and the decision between defining selector-based or independent classes is determined by designer preference and the organization of the style sheet.

Pseudo-Classes

A pseudo-class is similar to creating a class except it applies to different aspects of the same element that are to be distinguished from each other, as opposed to different elements themselves. For example, the anchor tag is used to create hyperlinks, but you may wish to stylistically distinguish unvisited links, visited links, selected links, or hovered-over links. Pseudo-classes enable stylistic control of the various forms of a single element; these rules use a colon between the element and the specific element form. Pseudo-classes that are frequently defined for the anchor tag are shown in Figure 10.7.

Pseudo-classes can be combined with classes; for instance, the independent class created earlier called "new" could be specified in a pseudo-class as shown in Figure 10.8.

```
a:link {color: red}
a:visited {color: blue}
a:hover {color: green}
a:active {color: black}
```

Figure 10.7 Pseudo-class use with anchor properties.

```
a.new:visited {color: blue}
```

Figure 10.8 A class used with a pseudo-class.

Sizing and Color Units in CSS

It is often necessary to specify sizes and positions in CSS, and these measurements can be provided in absolute, relative, or percentage terms. Absolute units include English and metric measures, or inches, centimeters, and millimeters, as well as typographic measures of points and picas, which are respectively, 1/72 of an inch and 12 points. Absolute measures are more relevant to the world of print and are problematic for most Web designs because the designer cannot anticipate the screen sizes of users. Even pixels (picture elements) are not really absolute units because their size is dependent on screen size, dot pitch, and the resolution setting of the hardware in use.

Percentage units are frequently used to control the amount of space allowed for elements within the browser window. Percentages can refer to a portion of the full screen or relate to a percentage of some other set measurement, most often the font size. The rule in Figure 10.9 has the body left margin set to 20 percent of the screen real estate and the line height set to a percentage of the chosen font size.

Regardless of the browser window size, the left margin as specified in this example would stay proportionately the same, and the line height, which controls line spacing, would be 125 percent of the font size. Using a percentage in the rule allows the spacing to remain proportional even if a user setting forces a different font size in the browser preferences. Note that the font declarations can be combined into one statement specifying the font size and line height by giving two point sizes separated by a slash, as in "**font: 12/15 Verdana**."

Relative measures include **px** for pixel and the **em** designation for a single character height. As noted earlier, pixels are relative measures because their sizes are dependent on a number of factors outside the designer's control. For instance, specifying a left margin of **40 px** looks quite different when viewed with screen resolutions 640 x 480 versus 1280 x 1024 or when viewed on a 15" versus a 20" monitor. The **em** unit is relative to the font size and equal to the height of a character. Again, the relative nature of this unit helps keep spacing proportional to the font if the font size in the style is overridden by the browser.

Color is also a property that can be specified in style rules using the RGB color model discussed in Chapter 8. The units that specify a color in this model are numeric representations of the amount of red, green, and blue, with 8 bits allowed for each additive primary color. Color values can be specified by name (e.g., red, blue, yellow, etc.), as percentages, or numerically with either

```
body {
margin-left: 20%;
font-family: Verdana
font-size: 12 pt;
line-height: 125%;
}
```

Figure 10.9 Using percentages as units of measure.

decimal (0–255) or hexadecimal (0-ff) notation. The color white could be specified in any of the following equivalent ways:

color: white

color: rgb(255, 255, 255)

color: rgb(100%, 100%, 100%)

color: ffffff

Hexadecimal is a common way to specify color in both HTML and CSS. If each pair of HEX digits is the same, the notation can be shortened to specifying only the first digit of each pair. So "**ffffff**" can be simplified to "**fff**." If only three digits are given, the omitted digit from each pair is assumed to be the same as the first when the rule is parsed.

CSS HACKS AND SHORTCUTS

As mentioned earlier, there are a number of hacks used in CSS to compensate for the variations among different browser interpretations of style rules. A hack refers to either an added rule or an odd application of a rule in order to achieve consistent page appearance across different browsers. The W3C Box Model defines the height and width of a box as that of the content area only. However, Internet Explorer prior to version 6 adds in the padding and border space to the overall dimensions of the box, resulting in different rendering than Firefox or later IE versions. For instance, consider the rules shown in the left side of Figure 10.10.

In most browsers, the rules on the left result in a "box" that is 130 pixels (100 + 10 + 10 + 5 + 5). However, in some versions of IE the full box size would be constrained to the content width given as 100 pixels, resulting in a smaller box. One fix is to address this by creating a "box within a box" and set the padding and borders to zero for the outer box. Another fix, shown on the right side of Figure 10.10, is a hack made possible by a difference between IE and other browsers regarding rule weighting; the **!important** designation is ignored by some versions of IE. Normally the **!important** weighting results in giving the

Rules that could result in two different box sizes depending on the browser	A sample "hack" to address this difference

#nav {
width:100px;
padding:10px;
border 5px;
}
	#nav {
	border: 5px;
	padding: 10px;
	width: 100px !important;
	width 130px;
	}

Figure 10.10 Box size definitions that require hacks with some browsers on the left; a hack fix on the right.

rule precedence over a later one, except in browsers that do not recognize this designation. Browsers that comply with the W3C definition of box height and width and that pay attention to the **!important** weighting would make the box 100 + 10 + 10 + 5 + 5 = 130 pixels. The versions of IE that would make the full box size equal to the width dimension ignore the **!important** weighting. In that case, IE would default to the precedence of the "last rule," which gives the width as 130 pixels, the same box size as the other browser. Although such hacks can be useful, the best practice is to avoid them as much as possible.

There are also some useful shortcuts in CSS. The color value shortcut, already mentioned, allows a single HEX digit to stand in for the double digit if the values are the same. Specifying a color as "**33cc55**" is equivalent to just using "**3c5**" to determine the amounts of red, green, and blue respectively. In addition, when specifying margins and padding, a single rule can list all four values with the assumption that the order is always top, right, bottom, left. Therefore, the rules shown on each side of Figure 10.11 are equivalent.

UNDERSTANDING THE CASCADE

There are multiple entities involved in the control of the presentational aspects of a Web page. Obviously, the author/publisher cares about the appearance of the site; the viewer wants, and has, some level of control. In addition, the device or software in use plays a role in page appearance and style application. The *cascade* part of the name for CSS reflects that these various overlapping directives interact and may result in multiple directives for the same HTML element. A defined order of precedence is necessary to resolve rule conflicts; generally, rules that are more local to the HTML are preferentially enforced over ones that are from more distant sources. At the lowest level, if there are no style rules, the browser controls presentation. However, if an external style sheet is referenced with a **LINK** tag those style directives override the browser defaults. Next, if a STYLE tag is in the head area with rules that apply to an element, those local rules override any external style sheet directions for that element. If a local STYLE container in the HTML uses both imported and local rules for the same element, the local rules "trump" imported ones. Inline styles using a style attribute in an element override all other conflicting style information.

Rules to individually specify margins	Single rule with four values in the declaration

{
margin-top: 1em;
margin-right: 2em;
margin-bottom: 3em;
margin-left: 4em;
}
	{
	margin: 1em 2em 3em 4em;
	}

Figure 10.11 Size designations on left and shortcut method to specify all in one statement on the right.

The styles applied to a specific element depend on the source of the style information for it. If an element is not specifically identified as a selector in a rule, the element's style properties are inherited from the next higher HTML element. For example, if there are no selectors for paragraphs, paragraphs then simply inherit the appearance properties specified for the BODY element. If there are rule declarations for some specific element and property, they are sorted by origin and weight. If there are two or more declarations for the same element, any explicit weighting is then factored in. For instance, a declaration can be given higher weighting by the inclusion of the **!important** designation, at least with browsers that respect it. The declaration in the following rule will be given higher weight in the precedence calculation by most browsers because of the **!important** designation.

```
#nav {margin-right: 1em! important}
```

After factoring in explicit weighting, the browser then sorts the rules by origin as described previously. Rules presented in style attributes for the elements themselves override rules in a more distant **<style>** tag; local rules within a **<style>** container override those imported into it with the **@import** notation; all these rules override those imported from an external style sheet file with the **LINK** tag. If two rules have the same level of weighing and origin, specificity is given precedence over rules that are more general. Finally, if this secondary sort does not resolve the rule conflict, the last occurrence of the rule is enforced over an earlier rule.

PUTTING IT TOGETHER: A CSS EXAMPLE

The best way to learn many of these techniques is by looking at examples and applying them with hands-on practice. The following example of a CSS style file and its action on a simple HTML document is provided to illustrate how CSS can control presentation, but this is no substitute for practice you do on your own. The following HTML file, rendered in the Firefox browser with styles turned off (there is a useful developer toolbar for Firefox that makes it possible to easily turn styles and scripts on or off), shows a non-styled HTML with lists of links. The table and final footer areas have no special formatting in this view, shown in Figure 10.12. The same file rendered in the Firefox browser with styles turned on and utilizing a CSS file is shown in Figure 10.13.

Note that the two menu lists have been positioned and formatted so as to be readily recognized as navigation areas; in addition, a hover over effect has been added to make them more interactive and animated (note the first link area on the vertical left list has changed from blue to gray with the mouse over). Other layout controls have made some text positioned as a sidebar, provided table formatting, and made the footer area appear centered and in color, making an appropriate area for contact information and a last modified date. The HTML code that is the source of both views of this page is shown in Figure 10.14. The callout notes inserted in the screen shot in Figure 10.13 give the names of the DIV containers that are referenced in both the HTML and the CSS file.

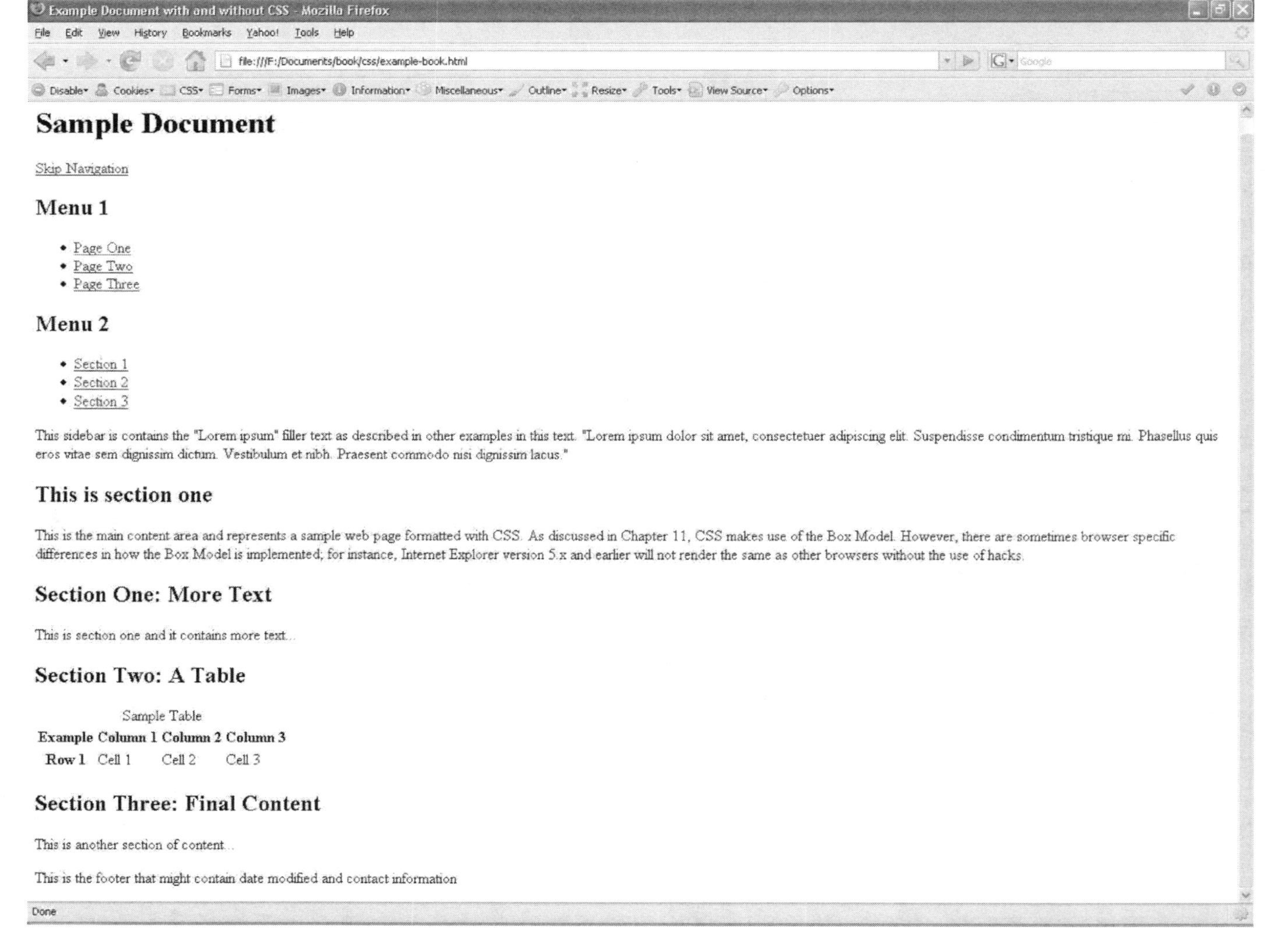

Figure 10.12 A screen shot of the HTML file from Firefox with styles turned off preventing the application of any style directives.

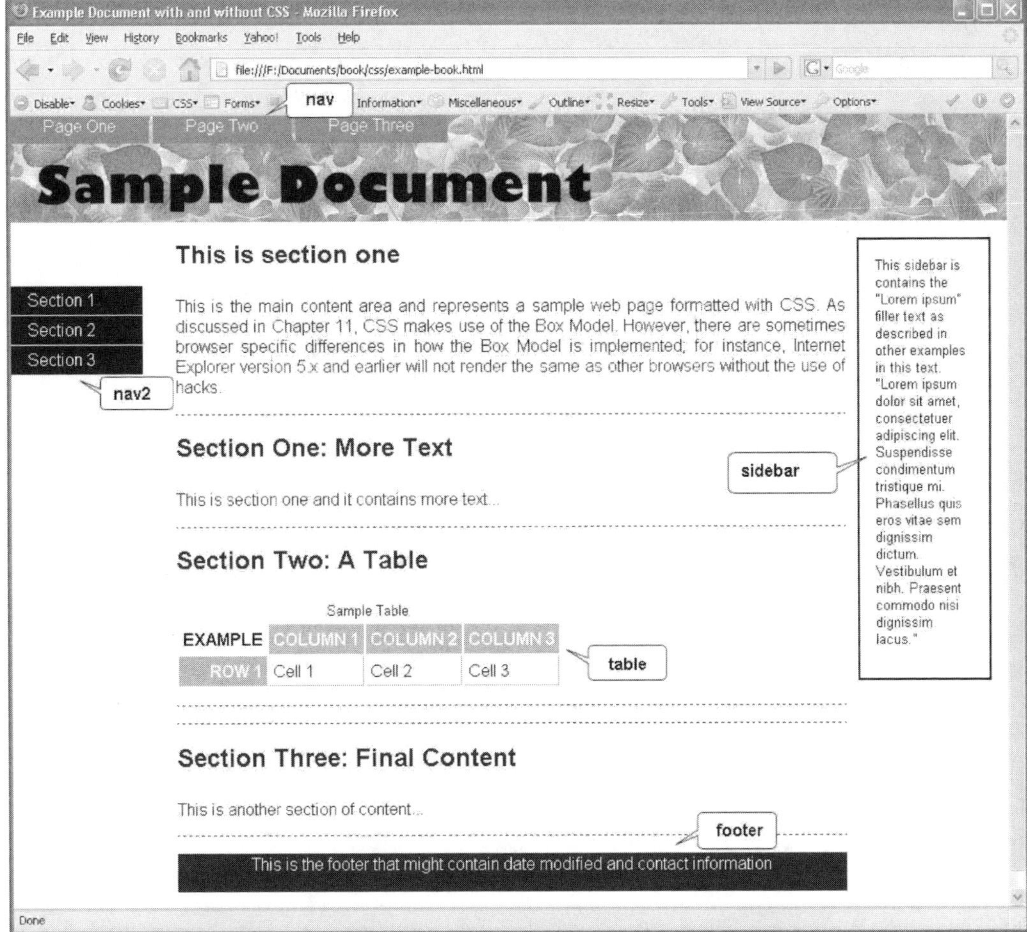

Figure 10.13 The same Web page as in Figure 10.12 with styles enabled.

These are explained in the series of figures that follow the HTML file in Figure 10.14.

The following figures present specific rules in the CSS file that change the HTML file's appearance to that shown in Figure 10.13. The rules all reside in the separate file **style-example.css** that is referenced in the HTML file LINK tag. For purposes of explanation, the rules from this file have been segregated into those that do not reference a specific HTML DIV container and those that do. The rules are listed on the left of each figure, and the explanation of their action is on the right. Figure 10.15 has a list of the CSS rules that do not have a **DIV** container specified.

The following figures are rules associated with **DIV** containers. Figure 10.16 has the rules for the "header" and "footer" **DIV** containers. Figure 10.17 shows the rules for the "nav" container, and Figure 10.18 has the "nav2" **DIV** container rules. Figure 10.19 shows the "maincontent" and "sidebar" div rules. Finally, Figure 10.20 has the rules for the "table" **DIV** container.

```
<html>
	<head>
		<title>Example Document with and without CSS</title>
		<link rel="stylesheet"" type="text/css" href="style-example.css" />
	</head>
	<body>
		<div id="header">
			<h1>Sample Document</h1>
		</div>
		<div id="skipnav">
			<a href="#content">Skip Navigation</a>
		</div>
		<div id="nav">
			<h2>Menu 1</h2>
			<ul>
				<li><a href="pageone.htm">Page One</a></li>
				<li><a href="pagetwo.htm">Page Two</a></li>
				<li><a href="page3.htm">Page Three</a></li>
			</ul>
		</div>
		<div id="nav2">
			<h2>Menu 2</h2>
			<ul>	<li><a href="#sec1">Section 1</a></li>
				<li><a href="#sec2">Section 2</a></li>
				<li><a href="#sec3">Section 3</a></li>
			</ul>
		</div>
		<div id="sidebar">
		<p>This sidebar contains the "Lorem ipsum" filler text ..."</p>
		</div>
		<div id="maincontent"> <a name= "content"></a>
			<div id="sec1">
			<h2>This is section one</h2>
		 <p>This is the main content area ... </p>
			</div>
			<div id="sec1">
				<h2>Section One: More Text</h2>
				<p>This is section one, and it contains more text...</p>
			</div>
			<div id="sec2">
				<h2>Section Two: A Table</h2>
				<div id="table">
				<table summary="Sample Table"> <caption>Sample Table</caption>
					<tr>	<th class="title">Example</th>
						<th>Column 1</th>
						<th>Column 2</th>
						<th>Column 3</th>	</tr>
					<tr>	<th class="row">Row 1</th>
						<td>Cell 1</td>
						<td>Cell 2</td>
						<td>Cell 3</a></td>		</tr>
				</table>
			</div>
			<div id="sec3">
				<h2>Section Three: Final Content</h2>
				<p>This is another section of content...</p>
			</div>		</div>
		<div id="footer">
			<p>This is the footer that might contain date modified and contact information</p>
		</div>
	</body>
</html>
```

Figure 10.14 The HTML file code for the Web page displayed in both Figure 10.12 and Figure 10.13. Note the DIV container names.

CSS Rules not associated with a DIV	Notes

* {
margin : 0;
padding : 0;
}
	The * is a wildcard for all element selectors, and the declaration starts the new page with all container margins and padding set to zero.

h2, p, ul, ol, table, fieldset {
margin-bottom : 1em;
}
	This will set the bottom margin for the selectors listed (fieldset is for forms) .

body {
font-family : arial, helvetica, sans serif;
}
	This lists the preferred font for all body content; fonts are listed in order of preference. For instance, if Arial is not available, Helvetica will be used; if neither are available, any sans serif font will be used.

a {
text-decoration : none;
}
	This turns off the default link formatting for anchor tags.

#skipnav {
display : none;
}
	This will suppress the display of the "skipnav" DIV container. However, if CSS is not enabled, the skipnav area will still be available.

Figure 10.15 Rules not associated with a DIV container.

DIV name	CSS Rule	Notes

header	#header h1 {
	background : url(banner.png) top left no-repeat;
	}
	#header h1 {
	display : block;
	height : 100px;
	textindent : -9999px;
	}
		These rules all apply to the header DIV container and will replace the H1 content wit image. A nonrepeating background image is set for this area, and within that area, the H1 content will be set off screen with a negative indent but remains available when viewed without CSS.

footer	#footer {
	clear : both;
	}
	#footer {
	color : #fff;
	background-color : #006;
	text-align : center;
	}
		This clears a space for the footer area and prevents any floating containers from getting in the way. Text and background colors are set, and text is center aligned.

Figure 10.16 CSS rules for the header and footer DIV containers.

DIV Name	CSS Rules	Notes

nav	#nav {
	position : absolute;
	left : 0;
	top : 0;
	}
	#nav h2 {
	display : none;
	}
	#nav ul {
	list-style-type : none;
	}
	#nav ul li {
	display : inline;
	}
	#nav ul li a {
	padding : 0.5em 2em;
	text-decoration : none;
	color : # fff;
	background-color : #555;
	}
	#nav ul li a:hover {
	color : #006;
	}
		These rules apply to the nav DIV container. The container is positioned, and specific selectors within the container are formatted as follows: H2 elements will not display; unordered list formatting is removed and list items made to flow across the screen with the inline display; and links within the list items are formatted by removing default formatting and specifying text, background, and hover colors.

Figure 10.17 The rules for the "nav" container.

DIV Name	CSS Rules	Notes

nav2	#nav2 {
	position: fixed;
	float : left;
	width : 7em;
	top: 10 em;
	}
	#nav2 h2 {
	display : none;
	}
	
	#nav2 ul {
	list-style-type : none;
	}
	#nav2 ul li a {
	display : block;
	width : 100%;
	padding : 0.25em 0 0.25em 1em;
	background-color : #004;
	border-bottom : 1px solid #eee;
	color : #fff;
	text-decoration : none;
	}
	#nav2 a:hover {
	background -color : #777;
	}
		These rules apply to the nav2 DIV container. The container is floated to the left side, and the fixed positioning declaration keeps this navigation area in the same screen location of 10 em from the top regardless of page scrolling. The container width is specified as 7 em. Within this container, H2 elements are suppressed, unordered list formatting is removed, and links within list items will be reformatted in a block display with padding, colors, and borders specified.

Figure 10.18 The rules for the "nav2" container.

DIV Name	CSS Rules	Notes

maincontent	#maincontent {
	margin : 0 9em 0 9em;
	}
	#maincontent {
	padding : 1em;
	text-align : justify;
	}
	#maincontent div {
	border-bottom : dashed 1px #006;
	margin-bottom : 1em;
	}
	#maincontent h2 {
	color : #006;
	}
		These rules apply to the maincontent DIV container and specify margins, padding, and text alignment. DIV containers within the maincontent area will have borders, and the color of H2 elements is set.

sidebar	#sidebar {
	float : right;
	width : 6em;
	margin-top : 1em;
	margin-right : 1em;
	}
	#sidebar {
	padding : 1em;
	border : solid 1px;
	}
	#sidebar p {
	font-size : smaller;
	text-align : left;
	}
		These rules apply to the sidebar DIV container, which will float to the right and be set at 6em wide. The padding, borders, and paragraph text formatting are all specified.

Figure 10.19 The rules for the “maincontent” and “sidebar” containers.

DIV Name	CSS Rules	Notes

table	#table caption {
	padding-bottom : 0.25em;
	text-align : center;
	font-size : smaller;
	}
	#table th {
	padding : 0.25em;
	text-transform : uppercase;
	color : #fff;
	background-color : #999;
	}
	#table th.row {
	text-align : right;
	}
	#table th.title {
	text-align : center;
	background-color : #fff;
	color : #000;
	}
	#table td {
	border-right : solid 1px #999;
	border-bottom : solid 1px #999;
	padding : 0.25em;
	}
	#table tr:hover {
	background-color : #ccc;
	}
		These rules will control the presentation of the table DIV container. The caption, headings, title, and data cells are all formatted. In addition, a hover color is added to highlight a row when the cursor passes over it. Note that this hover-over effect for table cells may not work in all browsers.

Figure 10.20 The rules for the table DIV.

With these simple rules, the HTML file is transformed in appearance, but if the styles are not desired or unavailable in a particular viewing environment, an acceptable version of the page is still available that presents the navigation links as linear lists followed by the content of the page.

SUMMARY

CSS is now a widely accepted standard for presentation and allows designers to have much better control of their Websites. The separation of presentation from content is an efficient strategy for managing style changes. CSS can also give the user some control of presentation by allowing for different views of the content that can accommodate the limitations of different devices and browsers. CSS is fairly easy to learn, but as with many technologies discussed in this text, hands-on experience is essential to become truly proficient in its application.

REFERENCES

Lie, H. W., & Bos, B. (1999). Cascading Style Sheets, designing for the Web. Reading, MA: Addison Wesley.

McClelland, D., Eismann, K., & Stone, T. (2000). Web design studio secrets (2nd ed.). Foster City, CA: IDG Books.

Powell, T. A. (2003). HTML and XHTML: The complete reference. Emeryville, CA: McGraw-Hill/Osborne.

W3C. (2008). Cascading style sheets home page. Retrieved May 2, 2008, from http://www.w3.org/Style/CSS.

W3Schools. (2008). CSS tutorial. Retrieved May 2, 2008, from http://www.w3schools.com/css/default.asp.

Chapter 11

Introduction to Web Programming

Web content can be easily created in HTML and presented with or without CSS styles; such static content residing in separate HTML files comprises a large portion of existing Web resources. However, HTML has limited options for interactivity, and content updates that take place at the individual file level are problematic for sites with a large number of pages to manage. One alternative is to utilize programming, often in conjunction with databases, to create more dynamic and interactive Websites. Dynamic content is that which does not already exist in some predefined HTML container but is generated on demand by a query or script action. A consequence of this approach is that search engines are unable to index these dynamic pages because they do not exist as autonomous and unchanging files residing on a Web server; database driven content therefore represents a significant portion of the invisible Web.

Programming can provide higher levels of interactivity with the user. Dynamic content and enhanced interactivity requires the use of various programming technologies that have been adapted to, or specifically created for, Web publishing needs. In addition to making pages more attractive, fun, and interactive, Web programming can handle a myriad of other important tasks including processing data from forms, formatting database queries and their output, automating administrative tasks, setting and utilizing cookies, and validating form input data. These capabilities, along with the possibility of dynamically generating a new or uniquely configured Web page based on user input or an event, makes learning about programming an important addition to the toolbox of the Web developer.

The starting point for this examination of Web programming is a general discussion of a few programming principles and terminologies that are specific to the Web environment; Schneider and Gersting (2000) provide a good source for introductory programming concepts. This introductory background supports the main agenda of this chapter, which is an examination of interpreted script programming using two popular languages for the Web: JavaScript and PHP. Web publishers quickly embraced JavaScript and PHP, both developed explicitly for the Web, because they are relatively easy to use and make many Website enhancements possible. This material is not presented from the perspective of a programmer (which I am not), but from the perspective that a basic understanding of these scripting technologies and an awareness of their potential is essential to all those involved in producing Web content and services.

CONCEPTS AND TERMINOLOGY

Programming begins with the idea of an *algorithm*. In simplistic, generic terms, this refers to a series of steps by which a problem can be solved. This definition can be extended to a wide variety of problems and formats describing the steps in the proposed solution. A cookbook recipe, a set of woodworking plans, or driving directions for a trip could all be thought of as describing the steps to solve a defined problem. Programs and scripts are a structured way to solve certain types of problems faced in Web development. In programming, the problem definition and its solution are described in limited, structured terms; the algorithmic solution is expressed in some specific programming language. As with all language, there is a vocabulary and syntax used for the instructions representing an algorithm. Instructions can be grouped together into a *function*. A function, also called a *subroutine* or *procedure*, is a set or block of instructions that execute together to yield a single result; these blocks can be reused in a modular fashion throughout a program. The block of statements associated with the function are enclosed within special punctuation, typically the curly bracket symbols { }. Functions are given names, and they may be predefined in a language or created as needed. Once defined, functions may be invoked later in the script; their action depends on user input or other events, such as a mouse click or a page loading. Information may be passed to a function in the form of a *parameter*, also referred to as an *argument*, when the function is defined. The term *variable* is used in many contexts and can be thought of generically as a placeholder for some value provided or assigned later. In programming, variables refer to named memory locations that store data of various types such as text strings, numbers, or Boolean data. A variable can be assigned a *null* value, meaning no data is stored. The rules for referencing variables or declaring them varies with the language used, but all script languages make use of variables.

A distinction is sometimes made between programming and scripting languages. Programming languages such as C++ or Java are written and then *compiled* into machine code; it is the compiled version that is run as an executable file. Scripting languages are not compiled but are interpreted line by line when they are run; they are considered a more lightweight form of programming. So, interpreted programs execute line by line on the fly, while compiled programs are converted to machine code by a compiler, turned into an executable format, and run in that form. To alter or debug compiled programs, the code must be corrected and the entire program must be recompiled before it can be tested; interpreted programs can be edited at the line level and run again immediately. Both the JavaScript and PHP languages are examples of interpreted script languages that do not result in compiled programs.

WEB PROGRAMMING

The scope of this overview includes only JavaScript and PHP, but this limited coverage is not intended to imply that they are the only or the best options for many applications; there are other programming languages that are equally important in Web development applications that are well-suited to various programming needs. While not covered in this chapter, a few of these other alternatives are highlighted.

An early Web programming development was programming associated with the Common Gateway Interface (CGI), which handled many types of information exchange between Web applications and servers, such as that needed for HTML form processing. CGI, as did the GUI Mosaic browser, came out of the National Center for Supercomputing Applications (NCSA) at the University of Illinois at Urbana-Champaign in 1993 (Brenner & Aoki, 1996). CGI was designed mostly for the UNIX environment and includes programs written in many different languages, including C++, PERL, and Python.

Beginning with Windows NT and Windows 2000, Microsoft has integrated the Internet Information Services (IIS) programs into its operating system. The IIS software enables Windows systems to run Web servers and other Internet services on a Windows PC. The IIS suite includes a set of Server Side Includes (SSI), a collection of software that enables many server-side programs; these are programs that run on a Web server when needed. The SSI software is usually associated with servers running Microsoft's IIS services, but these server-side programs are available for other platforms such as UNIX. Microsoft has developed a scripting technology for dynamic content that utilizes SSI software called *Active Server Pages* (ASP). ASP have embedded scripts that are processed on a server using the SSI programs. ASP have been coupled with the Microsoft.NET initiative, a broad framework utilizing XML, SOAP, and other technologies to create an Internet-based platform of Web services for Windows systems (Microsoft.NET, 2008). Other proprietary scripting languages such as Coldfusion (CFM), now owned by Adobe, have also been developed.

Java Server Pages (JSP) and Java servlets are another strategy for creating interactive, dynamic content. Servlets are Java programs designed to run on a Web server that can process the instructions contained in JSP pages (Harms, 2001). Because there is potential confusion between Java and JavaScript due to the use of "Java" in both names, their differences should be clarified. Developed by Sun Microsystems in the mid-1990s, Java is a full programming environment similar to C++. Java programming is an object-orientated programming (OOP) language consisting of classes of objects that can inherit properties by virtue of their class membership. Java programming results in compiled applications, applets, or servlets that can run on a Java Virtual Machine, available for all platforms. Java then, is a powerful, general purpose, cross-platform programming language for developing applications that can be used outside the context of the Web.

Java is usually used on the Web in the form of *applets* and *servlets. Applets* refer to programs called within a Web page, retrieved, and then run within the browser by the Java VM. However, when Java is used to create programs that run on the server, they are referred to as *servlets.* Servlets require that the Web server either have Java capability built-in to it or that a separate *servlet container* is installed to be the processing engine for the servlet code (Harms, 2001). Both strategies require knowledge of the Java programming language and result in a compiled program that runs on the Java VM.

The main point is that JavaScript and Java are not the same. JavaScript is a lightweight scripting language designed for the Web and intended to enhance HTML. The JavaScript syntax and its object model borrow significantly from the Java language, but they are quite different environments: JavaScript is interpreted by the browser, it does not result in a compiled binary file, and its use of objects is much more limited than Java.

DATABASES AND WEB PROGRAMMING

One of the important motivations for learning Web programming technologies is their application and usefulness in accessing databases via the Web. Riccardi (2003) provides a practical implementation of this, as do a number of other sources. The PHP language discussed later in this chapter is used extensively with Web database development, but it is certainly not the only choice available to the designer. Other options include the Ruby on Rails (RoR) development framework with the Ruby programming language (Ruby on Rails, 2008) or the JSP approach described earlier.

Databases are critical to the activities of most large enterprises and support commercial business transactions as well as information seeking. Because they come up in Web development, a brief review of key database concepts is provided here; more comprehensive coverage regarding database systems is available in many sources (Rob & Coronel, 1997; Hoffer, Prescott, & McFadden, 2002). Databases can be defined as any collection of data and facts that are stored for future retrieval for some process or information need. Computer technology has vastly enhanced the capabilities of database systems. The software that allows users to add, view, modify, or extract information from a database is called a *Database Management System* (DBMS). There are various types of databases, such as flat file databases, where a single table contains all the data; relational databases, where the data and the relationships among the data are stored in a series of interrelated tables; and object-oriented databases, where the data structures are modeled as objects, which can be grouped together to form classes.

The relational database type is a common choice for delivery of Web content. There are many options for relational database software applications, including Microsoft Access, Sybase, and Oracle. However, the flexibility of the open-source MySQL database software (recently purchased by Sun Microsystems) has made it an attractive alternative for those wanting to do Web development within an open-source framework. Relational databases use a powerful command language called the *Structured Query Language* (SQL). In the relational model, data and the relationships among data are stored in database tables; when these tables meet certain criteria they are called *relations.* SQL queries can be written to add or delete records, perform counts or calculations, or extract content from one or more tables to create useful subsets of records. When databases are available via the Web, data entry, query submission, and query results can be done through HTML forms in conjunction with script programming or with a content management editor. When combined with style sheets, the result is a dynamically generated Web page derived from the database query output. A full discussion of the relational model is beyond the scope of this chapter, but it is briefly described later in this section.

Databases play vital roles in all forms of Web commerce by storing customer and product data as well as tracking orders, shipping, and billing. Database solutions are also utilized as a technique to create and manage Website content. The use of databases for business transactional needs or to enable dynamic Web content where pages are composed "on the fly" is dependent on a well-designed database, appropriate queries, and script programming technologies that mediate the overall process. Databases are an important component of content management systems that allow distributed access to Website updates, so designers interested in this approach need to learn about these interrelated technologies.

On the surface, electing to implement a database approach to deliver Website content adds a number of formidable complications to site production. Someone has to design, model, and build the database and enter the data. SQL queries must be written, and a scripting language chosen and utilized to pass those queries to the database system. Static Web pages only require a Web server to respond to a client request, but database approaches require the installation of additional server-side software, such as the PHP engine or the Microsoft SSI software. In addition, if the database resides on the same server, performance issues might arise depending on the nature and scale of the site and the query load that results from its use. Caching techniques, discussed later, can address this issue. The most technically challenging parts of this process are developing the necessary scripts, programs, and style sheets that take user input, such as a followed link to create the appropriate query, and generate a well-designed response page.

As mentioned earlier, the open-source MySQL software is a popular choice for the backend database. Two of the programming solutions frequently used with MySQL are PHP scripting or JSP. There are many books that discuss the details of each strategy. PHP is so closely aligned with the MySQL database that both these topics are often treated together (Davis & Phillips, 2006; Meloni, 2000; Powers, 2006). The details of these implementations are beyond the scope of this chapter, but examples of PHP scripting are examined to introduce its syntax and capabilities.

Choosing a database approach to managing a Website involves an investment of initial effort, but it can have a significant payoff in long-term ease of maintaining and updating large, complex sites. A site comprising numerous static HTML pages requires checking many pages for each minor content update; any pages that are overlooked will continue to provide out-of-date or conflicting information. In a database driven site, content updates need to occur only in the specific database table that holds that information and can be done with simple Web-based editing software by anyone with access to the database.

This shares content responsibility with a large group throughout an organization. Content management software, such as the open-source FCKeditor, provides a text-editing environment that does not require HTML knowledge (FCKeditor, 2008). Another open-source CMS that is becoming quite popular is Drupal (http://drupal.org/) a feature-rich platform that utilizes PHP and MySQL technologies. In addition to CMS approaches, designers of database-driven sites can make use of a template/presentation engine such as Smarty (http://www.smarty.net/) that also includes page caching features. Web pages pulling information from the database are dynamically updated with the next request from a Web client, as diagrammed in Figure 11.1.

The relational database model uses a series of interrelated tables to store data and relationships among data. Each table is designed to store information for a single entity, defined as one of the "things" of interest. An entity might be employees, customers, or products. Entities are described by their attributes, which become the columns of the table; rows within a table are entity instances, or records. One field for each table is designated as a primary key, which is defined as a unique record identifier; this is often numeric, such as a person's ID number. A table may reference another table's primary key, which becomes a foreign key in that table. Primary keys and foreign keys create a relationship between the two tables that allows a query to join elements of each

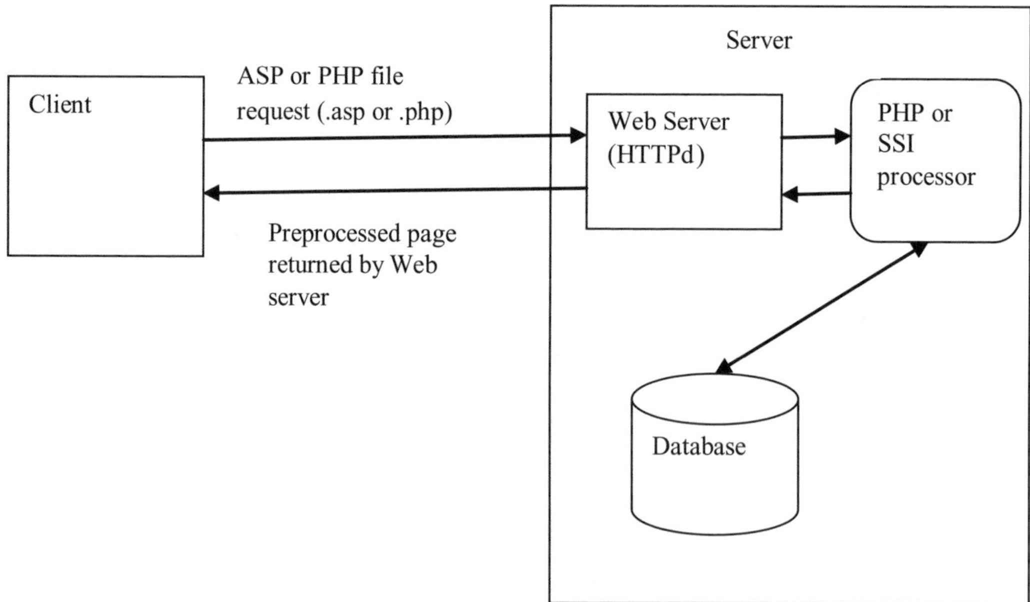

Figure 11.1 A client (browser) requests a file that contains ASP or PHP code. The Web server (HTTPd—d is for "daemon," i.e., a Web server) recognizes the corresponding file extension and hands the file to the appropriate script processor (the PHP engine or the Microsoft SSI installed on the server). The script is processed there; if the code contains a database query, it is passed to the DBMS, which may be on the same server as shown or on another host. The resulting content is returned to the requesting client by the Web server.

table together. Relational databases have strict design requirements, and the process of ensuring compliance with these rules is called *normalization.*

Relational database queries use SQL or a graphical equivalent of it. However, scripts can associate links with predefined queries or handle query formation using criteria from HTML forms, relieving users of the need to know anything about SQL. For example, a select query can draw data from one or more tables. A database table called "students" could be queried as shown below to display first and last names along with email addresses, sorted by last name:

```
SELECT Students.FirstName, Students.LastName, Students.
   EmailName FROM Students ORDER BY Students.LastName;
```

This SQL statement could be placed in a script that could also accept the database output and, along with style sheets, result in a dynamically produced Webpage.

SCRIPT PROGRAMMING BASICS

Scripts are special types of text files that contain commands and instructions that are interpreted by a parsing program or operating system. Script files are commonplace on both UNIX and PC systems. In the PC world, simple DOS-based scripts known as batch files were common and are still used to automate tasks. Shell scripts on UNIX hosts have an equally long history. Other types of scripts include login scripts for Novell networks and Microsoft's Visual Basic scripting language that supports macro creation in the Office suite.

Batch files are one of the simplest forms of a script program. Each line in such a script begins with a command, and the parameters (the object of a command) are passed to the commands. The text file that contains the commands is given a **BAT** extension to indicate its executable nature, and the script could be associated with an icon on the Windows desktop. While simple batch files are not as interesting as Web scripts, they illustrate key concepts of script programs: (1) Scripts are simple text files but are recognized as executable by their extension. (2) They are written according to the rules vocabulary of the program expected to interpret them. (3) They can contain comments. (4) They can utilize control structures such as conditional tests. (5) They are interpreted sequentially line-by-line unless there is some intervening control structure.

Microsoft uses Visual Basic script for macros in programs such as PowerPoint and Word. The VB script shown in Figure 11.2 can be used to add a simple interactive macro function to a PowerPoint object, such as presenting a quiz with feedback in the form of alert boxes. The nature of the questions and answers in this example are immaterial; the questions and answers could be about any topic. The point is the VB script controls the response for an incorrect or correct answer, as shown in Figure 11.2. The script uses simple programming techniques to create user interactivity within a PowerPoint slide show. Figure 11.3 shows the script alert box displayed when an incorrect response was chosen.

Macros in Visual Basic	Code explained
Sub Wrong()	Declares a subroutine called "Wrong"
MsgBox ("sorry, that's incorrect")	A MsgBox function that displays the content shown
End Sub	Ends this subroutine
Sub Right()	Declares a subroutine called "Right"
MsgBox ("Yes—good answer!")	A MsgBox with feedback for a correct answer
SlideShowWindows(1).View.Next	Advances the slideshow to the next slide
End Sub	Ends this subroutine
Sub Rightlast()	Declares a subroutine called "Rightlast"
MsgBox ("congratulations— you're done!")	A MsgBox showing a message for the end of the slideshow to conclude the quiz
End Sub	Ends this subroutine

Figure 11.2 A Visual Basic script used to define three macros in PowerPoint. Each can then be associated with different events.

Figure 11.3 Screen shot showing the alert box macro function when an incorrect response is selected by the user.

Script languages are very much a command world, so some familiarity with the unforgiving nature of a command line interface is necessary. Command-line environments have strict syntactical rules for command processing and are intolerant of spelling and punctuation errors, as are script processors. A misplaced quotation mark or comma, a mistake in spelling or case, or a mismatched curly bracket, and the script will fail. Another commonality with the command-line syntax is the ability to pass parameters (also called arguments) to a command. A parameter is what the command acts on, identified by its position on the command line. Parameters can be passed to functions as well.

The first Web clients and servers were on UNIX systems, and the people creating these sites usually had extensive experience with shell scripts as well as other programming languages. It is not surprising these early Web developers applied programming techniques to HTML, giving rise to a number of new scripting languages. Microsoft's ASP, JavaScript, and PHP resulted from an interest in enhancing the Web experience as well as extending the functionalities of HTML. Script code blocks can cohabitate within HTML or be stored as separate external files. External script files, referred to as *include files,* are recognized by the use of a specific assigned file extension; for instance, JavaScript files end in **JS**.

Script languages use a formal language and utilize the same types of internal control structures as other programming languages to determine the flow of their execution. Script programming languages are procedural, and the default control structure is sequential control; without some intervening instructions, scripts execute sequentially line by line. Intervening control structures include selection structures, which allow for IF–THEN conditional testing and repetition structures, which allow for looping of a section of code until some condition is false.

Software for Script Programming

Script files are simple text and, as with HTML, can be created in any text-editing environment. However, there are many specialized editors that make the task of script writing easier such as Microsoft's Script Debugger, Mozilla Venkman, or ActiveState's Komodo Edit. Most simple HTML editors also include various tools to support script authoring. Script testing and debugging depends on whether processing is on the client or server (a distinction explored in the next section). JavaScript functionality is integrated into Web browsers and most HTML editing programs, so these scripts are easily tested on a desktop PC without additional specialized software installed, and an Internet connection is not needed. Server-side languages, such as PHP, require that a script-processing engine is available along with a Web server for testing. If these components are installed on the PC testing can be done locally, otherwise testing is done after uploading the script file to a server with those capabilities.

Client-Side vs. Server-Side Programming

Web scripts are divided into two different types based on where they are executed. *Client-side* scripts are executed solely on the client host; *server-side* scripts execute on a server with a processing engine or container installed and configured to coordinate with a Web server. JavaScript uses client-side processing and PHP uses server-side processing. Not all client-side script languages work within all browsers. JavaScript was developed by Netscape, and while most browsers can process JavaScript that was not always the case. Visual Basic is a Microsoft technology; Internet Explorer can process it, but other browsers may not support it.

The distinction between client and server processing extends to Java programs as well, which are designed to run on either the client or the server. Java applets are downloaded with a Web page using the applet tag and are executed by the client Java VM. Java Server Pages are first preprocessed by some servlet, which is a Java program running on a server. This takes place within a separate server module called a *servlet container* such as the Jakarta Tomcat software; the resulting page is sent to the browser only after this preprocessing. Other server-side technologies previously mentioned are Adobe ColdFusion and Microsoft Active Server Pages (ASP), both of which utilize scripts within HTML documents extracted and processed by the server programs associated with each.

Server-side approaches depend on a successful hand-off by the Web server to some other specific container or processing engine that extracts and processes the code; this process is diagrammed in Figure 11.4. The Web server uses either the file extension or a designated directory location of the requested file to determine that the HTTP file request should be redirected to another program for preprocessing. After the code block has been executed and replaced by the script output, the file is passed back to the Web server to send to the client. Files that end in ASP, PHP, CFM, or JSP all indicate that the Web server program should send the file to another server program first.

Pros and Cons of Server vs. Client Execution

Client-side and server-side approaches each have advantages and disadvantages. Client-side scripts accompany the HTML with the result that all the code is easily available by simply viewing the HTML source code, which may or may not be desirable. The easy availability of the script code contributed

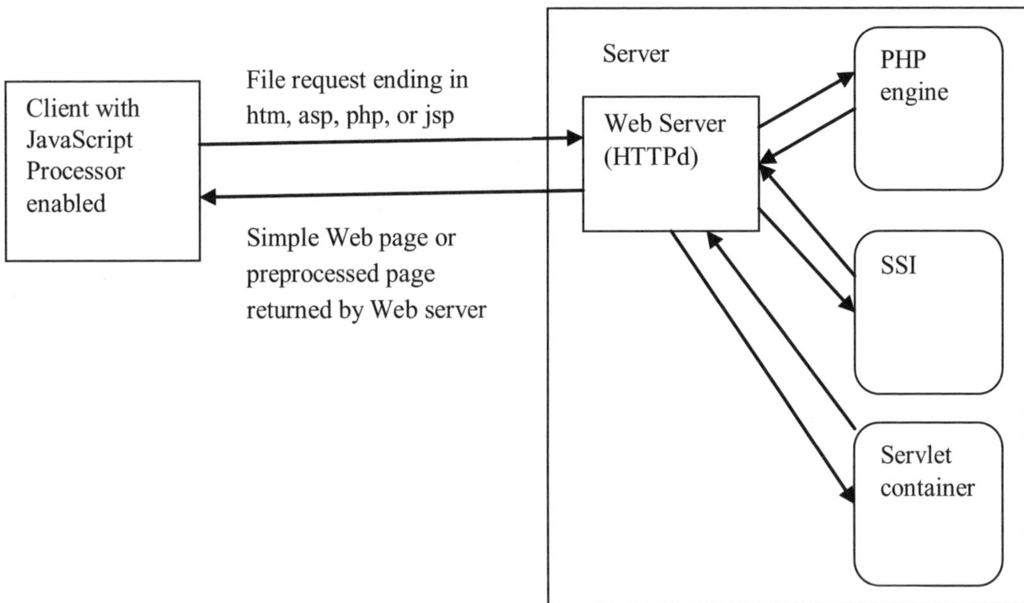

Figure 11.4 A client (browser) may request a static Web page ending with .HTM, or a file that needs additional processing such as those ending with PHP, ASP, or JSP. A file ending in HTM simply is sent to the client via HTTP. However, if the appropriate server-side software is installed, the Web server forwards PHP files to the PHP engine, ASP files to the SSI software, or JSP files to some installed servlet container, where the needed processing takes place. The output of that processing is then returned to the Web server in the same file container that contained the code; this output is then sent to the client for display. If that file happens to contain JavaScript code as well, that must be handled by the JavaScript capabilities of the client.

to the popularity of JavaScript because it can be viewed, copied, and adapted to new uses. Client-side approaches relieve the server of added processing demands and distribute them to the users. However, dependence on the client for processing can be problematic because the script functionality depends completely on the capability of the user agent employed. Standard Web browsers can process JavaScript, but there are mobile and assistive devices that cannot. Server-side approaches are better for accommodating those devices than client-side techniques.

Server-side solutions have advantages. The user only sees the output of the script action, and the script itself can remain private. Server-side approaches also avoid some of the previously mentioned accessibility issues of client-side techniques. However, because they can accept information or parameters from URLs, they can raise security issues (see the discussion of the PHP register globals issues later in this chapter). In addition, these technologies do add to the load of the server, which can create serious performance issues, especially if the script references other server components such as a database. These server load issues can be reduced with the addition of software that enables server caching of dynamic content. Commonly requested Web pages generated dynamically from a database can be cached on the server, and the cached copy can be sent in response to future client requests; a new query is performed only if the cached copy is older than a preset timeframe.

Programming Details for Scripts

Scripting languages are all similar in that they share many of the same objectives and functionalities. Although there are differences in the details of how specific tasks are handled, there are common themes and terms employed in all scripting languages. Some of these commonalities are described before examining the examples of specific JavaScript and PHP scripting that follow.

An immediate issue is the textual nature of script programs and the method employed to parse the commands within them. JavaScript and PHP are more rigorous languages than the simple batch files mentioned earlier. Batch files do not require a special instruction terminator other than the CRLF (the "carriage return line feed" ASCII codes) found at the end of each line, and echoed text does not need to be in quotation marks. This is not typically the case with other script languages; instruction terminators are expected to identify the end of the instruction line, and they require that quotation marks surround text strings. PHP requires the use of the semicolon character for the instruction terminator; although this is not enforced in JavaScript, it is considered good practice to use it. Both permit either single or double quotation marks to delimit strings. As with HTML, issues arise when text characters with special meaning to the parsing program are used as simple text. Just as character entities in HTML allow the display of characters such as the less than or greater than sign as textual content instead of a tag identifier, scripting languages use "escape sequences" to permit the use of characters such as quotation marks as simple text instead of a delimiter. The backslash character preceding a quotation mark is a way to tell PHP or JavaScript that in that instance the quotation mark is not a delimiter but instead is to be treated as any other character.

In JavaScript, variables are simply declared by providing a qualifying string name set equal to some value; any name may be used, but the usual convention is to use "var" as a keyword first, as in **var some_name = "some_value**." In PHP, variables can be declared with a name starting with the dollar sign, as in **$some_name = "some_value**." Figure 11.5 shows examples of variable declarations with value assignments; the first two are JavaScript, the third is PHP.

Sometimes scripts writers want to add, or *concatenate*, one string or variable with another; this requires an operator (usually "+") within a script. In addition to the concatenation operation, there are other standard operators used in scripting. The familiar operators from arithmetic and algebra are available and have the same role as special symbols that are associated with some predefined action. In addition to the standard arithmetic use of operators (+,–, *, and / for addition, subtraction, multiplication, and division), operators exist for assignment or comparison of values and for Boolean operations (AND, OR, NOT) as well. The common symbols for each operation are the same in both JavaScript and PHP and are listed in Figure 11.6.

Besides declaring individual variables with a one-to-one name-to-value mapping, it is often useful to reference a list of related name and value pairs, done with an *array*. Like simple variables, arrays have names and refer to memory locations where the array table is stored. Arrays use either a numeric or a name index to determine what part of the list is being referenced. For instance, a numeric key array associated with the days of the week is shown in Figure 11.7. Arrays are explored further in the PHP examples.

Scripts can respond to *events*, which are actions associated with some function within the script; events cause something to happen. Common trigger events can include a mouse hovering over some area, a click on a button or image, a page loading, or a page being exited. The set of codes associated with these events are *event handlers*.

Variable naming and assignment of values	Explanation
userID= "Miller";	In JavaScript, a variable can be simply given a name and assigned a value with the equal sign; the line at left creates a variable named "userID" and assigns it a string value.
var userID= "Miller";	Here the keyword "var" is used to formally declare this variable; while not required, it is good practice.
$userID= "Miller";	In PHP, variable names are preceded with a $. This line would create the variable "userID" and assign it the string value "Miller."

Figure 11.5 Examples of creating variable names and assigning them values in JavaScript and PHP.

Type	Operator	Description
Arithmetic	+	Addition
	-	Subtraction
	*	Multiplication
	/	Division
	%	Modulus (division remainder)
	++	Increment
	--	Decrement
Assignment	=	Assign value (x=y)
	+=	Assign value as with some added amount (x+=y)
	−=	Assign value as minus some amount (x−=y)
	*=	Assign value as multiplied by some amount (x*=y)
	/=	Assign value as divided by some amount (x/=y)
	%=	Assign value as modulus some amount (x%=y)
Comparison	==	is equal to
	===	is equal to (both *value* and *type*)
	!=	is not equal
	>	is greater than
	<	is less than
	>=	is greater than or equal to
	<=	is less than or equal to
Boolean	&&	and
	||	or
	!	not

Figure 11.6 Script operators used in JavaScript and PHP.

Key	Value
0	Sunday
1	Monday
2	Tuesday
3	Wednesday
4	Thursday
5	Friday
6	Saturday

Figure 11.7 A numeric key array with corresponding values.

JAVASCRIPT BASICS

This general discussion of structure and terminology can be applied to the two specific languages to be explored further in this chapter: JavaScript and PHP. JavaScript was created in 1995 by Netscape engineer Brendan Eich and released as part of Netscape 2 in 1996 (Shafer, 1996). The name was chosen partly to capitalize on the attention garnered by the Java language developed at Sun Microsystems, but as discussed earlier, the two languages are quite different. JavaScript is considered a lightweight programming environment designed to enhance HTML. Microsoft developed its own version of this technology called Jscript that was released with Internet Explorer 3.

JavaScript is an object-oriented language built on the view of a Web document as a hierarchically structured collection of objects, methods, and properties. *Objects* are defined in many programming languages. In broad terms, an object is some defined entity that is named and described with a set of identifiable attributes or properties that are assigned specific values. In the real world, objects are physical things such as a bicycle, which has properties such as color or wheel size that describe it. Script objects have properties but can also be associated with a method, which is a defined set of instructions the object can reference. In addition, parameters can be passed to an object.

When JavaScript was developed, each browser had its own object model, but this object view has been standardized with the W3C Document Object Model (DOM) (W3C, 2008). Document objects are created using the HTML tags associated with them; further, these objects may have a name attribute defined that identifies a specific object in a particular document. For instance, the tag **<form name = "myform">** defines a form object named **myform**. The JavaScript object model references the W3C DOM standard as well as the other DOM-like features from the earlier Browser Object Model (BOM). There is a subtle distinction between the two: The DOM is a model for a document presented by a browser, while the BOM includes information about the browser itself and defines specific browser-related objects such as the **window** object. JavaScript has a set of core objects that can be referenced in scripts, such as the **document** or **date** objects. JavaScript also permits new objects to be created as needed.

JavaScript uses the *dot notation* for objects and method. This syntax for objects provides object names and identifies associated child objects, properties, or methods. The dot notation convention separates these elements with a period (a "dot") that reflects the object hierarchy, as in the name "**document.form**" to reference a form object within a document, or "**document.write**" to identify a method that displays information within the document object. This convention is illustrated in some of the JavaScript examples that follow. The browser-centered object hierarchy begins with a window object that contains a document, a history, a location, and references to itself or a parent window. Documents contain elements that can be treated as objects including links, named anchors, paragraphs, forms, and lists. Examples of the components in this object hierarchy are shown in Figure 11.8.

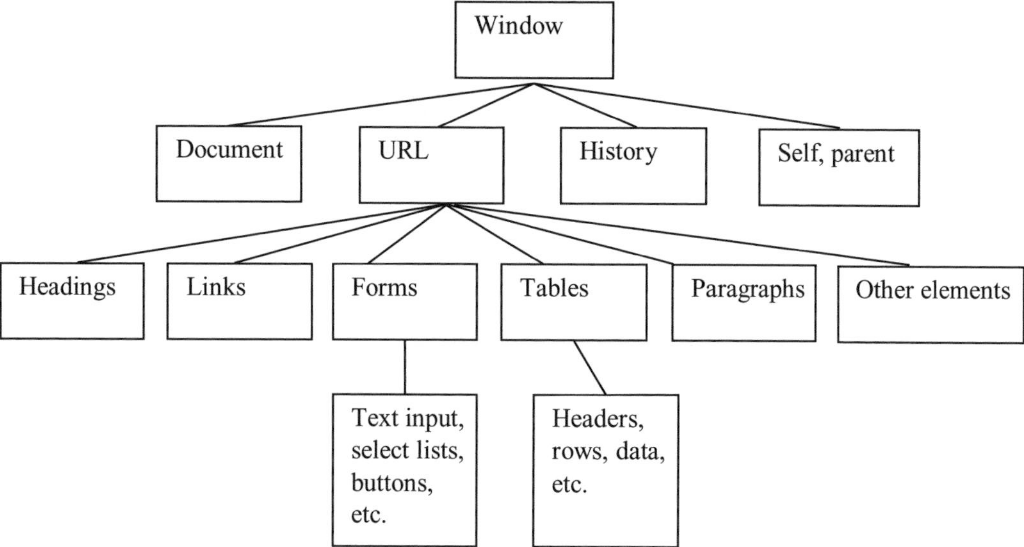

Figure 11.8 Examples of objects in the hierarchical browser object model view of Web components beginning with the window object.

The objects defined in this hierarchy have names, properties, and methods associated with them. The window object has the properties **self** (refers to the current window itself), **frames** (information about each frame window), **default status** (the status area at the bottom of the window that displays link addresses when the cursor hovers over them), or **top** (the window identified as the first opened window in the session). This window object also has methods associated with it, such as presenting a dialog alert box or other prompting dialog box, as well as methods for opening new windows or closing them. Document objects have a large set of properties and methods in JavaScript.

JavaScript Examples

JavaScript has been discussed rather abstractly up to this point, but better understanding results from examining examples that demonstrate these ideas. The first JavaScript example is the nearly ubiquitous first-time script everyone learns in scripting: the "Hello World" message that also displays the current date, shown in Figure 11.9.

This very simple script demonstrates a number of important aspects of JavaScript:

1. JavaScript code blocks can cohabitate within a standard HTML file container that ends with the HTM extension. The script is processed by the browser along with the HTML.

HTML with JavaScript	Output from a browser display of the HTML file with the script.

<!DOCTYPE HTML PUBLIC
"//W3C//DTD HTML 4.01
Transitional//EN">
<html>
<head>
<title>Our first JavaScript</title>
</head>
<body>
<h1>Example 1</h1>
<script language= "javascript1.2">
<!-- commenting out the script for old
browsers
document.write("Hello World!" +
"
");
var today = Date();
document.write(today);
// End hiding script -->
</script>
</body>
</html>
	Example 1
	Hello World!
	Tue Sep 25 13:38:09 2007

Figure 11.9 JavaScript code in an HTML container and its output as copied from a browser display.

2. The **<script></script>** tag pair is used to identify the JavaScript code block; the language attribute identifies this as JavaScript.
3. The script commands are nested within the <script> tag container. These commands could have been stored in an external file, called an include file. If this had been done, the source attribute for that external file would be defined (**src = "filename"**) to specify the location of the required script file. The external file would end in **JS** and would contain only the information that would have been placed between the beginning and ending script tags if the script had been placed in the HTML container (that is, the external file should NOT have any other HTML, such as starting and ending script tags).
4. The first line within the script is an optional HTML comment identifier so that browsers without JavaScript capability will ignore the entire script block. The comment begins with <!--which comments out that line for systems lacking the JavaScript interpreter; the ending--> ends the HTML comment block.
5. The line of code **document.write("Hello World!" + "<br>")** demonstrates an object with a method; the document object can "write" text into the page. It also shows that a parameter, in this case "**Hello**

```
<!DOCTYPE HTML PUBLIC "-
//W3C//DTD HTML 4.01 Transitional//EN">
<html>
<head>
<title>Example 2</title>
<script language="javascript">
        function ButtonOne()
        {
        alert("Hello World");
        }
</script>
</head>
<body>
<h1>Invoking JavaScript within a HTML
Page</h1>

<input type=button name="buttonJS"
value="click here" OnClick="ButtonOne()">

</body>
</html>
```

Figure 11.10 JavaScript code for "Hello World" interactive script.

World" + "**
**", can be passed to this object by its placement within the parentheses. The text to print in the page is in double quotation marks; the plus sign shows the concatenation, or adding, of two text strings. Note that one of the text strings printed in the page is just the HTML for a line break to separate this line of output from the next in the display.

6. The **var today = Date()** declares a variable called "today" and assigns it the value of the JavaScript predefined date object.
7. Finally, the line **document.write(today)** shows that a variable can be referenced in the document.write object.

Another simple script example is shown in Figure 11.10. Note that this script requires an event to trigger the alert function. The output of the script action in a browser preview is shown in Figure 11.11.

This script highlights a few additional points about JavaScript:

1. A function is defined in this script with the line **function ButtonOne().** It is declared with the keyword "function" and is called "ButtonOne()." Note that the function names end with a set of parentheses, which can be empty or contain a parameter to pass to the function. The block of statements in this function are contained within curly brackets and reference the alert object with the message parameter shown in parentheses.

Figure 11.11 The output of the JavaScript in Figure 11.10 previewed as it would appear in a browser after clicking on the button.

2. Functions are defined in the head area and are called in the body area by some event. In this example, a button was created, and the OnClick event is associated with the function defined in the head area.

The last example shows one version of a rollover effect with JavaScript. This last example in Figure 11.12 highlights these additional points:

1. A conditional test is used (the "**if. . .else**") to allow for different possible outcomes.
2. JavaScript comments, marked either by // at the beginning of a single comment line or with the start and ending tags /* and */

```
<html>
<head>
<SCRIPT LANGUAGE="Javascript1.2">
<!-- hide script from old browsers
if (document.images) {
/* check to see if browser can handle image objects; better than testing for many browser
versions */
        banner1 = new Image;
        banner2 = new Image;
//makes two image objects

        banner1.src = 'image2mo.gif';
        banner2.src = 'image1.gif';

        //fills objects with specific gifs
}
else {
        banner1 = "";
        banner2 = "";
        document.banner ="";
}
// for old browsers, leave objects empty
//end hiding script -->
</script>
</head>
<body>
<h1>An image rollover</h1>
<a href="" onmouseover = "document.banner.src=banner1.src"
onmouseout = "document.banner.src=banner2.src">
<img src="image1.gif" border="0" name="banner"></a>
</body>
</html>
```

Figure 11.12 JavaScript code for a rollover within an HTML file.

around a more lengthy comment, are helpful to those who might use or modify your scripts.

3. The object model can be used to do "browser sniffing;" that is, if a browser can work with the DOM model that indicates it is JavaScript capable. This is more efficient than testing for multiple browsers and versions as was sometimes done with older JavaScripts.
4. The banner document object is associated with the image by the name attribute value in the image tag.

With these examples, along with those you seek out in other sources, it is important to recognize that there is rarely "one right way" to create a script. For almost any problem there are many possible solutions that can be addressed with scripting, and there are thousands of examples available on the Web and in books on JavaScript that may address similar functions quite differently. JavaScript has many practical applications, including page redirects, automatic date-last-modified references, image and text effects, slide shows, navigation rollovers, and pop-out menus. While there are annoying and problematic JavaScript applications as well as some known accessibility issues, its usefulness in Web development is well established. JavaScript has also found new applications in conjunction with other Web technologies such as XML and CSS, which allow for dynamic styles that exhibit different behaviors based on user interaction. AJAX (asynchronous JavaScript and XML) is used with other APIs to create useful "widgets" in Websites such as tools that place location stickpins in a map (Purvis, Sambells, & Turner, 2006). Using the Google Map API in this manner is an example of a "mashup"; mashups and other Web 2.0 technologies are discussed in Chapter 16.

PHP OVERVIEW

The PHP scripting language grew out of an earlier language developed by Rasmus Lerdorf in 1995 called "personal home page tools." This was rewritten by Andi Gutmans and Zeev Suraski in 1997 and released as PHP 3.0. The new version of PHP was rechristened with the recursive name "PHP: Hypertext Preprocessor" (The PHP Group, 2008a). Currently in Version 5, PHP is a well-documented and supported language (see http://www.php.net for the documentation of this language).

PHP is a server-side language designed explicitly for Web development; hence the name "hypertext preprocessor." It supports interaction with databases including MySQL, Informix, Oracle, Sybase, and the Generic ODBC model. In fact, much of the interest in PHP is because of its suitability and well-established support for database interactions. As an open source solution, PHP is an especially good fit with the database program MySQL.

PHP Syntax

As with JavaScript, PHP code blocks can cohabitate within HTML documents or exist as separate script files. However, one difference from JavaScript is that all files that contain PHP code must end in the PHP extension even if the majority of the file is simple HTML. This is required for the Web server to recognize the needed handoff to the PHP processor. In addition, a PHP engine must be installed to accept this handoff. When the handoff takes place, the code blocks are extracted and replaced with the output of the script; this preprocessed file is what is returned by the server to the requesting client. Because of this difference, PHP code blocks are not seen within the HTML source code that the browser receives. It follows from this that any practical testing of the scripts described here requires access to a Web server with the PHP engine installed. If desired, this environment can be created on your desktop PC by setting up a Web server and the corresponding version of the PHP processor.

Although the look and feel of PHP seems familiar to those using JavaScript, it does have its own rules to learn. PHP can reference objects, functions, and variables, and it has the same operators and data types (strings, integers, floating point, and Boolean) that JavaScript does. As with JavaScript, names are case sensitive, and some names are reserved. It also has a mechanism to "escape" reserved characters; some characters that have a specific meaning to the parser can cause errors when used as simple text within a string, so it is necessary to have "escape" sequences available for those characters. Some key elements of PHP include:

1. PHP code blocks are identified by, and contained within, an identifying tag pair. There are three ways such a code block can be identified:
    a. With a **<?php and ?>** tag pair. Note that these are usually on the first and last lines of the code block with all the PHP coding in between (this is the most common and generally preferred method);
    b. With a simple **<? and ?>** tag pair used as above;
    c. With the code placed between a **<script language = "PHP"> </script>** tag pair.
2. Comments are permitted; single line comments use the double forward slash (//) but may also start with the pound sign (#). Multiple line comments begin with /* and end with */.
3. Each line within the code block requires an **instruction terminator,** which is the semicolon (;) character.
4. Variables can be declared with a dollar sign ($) immediately followed by a name. Names must start with a letter or underscore character and are case sensitive. PHP allows for different data types with variables, and they do not have to be specified when the variable is declared.
5. Arrays are a special type of variable that can hold a set of values and can be declared with **$array_name [key] = "some_value"** (see examples in the next section).
6. Functions are declared with the familiar **function name( )** where the parentheses can be empty or contain information that is passed to the function; information in the parentheses is called an argument. The block of statements associated with the function is contained within a set of curly brackets { }.

PHP: First Example

With these basics in place, an example is provided of a PHP script that is similar to the earlier JavaScript that displayed a message back into the HTML container. Figure 11.13 shows the code for "**hello.php**."

This simple code block demonstrates a few of the things that can be done with PHP. Some key observations about this script are:

1. Although the code is embedded in HTML, this file must end with the .php extension; otherwise, it is not handed off to the PHP engine for processing.
2. Because this code block must be preprocessed, the action of the script cannot be previewed on your desktop PC unless a local Web server is installed with the PHP engine. Alternatively, it can be uploaded to some remote host known to have both a Web server and the PHP engine. After processing, the Web server sends the file to the requesting client. If the source code is viewed in the browser, no PHP code is seen within it; it has been replaced with the output of the script.
3. Each line must end with a semicolon that serves as the instruction terminator.
4. The first line declares a variable called "myName."
5. The next lines contain echo commands. Echo is a common script command used to display some string. Here it simply places the string within the double quotes into the output. HTML code is treated

```
<!DOCTYPE HTML PUBLIC "-//W3C//DTD HTML 4.0
Transitional//EN">
<html>
<head>
        <title>my php test</title>
</head>
<body>
<?php
$myName = "Joe Miller";
echo  "<i>Hello world, I'm a PHP script</i>!";
echo  "<p>My name is $myName";
?>
</body>
</html>
```

Figure 11.13 PHP code in "hello.php."

the same as any other text in this string, and it can be "echoed" back into the file, providing markup instructions to the browser.

6. The next echo command contains another text line; it also references the variable declared earlier, displaying the string assigned to this variable in the output file.

PHP Arrays and Functions

The next PHP script file example introduces arrays and functions. Variables can store a single value with a name, but there are times when it is desirable to store multiple values with a single variable name. This is accomplished with an *array,* which is really just a two-column list that has been given a name. Each value assigned is called an *array element,* and each value is referenced by an index entry in the left column of the array. The index can use numbers starting with zero, creating an *enumerated array.* Alternatively, each index value can be given a name referred to as a key; this results in an *associative array.* For example, consider a set of values such as those shown in Figure 11.14.

Earlier, a function was described as a block of code that performs a specific task that may be predefined or created as needed. Functions are declared with a name followed by parentheses; the parentheses may be empty or hold arguments to pass to the function. Curly brackets are used to house the block of instructions associated with a function. The code shown in "**array-demo.php**" in Figure 11.15 demonstrates both the creation of an array and the use of functions.

The lines with the code **$genre[ ]** assign values to each key in the array; the use of numbers indicates this is an enumerated array, but string names could have been used instead of numbers resulting in an associative array. As with all variables, declaring them makes them available, but they do not have an action until they are referenced elsewhere in the code. This array is referenced in the count function, which results in the number 5 being displayed as the output. The values in parenthesis are parameters passed to each **foreach** statement; in this case, the instruction is for each successive value in the array to be associated with a new variable named "**$temp**" by looping through the array. The statement within the function, shown in curly brackets, displays each value along with the HTML code for a line break, forcing a new

Key	Value
0	Mystery
1	Horror
2	Film Noir
3	Comedy
4	Drama

Figure 11.14 A numeric key array of film genres.

Array-demo.php code	Output of array-demo.php
<!DOCTYPE HTML PUBLIC "-//W3C//DTD	**A PHP Array**
HTML 4.01 Transitional//EN">	5
<html>	Mystery
<head>	Horror
<title>test array</title>	Film Noir
</head>	Comedy
<body>	Drama
<h1>A PHP Array</h1>	
<?php	
$genre[0]= "Mystery";	
$genre[1]= "Horror";	
$genre[2]= "Film Noir";	
$genre[3]= "Comedy";	
$genre[4]= "Drama";	
echo count ($genre), " ";	
foreach ($genre as $temp)	
{	
echo "$temp ";	
}	
?>	
</body>	
</html>	

Figure 11.15 A PHP code block within an HTML file shown on the left, and the output of the script as it would be presented after preprocessing on the server shown on the right.

line for each element in the output page. One note about the variable **$temp:** Because it is declared within this function, its scope is limited to that part of the script, and it is not available for use outside this function. The distinction between local and global variables is discussed in the last example at the end of this section.

There are many useful predefined functions in PHP. For instance, the array in the previous example could also have been created using the array function with a single line of code as shown in Figure 11.16.

In addition to creating and manipulating arrays, other useful functions include those associated with environment variables. The **GETENV** function has a number of arguments including "**REMOTE_ADDR**" and "**HTTP_USER_AGENT**" that can report on the remote IP address and user agent type and version.

PHP and HTML Form Processing Example

This brief examination of PHP concludes with the creation of a PHP script that can accept data from an HTML form using the method POST; see Chap-

```
$genre = array ("Mystery", "Horror", "Film Noir", "Comedy", "Drama");
```

Figure 11.16 The array function used to create $genre. Compare this approach to that in Figure 11.15.

```
<!DOCTYPE HTML PUBLIC "-//W3C//DTD HTML 4.0
 Transitional//EN">
<html> <head> <title>Form that posts data to PHP</title>
</head>
<body>
<h2>A form that can calculate</h2>
<form method="post" action="calculation.php">
<p>Value one <input name="value1" type="text" size="10"></p>
<p>Value two <input name="value2" type="text" size="10"></p>
Calculation:<br>
<input name="calculate" type="radio" value="add">Add <br>
<input name="calculate" type="radio" value="sub">Subtract<br>
<input name="calculate" type="radio" value="multiply">Multiply<br>
<input name="calculate" type="radio" value="div">Divide <br><br>
<input type="submit" name="submit" value="do it!"><br><br>
<input type="reset" name="reset" value="clear">
</form>
</body>
</html>
```

Figure 11.17 Form code in HTML referencing a PHP script.

ter 5 to review HTTP methods and Chapter 9 for the HTML form code. Specifically, this PHP script can perform arithmetic calculations and report results. Remember, there are many ways such a PHP script could be created—there are similar examples in books and script library Websites, so this code is neither unique nor the only way to accomplish this task (Meloni, 2000). An additional note is that whether the example code works as written on a particular PHP-enabled server depends on how the PHP engine is configured. There is an issue with this version of the script related to the "register globals" discussion in the next section that may need to be addressed for successful execution.

First, you must have the HTML form that will reference the PHP script in the action attribute of the **<form>** tag. Therefore, two files are needed: the HTML file with the FORM code and the PHP script it references. The HTML code of such a form that will suffice for this example is in Figure 11.17.

The PHP script that accepts the posted data action that is referenced in the action attribute of the form is created next. The form code INPUT tags use NAME attributes that must match the variable names in the PHP script. The source of the data is either the user (for value1 and value2) or a set value attribute in the tag, as provided in the radio button input tags. Note that it is essential that the names used in the form input tags exactly match the variable names in the PHP script. The browser view of such a form is shown in Figure 11.18.

The PHP script code block is in the file calculation.php that is shown in Figure 11.19. Note that there should not be any HTML code preceding the start of this PHP code block. Also note how there are two different uses of the equal sign; a double equal sign is a comparison operation and a single equal sign is to assign a value. Figure 11.20 explains the function of different parts of this PHP script.

As noted earlier, this script may not work as written on all servers with PHP available. When scripts fail, the usual suspects are parsing errors caused by omitted semicolons or quotation marks. However, even if the code is reproduced exactly, a change in one of the default settings in the PHP engine setup could result in problems with how the variables are declared in this script—this issue is discussed next.

Global and Superglobal Variables

Until PHP version 4.2.0, the script as written above would usually work on any PHP-enabled server because up to that version, the setting for "register_globals" was turned on by default. However, with version 4.2 this default setting went to "off" (The PHP Group, 2008b). This harmless sounding change had a dramatic impact on a script working with form data like the one just described. The idea of the scope of a variable came up earlier in discussion of the **array-demo.php** script example; a variable defined within a function is local to that function and not available outside of it. However, there are global variables in PHP that have unlimited scope and can be referenced anywhere in a script. Further, PHP has **super_global** variables that store environment information in arrays. These are designated with a beginning **$_** such as **$_POST** for variables coming from a form using HTTP POST. Figure 11.21 lists the **superglobals** as documented at the PHP.net site.

With the **register_globals** turned on, PHP scripts could make use of request variables such as those in the calculation example without any prior variable initialization. However, doing so creates potential security issues for PHP scripts (The PHP Group, 2008c). To address this concern, newer PHP versions turn this setting to **off** by default. When that is the case, the previous script must be modified before it can work on these PHP-enabled servers, unless the administrator has overridden the new default.

There are many ways to address this issue in the script example. One solution would be to edit the PHP script and initialize each instance of a variable

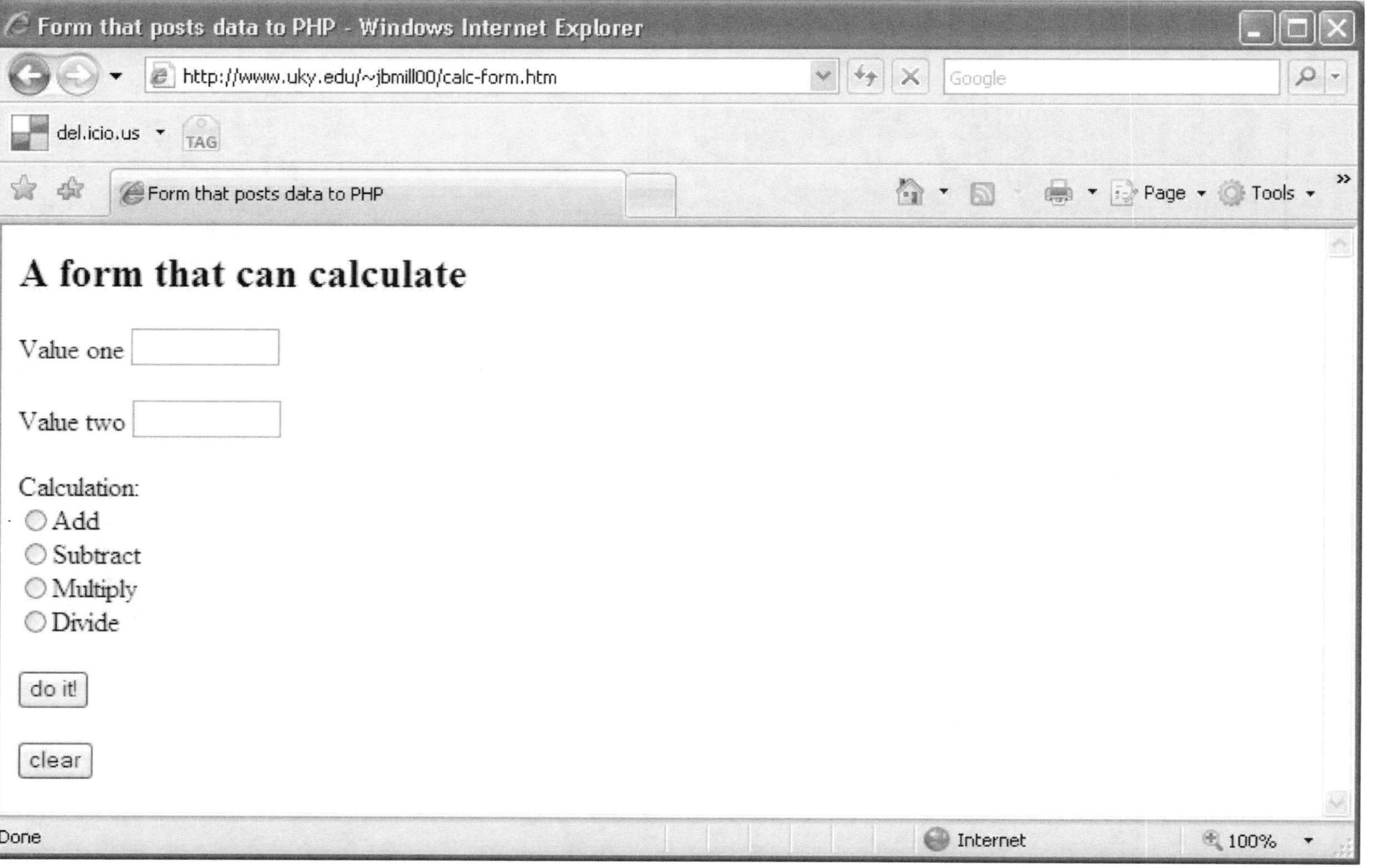

Figure 11.18 Browser view of the HTML form.

```
<?php
if (($value1 == " ") || ($value2 == " ") || ($calculate == " ")) {
header ("Location: http://www.uky.edu/~jbmill00/calc-form.htm");
exit;
}
if ($calculate == "add") {
   $answer = $value1 + $value2;
} else if ($calculate == "sub") {
         $answer = $value1 - $value2;
} else if ($calculate == "multiply") {
         $answer = $value1 * $value2;
} else if ($calculate == "div") {
         $answer = $value1 / $value2;
}
?>
<!DOCTYPE HTML PUBLIC "-//W3C//DTD HTML 4.0
Transitional//EN">
<html>
<head>
         <title>results</title>
</head>
<body>
 <h2>Calculation result</h2>
And the answer is: <?php echo "$answer"; ?>
</body>
</html>
```

Figure 11.19 Calculate.php script file contents.

representing data from the form with **$_POST['variable_name']**. For instance, **$value1** would then become **$_POST['value1']**. Doing this for every instance of such a variable can be tedious. Two other more efficient solutions are shown side-by-side in Figure 11.22. At the very beginning of the script, the three variables from the form POST action could be defined as shown on the left of Figure 11.22. Alternatively, another option would be to use the single extract function to import all variables with the superglobal **$_REQUEST** as shown on the right of Figure 11.22. The **$_REQUEST** superglobal consists of the combined array of **$_GET, $_POST,** and **$_COOKIE**.

These examples just scratch the surface of the many possibilities scripting provides the Web developer. Much of the success of Web 2.0 is due to the many popular widgets that scripts support, such as Ajax-enabled mapping functions.

<table>
<tr><td>Code</td><td>Explanation</td></tr>
<tr><td><?php</td><td>This starts the PHP code block; no HTML should precede this.</td></tr>
<tr><td>if (($value1 == “ ”) || ($value2 == “ ”) ||
($calculate == “ ”)) {
header (“Location:
http://www.uky.edu/~jbmill00/calc-form.htm”);
exit;
}</td><td>This is a conditional test to ensure that the user has provided two values and selected a radio button for the desired operation. If any of the posted values are null, the header function will reload the form page. The || symbols are for Boolean OR. If none of those conditions are true, this test is exited and the script continues.</td></tr>
<tr><td>if ($calculate == “add”) {
    $answer = $value1 + $value2;
} else if ($calculate == “sub”) {
    $answer = $value1 - $value2;
} else if ($calculate == “multiply”) {
    $answer = $value1 * $value2;
} else if ($calculate == “div”) {
    $answer = $value1 / $value2;
}</td><td>This series of if statements are to determine what operation was selected and what should happen for each selection. For instance, if the user chooses the button for Add, the value sent from the form will then match the first string in the series. Since that comparison will be true, the rest of the statement will execute resulting in an answer being stored as “$answer.”</td></tr>
<tr><td><body>
<h2>Calculation result</h2>
And the answer is: <?php echo “$answer”;
?>
</body></td><td>This is standard HTML with a second embedded PHP script; its sole job is to present the value now stored in $answer in the page.</td></tr>
</table>

Figure 11.20 The PHP file “calculation.php” and an explanation of the code.

PHP Superglobals	Definition
$_SERVER	Variables set by the Web server or otherwise directly related to the execution environment of the current script.
$_GET	Variables provided to the script via URL query string.
$_POST	Variables provided to the script via HTTP POST.
$_COOKIE	Variables provided to the script via HTTP cookies.
$_FILES	Variables provided to the script via HTTP post file uploads.
$_ENV	Variables provided to the script via the environment.
$_REQUEST	Variables provided to the script via the GET, POST, and COOKIE input mechanisms, and which therefore cannot be trusted.

Figure 11.21 Superglobal variables from PHP.net (2008b).

```
<?php
$value1 = $_REQUEST[‘value1’];
$value2 = $_REQUEST[‘value2’];
$calculate = $_REQUEST[‘calculate’];
...
```

```
<?php
extract($_REQUEST);
...
```

Figure 11.22 Two possible solutions to the register global issue for the calculate. php script.

SUMMARY

Web programming greatly extends the capability of HTML and, when combined with databases, provides the Web publisher with new options for content management. Such powerful techniques are an important addition to the technology toolbox of Web publishers. This is a broad, multifaceted topic that cannot be treated in depth in a single summary chapter, and far more expertise is needed to implement such solutions. Nevertheless, such an overview can at least highlight the wide range of programming solutions and develop an appreciation of the potential these technologies have to enhance and extend the Web experience. These Web programming techniques utilize both client-side and server-side technologies, and JavaScript and PHP represent important examples of each approach. The intent of this overview is to serve as a modest starting point for those interested in further exploration of the area of Web programming.

REFERENCES

Brenner, S. E., & Aoki, E. (1996). *Introduction to CGI/PERL.* New York: M&T Books.

Davis, M. E., & Phillips, J. A. (2006). *Learning PHP and MySQL* (1st ed.). Cambridge: O'Reilly.

FCKeditor. (2008). The text editor for the Internet. Retrieved October 1, 2007, from http://www.fckeditor.net.

Harms, D. (2001). *JSP, servlets, and MySQL.* New York: M&T Books.

Hoffer, J. A., Prescott, M. B., & McFadden, F. R. (2002). *Modern database management* (6th ed.). Upper Saddle River, NJ: Prentice Hall.

Meloni, J. C. (2000). *PHP fast & easy Web development.* Roseville, CA: Prima Publishing.

Microsoft.NET. (2008). Overview. Retrieved October 1, 2007, from http://www.microsoft.com/net/Overview.aspx.

The PHP Group. (2008a, June 6). History of PHP and related projects. Retrieved June 9, 2008, from http://us2.php.net/history.

The PHP Group. (2008b, June 8). Predefined variables. Retrieved October 1, 2007, from http://us3.php.net/variables.predefined.

The PHP Group. (2008c). Using register globals. Retrieved October 1, 2007, from http://us3.php.net/manual/en/security.registerglobals.php.

Powers, D. (2006). *PHP Solutions: Dynamic Web design made easy.* New York: Springer-Verlag.

Purvis, M., Sambells, J., & Turner, C. (2006). *Beginning Google maps applications with PHP and Ajax; From novice to professional.* Berkeley, CA: Apress.

Riccardi, G. (2003). *Database management with Web site development applications.* New York: Addison Wesley.

Rob, P., & Coronel, C. (1997). *Database systems: Design, implementation, and management* (3rd ed.). Cambridge, MA: Course Technology.

Ruby on Rails. (2008). Web development that doesn't hurt. Retrieved October 1, 2007, from http://www.rubyonrails.org.

Schneider, G. M., & Gersting, J. L. (2000). *An invitation to computer science.* Pacific Grove, CA: Brooks/Cole.

Shafer, D. (1996). *JavaScript & Netscape wizardry.* Scottsdale, AZ: Coriolis Group Books.

W3C. (2008). Document Object Model (DOM). Retrieved October 1, 2007, from http://www.w3.org/DOM.

ADDITIONAL READING

Afergan, M., Darnell, R., Farrar, B., Jacobs, R., Medinets, D., Mullen, R., et al. (1996). *Web programming desktop reference 6-in-1.* Indianapolis, IN: Que Corporation.

Burd, B. (2001). *JSP: JavaServer pages.* New York: M&T Books.

Deep, J., & Holfelder, P. (1996). *Developing CGI applications with Perl.* New York: John Wiley and Sons.

Heilmann, C. (2006). *Beginning JavaScript with DOM scripting and AJAX: From novice to professional.* New York: Apress.

Holman, B. K., & Lund, W. (1997). *Instant JavaScript.* Upper Saddle River, NJ: Prentice Hall.

Jamsa, K., Lalani, S., & Weakley, S. (1996). *Web programming.* Las Vegas, NV: Jamsa Press.

Strom, E. (1998). *PERL CGI programming: No experience required.* San Francisco: Sybex.

WEBSITES FOR SCRIPT PROGRAMMING

Coldfusion http://www.adobe.com/products/coldfusion.
JavaScript http://www.javascript.com.
Microsoft .NET http://msdn2.microsoft.com/en-us/netframework/default.aspx.
Microsoft ASP http://www.asp.net.
PHP home: http://www.php.net.
Python http://www.python.org.
Tutorials http://www.w3schools.com.

Chapter 12

XML Primer

Internet content comes in a multitude of formats representing the variety of digital documents found on the Web. These formats can be divided into those that use proprietary binary file types and those that use open text-based standards. Proprietary formats have many advantages and a long history that predates the Web. By combining the content with control codes for presentation and structure, binary formats are a highly efficient way to encode and present documents. However, this efficiency comes at a cost of exchangeability because users must typically have the software that created them. Other approaches that use simple text for content as well as codes to control presentational directives also have a long history in the digital world. Given their simplicity and portability, it is not surprising that Web founder Tim Berners-Lee used a text format to develop the HTML markup language, which has become the predominate form of Web content.

There are significant limitations to HTML markup, especially its inability to provide much information about what the content being marked up actually *means*. For instance, the markup tells you and a browser that the content is in a list but provides no information about what it is a list of—it could be a grocery list or a list of people in a department. Traditionally, data structuring that provides metadata in the form of field definitions is accomplished through the creation of a database resulting in a proprietary binary format. The Extensible Markup Language (XML) does for data structuring what HTML does for document presentation by providing an open text-based alternative to structure and exchange data. Since its introduction, a number of XML technologies have emerged to become part of today's Web, including RSS (Really Simple Syndication), SVG (Scalable Vector Graphics), SOAP (Simple Object Access Protocol), and WML (Wireless Markup Language).

XML overcomes the limited document structure of HTML, which is almost exclusively focused on presentation. Unlike HTML, which has a predefined set of elements, XML tags are extensible, that is, elements are not predefined and can be created as needed. XML allows the creation of self-describing documents with markup that conveys information about the content the tags contain.

XML is often equated with the Semantic Web but this is somewhat of an oversimplification. The Semantic Web initiative, as described by the W3C site, is "a common framework that allows data to be shared and reused across application, enterprise, and community boundaries" (W3C, 2001). Web founder Tim Berners-Lee has promoted the idea of the Semantic Web as the ultimate future Web, referred to by some as Web 3.0. Berners-Lee asserts an XML data-centered Web will enable direct data exchange among applications and enhance intellectual access to content through search engines designed to exploit its structure (Berners-Lee, 1999; Berners-Lee, Hendler, & Lassila, 2001). Although this vision would utilize XML, it also depends on other technologies and standards. Standards for the Semantic Web include the Resource Description Framework (RDF), which supports metadata exchange and interoperability, and OWL (Web Ontology Language), designed to facilitate content processing by applications. Both RDF and OWL are documented at W3C. This broader application of XML and interrelated Semantic Web topics are beyond the scope of this chapter.

This introduction to XML has three goals: (1) to introduce the nature of XML documents and the related ideas of well-formedness and validity; (2) to explore the codification of XML with DTDs or XML Schema Definitions (XSD); and (3) to consider how XML documents can be presented and transformed with styles. There are many excellent books on XML as well as many tutorials on the Web itself that provide in-depth coverage of these topics; an excellent short introduction to XML is by Yott (2005).

XML: THE EXTENSIBLE MARKUP LANGUAGE

XML, like HTML, was derived from the Standard Generalized Markup Language (SGML), which was developed to accommodate markup of digital data. SGML is not a specific markup language but a meta-language used as a standard for creating specific markup languages. The SGML standard evolved from IBM's General Markup Language and became an ISO standard in 1986. SGML is a very broad standard developed to accommodate multiple forms of digital publishing. SGML is not particularly suited to the more focused needs of Web developers. XML was first proposed at the SGML 96 Conference as a Web-centered, lightweight version of SGML. The goal was to create a dialect of SGML suited to Web processing that is similar to that of HTML, while retaining interoperability with those preexisting Web standards. In essence, XML is a "scaled down" subset of SGML optimized for the Web. Like SGML, XML is a meta-language, and it can be used to create many specific markup language implementations.

As with SGML, XML is a text-based standard, utilizing tags in ways that are similar to HTML. However, there are important differences. HTML tags are predefined within the HTML standard. In XML, potential tags are unlimited and self-defining; hence the markup is "extensible." XML is supported in two current versions; as of August 2006 version 1.0 is in its fourth edition, and version 1.1 in its second. Version 1.1 is not substantively different from the previous version except for its support of extensions to the Unicode 2.0 character sets (Bray et al., 2006).

XML VS. HTML

This examination of XML begins by identifying its commonalities and differences with HTML. On a superficial level, HTML and XML look quite similar: Both are text-based, and both define elements with tags that provide information to a parsing program. Each uses the less than (<) and greater than (>) symbols to identify tags; tags can have attributes defined that further refine them. However, there are some key differences: HTML uses a predefined set of tags and attributes, does not permit the creation of new tags as needed, and is designed to simply display or present data. In contrast, XML tags are unlimited and designed to structure data by describing what the content means; XML is therefore similar in function to that of a database. HTML creates some structure to the content, but only at the level of identifying the logical parts of the document, making HTML elements such as titles and headers distinguishable from other parts such as paragraph text. A search engine performing term weighting can use HTML information and text decoration, but the markup does not inform the program about the nature of the content itself.

Although XML documents are just text, they are not intended to be read that way by people. Programs parse the XML data and use styles or other transformation technologies that produce output for presentation. XML's strength is that it can accommodate data exchange between programs and transmit information across multiple platforms. Although there is considerable interest in its application to the future Web 3.0, XML is not intended to displace HTML. There is a huge volume of information in HTML format that will remain on the Web. In addition, HTML will likely remain a common output format for XML documents because Web browsers cannot directly process XML content. This is not surprising as browsers were designed specifically for HTML; they only show the tag coding of XML documents with hierarchical nesting unless additional presentational style information is provided. XML is more powerful and flexible than HTML, but it is also a less forgiving environment for the creator. Much current Web content created by nonexperts is not well-formed HTML; tag omissions and coding errors are commonplace. The forgiving nature of the HTML parser (the browser) tolerates many of these errors and usually presents the document in spite of coding errors. In contrast, XML documents must be well-formed; any code violations cause parsing errors that halt document processing.

XML KEY CONCEPTS

Even though XML is a subset of the broader SGML standard, it is still a large and complex standard. Some of the key summary points about this standard are:

- XML is a simplified subset of the SGML meta-language optimized for the Web.
- XML is for structuring data as opposed to determining how data will be displayed or presented. XML contains rules for using text formats to unambiguously define data structures in new markup languages.
- XML looks like HTML; it is hierarchical and uses tags to identify elements. Tags are identified with the less than and greater than symbols (< >), and they can have attributes in the form of name/value pairs. In HTML, the tag set is predefined; in XML, the tag set is extensible. XML tags are delimiters and what they mean depends on the program using it.
- XML is not intended to be a replacement for HTML.
- XML code can be viewed as text, but it is intended to be processed by some program.
- XML is "verbose by design"; that is, much of the file size will be associated with the markup text overhead that is responsible for the data structuring.
- XML is really a family of interrelated technologies, including XLINK (how links are made in XML), CSS (Cascading Style Sheets), XSDL (Extensible Stylesheet Language), and XSDLT (XLS Transformations).

Key Components of the XML Specification

The full XML specification is maintained by W3C and includes these key components:

- XML allows for the insertion of comments. Comments allow the insertion information that is for human consumption but ignored by the parser. Just as in HTML, comment declarations are identified by the less than sign, exclamation, and two dashes and end with a double dash and the greater than sign, as in: **<!--this is a comment-->**.
- XML allows for entity and character references. Text-based markup languages have parsing problems when certain reserved characters are needed to be simply treated as text. HTML has a long list of character entities; XML uses only a small subset of five of these for the following characters: ampersands, less than signs, greater than signs, apostrophes, and quotation marks. In addition to these special character entities, XML allows for the creation of a named entity to represent a string of characters that may occur frequently in certain documents such as a copyright statement or trademark. As in HTML, character and entity references begin with the ampersand character and end with a semicolon.
- XML allows for the insertion of processing instructions. These instructions are identified by the use of the less than sign followed by a question mark (<?) and contain information for the parsing

program. Processing instructions are not part of the XML content and are passed directly to the XML parser.

- PCData: This stands for "parsed character data" and is the information or content itself that is being structured by the markup. Anything that is not markup is parsed character data.
- XML permits empty elements. As in HTML, there is markup that does not apply to any content. There are a number of empty elements in HTML such as the image, line break, and horizontal rule tags (<img>, <br>, <hr>) all of which simply identify something that is supposed to display at that location; there is no content between the beginning and end tags of empty elements.
- XML includes the possibility of a DTD. This is the Document Type Definition, and XML languages were often designed to reference a DTD to model that specific markup language. The DTD contains all the tags, attributes, and rules for the markup language. A DTD is not required, so XML documents can be DTD-less, or alternatively, the strategy of creating an XML Schema Definition may serve the same role as a DTD.

XML and Data Structures

As noted earlier, database programs have traditionally been the primary tool for structuring data. Database programs result in files that are highly efficient containers for data structuring, but typically they utilize proprietary binary formats that require users to have the same program or software that facilitates data exchange. Data exchange among various programs is thus limited and depends on software and standards such as the Open Database Connectivity model. In contrast, XML has the advantage of being an open text-based standard not dependent on a specific program. While XML can structure data, it is not intended to displace database systems but to complement them. For instance, XML can serve as a data exchange format that retains much more meta-information than other common text-based exchange formats such as **CSV** (comma-separated value) files (Graves, 2002). The process of creating a database can be lengthy and includes systems analysis, modeling techniques, data dictionary creation, and prototype development. XML solutions often require a similar investment in the creation of a document model expressed in a DTD or XML Schema Definition; these document modeling languages are discussed later in this chapter.

XML key concepts can be summarized as follows: (1) XML is a meta-language that supports an unlimited number of document types. (2) XML documents are intended to be processed by programs that can make use of the data structures built into the markup. (3) XML vocabulary and rules may be codified in a DTD or XML Schema. (4) XML depends on a number of related technologies to enable data exchange and presentation of content for human consumption, as shown in Figure 12.1.

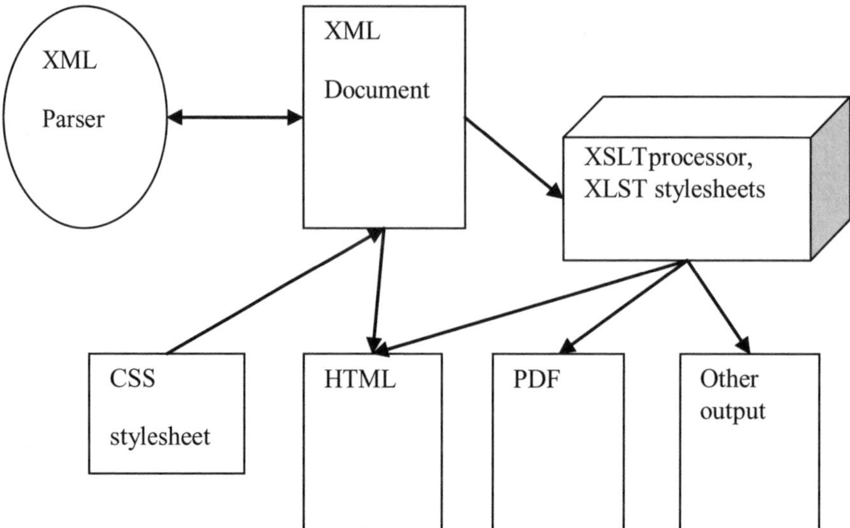

Figure 12.1 XML is designed to interact with many related technologies. The parser checks for well-formedness and validity; CSS can yield HTML views; XSLT transformations can process the XML into other forms.

Creating XML Documents

Any text editor can be used to create and edit XML documents. However, a word of caution about character sets used by simple text editors—when XML validation is attempted, if the encoding type used by the editor does not match the default or specified encoding directive to the validating program, errors occur. For instance, quotation marks may appear fine but come from a different character set and result in parsing errors. Most developers use XML-aware editors such as EditX and Microsoft XML Notepad. These programs have features such as tag auto-complete and attribute name support; some can also validate the XML.

An examination of examples of XML documents is informative before continuing with a more detailed analysis of XML. A sample XML document is referred to as an *instance document,* a single instance of some class of defined document type. While the term *document* often carries the connotation that the content is literally a narrative document such as a Web page or an article, this may or may not be the case in the context of XML. Here *document* is meant to refer to any XML container, whether or not it is literally a document in the sense a Web page is.

Two examples illustrate the structure of XML. In the first example, XML is used to create a catalog of bibliographic information for books, similar to the type of information that would be found in a library database; in the second, it is used to create a student directory. These hypothetical types of XML documents could look like those shown in Figure 12.2.

These XML documents begin with an *XML declaration,* which looks like a processing instruction because of the question mark in the tag but technically

XML-based book catalog	XML-based directory of student information:
<?xml version= "1.0" encoding= "UTF-8"?> <!DOCTYPE catalog SYSTEM "cat.dtd"> <catalog> <book binding= "soft" ISBN= "0-1111-2222-3"> <author alive= "no">P.G Wodehouse</author> <title>The Mating Season</title> <date>1949</date> <publisher>H. Jenkins</publisher> <city>London</city> </book> </catalog>	<?xml version= "1.0" encoding= "UTF-8" standalone= "yes"?> <directory> <student gender= "female"> <first_name>Mary</first_name> <middle_name>Jane</middle_name> <last_name>Smith</last_name> <address> <street>14 Oak Ave</street> <city>Middletown</city> <state>NJ</state> <zip>11125</zip> </address> <phone>777-968-1000</phone> <email>mjsmith@mail.com</email> </student> </directory>

Figure 12.2 Example of two possible XML documents.

is not (Harold & Means, 2002). This statement is not part of the XML document but provides the XML version information as well as other attributes, such as the text encoding being referenced and whether the document is standalone or not. In these examples, the XML version is 1.0, and both declarations specify the encoding to be UTF 8, which is 8-bit ASCII. The document on the right of Figure 12.2 also has the attribute and value **standalone = "yes"** to indicate that this is to be processed based on the generic rules of XML without a reference to a specific DTD or XML Schema Definition.

XML documents use tags to identify the elements and must begin with a *root or document element* tag. This is the top-level tag, which by definition has no parent. All XML documents must have a starting tag not nested within any other tag. XML documents have a hierarchical structure, and tags can be nested within tags. This tree-like structure is also referred to as a *node tree*, and each element is a *node*. Note that tag names are case-sensitive, and all tags must have end tags, including tags for empty elements.

The XML specification allows attributes to be defined; attributes describe a property of the element. The **<book>** tag in the first example has two attributes named "**binding**" and "**ISBN**." The set of defined element attributes are determined much as they are in the logical modeling phase of database design; they reflect the essential descriptive characteristics of an entity. How attributes are defined and how they are used varies in different XML languages. For instance, the designer has the choice of adding information as an attribute of an element or as a child element. In the example document on the right in Figure 12.2, "**gender**" could be defined as a separate child element of student, as with the child tag pair **<gender>female</gender>**, shown here with the PCData "female," or it could be defined as an attribute within the element **student.** The choice is dictated by the purpose of the information and how it will be used. Generally, data are stored as elements, and information about data (metadata) is stored as attributes.

Well-Formedness and Validity

XML requires that documents be *well-formed.* This means they must comply with the basic rules of XML as defined in the W3C standard. The key requirements are the presence of a root element; matching tag name pairs (the match must be exact in terms of upper and lowercase use); closing tags for all tags including empty elements; and proper tag nesting within tags. An instance document that complies with these rules is considered well-formed.

To be *valid,* the instance document must reference some DTD or XML Schema Definition and comply with it. DTD and XML Schema Definitions represent two ways to define a specific markup language and are compared in the next sections. For now, the main idea is that *validity* is a separate test beyond well-formedness. Validity requires verifying the document against a specific set of documented rules. XML permits the creation of documents without reference to a specific DTD or XML Schema Definition, so a document can be well-formed but not valid. Formalizing the rules of a particular XML language explicitly defines the language in a way that is useful to both parsing programs and to the people who use it. There are two main approaches to this process: the original DTD language derived from SGML and the newer XML Schema Definition Language. DTDs are considered first.

THE DOCUMENT TYPE DEFINITION (DTD)

The "**catalog**" XML instance document example in Figure 12.2 references an external DTD, but the "**directory**" XML instance document does not. Simple XML documents can be created without going to the trouble of documenting all the tags and rules formally in a DTD, and such an XML document is said to be "DTD-less." The decision to create DTD or not depends on the complexity of the markup language, the number of documents it will have to support, the number of people who might wish to create such documents, and the requirements of the programs developed to process them. There are advantages to precisely defining the tags, attributes, entities, and relationships of a markup language, and the DTD is one way to do this. However, writing a DTD is a complex task that involves learning a separate DTD language. Specifically, DTDs:

- Define and name all the entities and elements available in a document.
- Define the order elements will appear, their data type, and whether or not they are required.
- Determine the numeric constraints for the occurrences of elements by specifying whether they may occur not at all, once only, or multiple times.
- Define the nesting rules by showing child element lists for each element.

- Define all the attributes of each element, their data type, and any constraints on attribute values.

The use of a DTD for documenting XML tags, attributes, entities, and nesting rules was inherited from the SGML standard. DTD construction uses a specific syntax to make declarations, which adds to the learning curve for those using this approach to document a markup language. The familiar HTML was derived from SGML and uses a DTD; in fact, it has three DTDs: strict, transitional, and frameset. These are built-in to the browser, which serves as the HTML DTD processor.

A DTD can be internal, which means it is included within the instance document itself, or it can be external to the document, in which case its name and location must be specified. In addition, an XML document can have both internal declarations and an external DTD. The Document Type Declaration contains the information about the DTD that is in use and its location. Declarations always begin with a less than sign and exclamation point. If the DTD is external, the statement will be of the form:

```
<!DOCTYPE rootname SYSTEM "some.dtd">
```

In this declaration, **rootname** is a placeholder for the actual name for a root element in a particular XML language, and the location and name of the DTD file is provided in quotation marks preceded by the word SYSTEM in capital letters. If the DTD was internal, the DTD itself would follow a left bracket character within the DOCTYPE tag and end with a right bracket and greater than sign as will be discussed further in the next section. Such an internal DTD is immediately followed by the XML instance document as summarized in the code here:

```
<!DOCTYPE rootname [
DTD content follows here
• • •
]>
```

The XML document instance would then follow this internal DTD.

DTD Elements

To create an element, a declaration is made in the DTD that provides the element name as well as any child elements it can contain. In addition, special characters are used to indicate whether these nested elements occur zero or one time (?), zero to many times (*), or one to many times (+). The contents of the external DTD file "**cat.dtd**" shown in Figure 12.3 models the structure of the "**catalog**" document example from Figure 12.2.

Line 1 of this DTD defines an entity reference that allows the shortcut "NIP" to be used for the string "not in print" in these documents. Line 2 defines the root element **catalog** that contains the child element **book,** which must occur at least once, indicated by the plus sign after the element name. Line 3 declares that the element **book** has five child elements, listed in parentheses; the

```
1. <!ENTITY NIP "not in print">
2. <!ELEMENT catalog (book)+>
3. <!ELEMENT book (author*, title*, date*,
   publisher*, city*)
4. <!ATTLIST book
   a. binding CDATA #IMPLIED
   b. ISBN CDATA #REQUIRED>
5. <!ELEMENT author (#PCDATA)*>
6. <!ATTLIST author alive (yes | no) #IMPLIED>
7. <!ELEMENT title (#PCDATA)*>
8. <!ELEMENT date (#PCDATA)*>
9. <!ELEMENT publisher (#PCDATA)*>
10. <!ELEMENT city (#PCDATA*)>
```

Figure 12.3 A simple DTD for the book catalog; lines are numbered to match discussion in text.

asterisk character means all of these may occur zero to many times within the element book. Line 4 defines the attributes **binding** and **ISBN** for the book element; **implied** means an attribute does not have to be present, but **required** attributes must appear with the element. Line 5 defines the **author** element as PCData. Line 6 defines the attribute "alive"; this attribute is permitted to only have the value yes or no as indicated by the vertical pipe character, which is for Boolean OR.

The document declaration in the "**catalog**" XML document example shown on the left of Figure 12.2 indicates the DTD it references must be stored in the external file "**cat.dtd**." Alternatively, as noted earlier, the contents of this DTD file could accompany the instance document itself. If that were the case, the document and the internal DTD could appear as shown in Figure 12.4. Here, the DOCTYPE declaration line names the root element followed by a left bracket character instead of pointing to an external DTD file.

XML SCHEMA DEFINITION

The term *schema* has a broader context than just XML. With database systems, a schema is developed from the process of system analysis and the modeling of the database; the schema reflects the structure of a database and helps visualize or describe its organization. This is the general role of an XML Schema Definition. There are excellent Web-based resources and tutorials available on creating XML Schema Definitions (Vlist, 2001; W3Schools, 2008).

The DTD language was a holdover from XML's roots in SGML. The W3C developed the XML Schema Description Language (XSDL) in 2001 as an alternative to the DTD approach, and Version 1.1 was released in August 2007 (Sperberg-McQueen & Thompson, 2008). As with a DTD, an XML Schema Def-

```
<?xml version= "1.0" encoding= "UTF-8"?>
<!DOCTYPE catalog [
<!ENTITY NA "out of print">
<!ELEMENT catalog (book)+>
<!ELEMENT book (author*, title*, date*, publisher*,
city*)
<!ATTLIST book
        binding CDATA #IMPLIED
        ISBN CDATA #REQUIRED>
<!ELEMENT author (#PCDATA)*>
<!ATTLIST author alive (yes | no) #IMPLIED>
<!ELEMENT title (#PCDATA)*>
<!ELEMENT date (#PCDATA)*>
<!ELEMENT publisher (#PCDATA)*>
<!ELEMENT city (#PCDATA*)>
]>
<catalog>
<book binding= "soft" ISBN= "0-1111-2222-3">
<author alive= "no">P.G.  Wodehouse</author>
<title>The Mating Season</title>
<date>1949</date>
<publisher>H. Jenkins</publisher>
<city>London</city>
</book>
</catalog>
```

Figure 12.4 A DTD accompanying an instance document.

inition identifies the elements, child elements, nesting rules, cardinality, and attributes of a language but uses an XML language to create the document model as opposed to the DTD language. Some of the advantages and possible enhancements associated with the XML Schema approach are:

- Because the schema is XML-based, a separate DTD language does not need to be learned. An understanding of XML is all that is needed to create them, and XML editors can be used for this purpose.
- They support additional data types that were not available in DTDs.
- Standard XML parsers can check for well-formedness and validity; no separate DTD reader is needed for intermediary processing.
- Common attributes across multiple elements can be defined in an attribute group.
- Namespaces can be used to share XML vocabularies and resolve name conflicts.

One of the primary functions of an XML Schema Definition is to define names for elements and attributes, essentially creating a vocabulary. Before discussing the details of creating an XML Schema Definition (XSD), it is helpful to introduce how *namespaces* and *namespace prefixes* support XML vocabularies because the examples given here all use the "xs" prefix. A namespace identifies a specific XML vocabulary, which is referenced in the XSD by the use of an assigned tag prefix. Prefixes are text strings followed by a colon that precede the tag to form a qualified name. The default XSD tag's prefix is **xs** or **xsd** as in the example **<xs:element name = "something". . .>**. The use of the "xs" prefix ensures that the word "element" is taken to be part of the XSDL vocabulary and does not have some other meaning associated with it. For instance, a chemistry markup language could use the word to refer to an "element" in the sense of elements in the periodic table as opposed to elements in a XSD. Further, the namespace for the XSDL vocabulary is referenced as an attribute in the Schema root element with an XML namespace reference, which has the form shown below.

xmlns:xs = "http://www.w3.org/2001/XMLSchema

Namespaces will be discussed further later in this chapter.

XML Schema Definition Example

All XML Schema Definitions use the syntactical rules, but they can be expressed and organized in different ways. A simple schema can be developed by working backwards from the structure of an XML instance document. This is sometimes referred to as the "Russian Doll" method because elements and attributes are created in the XML Schema Definition based on the nesting of elements observed within the instance document (W3Schools, 2008). This approach is relatively simple; however, other organizational views of the XSD are possible, such as flat catalog view that groups elements together by whether they are simple or complex or a class-based approach that uses data types to organize the XSD. An instance document of the book catalog discussed earlier with DTDs is in Figure 12.5. It is the document sample from which an XSD will be made using the "Russian Doll" approach discussed later in this section.

The XML Schema Description Language is itself an XML language, so the Schema begins with the standard XML declaration, followed by the prefixed root element **schema** as shown in Figure 12.6.

This defines the root element as **schema**, and the tag prefix "**xs**" is assigned to indicate that all the elements in it are derived from the XSDL vocabulary. As noted earlier, the XSD accomplishes the same functions as a DTD; it must define the elements, their relationships, cardinality, and attributes. The XSDL syntax for defining elements and entities, as well as documenting their nesting rules, data types, attributes, and any numeric constraints on occurrences of elements, is different from the DTD element declaration format. Elements are defined in XSD in the form shown in Figure 12.7.

Elements are defined as either **complexType** or **simpleType**. Elements are ComplexType if they have child elements and/or attributes. SimpleType ele-

```
<?xml version= "1.0" encoding= "UTF-8"?>
<!DOCTYPE catalog SYSTEM "cat.dtd">
<catalog>
<book binding= "soft" ISBN= "0-1111-2222-3">
<author alive= "no">P.G. Wodehouse</author>
<title>The Mating Season</title>
<date>1949</date>
<publisher>H. Jenkins</publisher>
<city>London</city>
</book>
</catalog>
```

Figure 12.5 Book catalog XML instance document.

```
<?XML version= "1.0" encoding= "UTF-
8" ?>
<xs:schema>
...
</xs:schema>
```

Figure 12.6 The start of an XML Schema; root element is defined.

```
<xs:element name= "some_element">
        <xs:complexType>
                <xs:sequence>
        ...
                </xs:sequence>
        </xs:complexType>
</xs:element>
```

Figure 12.7 Building the XML Schema—defining elements.

ments are those that contain only data; they can have neither child elements nor attributes. In the generic XSD shown in Figure 12.7, the element's name is provided as the value of the "**name**" attribute. Because it is the complexType you can deduce it has either child elements and/or attributes defined. When child elements occur, they are nested within the **<xs:sequence>** tag pair. Each of the child elements themselves are either the complexType or simpleType. In addition, each element defined could have other attributes defined, for example those that constrain its minimum or maximum occurrences or its data type. Once the XSD has been created, it is typically stored in an external file that has the extension "**XSD.**" In this example, the XML Schema created has been named "**cat-schema1.xsd**." The contents of this file are in Figure 12.8; indentation is used to visually represent the nesting hierarchy of the elements.

```
<?xml version = "1.0" encoding= "UTF-8" ?>
<xs:schema xmlns:xs= "http://www.w3.org/2001/XMLSchema">
    <xs:element name= "catalog">
        <xs:complexType>
            <xs:sequence>
                <xs:element name= "book" maxOccurs= "unbounded">
                    <xs:complexType>
                        <xs:sequence>
                            <xs:element name= "author">
                                <xs:complexType>
                                    <xs:simpleContent>
                                        <xs:extension base = "xs:string">
                                        <xs:attribute name = "alive" type =
                                        "xs:string"/>
                                        </xs:extension>
                                    </xs:simpleContent>
                                </xs:complexType>
                            </xs:element>
                            <xs:element name= "title" type= "xs:string"/>
                            <xs:elemen   t name= "date" type= "xs:date"/>
                            <xs:element name= "publisher" type="xs:string"/>
                            <xs:element name= "city" type= "xs:string"/>
                        </xs:sequence>
                        <xs:attribute name= "binding" type= "string" />
                        <xs:attribute name= "ISBN" type= "string" />
                    </xs:complexType>
                </xs:element>
            </xs:sequence>
        </xs:complexType>
    </xs:element>
</xs:schema>
```

Figure 12.8 A "Russian Doll" style XML Schema (tested for validity at http://jiggles.w3.org/cgi-bin/new-xmlschema-check).

Note that one ComplexType element in Figure 12.8 is handled differently than the others. The <author> element in this XSD has an attribute but does not have child elements. When a complex element has only attributes and no subelements, it is still a complexType, but the attribute is defined as "**simple-content.**" This simple content information must be further refined by the **<xs: extension base = "some_datatype">** tag. The "**extension**" reference means the attribute that is declared is derived from, or *extends,* the data type given and indicates the type of information it carries, such as string text or an integer.

This XSD has been saved as "**cat-schema1.xsd**" in the same directory location as the instance document; that it is in the current directory location is deduced from the lack of any other path information to this file. The XSD is referenced in the document by including two pieces of information: first, that an XSD exists and should be used to validate this document, and second, its location. These directives are passed to the parser with the information shown in the following lines:

xmlns:xsi = "http://www.w3.org/2001/XMLSchema-instance"

xsi:noNamespaceSchemaLocation = "cat-schema1.xsd"

These attributes are added to the root element, as shown in Figure 12.9. The "nonamespace" reference informs the parser that this document does not use a specific namespace but does use a schema for validation.

XML Schema Organization

The XSD format created from following a document prototype creates a valid model but results in a view of the XSD that is hard for people to read and follow. Alternate XSD presentations can provide a more organized view that is easier for people to understand and modify if needed. For a complicated XSD, one of the two organizational methods mentioned earlier is often used—the flat catalog approach that groups elements by simple or complex types and the class-based approach that is organized by data types. To illustrate how these methods can improve the layout and appearance of the XSD, the "**cat-schema1.xsd**" file has been reorganized using the flat catalog approach. This view depends on separating elements by type. This organizational view depends on a clear understanding of what makes an element either "simpleType" or "complexType." As noted earlier, simple elements are those that contain only data; they cannot have child elements or attributes defined. ComplexType elements have child elements and/or attributes. Further, when

```
<?xml version = "1.0" encoding= "UTF-8" ?>
<!—two attributes have been added to the root element to indicate a schema is used and
where it is -->
<catalog xmlns:xsi= "http://www.w3.org/2001/XMLSchema-instance
xsi:noNamespaceSchemaLocation= "cat-schema1.xsd">
<book binding= "soft" ISBN= "0-1111-2222-3">
<author alive= "no">P.G Wodehouse</author>
<title>The Mating Season</title>
<date>1949</date>
<publisher>H. Jenkins</publisher>
<city>London</city>
</book>
</catalog>
```

Figure 12.9 XML namespace and Schema location reference added to the XML instance document.

a complex element has only attributes and no subelements, that attribute is defined as "simplecontent." This designation uses the **<extension base = "some_type">** tag to indicate the type of data it carries, such as text or an integer. The new view of the XSD has been saved as "**cat-schema2.xsd**" and is shown in Figure 12.10.

Note that this XSD accomplishes exactly the same functions as the first, but its structure is simplified by reducing the repeated nesting tag pairs that occur in the "Russian Doll" model, resulting in an XSD that is easier for people to read and logically follow. The simpleType elements are declared first, and those names are used to declare the complexTypes, which then use the **ref** attribute instead of **name**.

VOCABULARIES AND NAMESPACES

The element and attribute names used in an XML implementation become the vocabulary of that specific language. These vocabularies are not predefined and are up to the creator of the language. However, XML takes a modular approach and encourages the use of existing XML vocabularies where they can be applied in a new context. Making use of existing vocabularies is obviously an efficient strategy, but it introduces the problem of possible name collisions or conflicts when identical names represent different things. For instance, the element name "title" used as a tag could refer to the title of a book, but it could also have different meanings in other vocabularies, perhaps referring to a person's title in an organization, such as Dr., Director, Ms., or Professor. Similarly, an element that used the tag "table" could refer to a document object or a piece of furniture. If XML documents from different vocabularies are merged or if a single document depends on more than one vocabulary, the XML parser cannot resolve the different uses of the same tag without more information about its intended meaning. This is the function of namespace references.

Namespaces are referenced by binding an identifiable namespace to a particular vocabulary or to a specific prefix, and then adding that information to the document. The namespace identifier is in the form of a Uniform Resource Identifier (URI) or a Uniform Resource Name (URN). A URI looks like the familiar URL; the URN reflects a name for a URI that has some institutional persistence. Either will serve as a unique identifier for the namespace, but each has its own syntax when used. Namespace declarations using a URI followed by one using a URN are shown here:

xmlns = "http://somelocation/XML/namespace/example"

xmlns = "urn:namepace_identifier:namespace_string"

Either of these statements, when added as an attribute to the root element, establishes a default namespace for that document. A prefixed namespace reference can also use either a URI or a URN and would take the form:

xmlns:bk = "http://somelocation/XML/namespace/example"

xmlns:bk = "urn:namespce_identifer:bk"

```
<?xml version = "1.0" ?>
<xs:schema xmlns:xs=
"http://www.w3.org/2001/XMLSchema">
<! -- first simple elements are grouped together -->
<xs:element name= "title" type= "xs:string"/>
<xs:element name= "date" type= "xs:date"/>
<xs:element name= "publisher" type="xs:string"/>
<xs:element name= "city" type= "xs:string"/>
<! -- now define the attributes -->
<xs:attribute name="alive" type="xs:string" />
<xs:attribute name= "binding" type= "xs:string" />
<xs:attribute name= "ISBN" type= "xs:string" />
<! --  finally, complex elements are defined -->
<xs:element name= "author">
<xs:complexType>
<xs:simpleContent>
<xs:extension base = "xs:string">
<xs:attribute ref="alive" type="xs:string" />
</xs:extension>
</xs:simpleContent>
</xs:complexType>
</xs:element>
<xs:element name="book">
<xs:complexType>
<xs:sequence>
<xs:element ref= "title" />
<xs:element ref= "date" />
<xs:element ref= "publisher" />
<xs:element ref= "city" />
</xs:sequence>
<xs:attribute ref="binding" type="xs:string" />
<xs:attribute ref="ISBN" type="xs:string" />
</xs:complexType>
</xs:element>
<xs:element name="catalog">
<xs:complexType>
<xs:sequence>
<xs:element ref= "book" maxOccurs="unbounded" />
</xs:sequence>
</xs:complexType>
</xs:element>
</xs:schema>
```

Figure 12.10 A catalog style organization of the XML XSD described earlier (tested for validity at http://jiggles.w3.org/cgi-bin/new-xmlschema-check).

Both of these statements create a "bk" prefix that could then be used as an expanded name for any element in the document. For instance, the title tag would become <bk:title> to clarify that this instance of "title" is associated with the "bk" namespace. Certain letters are restricted and are not allowed in locally defined prefixes; the prefixes that start with letter "x" are used to identify prefixes reserved by the XML standard.

Although namespace identifiers may look like URL addresses, the XML parser does not retrieve or reference the external namespace file. They are just a unique identifier for a namespace, and their "location" does not need to be an active or real URL Web address.

XML enforces rules about what namespace is in effect and where the namespace is applied; this is referred to as the *scope* of the namespace. Namespaces are inherited in a descending fashion through the tag hierarchy. A namespace declaration at any level affects all the child elements below the location of the declaration unless another namespace declaration at a lower level overrides it. The sample XML document in Figure 12.11 has two defined namespaces.

In the Figure 12.11 example, a default namespace of "**http://somelocation/XML/namespace/example1**" is established, and it applies to all the child elements that are nested within it. However, a second namespace is referenced that creates the prefix "**bk**," and this associates the **title** tag with a different namespace. This prefix is available for use in any child element of the title element, but any element higher up in the hierarchy is out of the scope of this reference. Further, any child element of the title element that did not explicitly use the "**bk**" prefix is in the scope of the default namespace.

VIEWING AND PROCESSING XML

The universal client application for viewing Web content is, of course, the Web browser, and browsers were designed to handle HTML, not XML. Browsers vary in how they handle XML documents; generally, they simply display the full document instance and its accompanying markup in a nested hierarchical display. Other technologies must be combined with XML to enable browser display beyond the code view default.

```
<catalog xmlns= "http://somelocation/XML/namespace/example1">
<book binding= "soft" ISBN= "0-1111-2222-3">
<author alive= "no">P.G. Wodehouse</author>
<bk:title xmlns:bk= "http://somelocation/XML/namespace/example2">The Mating
Season</bk:title>
<date>1949</date>
<publisher>H. Jenkins</publisher>
<city>London</city>
</book>
</catalog>
```

Figure 12.11 XML namespace reference.

CSS and XML

As discussed in Chapter 10, HTML benefits significantly from the application of Cascading Style Sheets (CSS) to achieve separation of content from presentation directives. XML has no stylistic elements, and it is completely dependent on style languages or other forms of programming to handle data presentation. You can apply CSS to the XML environment, but CSS is not a complete solution, and other programming must be utilized to achieve the true potential of XML.

Simple CSS rules applied to XML use XML tags as selectors instead of the HTML tags used in previous examples of CSS rules. Again using the book catalog example, you can add a processing instruction that references a style sheet called "**bk.css**" that is located in the "**styles**" subdirectory, as shown in Figure 12.12.

A browser view of the XML before and after the application of CSS is shown in Figure 12.13 followed by the appearance with the CSS applied in Figure 12.14.

XML file with a reference to CSS	Contents of "cat.css"

<?xml version = "1.0" ?>
<?xml-stylesheet type= "text/css" href= "styles/cat.css" ?>
<catalog>
<book binding= "soft" ISBN= "0-1111-2222-3">
<author alive= "no">P.G Wodehouse</author>
<title>The Mating Season</title>
<date>1949</date>
<publisher>H. Jenkins</publisher>
<city>London</city>
</book>
</catalog>
	catalog {
	background-color: #eeeeee;
	width: 100%; }
	book {
	display: block;
	margin-bottom: 30pt;
	margin-left: 0; }
	author {
	color: #ff0000;
	font-size: 18pt; }
	title {
	color: #000000;
	font-size: 18pt; }
	date {
	display: block;
	color: #0000ff;
	font-size: 18pt; }
	publisher {
	color: #ff0000;
	font-size: 18pt; }
	city {
	color: #000000;
	font-size: 18pt; }

Figure 12.12 Left: An XML document that references CSS. Right: The contents of the "cat.css" file.

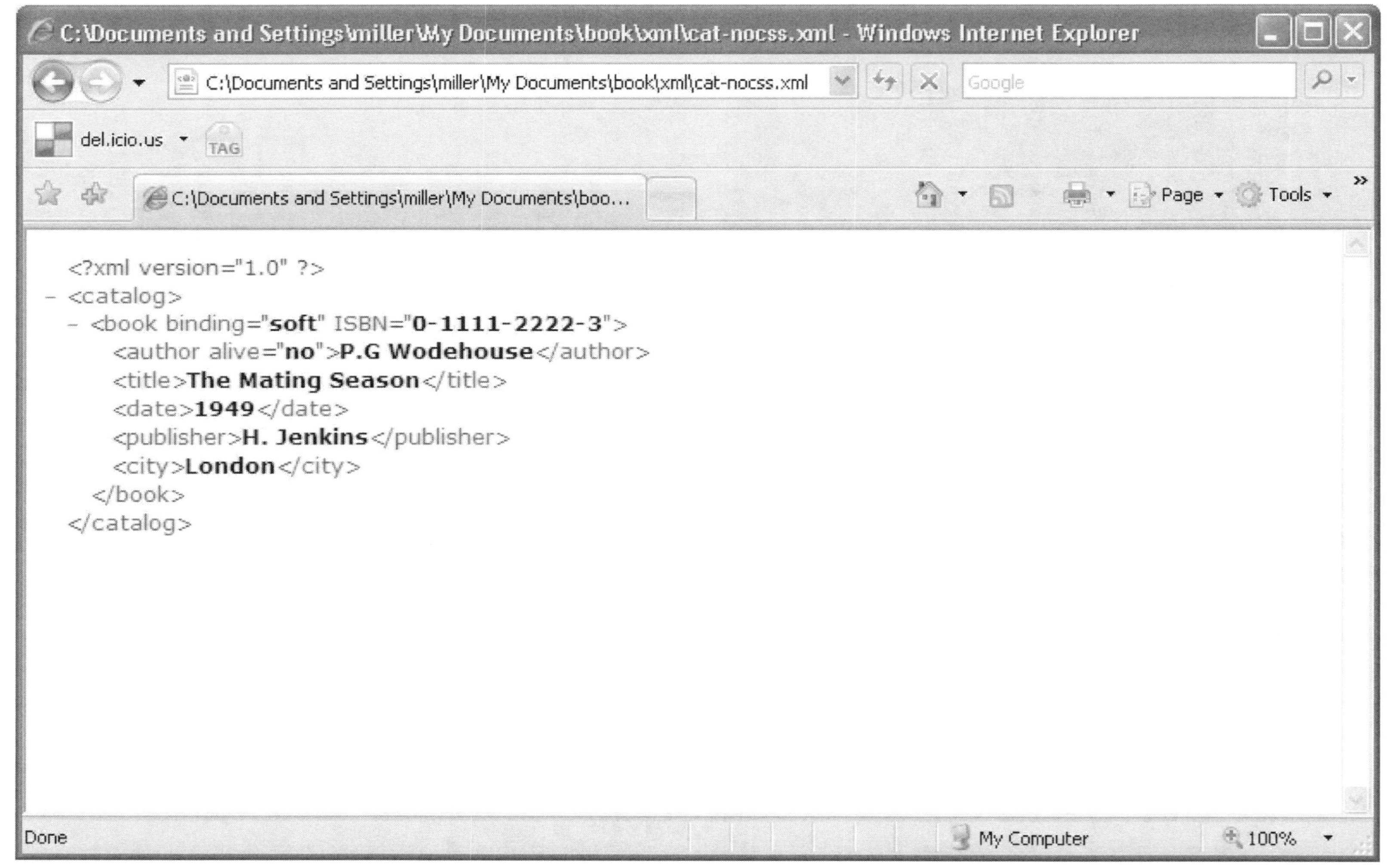

Figure 12.13 A browser view of an XML document without CSS applied.

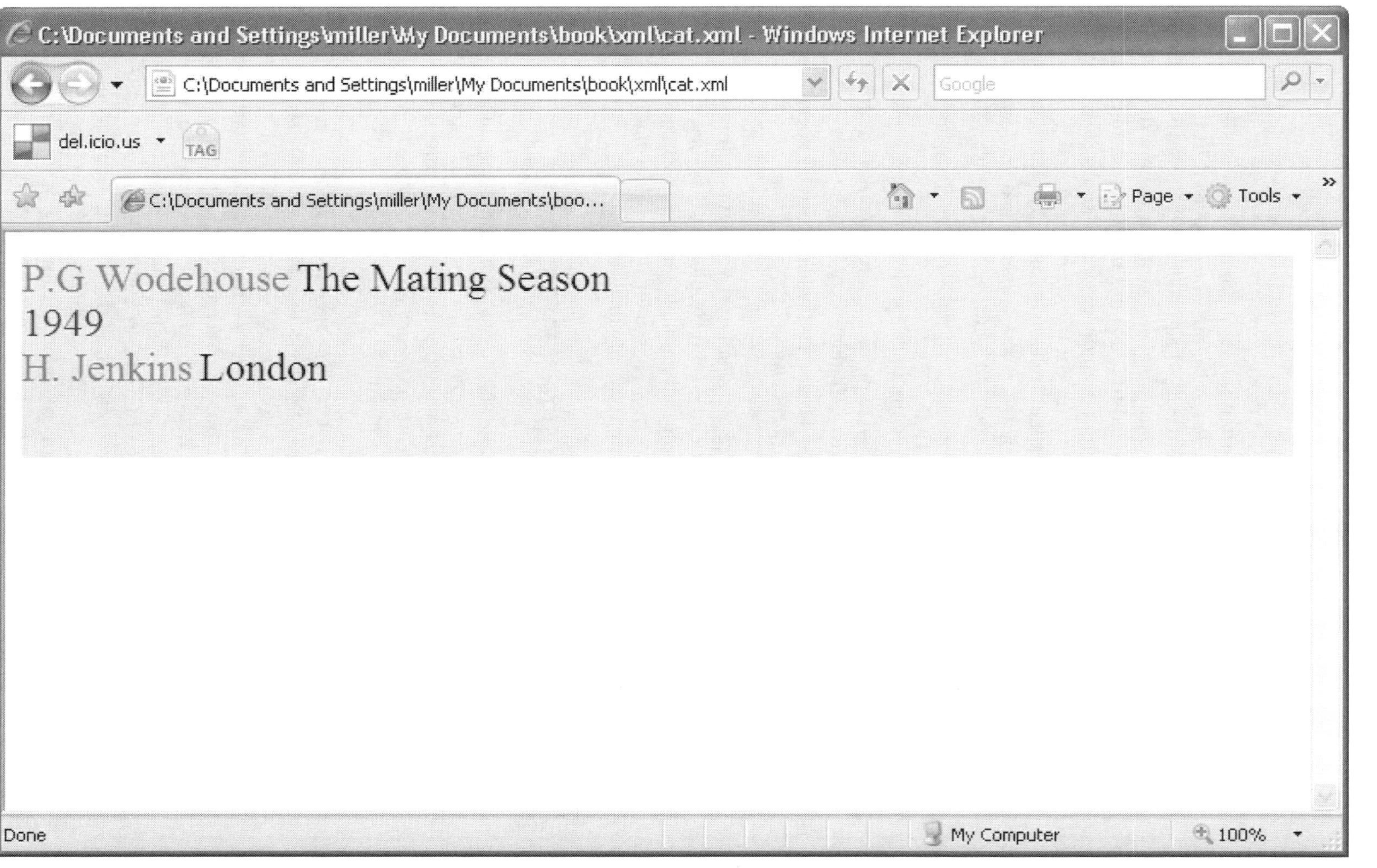

Figure 12.14 A browser view of an XML document with CSS applied.

XSL

CSS is relatively easy to learn, and most browsers can utilize it, but it is not a true programming language. It therefore has some limitations in the context of XML, specifically: (1) XML elements must be displayed in the order in which they occur and cannot be rearranged as needed. (2) CSS cannot handle computations or logical "if-then" conditional tests, and it cannot dynamically generate text blocks. (3) CSS is limited to utilizing simple parent-to-child relationships in its organization. XSL has been developed by the W3C as a family of related technologies to address document transformation and presentation in a more robust way. The Extensible Stylesheet Language (XSL) was introduced in October of 2001, and version 1.1 was released as a W3C recommendation in December 2006. According to W3C, XSL is a set of three interrelated technologies:

- XSL Transformations (XSLT), a language for transforming XML;
- XML Path Language (XPath), an expression language used by XSLT to access or refer to parts of an XML document; and
- XSL Formatting Objects (XSL-FO), an XML vocabulary for specifying formatting semantics. (W3C, 2008a, para. 1–2)

XSL is a programming language with support for built-in functions and features that make it more sophisticated than simple CSS. The two main components are XSL-Formatting Objects, which allow for text properties and formatting similar to CSS, and XSLT, which allows for the transformation of XML documents to other formats such as HTML or PDF.

XML-RELATED TECHNOLOGIES

In addition to XSL, there are other XML-related technologies that a more comprehensive treatment of XML could consider. These related topics are not discussed in detail beyond the brief descriptions listed here, but those interested in creating actual XML applications would want to explore them further. A partial list of related technologies includes:

- The Document Object Model (DOM) has been discussed in several area of this text. Generically, DOM refers to a hierarchically structured object-centered view of a document. This view of DOM is codified within the 1998 Level 1 DOM Specification at W3C, described as "a platform-and language-neutral interface that will allow programs and scripts to dynamically access and update the content, structure and style of documents" (W3C, 1998). New features have been added to this model with the release of Level 2 in 1999, which added CSS and query support. Level 3, released in 2004, allowed for programs and scripts to dynamically access and modify content. In the context of XML applications, DOM is a collection of routines, procedures, and tools that exploit the tree structure inherent in XML to build

XML-processing software (Harold & Means, 2002). Such a collection of routines and tools is referred to as an API or Application Program Interface.

- The Simple API for XML (SAX) is an event-based API originally designed as Java API, which is probably why so many books on XML also attempt to cover the Java programming language. Many XML parsers and validators are developed with the Java programming language.
- The Simple Object Access protocol (SOAP) is defined at W3C as "a simple and lightweight mechanism for exchanging structured and typed information between peers in a decentralized, distributed environment using XML" (W3C, 2000). SOAP creates messages and exchanges them between applications in a stateless fashion, usually via HTTP. Essentially, it is one of several Web service models that facilitate interoperable machine-to-machine program interactions. This protocol consists of three components: (1) the SOAP envelope that defines the message, (2) the encoding rules for defining data-types, and (3) the SOAP RPC representation. RPC stands for the Remote Procedure Call that controls one application or can execute another on a remote server.
- Scalable Vector Graphics (SVG) version 1.1 is a 2003 W3C language specification for describing two-dimensional graphics and graphical applications in XML (W3C, 2008b).
- Asynchronous JavaScript and XML (AJAX), as the name implies, uses JavaScript and the AJAX engine to send data asynchronously between client and server, facilitating interaction with a page and resulting in reloading specific components without having to retrieve the full page. AJAX has application to both dynamic HTML as well as XML applications.
- Resource Description Framework (RDF) is an XML-based metadata interoperability standard and is viewed as one of the key components of the Semantic Web. The RDF description framework is an XML application that associates a resource description and the resource through a URI. The RDF description is based on identifying the set of essential resource properties, each in the form of a property type and value pair. The RDF standard has a default namespace that can be extended to include one or more specific metadata namespace. For instance, the Dublin Core (DC) metadata scheme was developed by OCLC to facilitate simplified cataloging of Web resources. Dublin Core contains the type of metadata elements typically found in a library catalog such as author, title, description, and so forth. An RDF container could include a DC reference as an identified prefix as shown here: <rdf:RDF xmlns:rdf="http://www.w3.org/1999/02/22-rdf-syntax-ns#" xmlns:DC=http://purl.org/DC#">. The DC prefix would then qualify elements as being in the Dublin Core set for cataloging, such as <DC:author> or <DC:title> (W3C, 2004).

- XHTML is a reformulation of HTML to comply with the stricter requirements of XML. XHTML is given more attention at the end of this chapter.

XML IMPLEMENTATIONS

There are a large number of XML-based languages and standards in use, and as noted earlier, it is considered a key element in the development of the Semantic Web. XML is the foundation of the various RSS news feeds and blogs. RSS has different formats, and the acronym has several definitions, including Really Simple Syndication, Rich Site Summary, or RDF Site Summary, depending on the source. Other XML implementations include specialized languages like MathML for handling equations and the Encoded Archival Description language (EAD) used to create finding aids in library special collections. Library standards based on XML also include the Metadata Object Description Schema (MODS) and the Metadata Encoding and Transmission Standard (METS) at the Library of Congress. Another XML-related technology is XHTML, the XML-based reformulation of HTML described next.

XHTML

The XML standard has influenced the development of HTML. Because many predict the Web may make significant use of XML in the future, it makes sense to prepare current HTML documents to facilitate that transition. The XHTML standard is a reformulation of HTML to make it comply with the more rigorous rules of XML. Essentially this eliminates much of the "bad" HTML that has been acceptable on the Web and is permitted in most browsers. XHTML will ensure that new Web pages are both well-formed and valid. The main rules that XHTML enforces that HTML is lax about are:

- Documents must begin with a DOCTYPE declaration that references one of the three XHTML DTDs, strict, transitional, or frameset. The strict DTD disallows deprecated tags and attributes allowed by the looser transitional DTD. The frameset DTD is the same as the transitional with added frameset and iframe tag support.
- The root HTML element must be present.
- Tags and attributes must be written in lowercase.
- All tags, including empty elements, must have an end tag.
- All attribute values must appear within quotation marks.
- Nesting order is strictly enforced; any tag nested within another must also end within the parent tag.

In anticipation of more XML content and applications, all Web content produced with HTML should ideally be compliant with XHTML standards. For preexisting content created in the more forgiving world of simple HTML, there are programs that can "tidy up" the markup and attempt to auto-convert it to comply with the XHTML standard.

SUMMARY

XML is a meta-language that has many immediate applications and is likely to become increasingly important in the future Web. The core idea of XML is to facilitate the creation of languages to structure content in ways that are not possible in simple HTML and to facilitate data exchange among programs. The two main approaches to defining an XML implementation are through the creation of a DTD or an XSD. Both techniques formally define the elements, attributes, the nesting rules, and their numeric constraints. However, DTDs are an older technology carried over from the SGML standard, and XSD represents a newer and generally preferred approach to creating a formal document model. XSDs are written according to the rules of XSDL. An XSD can be created by "working backwards" from a sample document using the "Russian Doll" strategy, but there are other ways to organize and present an XSD, such as with a flat catalog view or with a class-based approach that uses data types as the organizational theme. Because XML is extensible, the vocabularies for different languages are not predefined. Words used to identify elements may overlap with other vocabularies where the term has a different intended meaning, so namespaces provide a mechanism to identify and separate these vocabularies.

The presentation and display of XML documents is problematic in Web browsers because these languages are not HTML. A browser can only show the XML code, but CSS can be used to provide formatting of the XML document when viewed in a browser. However, CSS has limitations, which are addressed in the more powerful programming language of the XSL specification.

There are many XML-related technologies and standards, such as XHTML, DOM, SAX, and AJAX. With this brief overview of the world of XML, it is apparent that a discussion of this environment quickly leads to many related topics for further exploration.

REFERENCES

Berners-Lee, T. (1999). *Weaving the Web: The original design and ultimate destiny of the World Wide Web by its inventor.* New York: HarperCollins.

Berners-Lee, T., Hendler, J., & Lassila, O. (2001). The Semantic Web. *Scientific American, 284*(5), 10.

Bray, T., Paoli, J., Sperberg-McQueen, C. M., Maler, E., Yergeau, F., & Cowan, J. (2006). Extensible markup language (XML) 1.1 (2nd ed.). Retrieved May 1, 2008, from http://www.w3.org/TR/xml11/#sec-xml11.

Graves, M. (2002). *Designing XML databases.* Upper Saddle River, NJ: Prentice Hall.

Harold, E. R., & Means, W. S. (2002). *XML in a nutshell* (3rd ed.). Beijing: O'Reilly.

Sperberg-McQueen, C. M., & Thompson, H. (2008, July). W3C XML Schema. Retrieved September 27, 2008, from http://www.w3.org/XML/Schema.

Vlist, E.v.d. (2001, October 17). Using W3C XML Schema. Retrieved October 10, 2007, from http://www.xml.com/pub/a/2000/11/29/schemas/part1.html.

W3C. (1998, October 1). Document Object Model (DOM) level 1 specification. Retrieved October 10, 2007, from http://www.w3.org/TR/REC-DOM-Level-1.

W3C. (2000, May 8). Simple Object Access Protocol (SOAP) 1.1. Retrieved October 10, 2007, from http://www.w3.org/TR/2000/NOTE-SOAP-20000508/.

W3C. (2001). Semantic Web activity. Retrieved October 1, 2007, from http://www.w3.org/2001/sw.

W3C. (2004, February 10). RDF primer. Retrieved October 10, 2007, from http://www.w3.org/TR/REC-rdf-syntax.

W3C. (2008a, April 27). The extensible stylesheet language family (XSL). Retrieved May 1, 2008, from http://www.w3.org/Style/XSL.

W3C. (2008b, May 26). Scalable vector graphics: XML graphics for the Web. Retrieved June 10, 2008, from http://www.w3.org/Graphics/SVG.

W3Schools. (2008). Introduction to XML schema. Retrieved October 1, 2007, from http://www.w3schools.com/schema/schema_intro.asp.

Yott, P. (2005). Introduction to XML. *Cataloging & Quarterly, 40*(3/4), 213–235.

ADDITIONAL READING

Fitzgerald, M. (2004). *XML hacks: 100 industrial-strength tips & tools.* Beijing: O'Reilly.

Ray, E. T. (2003). *Learning XML.* Sebastopol, CA: O'Reilly.

Rockwell, W. (2001). *XML, XSLT, Java, and JSP: A case study in developing a Web application.* Indianapolis: New Riders.

XML Guild. (2007). *Advanced XML applications.* Boston: Thomson.

WEB REFERENCES

EAD http://www.loc.gov/ead.

RDF http://www.w3.org/TR/REC-rdf-syntax.

SOAP http://www.w3.org/TR/2000/NOTE-SOAP-20000508.

XML http://www.w3.org/XML.

XML Schema http://www.w3.org/XML/Schema.

Part 3

Internet Content and Information Retrieval

Part 3 is devoted to the topic of Internet information resources and their retrieval using Web search services. The section begins with an examination of the sources and types of content available on the Internet and the various file formats in which it resides. Chapter 14 is an overview of textual information retrieval concepts and models, which provides the foundation for Chapter 15 on Internet search engines. That chapter includes a brief history of Internet searching; an examination of search engine functions and limitations; a description of the process they use to create a searchable index; relevance ranking issues; link analysis applications; and personalization and visualization techniques. This section concludes with a chapter examining the impact of the Internet on libraries and the information professions, as well as exploring new applications and opportunities presented by Web 2.0 technologies.

Chapter 13

Internet Content

Internet technologies are exciting, but *content* is what has driven much of the success of the Internet. There is a plethora of file types and formats making up the diverse forms of content accessible via the Internet. Many content forms are static files; other content sources are dynamic pages drawn from a database or other sources. Content residing in static forms is characteristic of Web 1.0; dynamic content production is more characteristic of Web 2.0 approaches. However, even with the rise of dynamic sources, a huge volume of Web content is still in the form of autonomous files placed on a Web server that can be requested by Web client software. These static formats are also important because they comprise much of the indexable Web that is accessible via a search engine. These static formats include a huge number of HTML files as well as a variety of other documentary and multimedia file types processed directly by Web browsers or by a helper/plug-in application. Collaborative content management approaches have become increasingly popular, and software for wikis, blogs, and podcasts makes it easy for groups of content specialists to create and modify Web pages without having to master all the underlying technical issues of HTML markup and server access. This discussion of static, indexable Web content begins with a technical description of file basics and then examines the major important file types for Internet-delivered documentary and multimedia content; Kientzle (1995) has a good overview of many Internet file format types.

Internet-based content has become a primary information resource for many, which has raised concerns about the quality of these sources. Many resources found as the result of Internet search are of questionable quality and authority, and librarians and educators have responded by seeking to promote information literacy skills. Information literacy is a necessary and critical skill set for information seekers in the twenty-first century. Information must not only be found, but it must also be evaluated and its appropriateness to an information need judged. This chapter on Internet content types therefore concludes with discussion of some accepted guidelines for evaluation of Internet content.

CONTENT CHALLENGES

Preparing content for presentation on the Internet presents both technical and epistemological challenges. The technical issues include preparation of content for migration to the Web, deciding whether the content should reside in static files or be generated dynamically, and identifying the best format for content delivery to a mass audience. In addition to format decisions, epistemological issues exist that require determining what the resource is about, how to represent it, and its ultimate usefulness to the user.

The focus of this discussion is primarily on static content formats, but a broader discussion of Internet content could explore a number of related issues that present legal, policy, and ethical dilemmas for libraries. The vast amount of "invisible Web" content, the challenges and controversies surrounding Internet content considered inappropriate (e.g., pornography and hate speech), and the possibility of deliberate misinformation make finding and using Internet information problematic. In addition, governmental restrictions imposed by new security concerns that limit or prevent access to previously available government information raise freedom of information issues. A few of these issues are explored in this chapter in the section on content evaluation. However, the main focus of this chapter is on technical aspects of content formats, not these related ethical and policy issues.

FILE BASICS

Most Internet content resides within static file containers that reside on Web servers and are available for delivery on request through client–server HTTP interactions. A file is a container of digital information stored and retrieved under some name. Most, but not all, computer systems view the digital information that makes up a file as a stream of bytes each containing 8 bits. Files have two key properties: they are *portable* and *persistent;* that is, they can easily be copied or moved from one location to another, and they do not disappear when the computer is turned off.

Although most file types are viewed as a stream of bytes, how a program interprets those bytes can vary. By convention, computer files are either *text files* or *binary files.* In ASCII text files, each byte value is associated with a character in an established code. ASCII is a 7-bit code where the eighth bit is used for error checking; extended ASCII uses all 8 bits in the code set. An 8-bit code permits a character set of 256 symbols; for non-Western character sets, different versions of the Unicode standard have 16 or 32 bits for character addressing, representing much larger sets of possible symbols.

Binary files (8-bit files) contain byte values that are not intended to be associated with ASCII characters; these bytes perform other functions that provide instructions or control codes to a program. Programs that create binary file types require the same program for successful viewing. For instance, Word documents, Excel spreadsheets, or Access databases are all proprietary Microsoft formats that require those programs for subsequent access to the content. A simple test for text files is to attempt to view the contents of any such file in a text editor such as Notepad; a text file is readable as text, but a binary file produces random odd-looking characters. The large numbers of proprietary formats represent the various requirements developers must consider when creating a new program. These include file size constraints, the speed of writing and reading the file to disk, and the possible need for random access to different parts of the file. Most Windows PC files are identified to programs and users alike by a naming convention that assigns a standard three- or four-character extension to the filename. An operating system then associates extensions with the appropriate application.

Proprietary formats are well-adapted to the particular needs of a program and result in highly efficient, compact containers that preserve the content along with data structuring and presentation information. The downside of proprietary formats is that they present barriers to those who do not have the same program that created them, or at least some converter or reader program. For instance, the world of word processing now dominated by Microsoft Word was once much less homogenous; people in a work group might have used WordStar, WordPerfect, Word, or some other preferred program. This made data exchange problematic and often resulted in the need to exchange documents in the lowest common denominator format of simple ASCII text. Files that needed to be edited and shared by many types of computers often were saved in text formats such as TXT (text) or RTF (Rich Text Format).

The Internet is designed to facilitate information sharing using text protocols, making the ASCII standard a natural choice for Web documents. All the Internet protocols, including the Web, move information as streams of 8-bit characters interpreted according to the ASCII standard, and encoding schemes are required to facilitate transfer of proprietary binary formats. The majority of Web content is in the HTML format; these files are a subset of the universe of ASCII text files. However, the choice of a simple text file format for Web pages presents its own set of tradeoffs. On the positive side, text files are very portable and do not require expensive proprietary software; in addition, all operating environments have some form of text editing capability such as the vi or emacs editor on UNIX systems, the Edit program with DOS, and Notepad in Windows. The downside of text formats is that presentation information and logical structure available in other formats can be lost. HTML addresses this issue by using tags that are themselves simple text but inform the displaying program how to present the data or define document structural elements such as titles or headings.

STANDARDS AND FORMATS

In an open environment like the Internet, the priority given to portability led to a handful of formats becoming the standards for documents and accompanying graphics. How do such standards come about? Standards might really just reflect accepted practice, which does not necessarily imply a best practice has been adopted. Ideally, standards are the result of expert opinion and are codified through adoption by some standards organization, but they may also be de facto standards that emerge from common use. For instance, the GIF format commonly found on the Web was initially a proprietary format, the CompuServe graphics interchange format. This format made use of a patented compression technology owned by Unisys, which resulted in licensing issues that were eventually resolved. The GIF format was adopted early on in Web publishing, and the capability to display GIF was incorporated into all graphical browsers. Another format, the Portable Network Graphic (PNG), came about through the efforts of a committee seeking to create a better open standard for Web graphics that would be free of the initial licensing constraints associated with GIF; Chapter 8 has more discussion on these graphics formats. HTML is an open standard, but another common Web format, PDF (Portable Document Format), was developed and owned by Adobe. As of July 2008 it became an ISO (International Organization for Standardization) open standard. PDF requires the free Adobe reader software for display, and PDF files can be created with Adobe Acrobat software or with other options such as PDF Creator from SourceForge.net (http://sourceforge.net/projects/pdfcreator/).

PRESENTING CONTENT ON THE WEB

When planning to present content on the Web, a number of questions must be addressed about the best way to represent the content digitally and the most appropriate final output format for the end user. The first issue depends in part on whether the content currently exists in a digital version; perhaps it is in a simple text file or in some proprietary file format. If there are digital versions, the next step is to determine if the program that created the file format is still available; in the case of older formats, the lack of an appropriate displaying program could render the file useless. If there are no digital versions and the content is available in hard copy only, there are other issues to consider, including the quality of the original as well as whether a digital image of the original is sufficient or if an editable text version is required. If editable text is needed, one option is to use OCR (optical character recognition) software to create a digital copy, but this option depends on the quality of the copy to be scanned. If a document image is sought, decisions must be made regarding the appropriate scan resolution needed to give an adequate rendering of the document. The most popular solution to emerge is scanning to the PDF format, which retains both image appearance and searchable text capabilities.

Once some of the input issues are resolved, the next step is to consider the output format. If the digitized document is presented as an image, the format choices are limited to those permitted in a Web browser (GIF, JPG, and PNG). However, presenting textual content in an image format requires high resolution scanning to make the text readable, resulting in very large file sizes. Image views of text are more commonly used for older, handwritten documents where the goal is to reproduce the look of the original. Proprietary document formats such as MS Word may be an option for some content if the target audience can be expected to have that program. However, because proprietary formats are problematic for many users, a more appropriate output format would be HTML, viewable in any browser, or a scan to PDF, which only requires the installation of the free Acrobat Reader software. Each choice has its own set of costs and tradeoffs. The final choice of a format is up to the content producer who must consider the needs of the target audience, the nature of the resource, and whether the resource is intended for display on a screen or destined for some other output device such as a printer. For instance, many forms that were once filled in manually are now made into HTML forms or PDF files that allow the form to be completed online and then printed out or saved. Format choices are also influenced by expectations of how the document is to be used; for instance, the Web is often used as a means to provide access to documents that are meant for printed output as opposed to screen viewing.

COMMON DOCUMENT FORMATS

The HTML format is by far the most common file type on the Web. Nevertheless, there are many other specialized formats encountered on the Web. The Adobe PDF has become common and is a de facto document standard. PDF is similar to the document description language used in Adobe PostScript but better suited for online display and browsing. PostScript is a "page description language" with instructions to a PostScript device on how to format the content. PostScript documents are intended for output on a PostScript printer that has the program to interpret these instructions. Many word processors and desktop publishing programs can convert internal fonts to PostScript instructions, which results in a consistent layout in the finished product that is device independent. The PostScript format is great for document description but not very good for document interchange. When this format is encountered on the Internet the intent is to make a document available for download and subsequent printing on a PostScript printer. The common extensions for these files are **PS, EPS, PFA,** and **PFB**. When viewed in a text editor, the first line of these files is a comment line that identifies the specific file type.

The portable document format (PDF) has a hierarchical structure and a document directory that allows random access to different parts of the document. PDF files use the **PDF** extension and are technically a type of text-based format but are transferred as binary files. As with postscript files, the first line in the file contains the PDF version in a comment line if it is opened in a text editor. While the reader program is a free download, PDF files require the Acrobat software or other software such as PDF Creator to create or modify PDF files or convert Word documents to PDF. Now that PDF is an open standard published by ISO, there are fewer ownership concerns. There are a number of other document formats, some of which are listed in Table 13.1.

COLLABORATIVE CONTENT

Web 2.0 technologies, discussed again in Chapter 16, have enabled a large number of powerful collaborative content management and social networking

TABLE 13.1 Common Document Formats Found on the Web

Extension	Format	Description
HTML	Hypertext Markup Language	Text files marked up in HTML to become static Web pages
SHTML	HTML page with some dynamic content; usually implies some server-side include (SSI)	A SSI is usually some value for a defined variable, such as an environment variable (like date/ time).
ASP	Active Server Page	ASPs are Web pages that contain programming in Visual Basic or JavaScript. When a server gets a request for an ASP, it executes the embedded code. Used as an alternative for CGI scripts, which allow interactivity with databases, etc.
PDF	Adobe Portable Document Format	Similar to postscript but designed for portability and exchange
TXT	Text	Simple ASCII text file
RTF	Rich Text Format	Text format with some formatting retained
CFM	Cold fusion	Adobe (formerly Macromedia) format for Web programming applications
DWF	Design Web Format	Autocad drawings

tools. Blogging, news feeds and aggregators, podcasting, and collaborative content management with wikis have been added to the earlier Internet tools of email discussion lists and Usenet groups. Although content generated by some of these communication tools, such as instant messaging and chat, tends to be somewhat ephemeral, others enable collaborative content production that results in new sources of searchable information accessible by both the participants and the public.

Email Discussion Lists and Usenet

Email discussion lists were early collaborative content tools of the Internet and are still extensively used. Programs such as Listserv or Majordomo can create group lists, manage subscriptions, and archive list content. Discussion lists exist around many topics and specialties in the library profession, and they serve as an important repository of human expertise and problem solving on a wide range of topics. Usenet groups are another form of a virtual community that grew out of the availability of Internet email. Instead of having messages "pushed" to each member as in discussion lists, users post messages to a common area where others can read them or reply. These groups are similar to the old "computer bulletin boards" that were common in the pre-Web computer era. Usenet groups represent every imaginable interest, and extensive lists of these groups can be found on the Web. For instance, Google Groups lists thousands of groups on a huge range of topics with many interested participants. Much of this content is archived and searchable if desired; some can be subscribed to with RSS feeds much as with a blog.

Blogs, News Feeds, and Podcasts

A huge source of new content is the proliferation of blogs, news feeds, and podcasts now common on the Internet. The foundation technology for these tools is the RSS (Really Simple Syndication) protocol, an XML-based standard. As interest in Web 2.0 has grown, these technologies have all become hot topics. Blogs are a Web published narrative of an individual or group, a shared "Weblog," that is updated regularly. The blogger frames the discussion by initiating the threads and determines if, and how, reader comments can be added. Some blogs are very personal narratives, and others may focus on a particular subject area. Blogs have some of the feel of both Usenet and discussion lists, but there are several important distinctions. They are much more interactive, and they have reached a much wider audience. It is likely that many people who never participated in Usenet groups or email discussion groups have now discovered the blogosphere; a 2008 Pew Internet and American Life Project survey estimates that one in 10 U.S. adult Internet users *have* a blog, to say nothing of how many more may just read them (Lenhart & Fox, 2006). In addition, most traditional news sites offer blog subscriptions to their readers. Blogs have received much media attention, and the buzz generated on a blog can result in the story being picked up by more mainstream news outlets. The Drudge Report, founded by blogger Matt Drudge, is a news aggregator that began as a simple email list but has become a news source competing with major media companies, breaking stories such as the Monica Lewinski scandal. His feeds are now available to mobile devices (Wellman, 2007). What began as just a personal, but public, journal for individuals is now a successful information outlet that competes with traditional media.

The software to create and manage blogs can be installed locally or accessed on a Web hosting service, such as Bloglines (http://www.bloglines.com/) or Blogger.com (http://www.blogger.com/start). Local reader software or reader Websites are also available for people following syndicated blog content. Blogs have found many applications in libraries to share and push content both internally and to the broader community. Some library blog topics include reference "frequently asked questions," general announcements, new books, book clubs, and specialized areas such as business or health sources. Blogs are even used as a collaborative content management approach to create home pages (Carr, 2008).

Podcasts represent another important content stream. Podcasts are digital audio programs delivered using RSS and can be downloaded to MP3 players; they can be described as audio blogs. Not only is it easy to find and hear podcasts, but with a few simple tools, anyone can become a producer of a digital radio show. Podcasts are also showing up in many library venues, such as a replacement for cassette tape audio tours or stories for kids. In many ways, podcasts and the blogosphere have become the new form of "talk radio" where anyone can reach a mass audience on any topic.

Wikis

The wiki (from the Hawaiian for "quick") is software that allows anyone to add or edit Web content without having to know HTML. Wikis have become an important source of Internet-based reference, such as that found at wikipedia.com, but some controversy surrounds wiki use as a reference tool because of the lack of quality control mechanisms. There are documented instances of malicious or biased editing in Wikipedia, but there is also evidence that its accuracy compares favorably with traditional encyclopedias (Giles, 2005). Aside from reference, Wikis present new opportunities to build and share content in many forums, and their use is growing. Some of these applications in libraries are discussed further in Chapter 16.

MULTIMEDIA ON THE WEB

One of the powerful and engaging aspects of the Web is the capability to embed multimedia elements into Websites. Not only does this provide for entertainment, but it is also a powerful educational tool because different learning styles can benefit from alternate views of textual content. The ease with which multimedia can be presented on the Web depends in part on whether the content was "born digital"; analog formats must be converted to digital, which can involve a significant effort. There are a number of technologies and formats used for Web multimedia.

Sound and Video Files

Conversion of analog sound to digital signals requires sampling the wave amplitude with an Analog to Digital Converter (ADC); and playback of digital audio requires a complementary Digital to Analog Converter (DAC) to recreate the sound waves people hear. As discussed in Chapters 1 and 8, sampling rates determine the quality of the conversion. Sampling technologies are based on the Nyquist-Shannon Sampling Theorem or its modern variants ("A New Wave," 2002). For instance, conversion of analog music to CDROM typically uses a sampling rate of 44.1 kHz, which is sufficient to represent the analog version accurately (Watkinson, 2000).

The capability for this type of conversion is available on most PCs in a separate sound card or with an integrated sound card on the motherboard. Audio destined for Web delivery could come from a variety of media sources, such as CDROM, audio tape, vinyl record albums, or MP3 files. Audio in MP3 is already Web ready, and CDROM sources are easily ripped to MP3 format. Audio tape and vinyl records take more effort, but there are devices for each type of media that can be connected to a PC via a USB port.

Much video is now born digital, and video capture cards are available for converting older analog video formats such as VHS tape to digital. Once again, the amount of sampling determines how accurately the digital version represents the full frequency ranges of the original analog form, which in turn determines final file size. The availability of newer digital recording devices has made it easier to work with both audio and video content directly on the PC.

Digital formats for multimedia are designed with a variety of compression strategies to keep file sizes as small as possible. For instance, when recording an audio lecture, much of the recording is actually saving "silence" (the pauses between words), and clever algorithms can compress the amount of digital information needed to represent those background periods of silence. The information captured for video can be thought of as a form of "3D"; video is a series of two-dimensional pictures where the third dimension is time. Because much of the image captured over this timeline is background that does not change from frame to frame, programs need only focus on the information that updates what is different in the new frame from the previous one. When enough of the frame is different from the previous one, a new "base frame" is used for this updating process. Production values for Web-delivered video are an important consideration, and a video professional can advise about the studio environment, appropriate lighting, and stage directions because excess movement of the participant can affect the quality of final product. In addition, bandwidth issues associated with different display preferences should also be considered.

Even with high-compression formats, digitized video can require huge amounts of data to be stored. Fortunately, disk storage has become cheap, and many terabytes of storage for video can be quite affordable. Bandwidth is critical for the user viewing experience, and a high data transfer rate must be sustained to avoid "jerkiness" in the playback. The older VHS video standard displays 30 frames per second, which gives the illusion of smooth, continuous motion. The amount of digital data that must be captured depends on both the frame rate chosen and the size of the video image on the screen. Early PC video formats typically used lower frame rates and did not utilize the full screen; the early Apple QuickTime format used 15 frames per second and often displayed video in a small window. The AVI (audio visual interleave) format was developed in 1992 by Microsoft for Video for Windows. Another format is AMV video (also called MTV), a proprietary format based on AVI. The large file sizes associated with many video formats create a bandwidth problem for some users, especially those with slower dial-up connections; any video streaming is problematic without broadband connectivity.

Fortunately, there are technologies and formats that make multimedia much more Web friendly. The MPEG (Motion Picture Experts Group) standard is a lossy compression method that has evolved into multiple formats used for high-quality audio and video such as MPEG-2 for DVD movies. MPEG-3 (usually now abbreviated as MP3) was combined with MPEG-2 and compresses CD-quality sound by a factor of 12 while maintaining high fidelity; it is the format responsible for the success of MP3 players. MPEG-4 (MP4) is the latest iteration of this format designed specifically for digital video and video streams.

For both audio and video, streaming technologies allow a bandwidth dependent data stream to take place between client and server. Prior to this approach, a media file had to be downloaded in its entirety before playback could begin, which resulted in long download times before the user could even see if the media was of interest. Some video-streaming technologies include VDOLive, Stream Works, and **RA, RV,** and **RAM** files from RealMedia. The **RA** format is audio, and **RV** is video with or without audio. **RAM** files stand for "Real Audio Metadata" and are text files where the browser receives the RAM file, launches Real Player, and then requests the various content sources listed as separate URLs in the RAM file from a Real Server. There are other technologies being developed that utilize clever streaming strategies; for instance, the SMIL (Synchronized Multimedia Integration Language) standard is an XML-based markup language being developed by W3C that enables Web producers to divide content into separate files and streams but display them together.

Macromedia Flash

A relative newcomer that is having a significant impact on Web multimedia is Adobe Flash, formerly Macromedia Flash or Shockwave Flash. Flash files are very bandwidth-friendly vector graphic animations that require the free Flash player from Adobe. Programs such as TechSmith's Camtasia software produce screen capture movies or audio-enhanced PowerPoint presentations that can be output as Flash for Web publication. The resulting Flash movies are quite compact in size; for instance, PowerPoint presentations with audio output as Flash can result in a package that is about one-half the size of the comparable AVI or PPT file. Some common multimedia formats are listed in Table 13.2.

COMPRESSION AND ENCODING FORMATS

Most multimedia files automatically use some level of compression as part of the format. However, compression in and of itself is also useful to minimize

TABLE 13.2 Some Common Multimedia Formats

Extension	**Format**
AU	Unix audio file
WAV	Windows audio—wave file
AVI	Audio/Video Interleave—Windows
MOV	AppleQuickTime
RA	RealAudio
RM	RealMedia
RAM	Real Audio Metadata
RPM	Playback in a Web page
SWF	Macromedia Flash

file sizes or combine multiple files into a single package for downloads or data packaging for sharing via the Internet. There are a number of formats specifically designed to accomplish such compression. As with proprietary formats, there is a tradeoff involved; namely both the sender and the recipient of the files need specialized software in order to compress and then subsequently uncompress them. A well-known compression file format for the PC is the **ZIP** format, which can create highly compact archive files. ZIP files require separate software, but the Windows platform is now able to create and use ZIP archives. There are also self-extracting **EXE** files that automatically uncompress when run. There are formats specific to other platforms as well, including UNIX TAR (tape archive) files and the Stuffit format for Apple. However, these compressed file formats can also serve as a means to package and hide a virus, worm, or Trojan horse program with some other program or data sent by email attachment. This is another reason it is imperative to have antivirus software that can examine compressed files for embedded malicious programs.

Related topics to this discussion are the encoding schemes used to facilitate the movement of binary data using the text-only protocols of the Internet. Encoding schemes create a text representation of binary data and then convert it back to binary on the receiving end. Examples include UUEncode and UUDecode (uue files), BinHex (an Apple format that converts binary file into a hexadecimal format), and MIME (Multipurpose Internet Mail Extensions), a scheme that automates the process of encoding and decoding of binary data used by most email client software.

INTERNET RESOURCE EVALUATION

Promoting information literacy has become a much-discussed role in librarianship. The American Library Association (ALA) defines information literacy as the set of skills and abilities to "recognize when information is needed and have the ability to locate, evaluate, and use effectively the needed information" (ALA's Presidential Committee on Information Literacy, 2006). Evaluation of information is a key component of information literacy. Information professionals must assist their clientele in assessing the appropriateness and validity of the information they find by applying critical thinking skills to the Web environment. The development and broad acceptance of the Internet as a primary information source by both the public and within libraries has made the issue of evaluation a necessary one. Access and use of the Internet has grown significantly over the last decade; nationally, nearly all colleges and K–12 schools have access to the Internet (Wells, Lewis, & Greene, 2006). In 1997, 79 percent of public libraries had access; by the end of the 1990s that grew to 95.6 percent; currently, virtually all public libraries offer free Internet access (ALA Research Series Report, 2007).

The issue of evaluation is confounded by the lack of any overarching control of Internet content, the malleability of digital content, and the ease and speed of Web publishing. In traditional publishing, a number of gatekeepers are involved in selecting and vetting content. Publishers have a stake in protecting their reputation, and they employ multiple strategies to ensure quality, including peer reviews of work prior to its acceptance and reviews by editors who examine content for both factual errors and overall quality. In addition, the cost of production and marketplace dynamics combine to limit the world of printed output. A print-dominated world still had self-published fringe literature, but the cost and effort of self-publishing and the accompanying distribution challenges limited its dissemination. In the online world, anyone and everyone can easily become a content producer with potentially a worldwide audience with a blog or a Website. The potential for misinformation, intentional or not, is great. Blogs and other forums have created new avenues for news but lack the established checks expected of traditional venues, and the "buzz" generated by a controversial blog report often becomes the story in and of itself, regardless of its merit. The democratization of content production is then a two-edged sword; the Internet has been a great leveler of media, creating great opportunities for those who could not get access to a broader audience, but with the cost of added effort on the part of the information consumer to ascertain its validity.

There is a large amount of marginally useful or incorrect material on the Internet. The early Web enabled "vanity publishing" relating to vacations, pets, or other personal pages, but there were the barriers of technical skills and server space. Web 2.0 and the social networking phenomenon has removed many of these barriers and vastly increased the use of the Internet for personal narratives. There are significant issues posed by inappropriate and problematic materials such as pornography and hate literature. Some of these materials might be illegal; others may be offensive to many users but qualify as constitutionally protected speech. This has generated ongoing debates regarding government legislation and library policies designed to address this problem, often with the stated intent of protecting children.

A Pew Report survey revealed that most college-age students see the Internet as their primary information resource and see little or no reason to engage libraries or information professionals in their information seeking (Jones & Madden, 2002). A concern of many in the library profession is not simply the competition the Internet presents, but the likelihood that people may be depending on, at best, poor quality unauthenticated resources or, at worst, dangerously inaccurate ones. In addition, there is the added "halo" effect that some Internet information seems to carry: the belief by some that if they find it on the Web, it is accurate and true.

Resource evaluation includes both an assessment of the content as well as consideration of the page design and presentation. Both can be evaluated, but clearly content assessment should be the higher priority. A number of framing questions facilitate the process of content assessment, such as:

- What is the apparent purpose of the site?
- What is the authority of the resource? For instance, is the author well-known or clearly identified? Is the information verifiable in other sources? How objective is the perspective? Is there an obvious agenda or bias?
- What about the publisher of the content—is it clear who sponsors the page? What is the domain location of site (gov, edu, com, etc)?
- How complete is the information? Does it represent original content or just point to other sites?

- How current is the site? When was it created or last modified?
- What is the apparent audience level?
- Is there evidence of scholarship, such as citations that can be checked?
- Has the page been reviewed or recognized as important by others?

Information professionals have developed a number of educational strategies aimed at different audience levels to formalize critical thinking skills as applied to Internet resources. School media specialists have been particularly active in this area, striving to instill critical thinking early on with their students. Rubrics have been developed to help students structure the evaluation process. One example is "The five W's": Who wrote it? What does it say? When was it created or modified? Where does the information come from? Why is it useful? (Schrock, 1998). Another example is known by the acronym CARS: Credibility, Accuracy, Reasonableness, Support (Harris, 2007). Both of these simple rubrics can help students begin to develop a life-long habit of critically evaluating Web content.

Although secondary to content, design also factors into evaluation. The best content is not very useful if presented in an unreadable style or without good navigation. Some of the key aspects to consider regarding design issues are:

- Graphics: Are they appropriate to the design or do they get in the way? Are the images sized appropriately? Do they load in a reasonable amount of time?
- Readability: Is the font size and style appropriate? Is there adequate contrast with the background color?
- Is there good navigation? Is it easy to get to the home base of site? Is it easy to navigate from each page to other major parts of the site?
- Is there a logical division and organization of the content?
- Is there good use of hypertext?
- Has access for the disabled been considered, such as the use of alternate text for images?

Evaluation of Web and Internet resources is a central component of the information literacy skills needed by information seekers in the twenty-first century.

SUMMARY

The Internet has greatly enhanced both the amount of information available and the ease of access to it. Internet information sources can be divided into two primary types: content that is dynamically generated and that which is found in autonomous file containers that reside on some Web server. The main focus of this chapter is the various forms of static Internet content found in a number of common documentary and multimedia formats. In addition to these static content forms, various interactive formats such as blogs and wikis that have added new information sources are also considered.

The choice of a content format can become a barrier to information use, so Web publishers must balance the advantages and limitations each format presents. The goal of Web publishing is to provide useful information with well-designed content free of format and accessibility barriers to some community. Information consumers must sort through many sources of content and critically evaluate each. Information literacy skills are essential to this process and information professionals are engaged in all these activities both as producers of original content and by assisting their clients in the evaluation of the information sources.

REFERENCES

American Library Association's (ALA) Presidential Committee on Information Literacy. (2006, July 24). Final report. Retrieved May 18, 2008, from http://www.ala.org/ala/acrl/acrlpubs/whitepapers/presidential.cfm.

American Library Association (ALA) Research Series. (2007). Connect communities: Public library funding and technology access study 2006–2007 report. Chicago: American Library Association. Retrieved May 1, 2008 from http://www.ala.org/ala/ors/plftas/finalreport.pdf.

Carr, N. (2008). *The big switch.* New York: W. W. Norton & Company.

Giles, J. (2005). Internet encyclopedias go head to head. *Nature, 438,* 900–901.

Harris, R. (2007, June 15). Evaluating Internet research sources. Retrieved October 1, 2007, from http://www.virtualsalt.com/evalu8it.htm.

Jones, S., & Madden, M. (2002, September 15). The Internet goes to college. *Internet and American Life Project.* Retrieved October, 2007, from http://www.pewinternet.org/pdfs/Pip_College_Report.pdf.

Kientzle, T. (1995). *Internet file formats.* Scottsdale, AZ: Coriolis Group.

Lenhart, A., & Fox, S. (2006, July 19). Bloggers: A portrait of the Internet's new storytellers. *Internet and American Life.* Retrieved October 1, 2007, from http://www.pewinternet.org/pdfs/PIP%20Bloggers%20Report%20July%2019%202006.pdf.

A new wave. (2002). *The Economist, 362*(8256), 68.

Schrock, K. (1998). 5 W's for evaluating Web sites. Retrieved October 1, 2007, from http://kathyschrock.net/abceval/5ws.htm.

Watkinson, J. (2000). *The art of digital audio* (3rd ed.). Oxford: Focal Press.

Wellman, S. (2007, December 5). Drudge Report goes mobile. Retrieved May 19, 2008, from http://www.informationweek.com/blog/main/archives/2007/12/drudge_report_g.html.

Wells, J., Lewis, L., & Greene, B. (2006). *Internet access in U.S. public schools and classrooms: 1994–2005.* Washington, D.C.: U.S. Department of Education.

WEBSITES OF INTEREST

ALA recommended sites at http://www.ala.org/parentspage/greatsites/criteria.html.

Evaluation tools at http://discoveryschool.com/schrockguide/eval.html.

Chapter 14

Information Retrieval

The goal of this chapter is to condense the essential concepts and classical models of information retrieval (IR) into a summary overview necessary for the discussion of Internet search engines in Chapter 15. Battelle (2005) describes Internet search as the most transformative technology since the development of the PC in the 1980s, and the IR models and strategies unique to its development are the focus of Chapter 15. However, Internet search technologies are an application of the general principles of information retrieval, so familiarity with IR principles, performance measures, and classic IR models is a prerequisite to that discussion. IR is a complex and diverse topic, and the coverage of it here is admittedly superficial and presumes some familiarity with these topics. Those who have not yet had such exposure to IR or who wish to explore it in more depth should consult one of the many excellent texts referenced throughout this chapter.

INFORMATION RETRIEVAL

Information retrieval is a broad topic covered in many different texts (Baeza-Yates & Ribeiro-Neto, 1999; Chu, 2003; Korfhage, 1997). A good starting point for this overview is to begin with a few definitions of IR provided in these and other sources. Bawden (2007) interprets IR as a process, describing it as "the purposeful searching for information in a system, of whatever kind, in which information—whether in the form of documents, or their surrogates, or factual material ('information itself'), are stored and represented" (p. 126). Baeza-Yates and Ribeiro-Neto (1999) describe IR as the "part of computer science which studies the retrieval of information (not data) from a collection of written documents" that "aim at satisfying a *user information need* usually expressed in natural language" (p. 444). Korfhage (1997) provides a definition of IR particularly suited to the focus of this discussion, describing IR as "the location and presentation to a user of information relevant to an information need as expressed by a query" (p. 324). Essentially, IR systems function as an intermediary between information resources and a user's information need, as shown in Figure 14.1.

Definitions of IR therefore depend on a number of associated concepts, specifically the nature of *information*, how it is represented and stored, and how it is sought and selected from the potentially large amount of other, nonrelevant information in the system. Defining "information" is the first challenge faced in any exploration of IR. This common sense concept is surprisingly difficult to define, mainly because it has many different possible meanings in different contexts. How is information the same or different from the related concepts of data, knowledge, or even wisdom? It is intuitively understood that words, images, music, and pictures all represent forms of information, but so do aromas, the color of a threatening sky, and facial expressions. A broad summary definition from Case (2007) is that "*information* can be any *difference* you perceive, in your environment or within yourself. It is any aspect that you notice in the pattern of reality" (p. 5, emphasis by the author). A more limited view of information emphasized in this discussion leading to Internet searching considers information to be usually in the form of recorded textual information that can be processed and represented in a system for subsequent retrieval.

Calven Mooers introduced the term *information retrieval* in his 1948 Master's thesis at M.I.T (Morville, 2005). Since that time, IR systems have utilized various strategies to represent, store, and facilitate retrieval of information by accepting and processing queries that represent some information need. The information is typically in the form of documentary resources as represented by sets of symbols that can be manipulated by both people and computer programs and that have meaning to the user. Textual information uses symbols such as letters and digits that are on a page or in digital systems, magnetic charges on a disk, or some other electronic representation. One of the first IR technologies used punch cards with notches for index terms; these cards were physically manipulated to segregate matching cards from the rest of the set. Cards representing nonrelevant retrievals that fell out with the relevant ones were called *false drops*, a term still used to describe nonrelevant retrievals returned in a search.

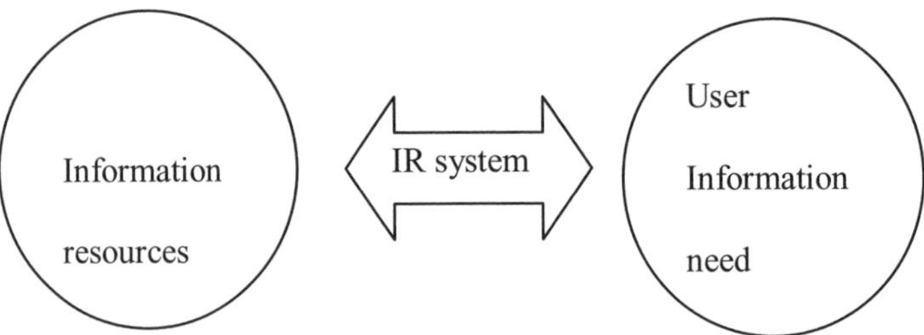

Figure 14.1 IR systems serve as an intermediary between information resources and someone with an information need.

Database management systems often use a command-based query language to extract records that match some query parameters. Relational databases are one type of database system and are briefly discussed in Chapter 11 in conjunction with dynamic database-driven Websites. Relational databases use a command language known as SQL (Structured Query Language), often in the form of a "select" statement. While the backend processing of search engines may utilize SQL, the user interface typically allows open-ended keyword searching that does not require the user to utilize its formal command-based syntax. Websites or search engines that deliver information from databases typically utilize scripts to transparently handle that part of the query process. Database management systems and their specific query languages are an important area in the field of IR but are outside the scope of this book.

TEXTUAL IR SYSTEMS

Textual information retrieval systems are the initial focus of this overview, and there are excellent sources that treat this area of IR in more depth (Meadow, Boyce, & Kraft, 2000). Beginning in 1990, the Text Retrieval Conference (TREC) has advanced many new technologies by providing a test bed for research and development activities in the field of textual IR. Internet search engines have adopted many of the developments and technologies that have resulted from TREC initiatives. The TREC has the following stated goals:

- to encourage research in information retrieval based on large test collections;
- to increase communication among industry, academia, and government by creating an open forum for the exchange of research ideas;
- to speed the transfer of technology from research labs into commercial products by demonstrating substantial improvements in retrieval methodologies on real-world problems; and
- to increase the availability of appropriate evaluation techniques for use by industry and academia, including development of new evaluation techniques more applicable to current systems. (The Text REtrieval Conference, 2008, para. 2)

In addition to supporting textual retrieval, TREC activities have diversified to include nontextual IR research, such as the track on retrieval from digital video launched in 2001 (Smeaton, 2007). Multimedia IR is briefly discussed later in this chapter.

In general, text-based retrieval begins with the presumption of some set of documents and user information needs that can be satisfied with the successful retrieval of one or more specific documents within the document corpus. The first challenge is to process and represent the documents in the IR system. Document representation can be accomplished through the creation of a surrogate, which can be a summary or abstract, a metadata record, or indexes of individual words or phrases either assigned to, or derived from, the document.

As the name implies, metadata is generally information that describes or defines some other information object, often according to a specific set of rules. Such a structured description of an information object can then serve as a surrogate for that object in an IR system. One example of such a metadata-based document surrogate is the bibliographic record that is created and stored in library catalog databases. These records represent information objects (e.g., books) and provide access points to them that are used for their retrieval. The card catalog of days gone by is a classic example of a searchable collection of document surrogates. The bibliographic record on each card represented the item of interest. The duplication of cards by access point allowed searching by author, title, and subject, and each card for an item pointed to a physical location with a call number. Such highly organized and labor-intensive catalogs worked well with the relatively small and well-defined collections maintained by librarians dedicated to the task. Modern computer-based catalogs allow for the creation of indexes using all these access points as well as on any keyword occurring in the surrogate record. These index terms point to the surrogate record, which in turn points to the physical or digital item in a collection. Full-text digital resources in libraries are searchable through keyword indexes but are also often organized according to some scheme or utilize metadata to enhance intellectual access to them. As highlighted in the next chapter, there is little organizational structure or formal metadata available to facilitate access to most Internet resources; one of the benefits of the future Semantic Web based on XML envisioned as Web 3.0 would be the opportunity for metadata-enabled Web searching. Most Internet search engines use indexes for document representation in the form of an inverted file, as described in the following section.

INDEXES AND INVERTED FILES

Indexes consist of an ordered list of terms that provides a link to the document, or documents, it represents. Index terms can be manually assigned by an indexer or generated automatically by extracting terms either from the documents or from their surrogates. These two approaches will be compared later. The importance and usefulness of an index, such as the one found at the end of a book, is well understood as a means of locating information. An index provides a list of terms, often arranged alphabetically, associated with record identifiers and facilitates quick lookups by common access points. Indexes are highly effective IR tools that eliminate the need for a sequential string search through a large set of records. For instance, in the library database example, separate indexes exist for author names, title words, subject heading terms, and a combined keyword index derived from all record fields. The index of a book is a collection of keywords showing the page numbers where the term occurs. The book example also reveals some of the limitations of an index; its usefulness depends on the term of interest being included in the list and also how well the keyword represents an associated concept. Computer technology and digital resources facilitate the automatic parsing of a document's full text into one or more indexes. An index term can point either to the set of documents that contain it, a record level index, or the specific documents with mapping of each term occurrence, which is a word-level index.

The net result of this process is an *inverted index*, sometimes referred to as an *inverted file index* or simply an *inverted file*. The inverted index is defined as a data structure that provides a list of words to serve as access points into a set of texts. Each index entry is associated with the list of texts in which it occurs, and perhaps also the location of the word within each of those individual texts (Black, 2008). The process of associating index terms with unique identifiers of specific objects is the process of inversion. When the locations of the terms within a document are also mapped, the process is referred to as *full inversion*. Although some sources distinguish an inverted index from an inverted file index (Black, 2006), for the purposes of this discussion, these are considered synonymous and will be used interchangeably. The inverted file is a well-known structure that facilitates quick lookups using common access points, and many IR systems and Internet search engines make use of them.

Flynn (1987) explains this structure with an example of a record level inverted file derived from a simple data file, and a similar example is provided here. The data file is about a wine collection and has information about the vineyard, the type of wine, the variety of grape, and the vintage year. Each record has a unique identifier, in this case a unique numeric key, assigned at the time of the record creation. A portion of this hypothetical database appears in Figure 14.2.

This example highlights two important points. First, the records need unique identifiers assigned that are referenced later. Second, any field can be a candidate for inversion; any field that might be the source of a common query is often inverted. For instance, if a query seeks to list all red wines of a specific variety, the database engine could perform a sequential search of each full record looking for records that contain text string matches with the query. However, if this is a common query, a more efficient strategy is to utilize an inverted file structure. The result is a list of the possible values for the inverted field along with pointers to matching records. Inverting on the "Type" field yields the inverted file structure shown in Figure 14.3.

Likewise, similar inverted files could be constructed for the vineyard, variety, and year fields. These key indexes make future lookups more efficient

ID	Vineyard	Type	Variety	Vintage
001	Yellowtail	Red	Merlot	2004
002	St Michele	Red	Cabernet Sauvignon	2006
003	Falkenburg	White	Riesling	2005
004	Little Boomey	Red	Shiraz	2006
005	Montes	White	Chardonnay	2004
006	Macmanis	Red	Pinot Noir	2002
007	Lancers	Rose	Portuguese	2005
008	Bonterra	White	Sauvignon Blanc	2006
009	Wolf Blass	Red	Cabernet Sauvignon	2000
010	Louis Jadot	Red	Beaujolais	2007

Figure 14.2 A portion of a database table.

Type	Records
Red	001, 002, 004, 006, 009, 010
Rose	007
White	003, 005, 008

Figure 14.3 Inversion on the field named "Type."

and facilitate set manipulation with Boolean searching for records that match multiple criteria.

Inverted indexes can be constructed using words from full-text sources as well, often at the word level. This requires some form of document processing. The document is broken up into its component terms, stopwords are removed, and pointers are created for the set of documents that contain the term. *Stopwords* are words deemed meaningless as access points and include articles, prepositions, and conjunctions. Other information about the term may also be stored, such as the term's frequency, its position in the document, the structural part of the document it came from, and the overall length of the document. Such information can be used to determine the *weighting* of the term by the retrieval system; for instance, a term that occurs multiple times in a document would be assigned a higher weight. This is the type of information typically associated with Internet search engines' indexes.

The resulting index is comprised of vocabulary derived from the texts, and the term's location in a text is associated with an address. Computer systems can keep track of the entire set of individual characters that make up a document, or they can treat the document as a group of logical blocks of text. Index term occurrences can therefore be based on their character positions, their location in some block of text, or the word position within the entire document. The tracking of terms in a document reflects the level of *addressing granularity,* which determines how term occurrences can be manipulated with proximity or phrase searching. Inverted file index structures are used with Internet search engines such as the Google index; the use of the inverted index in that context is discussed in the next chapter.

VOCABULARIES

When processing queries, an IR system must match query terms against the terms used to represent the document; both index creation and subsequent queries therefore depend on some vocabulary or lexicon. In the indexing process, term selection may utilize controlled or uncontrolled approaches. When terms are drawn from controlled vocabularies, they come from a restricted set of predetermined words. In uncontrolled vocabularies, terms are unrestricted keywords, often derived from the natural language of the document itself. Each choice determines the appropriate lexicon of possible query terms. Indexing terms derived from unrestricted natural language may be presented to the system in a variety of ways. A natural language processing (NLP) search system implies that queries may be posed as a natural conversational fashion as opposed to a specified, structured format. The AskJeeves search engine, now Ask.com, is an example of a Web search engine utilizing this conversational approach to query formation. However, the ambiguity of natural language poses many challenges to NLP systems. For instance, questions such as "who is the richest man in the world?" sound straightforward but this search performed recently in Ask.com resulted in a number of different answers; the top retrievals at that time were for a PBS program on Andrew Carnegie and a promo for an upcoming movie with those terms in the title. Broad conclusions should not be drawn from just one search on a free search engine, but these results highlight the difficulties of this approach. Not all keyword IR systems allow natural language queries. Term selection may be unrestricted, but query formation may require specific formatting, such as putting term phrases in quotation marks or adding an index name prefix or suffix to the query terms (e.g., "Bruce Springsteen" or "Wodehouse:author").

Controlled Vocabularies

A controlled vocabulary is an indexing language where the semantics and syntax for query terms are formally defined and applied by human indexers. In this approach, the representation of the resource is restricted to a predefined set of words; both the index terms and successful queries must utilize the same defined lexicon. Often a thesaurus is available, guiding users to appropriate terms and illustrating term interrelationships. This structure leads searchers to similar, broader, narrower, and related terms as well as explaining the scope of the term. Controlled vocabularies are often associated with descriptor terms that reflect the intellectual content, but other controlled "authority lists" can be created to standardize names of people, places, or subjects.

Controlled vocabularies are used in many forms to represent the intellectual content of an information resource with descriptors, subject heading lists, or classification schemes. For example, two such controlled vocabularies are the ERIC Descriptors Educational Resources, developed by the U.S. Department of Education, and MeSH Medical Subject headings developed by the National Library of Medicine. Controlled vocabularies can enhance search precision and reduce term selection problems. In addition, controlled vocabularies facilitate exploratory searching by leading someone unfamiliar with a discipline to new terminology that could be useful in a search. However, these advantages come with a cost to both the indexer who must assign them and the searcher who must be familiar with the preferred vocabulary and its structure.

Because the stated purpose of this overview is to develop needed background for an examination of Internet search engines, it is reasonable to ask how controlled vocabularies relate to Internet search. The short answer is that they are not used for most Internet searching. In fact, if anything the trend seems to be moving away from controlled vocabularies approaches and toward user-generated tag clouds known as folksonomies. In the early 1990s, just as the Web was about to burst on the scene, librarians were exploring cataloging of Internet resources; an OCLC study suggested full MARC cataloging could be applied to Internet content (Dillon, Jul, Burge, & Hickney, 1993). This quickly was recognized as untenable with the rapid growth of the Web. However, new metadata schemes, such as Dublin Core, are more nimble approaches that, when combined with controlled vocabularies, could offer improved precision when used with "metadata aware" search engines. In addition, the promise of the XML-based Semantic Web could create pools of more structured Internet with additional opportunities for controlled vocabularies.

Automatic Indexing

Automatic indexing uses the natural language of the documents themselves to represent them and permit queries formed from a natural language vocabulary with unrestricted term selection. A given document word set contains two subsets: (1) words that represent content, which are usually nouns; and (2) words that are simply grammatical in nature, which do not convey meaningful content. Analysis of term frequencies reveal a relationship known as Zipf's law, which finds an inverse relationship between a term's rank and its frequency; so terms occurring with very high frequency have little to do with its content, and terms that occur few times have high ranks (Korfhage, 1997). As noted previously, automatic indexing begins with document processing to extract terms followed by the elimination of stopwords, which have a solely grammatical function such as articles and prepositions. Terms are sorted into an index that is wholly derived from the document lexicon itself. Document processing could extract terms only from specific locations in a document, such as a title, or from the full text. In addition, term weights can be calculated using parameters such as term frequency, its location in the document, its proximity to other terms, and overall document length.

Because automatic natural language indexing and searching is limited to the lexicon of the documents and the imagination of the searcher, it can result in document representation that is not as rich or precise as that achieved by a content expert using controlled vocabularies and a higher probability that queries that may not utilize appropriate terms. However, automatic natural language indexes have several advantages: They are less costly to produce, and the user query terms are not restricted to a predefined vocabulary or descriptor language. Their hidden cost is in a potential loss of search efficiency due to generally less precise search results and a higher proportion of nonrelevant retrievals. As described earlier, these nonrelevant retrievals in a retrieval set are *false hits* or *false drops*. The ambiguity of natural language makes the problem of false hits almost inevitable.

Query Formation

Queries formed with either controlled vocabularies and uncontrolled natural language are problematic due to *synonymy*, *polysemy*, and *homonymy*. Deciding on the appropriate term to represent a concept or thing is a challenge because of the complexity and ambiguity of natural language. *Synonymy* refers to the fact that there are usually many words that could represent a concept. Is it a car or an automobile, a film or a movie? A search system can include some term variants by truncation to a term stem, such as including singular and plural word forms, but synonyms are more difficult to address automatically. *Polysemy* refers to one word that may have related but quite distinct

A top retrieval from ERIC using the keyword "ADD"
Course Shopping in Urban Community Colleges: An Analysis of Student Drop and **Add** Activities (EJ762247) Author(s): Hagedorn, Linda Serra; Maxwell, William E.; Cypers, Scott; Moon, Hye Sun; Lester, Jaime Source: Journal of Higher Education, v78 n4 p464-485 Jul-Aug 2007 Pub Date: 2007-00-00 Pub Type(s): Journal Articles; Reports - Evaluative Peer-Reviewed: Yes Descriptors: Community Colleges; Urban Schools; Course Selection (Students); Student Behavior; Two Year College Students

Figure 14.4 A retrieval from the ERIC database using the term "ADD."

meanings depending on the context. The term "foot" could refer to anatomy or to the base of a mountain; "mouth" could be a body part or the end of a river; a "church" could be an institution or a physical building. *Homonyms* refer to words that are either pronounced or spelled the same but have distinct meanings. For instance, a "router" could be a network device or a woodworking tool; "lead" could be the metal, a person who leads, or the terminal end of a wire; "lie" could refer to an untruth, a verb for a physical action, or describe the position of a golf ball. Term ambiguity and subsequent term selection issues often results in the retrieval of many records that are nonrelevant to the intent of the query, as well as the nonretrieval of relevant ones.

To illustrate the usefulness of a controlled vocabulary in choosing query terms, an example is provided of a search of the ERIC database of education research. A hypothetical teacher interested in exploring the topic of Attention Deficit Disorders enters the query term "ADD." The top retrievals this keyword search returns all use the word "add" in the title or abstract, but often in a different context. In the retrieved article shown in Figure 14.4 the word "add" appears not as the acronym ADD but in the sense of "adding" something.

The ERIC database has a controlled vocabulary documented in a thesaurus the searcher can reference. The thesaurus has an entry for "Attention Deficit Disorders" as a descriptor, as well as appropriate broader, narrower, and related terms shown in Figure 14.5.

Using the recommended descriptor in a new search results in a more precise retrieval set for the subject sought. The use of a controlled vocabulary, if available, is especially helpful in an initial exploratory search, which can lead to new terms for further searching. However, note the added precision comes with a cost to the searcher—they must not only know of the ERIC Thesaurus but take the time and effort to consult it to locate the better term.

PERFORMANCE MEASURES

The goal of retrieval systems is to provide documents that are *relevant* to the query. People tend to think of relevance in a way that is analogous to how

The ERIC Thesaurus entry for Attention Deficit Disorders	
Attention Deficit Disorders	
Descriptor Details	
using Attention Deficit Disorders as a search criteria	
Record Type:	Main
Scope Note:	Developmentally inappropriate inattention and impulsivity
Categor y:	Disabilities
Broader Terms:	Disabilities;
Narrower Terms:	n/a
Related Terms:	Attention; Attention Span; Behavior Disorders; Emotional Disturbances; Hyperactivity; Learning Disabilities; Neurological Impairments;
Used For:	Methylphenidate; Ritalin;
Use Term:	n/a
Use And:	n/a
Add Date:	06/21/1983

Figure 14.5 The ERIC Thesaurus entry for Attention Deficit Disorders.

the judicial system views the concept of obscenity, "you know it when you see it." People evaluate a retrieval set based on an internal sense of whether the documents satisfy an information need; those that do are "relevant." Automated ways to determine rank relevance are a significant challenge for IR systems; several algorithmic strategies for assessing relevance are examined with search engine technologies in the next chapter, including various forms of hypertext link analysis. Regardless of how relevance is determined, there are several standard measures of the effectiveness of a retrieval system: *recall*, the proportion of the potentially relevant documents that were actually retrieved, and *precision*, the number of relevant documents within a given retrieval set. Recall is represented by the formula shown in Figure 14.6.

Applying this to an example, assume a database of 10,000 documents has 250 documents potentially relevant to some information need, for instance, information about breast cancer treatments. A search with perfect recall would then retrieve all 250 of these. If only 125 are retrieved, then recall is 125/250 or 50 percent. Note that this determination is problematic as it presumes one can know or estimate the total number of relevant documents that exist in the collection.

Precision measures the effectiveness of a search in terms of the proportion of relevant documents within all retrieved documents. Precision is represented by the formula shown in Figure 14.7.

Continuing the previous example, assume the query "breast + cancer + treatment" retrieves 300 documents. If an evaluation of each shows that 200 are relevant, then the precision of the search is: P = 200/300 or 66 percent.

$$R = \frac{\#of\ relevant\ documents\ retrieved}{Total\ \#\ of\ relevant\ documents\ within\ the\ collection}$$

Figure 14.6 Recall measure calculation.

$$P = \frac{\#\ of\ relevant\ document\ retrievals}{Total\ \#\ of\ documents\ retrieved}$$

Figure 14.7 Precision measure calculation.

In an ideal world, searches would result in both perfect recall and precision. However, this is rarely the case because strategies to improve one measure usually reduce the efficiency of the other. For instance, an attempt to improve recall by "casting a wider net" through expanding the term set used in a search usually reduces precision by also gathering up a larger number of false hits. Conversely, attempts to improve precision by using more focused term selection usually results in lower recall.

Another highly important but more subjective measure of retrieval effectiveness is the time and effort required to process a query and display relevant results; both usability and search effort are critical factors. Clearly, a retrieval system that took many minutes to perform a search or that was difficult to use would not be acceptable to most users. The quantification of "too long" or "too difficult" is a judgment made in the context of the size and complexity of the corpus searched as well as the motivation and expertise of the searcher. The effort needed to use a system is inversely proportional to its acceptance by users. This was formally postulated by Zipf (1949) in his well-known "Principle of Least Effort" that postulated that "each individual will adopt a course of action that will involve the expenditure of the probably least average of his work" (p. 543)—that is, the least effort.

The truth of this principle is especially apparent in the preference shown by users for Internet search engines over more complex library systems for information seeking. Even in the context of Internet searching, searchers as a rule seem to abandon sites that are complex or hard to use in favor of those that permit easy, fast keyword searches.

CLASSICAL IR MODELS

The three main classical IR models are the *Boolean, vector space,* and *probabilistic* models. These are not necessarily mutually exclusive, and Internet search engine technologies have utilized elements of all three models. In keeping with the overview goal of this chapter, the mathematical details and formulas associated with the vector space and probabilistic models are not discussed because the intent is to develop a "big picture" view of these topics to support an examination of Internet search in Chapter 15. In addition, this overview does not include the enhancements or alternatives that extend these models such as fuzzy Boolean, Latent Semantic Indexing (LSI), and the neural net model. More detail on all these models is found in the references and suggested readings with this chapter.

Boolean IR

The Boolean model is based on set theory and Boolean algebra, and it is the most straightforward of the various retrieval models. Boolean logic has three operators: AND, OR, and NOT. IR systems utilizing Boolean logic permit you to "post-coordinate" the terms used in a query statement by connecting them together with any of these three operators. Boolean logic is represented truth tables; numbers in these tables represent the presence or absence of a term and whether a record is retrieved. The generic example below shows the result for a two-term search using Boolean AND. For instance, substituting "cats" and "dogs" for the terms, a Boolean search for "cats AND dogs" only retrieves records that contain both terms.

term1 AND term2 → only records with both terms are retrieved.

term1 OR term2 → Records with either one or both terms present are retrieved.

NOT term1 → Any record with term1 is eliminated from the retrieval set.

The Boolean algebra for these AND combinations is shown in Figure 14.8. The results of Boolean OR and Boolean NOT follow in Figures 14.9 and 14.10.

Operand	Operator	Operand	Result
0	AND	0	0
0	AND	1	0
1	AND	0	0
1	AND	1	1

Figure 14.8 Boolean AND truth table.

Operand	Operator	Operand	Result
0	OR	0	0
0	OR	1	1
1	OR	0	1
1	OR	1	1

Figure 14.9 Boolean OR truth table.

Operand	Operator	Result
0	NOT	1
1	NOT	0

Figure 14.10 Boolean NOT truth table.

Boolean logic permits the formation of complex queries using combinations of these multiple operators, which follow established rules of operator precedence (NOT, AND, OR). Statements within parentheses are always processed first, so they are often used for complex Boolean statements to group expressions and control processing order.

The main limitation with standard Boolean retrieval is there must be an exact match with the query terms. The Boolean model is binary in nature; that is, a document is relevant and retrieved or not retrieved depending on an exact string match. There is no "partial match" with simple Boolean; extended "fuzzy" Boolean does not have this limitation. The choice of query terms is therefore critical to successfully retrieving relevant documents, and the outcome of Boolean searching depends on how well the terms chosen to represent a concept match those in the index. All the issues discussed earlier regarding synonymy, polysemy, and homonymy are particularly relevant to Boolean searching.

There are several ways that a system could assist a searcher in identifying the best terms or extending the set of matches for the term used. Controlled vocabularies reduce term ambiguity and provide guidance on term selection with a thesaurus that identifies appropriate terms as well as term relationships. Even without a controlled vocabulary, the retrieval system may permit term truncation symbols that serve as placeholders for characters. The IR system could also automatically expand the term set used in the query by *term stemming* to take a word to its root form. Both these approaches add term variants to the query and expand the set of possible matches. In addition, search engines can provide term suggestions, auto-correct misspellings, auto-fill questions based on popular queries, and offer to search for results similar to a selected retrieval.

Vector Space Model

The vector space retrieval model described by Salton and McGill (1983) attempts to identify relevant documents through a mathematical computation of similarity between query and document vectors. This computation results in an estimate of relevance based on a computed degree of similarity measure, also referred to as the Retrieval Status Value (RSV). This approach avoids the binary limitations of the Boolean model and allows for system generated term weighting. As the name implies, the calculation depends on creating document and query vectors and placing them in a multidimensional vector space for a similarity comparison. The similarity measure, typically the cosine of the angle formed between the two vectors, is calculated to algorithmically determine relevance. Higher cosine values mean smaller angles between the query and document vectors, which imply a higher relevance ranking; smaller cosine values mean less similarity between the query and document vectors and a lower relevance.

The process of term weighting is a highly useful feature of this model. To understand how term weights are generated, suppose a collection of documents (d_1. . . d_n) has been processed and found to contain a set of unique terms numbered (t_1 . . .t_t), which therefore comprise the entire set of term vocabulary. Each term derived from the document set can be assigned a weight; this could be a binary value (0 if absent, 1 if present) or, more likely, some intermediate weight value based on the term's frequency in a document. In addition to raw frequency measures, the uniqueness of the term can factor into its weighting as well; intuitively, it is logical to assume that terms occurring in many documents are less useful as descriptors than terms occurring in relatively few documents. This information is represented in a documents-to-terms matrix or array, as shown in Figure 14.11.

The matrix results in t-dimensional vector space, and because many specific documents would not contain many of the potential terms, the matrix would contain many zero values. Each term is an axis in a Cartesian coordinate space, and both documents and queries could be represented as vectors within the term vector space. A simplified view of such possible vector comparisons is in Figure 14.12.

This model has several distinct advantages: It permits partial matches based on index term and query word weighting and provides an algorithmic process to perform relevance ranking. However, one drawback is its computational complexity, especially in the context of a large-scale, heterogeneous document collection such as the Web. Computing term weighted vectors for

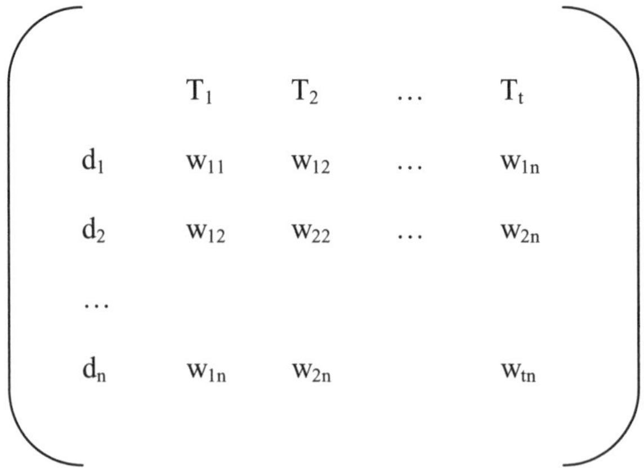

Figure 14.11 A document-term matrix. A set of *n* documents contains a set of *t* terms, each of which has been assigned a weight *w*, based on the term's frequency and other factors.

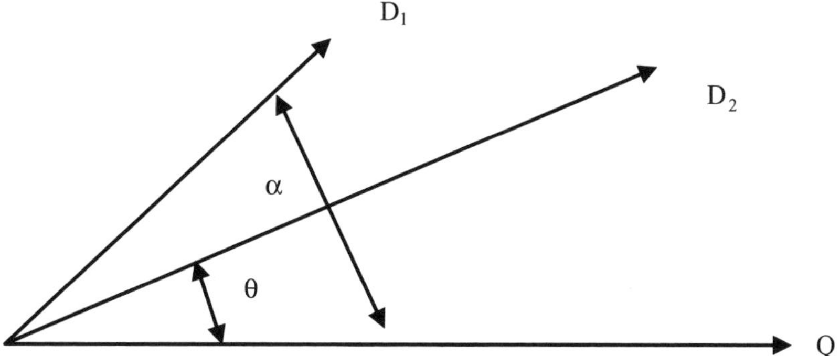

Figure 14.12 Document vectors 1 and 2 form angles α and θ respectively with query vector Q. The cosine of these angles will determine the degree of similarity; the angle formed with D_2 has a higher cosine value and is therefore more similar to the query than document D_1.

every Web document followed by similarity computations with queries would be a daunting task for any system. However, there are techniques that make this approach more tenable for such a large corpus of documents; for instance, an initial term lookup in an inverted file can eliminate documents with none of the query words and greatly reduce the candidate set of documents for subsequent vector similarity calculations. The application of this approach to Web IR is discussed in the next chapter.

Probabilistic Model

The probabilistic model, also referred to as the *Binary Independence Retrieval* (BIR) model, uses a statistical approach to estimate a probability of relevance to a query. The model presumes some ideal retrieval set that perfectly satisfies a query and attempts to identify that set. The model uses binary term weighting and a recursive statistical technique to estimate the probability that a document is either relevant or not relevant to the query. The Google developers describe the PageRank algorithm as a recursive technique to develop a probability estimate (Brin & Page, 1998), so the notion of probability will come up again with the discussion of Google in Chapter 15.

NONTEXTUAL IR

Retrieving multimedia content presents many challenges to IR systems and their designers. The Web has seen a huge proliferation of such content, and finding a specific media object has become more difficult as the quantity and diversity of these media has grown. For instance, one of the most common type of media available on the Web are the various types of graphic images; as of 2007 there were an estimated 10 to 20 billion of them not including those in private photo collections stored online (Rorissa, 2007). Search options and retrieval success when seeking an image depends in part whether they are housed and maintained in structured databases or simply integrated within general Web pages. Textual IR dominates Web search, but Goodrum and Spink (2001) found searching for images comprises a significant portion of Internet information seeking activity. In addition, their analysis confirmed the difficulty of image searching for users of the Excite search engine.

Users of specialized image databases may fare better given the nature of the image content and specific IR systems designed for those collections. Examples of such databases include the Library of Congress American Memory Project (http://memory.loc.gov/ammem/index.html), NASA's Multimedia Gallery (http://www.nasa.gov/multimedia/highlights/index.html), the National Institute of Health's Visible Human Project (http://www.nlm.nih.gov/research/visible/visible_human.html), as well as many art gallery databases. In addition to these projects, there are highly specialized IR systems designed for scientific and medical databases that contain mammogram or tissue sampling images, or law enforcement databases for fingerprint or facial recognition (Castelli, 2002). However, the large number of diverse image sources found on the broader Web can be more problematic for content-based pattern recognition programs. Other media types present their own set of challenges; for instance, content in a podcast is often in MP3 file format. Audio files and documents both contain textual content, one spoken, and the other written. However, the full text of the document is keyword searchable, but the podcast is not, unless a transcript accompanies it.

There are two main approaches to multimedia IR that can be used separately or in combination with each other. Cheng and Rasmussen (1999) describe these as *concept-based* and *content-based* IR approaches. Concept-based indexing and retrieval uses the same techniques employed for textual IR and involves the creation of a textual description for the media object that can be used by the system. The source of the textual description can be the object itself, the HTML code that references it, or a more rigorous application of metadata by a human indexer or a program. Textual information can come from the object filename, a transcript, or a song's textual lyrics, or in the case of Web page images, from the alternate text or a caption. However, these sources of derived descriptive text are limited and sometimes not very useful; for instance, filenames may be nothing more that an automatic code and number such as "**DSC00268.jpg.**" Alternate text or captions are often missing or applied inconsistently, resulting in poor, nonstandardized description. The creation of transcripts from audio content is not as easy as getting text from documents with OCR software, but there are voice recognition programs that do a reasonably good job of converting audio into text. The application of more rigorous standardized metadata can provide enhanced intellectual access, but it is a labor-intensive process. Alternatively, users themselves might contribute the descriptor tags they find meaningful and useful to multimedia. The large-scale Internet media search sites YouTube and Google Image search permit user tagging as a way to enhance access to visual content. Such a "tag cloud" of descriptors results in user-based taxonomies known as "folksonomies."

The other main IR approach is Content-Based IR (CBIR), which uses programs that try to assess the actual content of the multimedia object in terms of color, form, or texture by examining pixels, waveforms, shapes, or other properties. The system then attempts to use pattern matching within the media objects, for instance, to correlate image shapes with people, animals, structures, or other features to determine what it contains and what it is about.

The choice between these two strategies determines the query formation options. If concept-based textual indexing is used, the searcher encounters many of the same issues already discussed regarding term selection and natural language ambiguity. If a controlled vocabulary has been used the searcher needs to be aware of it to be directed to the appropriate terms. Content-based queries attempt to use features of the media object itself. This is done either in an iterative approach based on sample retrievals that allow the user to request more objects that look or sound similar to an initial retrieval, or by attempting to match user specified patterns derived from colors, shapes, or sounds. These strategies are discussed further in the next sections.

Concept-Based Indexing: Textual Descriptors and Metadata for Multimedia

As noted previously, textual description can be derived from the content of the object itself, its caption, or associated alternate text. Deeper levels of indexing involve human intervention, but describing multimedia objects such as photographic images or music is subjective, and they are consequently difficult to describe consistently. "A picture is worth a thousand words" and "beauty is in the eye of the beholder" are two old adages relevant to this discussion. One of the major difficulties is that images are typically both *of* something and *about* something, and those might not be the same thing; this process is complicated further by cultural influences (Berinstein, 1999). A photograph of a beach scene may include boats, waves crashing, sand dunes, people doing different things, and a beautiful sunset. The elements emphasized in the description of this landscape depend on what elements strike the viewer as important, and that assessment takes place at different levels because images are both literal and symbolic. For instance, a picture of a shrouded figure with a scythe could be described as a farmer in a hooded dark cloak, but many others would immediately recognize it as representing death. A picture of the planes hitting the Twin Towers is not just an image of a plane crash, but of a terrorist attack. Images, color, and symbols all reflect emotion and moods, and these second-level meanings are not the same for all viewers.

Textual descriptions for images and other media objects can be highly structured or relatively flexible and open-ended. On one end of the spectrum, there are established controlled vocabularies to assist in standardized description, such as the Getty Vocabularies that include The Art and Architecture Thesaurus, the Union List of Artist's Names, and The Getty Thesaurus of Geographic Names. At the other end, there are the user driven folksonomies that comprise the uncontrolled vocabulary tag clouds assigned to images and videos on Websites such as YouTube and Flickr.

Content-Based IR for Multimedia

An alternate approach to IR of multimedia is the development of programs that can "see" the image or "hear" the sounds in a way that is analogous to how human sight and hearing match sensory data to conceptual models. Some technologies have been around for some time, for instance OCR (optical character recognition) programs for "reading" text as well as handwriting and speech recognition tools. However, because images are viewed at differing levels of abstraction, automated semantic representation is difficult. Programs can handle lower levels of abstraction, such as defining certain pixel areas as shapes that represent a tree or a person, but higher-level semantics is more challenging. Some of the more successful examples come from narrower applications, such as fingerprint image databases or medical imaging. Systems like the IBM "Query By Image Content" allow pattern matching based on image attributes such as shapes, colors, or textures. One example of QBIC color matching is used in a database at the State Hermitage Museum in St. Petersburg; users can choose colors from a palate, set the relative amounts of each color, and search their digitized art by these color patterns. The visual search company Pixlogic (http://www.pixlogic.com/) has developed iterative software that allows both shape and color pattern matching (Pepus, 2007). Another approach to image IR is "Query By Example" (QBE), where the system seeks more matches that are similar to a user-selected or generated example image. With this approach the challenge is to locate an appropriate example as the starting point. These approaches can be combined, for instance QBE could be used to retrieve an initial image set and then QBIC applied to focus on certain shapes, colors, or textures, as the shopping site Like.com (http://www.like.com) attempts to do (Baxter & Anderson, 1996).

TYPES OF SEARCHING

Inherent in the definition of IR are the broad notions of information seeking and information behavior. Case (2007) describes information seeking as "a conscious effort to acquire information in response to a need or gap in your knowledge" and considers the importance of both active and passive information behaviors associated with it (p. 5). Although a broader discussion of this area is beyond the scope of this book, one facet of information seeking is particularly pertinent to the next chapter on Internet searching. Information *searching* behavior, described by Wilson (2000) as "the 'micro-level' of behavior employed by the searcher interacting with information systems of all kinds," is relevant to Internet search (p. 49). Rosenfield and Morville (1998, pp. 102–103) describe four broad categories of information searching that influence the choice of the best search strategy:

1. The *known item search*, where a specific information item is sought. Examples include a specific citation for an article or a quick factual lookup such as the name of a capital city or stock quote.
2. The *existence search*, where it is not known if the information exists, or if it does, how it might be described. The difficulty of looking up

a feature in software help is illustrative of this type of search; you might know the software can do a needed task, but not know how it is described or categorized in the program's documentation.

3. The *exploratory search*, where a topic is not well-known or understood making term selection problematic (the dilemma of "how can you look it up if you don't know how to spell it?").
4. The *comprehensive search*, where a topic might be well-known, but all possible information on it is desired. For instance, literature reviews on a potential research area where everything that has been done on a topic is sought.

These different types of searching frame the examination of Internet search, which is the focus of the next chapter. Internet search includes the application of IR to principles by the various search engines, metasearch services, and directory subject guides that comprise the main avenues people use to seek Internet-based information. Each of these various services can accommodate these four general types of search. A URL published in the newspaper or given in a company brochure is a type of known item search. Web directory services or subject guides facilitate the initial steps of an exploratory search. Both existence and comprehensive searches are more challenging and can be problematic for any IR system because it is difficult to prove that something does not exist or that all information on a topic has been located. A Web search engine is the usual starting point for these searches, and a metasearch engine that broadcasts the search to multiple search engines is a particularly useful strategy to enhance the comprehensiveness of a search. Although the Web was developed to facilitate browsing, the scale of the Web makes simple browsing ineffective unless the search is initially focused by one of the techniques described previously.

SUMMARY

Search has become a defining technology of the Internet. Search engines utilize the principles of general textual IR systems as described in this overview, which examined performance measures, document processing, and the retrieval models that are relevant to understanding Internet search engines. In addition, the Internet is driving many exciting developments in nontextual, multimedia information retrieval. Internet search engines represent IR systems capable of accommodating the various types of searching performed by people seeking Internet information, and this IR overview frames the discussion in Chapter 15 of search engine technologies.

REFERENCES

Baeza-Yates, R., & Ribeiro-Neto, B. (1999). *Modern information retrieval.* New York: ACM Press.

Battelle, J. (2005). *The search.* New York: Penguin Group.

Bawden, D. (2007). Information seeking and retrieval. *ALISE, 28*(2), 126.

Baxter, G., & Anderson, D. (1996). Image indexing and retrieval: Some problems and proposed solutions. *Internet Research, 6*(4).

Berinstein, P. (1999). Do you see what I see? Image indexing for the rest of us. *Online, 23*(2), 85–88.

Black, P. E. (2006). Dictionary of algorithms and data structures [online]. Retrieved September 13, 2008, from http://www.nist.gov/dads/HTML/invertedFileIndex.html.

Black, P. E. (2008). Dictionary of algorithms and data structures [online]. Retrieved September 13, 2008, from http://www.nist.gov/dads/HTML/invertedIndex.html.

Brin, S., & Page, L. (1998). *The anatomy of a large-scale search hypertextual Web search engine.* Paper presented at the Proc. Seventh World Wide Web Conference, Brisbane, Australia.

Case, D. O. (2007). *Looking for information: A survey of research on information seeking, needs, and behavior* (2nd ed.). New York: Academic Press.

Castelli, V. (Ed.). (2002). *Encyclopedia of library and information science* (Vol. 71). New York: Marcel Dekker, Inc.

Cheng, H.-L., & Rasmussen, E. M. (1999). Intellectual access to images. *Library Trends, 48*(2), 291–302.

Chu, H. (2003). *Information representation and retrieval in the digital age.* Medford, NJ: Information Today.

Dillon, M., Jul, E., Burge, M., & Hickney, C. (1993). *Assessing information on the Internet: Toward providing library services for computer-mediated communication.* Dublin, OH: OCLC Online Computer Library Center, Inc.

Flynn, R. R. (1987). *An introduction to information science.* New York: Marcel Dekker.

Goodrum, A., & Spink, A. (2001). Image searching on the Excite Web search engine. *Information Processing and Management, 37,* 295–311.

Korfhage, R. R. (1997). *Information storage and retrieval.* New York: Wiley & Sons.

Meadow, C. T., Boyce, B. R., & Kraft, D. H. (2000). *Text information retrieval systems* (2nd ed.). San Diego, CA: Academic Press.

Morville, P. (2005). *Ambient findability.* Sebastpol, CA: O'Reilly Media, Inc.

Pepus, G. (2007). Smart image and video search. *KM World, 16*(6), 6–9.

Rorissa, A. (2007). Benchmarking visual information indexing and retrieval systems. *Bulletin of the American Society for Information Science and Technology, 33*(3), 15–17.

Rosenfield, L., & Morville, P. (1998). *Information architecture for the World Wide Web.* Sebastopol, CA: O'Reilly.

Salton, G., & McGill, M. J. (1983). *Introduction to modern information retrieval.* New York: McGraw-Hill.

Smeaton, A. (2007). TRECVid-Video evaluation. *Bulletin of the American Society for Information Science and Technology, 33*(3), 21–23.

The Text REtrieval Conference. (2007, August 8). Overview. Retrieved May 1, 2008, from http://trec.nist.gov/overview.html.

Wilson, T. D. (2000). Human information behavior. *Informing Science, 3*(2), 49–56.

Zipf, G. K. (1949). *Human behavior and the principle of least effort; an introduction to human ecology.* Cambridge, MA: Addison-Wesley.

ADDITIONAL READING

Chan, L. M. (2007). *Cataloging and classification: An introduction* (3rd ed.). Lanham, MD: The Scarecrow Press, Inc.

Chowdhury, G. C. (1999). *Introduction to modern information retrieval.* London: Library Association Publishing.

Lancaster, F. W. (1979). *Information Retrieval Systems: Characteristics, testing, and evaluation.* New York: John Wiley.

Yang, K. (2005). Information Retrieval on the Web. In B. Cronin (Ed.), *Annual review of information science and technology* (Vol. 39, pp. 33–80). New York: ASIST.

Chapter 15

Internet Search

Internet search is second only to email in popularity among Internet activities (Rainie, 2005). Search is not just an individual means to an end, but search patterns also are sociologically significant as a measure of broader collective interests. Google Trends tracks the most popular searches of the day and provides a fascinating snapshot of what is culturally significant at any given time. This phenomenon represents a "database of intentions" (Battelle, 2005) and is a cultural artifact that records shifting societal trends over time. While this is an intriguing result of the totality of individual searches, it is the individual's search activities and search engines' technologies, which respond with useful, relevance ranked results, that are the focus of this chapter.

Internet search as described here is information retrieval applied to the more limited, specific context of using search engines to find Web pages or other forms of content that are relevant to a query. The focus is on the general process employed by search services to create a searchable index, process a query, and rank the results. The theoretical and mathematical underpinnings of these systems are considered only to the extent needed to support a general understanding of the way search engines work and the consequent implications for searchers.

THE CHALLENGES OF INTERNET IR

Internet information retrieval is challenging to both Internet searchers and search engine designers for a number of reasons. Issues include the extremely large volume documents available; the myriad of formats and languages in which content resides; the lack of any consistent quality control applied to published content; the presence of inappropriate and misleading information; the problem of the "invisible" Web; and the lack of any overarching organizational scheme or controlled vocabularies.

The Size and Currency of the Web

One of the first and most significant issues encountered by all Internet search systems is the sheer volume of documents that are available. Information retrieval (IR) technologies that work well in a smaller document universe do not necessarily scale up to the Web environment. The numbers of documents that make up the Internet universe are huge and so are the retrieval sets returned by most searches, making relevance ranking both critical and problematic. Accurate estimates of the number of static Web pages are difficult to come by, and many search engines, including Google, have stopped providing data on index size. However, there have been attempts to take a census of Internet content over the history of the Web. Earlier surveys reported the search engine AltaVista indexed 30 million pages in 1996, 90 million in 1997, and 150 million by 1998 (Sullivan, 2005). Other statistical methods yielded an estimated 320 million pages by the end of 1997, which grew to about 800 million by 1999 (Lawrence & Giles, 1998, 1999). By 2005, the estimated size of the Web had ballooned to 11.5 billion pages (Gulli & Signorini, 2005). Two years later Boutell.com, a software and Internet service company, calculated that there were 29.7 billion pages, but they readily acknowledge this extrapolation is based on a number of fuzzy assumptions for server counts, the "average" number of pages at each site, and Yahoo's index size, making this little more than a good guess (Boutell.com, 2007). That estimate is also close to the 27.6 billion pages reported by de Kunder (2008). Another recent estimate (Gil, 2008) suggests there are 71 billion static Webpages. Although these data demonstrate that accurate and consistent measures of Web size are problematic, it is clear that the Internet content pool is huge, and it continues to grow at a rapid rate.

In addition to Web size, currency of the content is also a concern. Many pages found in a search are woefully out-of-date, devaluing their information. Many URLs referenced in both printed works and as Web hyperlinks represent dead or invalid sources where the content has disappeared or been relocated without a forwarding link. Estimates suggest that almost a quarter of the articles published with URL references may fall into this category (Lawrence et al., 2000). Kahle (1997) early on highlighted the need for and the value of archiving the potentially transient content of the Internet; there are Websites devoted to this purpose. One notable attempt to create such a repository is the Internet Archive project with its "wayback machine," which permits a search for pages that are no longer active as well as for earlier versions of a current page.

Format Issues

Another challenge is the diversity of content formats available in terms of both the file formats (other than simple HTML) and in the language of the content itself. Barriers associated with file formats are discussed in Chapter 13. Inappropriate content such as pornography is also an issue, and most search engines have the capability to filter such content. However, Internet searches still yield content that is not only nonrelevant but also potentially offensive to some users.

For a time, OCLC (the Online Computer Library Center) presented a "snapshot" of the Web for a given year. In the last of these studies, OCLC estimated that there were about 9 million discrete sites each with potentially many pages and that about 35 percent of these were public sites that did not require any authorization or fees (Online Computer Library Center, 2002). They reported that 16 percent of all sites were related to the information industry; 14 percent were related to professional and technical consultants; 12 percent associated with retailers; and 3 percent, or about 102,000 of the total, constituted "adult" sites. Although this explicit content represented a relatively small proportion of total Web content, the ease of access to it is a concern for parents and providers of Internet access to the public. That report found that, in 2002, 72 percent of the Web was in English, 7 percent in German, 6 percent in Japanese, and 3 percent in each Spanish and French. While these numbers have surely shifted over time, these data reflect the concern that the "global" Internet is dominated by Western language content and, more specifically, English language content. The potential for cultural and language bias is a source of controversy for the Google book digitization initiative, with some outside the U.S. asserting non-English works are being marginalized in this effort (Jeanneney, 2006).

Quality of Information

Separate from the potential retrieval of offensive or pornographic content, there is a wide range in the overall quality of the information resources retrieved with Internet search. Evaluation of Web content is discussed in Chapter 13, but it is an IR issue as retrieval sets are often cluttered with items that initially appear to be highly relevant but whose quality is poor, are aimed at a different audience level, or contain deliberate misinformation.

Search engine technologies are susceptible to manipulative techniques designed to influence relevance-ranking algorithms. These attempts have a back and forth cycle; as search engines respond, those seeking an advantage in the retrieval ranking game develop new techniques. For instance, *term stuffing* was somewhat common in the early Web until search engines developed technologies to recognize and combat it. Term stuffing is the repeated placement of keyword terms in a document in a way that is not visible to the user. It might involve placing terms in the HEAD area that are not displayed by the browser or the use of identical font and background colors to fill the "white space" of a document with terms that are present but not visible; either approach could influence an algorithm that correlates term frequency with document relevance. In addition, it is possible to add misleading meta-tag content. Google's Page Rank has been manipulated through the development of "link bombs," which are the result of a coordinated effort to manipulate document linking that brings a targeted page to the top of a retrieval set. This issue is discussed further in the section on Google later in this chapter.

The Invisible Web

The "invisible" Web is content not accessed by most search engines, and it represents a huge pool of largely unavailable content. There are many ways content can become "invisible" to a search engine: The content could be protected behind a firewall; reside on a server using the robot exclusion protocol; be part of a page with a META tag that excludes the page from being indexed; use a file format that cannot be directly indexed; or be derived from a database. Dynamic database driven pages do not really exist until a query creates them, so there is no autonomous static file for the search engine to harvest. As database driven approaches become more common, Web crawlers do not reach an ever-increasing pool of this type of content. There are estimates that the invisible Web could contain 400–500 times the content that is available on the indexable Web (Bergman, 2001). Zillman (2007) estimates that the total invisible Web from all sources that cannot be found by traditional Web crawling search engines could represent about 900 billion pages. Of that total, it is estimated that about 220 billion pages result from database-driven sites alone (Gil, 2008). Separate from how reliable such figures are, there is no doubt that significant amounts of content are not found by standard search engine approaches, which influences the comprehensiveness of Internet search as it exists today.

Web Organization

In addition to these problems, the general lack of controlled vocabularies, structured metadata, and organizational schemes also limits Internet search effectiveness. Unlike many formal information systems, there is little organization to the Web, and keyword searching is the primary access strategy. There have been attempts to create Internet directories using more formal organizational approaches such as the Librarians Index to the Internet, Drexel's Internet Public Library, Library and Archives Canada, and the BUBL LINK Catalogue of Selected Internet Resources in the United Kingdom. Such efforts attempt to provide more structured access to Internet content for academic subject access.

There is an emerging interest in creating a metadata enhanced Web to improve intellectual access to Internet resources. Metadata initiatives, such as OCLC's Dublin Core, which is a structured framework for those wishing to utilize metadata, and the broad goals of the "semantic" XML-based Web promoted by Tim Berners-Lee, (Berners-Lee, Hendler, & Lassila, 2001) represent two such approaches. Although these offer exciting opportunities for enhancing information access, their use is still the exception rather than the rule, in part because the creation and use of structured metadata is labor intensive. There is also some evidence that metadata strategies do not always necessarily improve search accuracy. One study examined queries of a university Website that utilized subject metadata and found that metadata-enabled searching actually underperformed when compared to using anchor text, which resulted in better answers to queries (Hawking & Zobel, 2007).

A SHORT HISTORY OF INTERNET SEARCHING

From the start of the Internet in 1969 to 1990, there was comparatively little content of interest to the public and little need for Internet search as used today. Most early Internet activities were limited to email communication, telnet access to remote hosts, or the use of FTP to access file repositories. These FTP sites could contain large numbers of files, and locating a specific file of interest was difficult. One of the first Internet search technologies, called Archie and developed in 1990 at McGill University, was designed to facilitate search of these repositories. Archie was short for "archives" and consisted of an index created by a program that harvested information from the various anonymous FTP sites.

The gopher protocol, developed at the University of Minnesota in 1991, utilized a hierarchically structured menu system to access Internet content. This service grew rapidly, and by 1994, there were about 10 million items on about 5,500 gopher servers on the Internet, making simple browsing ineffective as a search strategy. The VERONICA indexing service was an index of all the terms used in gopher menus and document titles, making direct access to gopher documents possible. VERONICA was supposedly an acronym for the "very easy, rodent oriented net-wide index to computer archives," but also named to follow the development of Archie with another of that comic book's characters (Vidmar & Anderson, 2002). The indexing was not of the document full text, so how well the index term represented the actual intellectual content depended in large measure on how descriptive the menu or title words were. The VERONICA service had several mirror server sites, but as demand grew, the service was frequently overwhelmed. Jughead was a similar Gopher search service developed in 1993 at the University of Utah; its name was also drawn from the Archie comics. This service was not very different from VERONICA and some speculate its development was in part simply to complete the trio of search services named after the comic series characters (Vidmar & Anderson, 2002). These early services allowed for Boolean searching and word stemming with truncation symbols, but advanced searching required a complex set of search option modifiers represented with a dash and a letter. The command-based search interface was not particularly intuitive compared to search engines of today.

Also in 1990, Brewster Kahle of Thinking Machines Corporation (who went on to codevelop the Internet Archives project) along with other corporate partners developed the Wide Area Information Server (WAIS). The software could create a database of weighted terms that was searchable with natural language and yielded a relevance ranked output. This technology was an early precursor to the modern search engine.

Tim Berners-Lee developed the World Wide Web during this same period. In late 1991, he publicly demonstrated the Web for the first time at the Hypertext '91 Conference in San Antonio, Texas. The original WWW ran on a server at CERN, which is where it was developed, and access to it was through text-based browsers running on UNIX hosts. In 1993, NCSA released the Mosaic graphical browser, and by the next year, there was an explosion of Internet traffic, increasing an astounding 1500 percent (Cheong, 1996). The saying "if you build it they will come," which is often applied to the Internet story, apparently should be restated as "if you build it and *make it really easy to use and useful to people's lives,* they will come."

Initially, you could browse the embryonic Web simply by logging into the info.cern.ch site with a telnet connection. However, as the Web grew in scale, simple browsing was no longer a viable strategy without the initial ability to identify promising starting points for browsing. In 1993, the ALIWEB (Archie-like index of the Web), one of the first Web crawlers, was developed. ALIWEB harvested and combined local index files created by a webmaster into a large-scale searchable index. Oliver McBryan developed the WWWW (also called the W4 worm) in 1994, and it expanded automatic indexing to include Web page title words and URLs (Vidmar & Anderson, 2002). Advances in Repository-Based Software Engineering (RBSE) resulted in two companion "spider" programs; one that would find URLs and another that would retrieve and index the documents associated with those URLs. The robot programs that automate the process of creating a searchable index for Web resources are the foundation technologies of modern Web search engines.

The development of these crawler programs in 1994 led to the rapid development of various search engines that continues to the present. The directory services EINet Galaxy and Yahoo, as well as the WebCrawler, Lycos, and Excite search engines, were all developed that year, followed in 1995 by Infoseek, AltaVista, and Inktomi. Northern Light appeared in 1997 and introduced the innovation of categorizing results into folders. Google, released in 1998, quickly became the most popular of the search engines. The metasearch engine, which allows a query to be processed by multiple search engines simultaneously, appeared in 1995 with Savvysearch and Metacrawler, soon joined by AskJeeves and Dogpile, among others.

INTERNET SEARCH SERVICES

Internet search services consist of three fundamental types: the Web directory, the search engine, and the metasearch engine. Early in the development of these services, the lines between them were sharply drawn, but now there is a good deal of functional overlap; most directory services also have a search option, and many search engines support a directory.

Directories

Directory approaches involve the creation of a categorized list of topics, usually with hierarchically structured menus. Resource selection and categorization may take place automatically or with human intervention. The human intervention may be by employees of the service or by the Web community at-large. Directory services can be especially effective when someone wishes to explore or expand a known topic. Directories provide useful starting points for an exploratory search by identifying the various facets of the topic. One of the difficulties with directories is that the topic headings chosen by their creator may not reflect categories or terms that match how the user thinks of the topic; the issues of polysemy and synonymy discussed in Chapter 14 are relevant here. One solution is to standardize the categorization scheme and to make a subject thesaurus available. A directory service must also define the comprehensiveness with which it attempts to represent all possible topics as well as define the intended target audience. Directories for general audiences may have top-level categories for sports or entertainment as opposed to academic topics, which limits their effectiveness for more serious research. Hierarchical directory menus can also be problematic because a user must decide on the best entry point to the directory tree structure and then drill down far enough to determine if that initial choice was correct. To make directory use more efficient, most provide a search feature that assists the user in identifying the most appropriate entry point rather than requiring the exploration of many menu layers to find an entry.

One example of a directory service is the one created by Yahoo. Yahoo began its business with its directory service but has since evolved into a complete Web portal offering a variety of other services such as mail, Web search, Yahoo Answers, and Yahoo messenger. Yahoo built its reputation on the claim that although it did not have the "biggest" index, it provided access to the "best" Web content on a given topic because of its resource selections. Figure 15.1 shows the top-level directory categories for the Yahoo site as of 2007.

The DMOZ Open Directory project is another example, but instead of employing selectors, it uses the community of the Web itself. This collaborative approach allows individuals interested in a topic area to contribute selections to it. Figure 15.2 is a screen shot of the DMOZ Open Directory categories.

Search Engines

The number of search engines grew rapidly from 1994 on, and there are hundreds of Internet search engines to choose from today. Although they offer different features, most use similar technologies to automatically create a searchable index and process submitted queries. They all seek to rank results by relevance, but the details of that process are often proprietary algorithms that distinguish one service from another. Search engines facilitate the exploration of a topic with simple key word searching; they are a particularly useful starting point for both a known item type search and for an existence search, where the user needs to determine if information on a topic is even available.

Search engines vary considerably in index size and focus; some attempt to index as much of the Web as possible, while others focus on a smaller, more specialized niche. There is also much variation in the type of materials indexed; all index HTML content, but many also index content in other formats such as PDF. As with directory services, search engines have expanded to become complete service portals; services may include email, maps and driving directions, satellite imaging, image search, language translation, and access to other types of digital content such as that provided by Google Scholar and Google Books.

There is considerable variation in both the user interface and in the search features allowed. Many search engines favor the simple design that has been so successful for Google, relying on a single text box for users to enter keywords; others provide a more complex set of options on the initial search screen. Even the simple text box approach has potential pitfalls depending on how well the user understands the assumptions made by the search engine designers. A multiple word search has a number of implicit assumptions, and to understand the outcome of a query the searcher must be aware of these

The Yahoo Directory
Arts & Humanities
Photography, History, Literature...
Business & Economy
B2B, Finance, Shopping, Jobs...
Computers & Internet
Hardware, Software, Web, Games...
Education
Colleges, K-12, Distance Learning...
Entertainment
Movies, TV Shows, Music, Humor...
Government
Elections, Military, Law, Taxes...
Health
Diseases, Drugs, Fitness, Nutrition...
News & Media
Newspapers, Radio, Weather, Blogs...
Recreation & Sports
Sports, Travel, Autos, Outdoors...
Reference
Phone Numbers, Dictionaries, Quotes...
Regional
Countries, Regions, U.S. States...
Science
Animals, Astronomy, Earth Science...
Social Science
Languages, Archaeology, Psychology...
Society & Culture
Sexuality, Religion, Food & Drink...
New Additions
10/4, 10/3, 10/2, 10/1, 9/30...
The Spark Blog

Figure 15.1 The Yahoo Directory top-level categories (http://dir.yahoo.com/).

assumptions. For instance, what happens when more than one word is entered in the query box? Is the default to process these multiple word searches as a Boolean AND (all the words) or a Boolean OR (any of the words)? Does word order make a difference? Does the use of capital letters in the search terms affect how the search is processed? The answers to these questions do matter, and various search engines handle them differently.

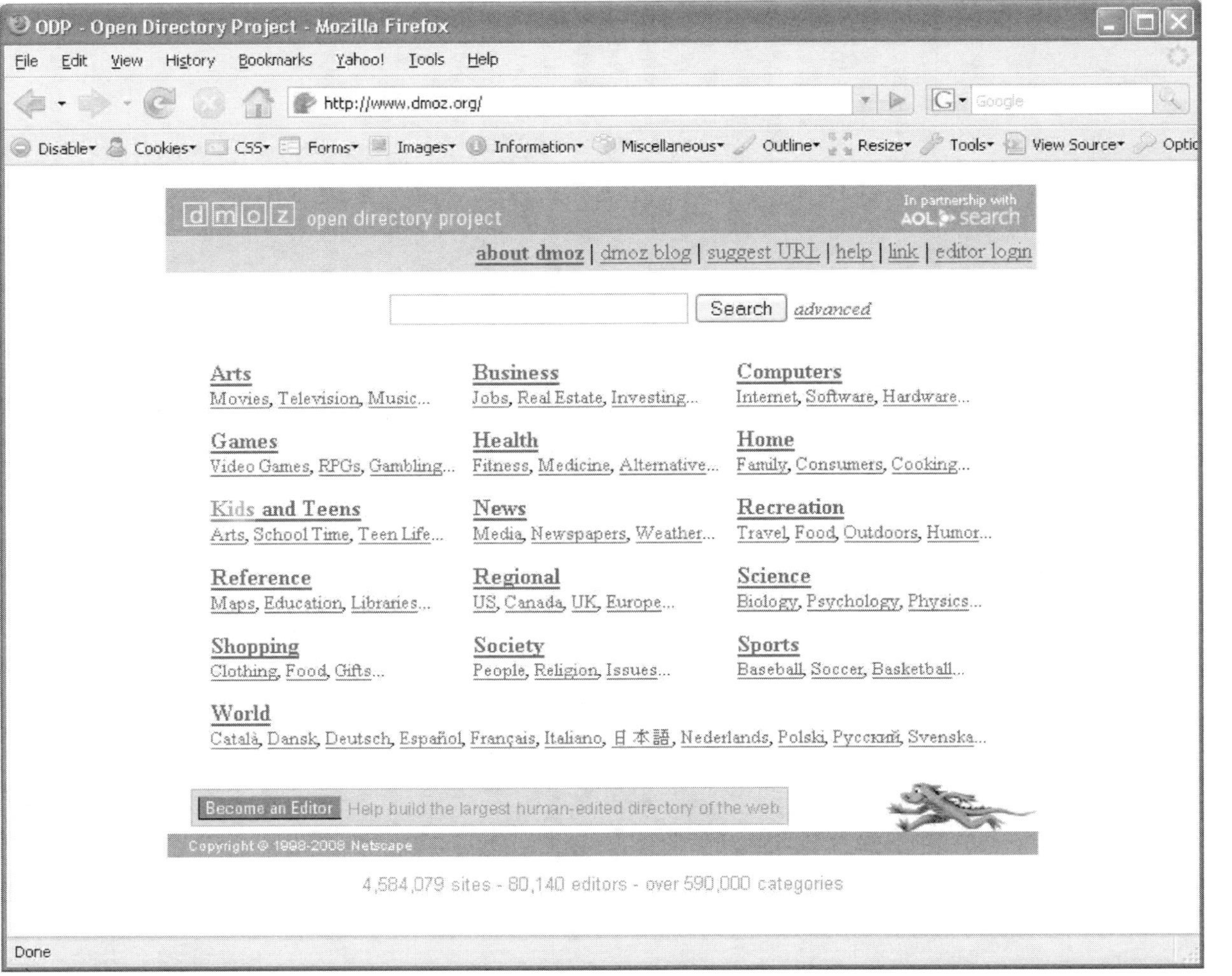

Figure 15.2 The DMOZ Open Directory Project.

Many search engines have common approaches to advanced search features such as the use of quotation marks to indicate a phrase search, or the use of a plus (+) or minus (–) sign to force a term to be present or absent. For instance, a searcher interested in World War I zeppelins but not the rock group Led Zeppelin might be able to exclude potential false hits by the search "zeppelin –Led." In addition, many search engines allow for complex Boolean searching as well as restriction techniques such as limiting results to date ranges, media type, or Internet domain location. All these features require some exploration of the advanced options that ideally are well-documented on the site.

Metasearch Engines

Metasearch engines enable simultaneous search processing by many individual search engines. This approach is very useful for existence searches, and it is especially helpful for comprehensive searches, where as much information as possible is sought on a topic. There are large differences in the coverage of the major search engine indexes. As will be discussed later, there is evidence that there is surprisingly little overlap among them (Dogpile.com, 2007; Mowshowitz & Kawaguchi, 2002; Notess, 2002). Consequently, the total reliance on just a single search engine very likely results in the omission of potentially important retrievals. The metasearch engine attempts to solve this problem by broadcasting the query to multiple search engines or by creating an index that combines multiple indexes. The metasearch engine removes duplicate retrievals from the resulting set and sorts the output by the search engine it came from or with some type of dynamic categorization.

There are disadvantages to the metasearch approach. First, the search results are dependent on the underlying search engines the metasearch happens to include, and sometimes that array of search engines is not optimal for a particular search. Second, not all search engines support the same feature set, and various "power searching" options are often not available. Even when a metasearch engine allows inclusion of advanced search options, the search results may still be different from what would be obtained directly from the individual search engine itself. Popular metasearch engines include Meta crawler.com, Dogpile.com, and Mamma.com. Figure 15.3 shows the Mamma. com interface.

THE ECONOMICS OF SEARCH ENGINES

On the surface, the economics of search engines seems somewhat puzzling as they apparently provide services with no cost to the user. Before Web search engines, online services such as DIALOG and Lexis-Nexis developed a business model that required user accounts to be charged for searching based on the amount of time connected, the number of searches performed, the number of records viewed or printed, or some combination of these approaches. There were a few early attempts to mimic this fee-based model with Web search, but the overall Internet culture of "free access" worked against it. For instance, InfoSeek initially began with a pay as you go model but abandoned it by 1996.

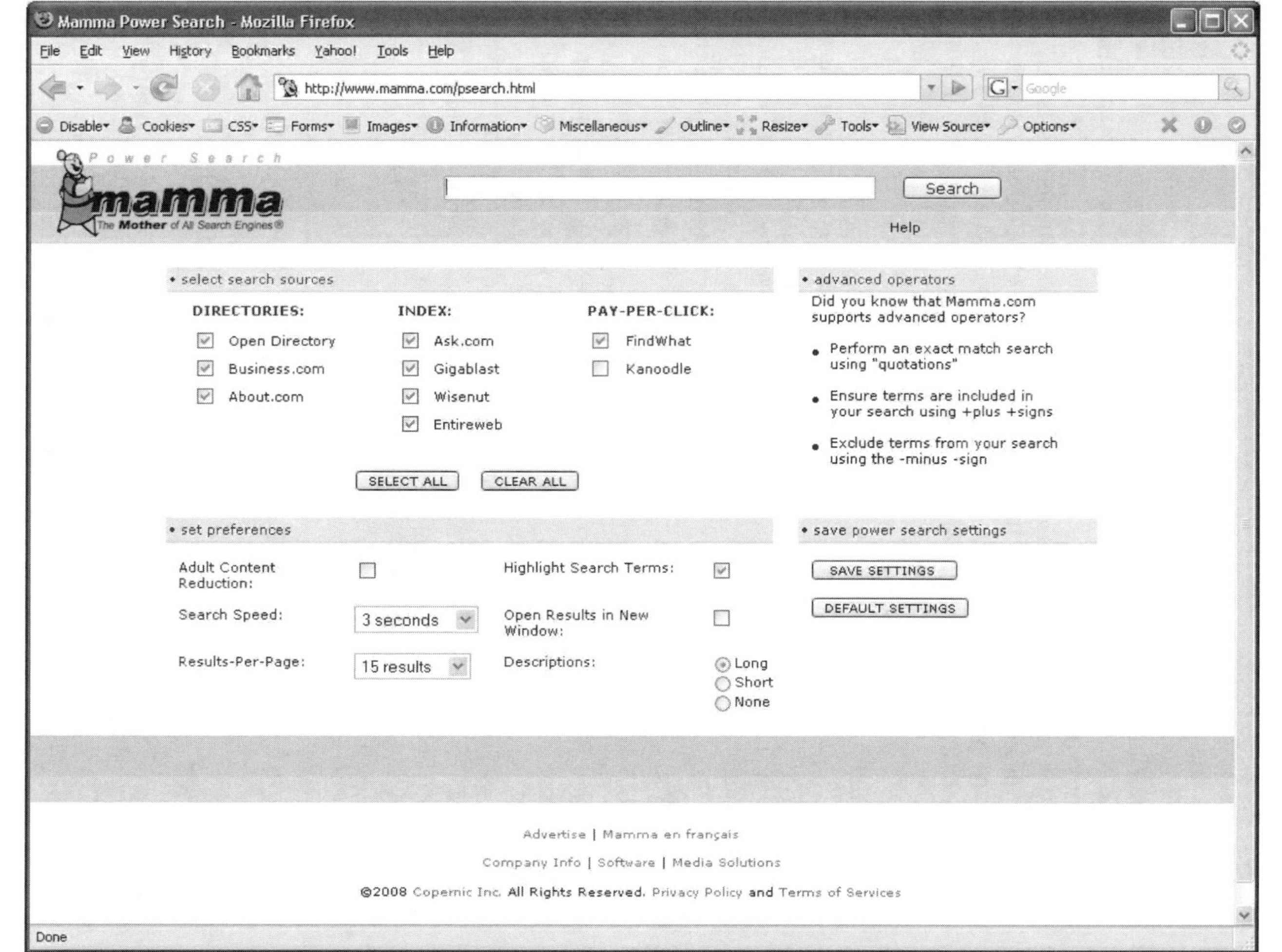

Figure 15.3 The options for the metasearch engine Mamma.com.

There are also opposite precedents—the Northern Light search engine began as a free service but switched to a fee model that has found success in a corporate marketplace. The economic model of search engines is similar to that of commercial television—it is technically free, but a number of minutes for each program slot are devoted to advertising that viewers may or may not want to watch.

Search engines are technology companies, but they are also media companies because most of their revenue comes from advertising (Mills, 2005). These companies have been quite successful financially; for instance, Google and Yahoo reported revenues of $6.139 billion and $5.3 billion, respectively, in 2005. Advertising income is generated in a variety of ways: paid banner ads, which all users see; the "click through" model, where payment is based not just on ad placement but on the number of users who click through to the site; and the pay-for-action approach where advertisers pay when the ad leads to a specific action such as a sale (Broder, Fontoura, Josifovski, & Riedel, 2007). There are also sponsored links that result from "term leasing," where advertisers bid on associating their link with a specific search term. Sponsored link ads targeted to the search query may be useful for certain types of searches, but they can also be distracting. Most search engines distinguish sponsored links from other retrievals by visually segregating them from the rest of the retrieval set. There are concerns that payment by advertisers could influence the ranking process in ways that would not be apparent to the user. A related issue is the potential for search engines to track user searching and sell or report this information to a third party. Privacy concerns also arise with personalized searching based on a user-supplied profile.

Search engines have other potential sources of income such as payments from ISPs or corporations for inclusion of a toolbar or link to the search engine, or revenue from marketing the search technology as a site search appliance. Nevertheless, the dominant economic activity that supports most of these companies is income from various types of advertising. There have been many buyouts and mergers of these services, and many services "outsource" certain functions to another engine or directory. The importance of search as a technology business model is evidenced not just by Google's financial success but also by Microsoft's interest in acquiring Yahoo.

SEARCH ENGINE SIZE AND INDEXICAL BIAS

Over the years, search engines engaged in promoting their index size both in relation to other search indexes and to the estimated size of the entire Web. Sites such as Search Engine Watch and Search Engine Showdown compared index sizes of various search engines over time, but many services no longer report these data. However, it is reasonable to expect that some of the trends from previous index size studies indicate there could be potentially large differences in the comprehensiveness of these indexes. Figure 15.4 shows the results of one such comparison done by Notess (2002). As of mid-2008, Gil (2008) estimates that Google indexes 12.5 billion Webpages, an impressive accomplishment to be sure, but even that represents only about 17 percent of his estimate of the total number of Webpages.

Search Engine	Showdown Estimate (millions)	Claim (millions)
Google	3,033	3,083
AlltheWeb	2,106	2,112
AltaVista	1,689	1,000
WiseNut	1,453	1,500
Hotbot	1,147	3,000
MSN Search	1,018	3,000
Teoma	1,015	500
NLResearch	733	125
Gigablast	275	150

Figure 15.4 Chart data from showing 2002 index size comparison (Notess, 2002).

Studies comparing results of a standard query sent to various search engines have documented significant differences in index coverage. Notess (2002) examined index overlap by analyzing the results of 4 simple, standardized searches on 10 different search engines. He found 334 total hits, 141 of which were specific Web pages. Of that set, about half (71) were found by only 1 of the 10 search engines; another 30 of these unique hits were found by just 2. A research report from the metasearch engine Dogpile reports three different studies from April 2005, July 2005, and April 2007 that compared large sets of user-defined queries across common search engines. The first examined the results of 10,316 queries across Google, Yahoo, and Ask Jeeves and found that only 3.2 percent of the first screen results were the same for a given query. The July 2005 study examined over 12,000 queries and found that only 1.1 percent of the first pages results were the same across these four search engines. The April 2007 study of over 19,000 queries found that on average only 0.6 percent of the results for a given query were the same across the tested search engines. The researchers concluded that the results provided by different search engines are fairly unique (Dogpile.com, 2007).

Index overlap is also described as *indexical bias*. The word *bias* can have a negative connotation, but in this context, bias refers simply to the hidden assumptions that are inherent in the design and implementation of search engines. Mowshowitz and Kawaguchi (2002) examined indexical bias differences among search engine indexes, finding that the identical query of "home refrigerators" resulted in considerable differences among the top 50 retrievals gathered from nine well-known search engines. They reported 309 of the 450 retrievals examined were distinct, representing 231 unique sites. Examining the URL strings for the retrieved sets revealed very different frequency patterns of well-known brand names; for instance, the brand name "Amana" in a URL appeared only once and with just one search engine.

These studies reveal that search engine index overlap, or indexical bias, is of theoretical interest and a practical concern. They suggest that comprehensive searching therefore benefits from the use of more than a single search engine in order to compensate for inconsistent and variable index coverage. Metasearch services, even with their limitations, can be a useful strategy to address this issue.

INTERNET SEARCH ENGINE ANATOMY

Search engines and their associated programs perform the essential functions that facilitate Web search. They identify URLs of pages to index, manage the resulting URL database, harvest content from identified resources and parse it into an index, provide the search-user interface, accept queries and match them to the index, and present ranked output to the user. Along the way, these activities perform other useful secondary functions, such as providing estimates of the size of the indexable Web, identifying dead links, and caching pages to create an archive of pages no longer available. What follows is a general description of this process; Maze, Moxley, and Smith (1997) provide additional details.

The URL Database

The first step to building a search engine is to identify Web URLs. Most search engines accept URLs submitted by content producers, but the vast majority of the URL database is the result of the actions of spider programs. The process of automated discovery begins with a Web crawler program, also known as a spider or more generically, a robot, retrieving all URLs it can locate. Set loose on the Web, these programs follow every link they find according to program parameters that determine how they are to proceed. Spider programs may follow Web links using a breadth-first or depth-first strategy. Breadth-first, the most common method, is when the crawler follows the first link in a page and then all the links in that secondary page before returning to the first page to repeat the process with the next link it contains. In the depth-first approach, the first link in each page is followed, so the first link in a second-level page would be followed, and then the first link in that page, and so on with the result that the spider drills down as far as it can before returning to the original page with that first link. Both approaches require a queue of URLs to be tracked; the breadth-first approach adds new links by appending them to the end of the queue in a "first in first out" strategy; depth-first spiders use a "last in first out" strategy that adds new URLs to the front of the queue. Spiders differ in how deep into a site they are programmed to go and in whether they follow all links in a page or just a sampling of them. These programming directives to their spiders are responsible for the differences in size and coverage among search engine indexes. The URL database is then sorted and de-duped, resulting in the grouping together of all items from the same domain. Many Internet resources are not included in this process. There are a number of ways content may be overlooked by a Web-crawler, including:

- Non-HTML formats such as PDF files as well as other formats are often not indexed. However, the formats indexed by search engines vary; Google started indexing PDF in February 2001.
- HTML coding can affect spider crawling results. For instance, frame-set files may be independently crawled, resulting in access directly to those pages outside their intended viewing context. In addition, JavaScript code in the HTML is ignored by indexing programs, so pages that depend on scripts are not fully represented in the index.
- Spiders cannot access sites that require authentication or registration.
- Images that appear in a page are indexed only by the filename or with alternate text in the image tag, if available, making image search problematic.
- The Robot Exclusion Protocol, a "netiquette" for robots that is respected by most search engines, can turn away the spider. The site administrator can insert a file called robot.txt with restrictions to the visiting robot to keep away from the server or restrict specific areas on it.
- The Robot Metatag with the "noindex" directive within a specific page turns the spider away from that page.
- Dynamic Web content does not exist as a static HTML page to harvest, so it cannot be indexed.

These nonindexed sources by definition become part of the "invisible" Web previously described. However, Web developers may be interested in ensuring a page is included in a search engine index as opposed to keeping it private. One solution is simply to submit the URL; most search engines allow a content creator to submit a site requesting inclusion. The other main way to increase the odds of inclusion is to increase the number of page in-links.

Creating the Index

The next step in the creation of the index involves a robot crawler program, sometimes called a harvester. Its job is to visit the pages in the URL database and harvest content for parsing into an index. The amount of content gathered varies; typically, it is the entire page, but it may be just the head area along with a portion of the body content. The collected pages make up the document store. Stopwords are typically (although not always) eliminated as nonmeaningful terms, and the remaining document terms are melded into an index in the form of an inverted file. Each term has a pointer back to the documents the term appeared in as well as other information such as its frequency and position. The result is a record that can include the term location in a document, the number of occurrences of the term, the total number of words in the entire document, and the HTML tagging associated with it, all of which provide data to the relevance-ranking algorithm.

The User Interface

The user interface provides the functionalities needed to present a query to the query processor. The interface is an HTML form, and scripts process the data the user submits and translate it into an acceptable query for the back-end server. The conversation that takes place between the client and server with such a form uses a GET or POST method, discussed with HTTP.

Such a form interface can be quite simple, as with the well-known single text box of the Google search, or more complex with many options the user can select. There are many design issues embedded in the creation of this interface that affect its success and use. The best underlying search engine technology will not compensate for a poorly designed, cluttered, and difficult-to-use interface. There is an obvious tension between the competing objectives of providing a clean, easy--to-use interface with the concurrent economic need to place banner ads and sponsored links within the same page. Some design tradeoffs tip the balance one way or the other. Some sites do not place any ads on the initial search screen and clearly segregate them in the results, while other services seem to pack in as many ads and pop-ups as possible. The availability of online help and the ease of finding it is another interface issue that differentiates search engines. Some services provide excellent documentation with many search examples; others are almost totally lacking in such documentation.

Query Processing and Relevance Ranking

Once submitted, a query processor handles the search and then ranks the results. These are separate search engine modules, but taken together, they comprise a key functionality that distinguishes one search engine from another. Query processing involves converting the natural language of the searcher into a query the system can accept, executing it, and returning a retrieval set. The ranking module determines the size of the set presented and the ranking order. Most search engines view their query processing and result-ranking algorithms as proprietary information and, consequently, do not make all the details of this process available.

Search engines make use of the classic IR models discussed in the previous chapter, applying them individually or in some combination. Many rely on the Boolean model, but term weighting expands strict Boolean to incorporate factors such as the number of occurrences of the term compared to the size of the document and the order of the terms in the query. A simple Boolean search of the inverted file usually determines an initial retrieval set; this set might be returned to the searcher as is, or if it is large, further processing using term weights could be performed. Some search engines have adopted a vector space approach. The Inktomi search engine utilized the vector space model, but the full implementation of this model is constrained by both computational expense and scalability issues (Langville, 2005). Search engine use of the probabilistic model is also limited by its complexity and scalability limits. However, some probability related approaches have been successful; the creators of the Google Page Rank algorithm describe it as an attempt to determine a probability distribution derived from link analysis.

Link Analysis and Retrieval Rankings

Link analysis can have multiple connotations depending on the kind of "link" that is examined. The term is used in the context of national security intelligence gathering and data mining, where it applies to following communication links to determine a social network of connected people. In the context of Internet search, however, it refers to algorithmic ways of exploiting the hypertext structure of the Web to influence the filtering and ranking of a retrieval set. Conceptually, link analysis is similar to citation analysis in the core idea that a measure of the importance of a work within a discipline is associated with both its citation frequency and the prestige of the sources that cite it; it is reasonable to assume that a work cited many times is important in that discipline. Citation analysis provides a metric for measuring the impact of journals known as the *journal impact factor* (Garfield, 1972). In the hypertext Web, embedded links are a form of citation, so it is not surprising that link analysis could contribute to both creating retrieval sets and their subsequent ranking. However, link analysis techniques, while tied to the idea of citation analysis, do not depend exclusively on simple numbers of links to determine a measure similar to Garfield's impact factor. There are notable differences between citation patterns within printed scientific literature and the nature of Web hyperlinks that must be considered in search engines implementations (Chakrabarti et al., 1999). The goal of a search engine is to deliver Web pages that are judged both *relevant* and *authoritative*. Although this judgment is ultimately a human one, link analysis techniques can provide viable algorithmic solutions.

Two models for hypertext link analysis have been used in Web search; perhaps best known is PageRank developed by Sergey Brin and Lawrence Page, the Google founders. However, Brin and Page were not the only ones working on link analysis during the 1990s. During the same general period they were developing Google at Stanford, Jon Kleinberg had developed the Hypertext Induced Topic Search (HITS) model (Kleinberg, 1999). Although Kleinberg did not develop this concept into a public company as did the Google developers, a prototype engine called Clever was developed (Chakrabarti et al., 1999). In addition, the Teoma search engine also adopted this algorithm (Langville & Meyer, 2006). Both the HITS and PageRank models are of interest to this discussion.

Relevance is not easy to determine automatically, and the nature of the query plays a role in how difficult the task is for a program. Very specific queries are easier to handle as the retrieval set tends to be relatively small, and the judgment of relevance is based on the presence or absence of the "answer" sought. However, general queries usually retrieve larger sets, and the degree of fit to the query is harder to automatically assess. Kleinberg (1999) observed that specific queries are affected by the *scarcity problem,* that is, there may be few pages relevant to a very specific query and it may be difficult to find them, and broad queries give rise to the *abundance problem,* that is, the set of pages returned can be too large for a person to digest. Further, he notes that within a very large retrieval set, a process that would filter the set to retain the most *authoritative* sources is desirable, and this is the primary goal of the HITS model he developed.

Assessing authority is the subjective process of assessing the significance and trustworthiness of the information presented. Kleinberg's (1999) work suggests that link analysis can provide an algorithmic solution to this problem. The key idea of HITS is that if Page A links to Page B, then the creator of Page A must have deemed Page B to be worthy of the link; in that way Page A has *conferred* some degree of *authority* to Page B.

In the HITS model, pages are *nodes.* The model presumes that a query has yielded some initially large retrieval set, and that set is further restricted to a relatively small subset consisting of the highest ranked retrievals. This subset is referred to as the *root set,* and it can be expanded to form a base set by including other pages identified by having links to and from any of the root set pages. This expanded set can then be further refined through link analysis with the goal of finding pages that are not just relevant but also the most *authoritative.* The HITS model attempts to identify these computationally. Within the root set, there are pages that link to other pages within that set. The number of pages that link to a given page provides a measure of the *in-degree* for that page, and the number of pages it links to is the *out-degree* of that page. Pages with a high measure of out-degree are *hubs,* and pages with high in-degree are *authorities.*

In this model, good hubs point to good authorities, and good authorities are linked to good hubs, as diagrammed in Figure 15.5. This sounds circular, as does the PageRank process discussed later, but Kleinberg's (1999) work showed that if this iterative algorithm is run a sufficient number of times, the results converge to values that turn out to be useful in determining relevance. In his model, the identification of hubs and authorities is therefore mutually

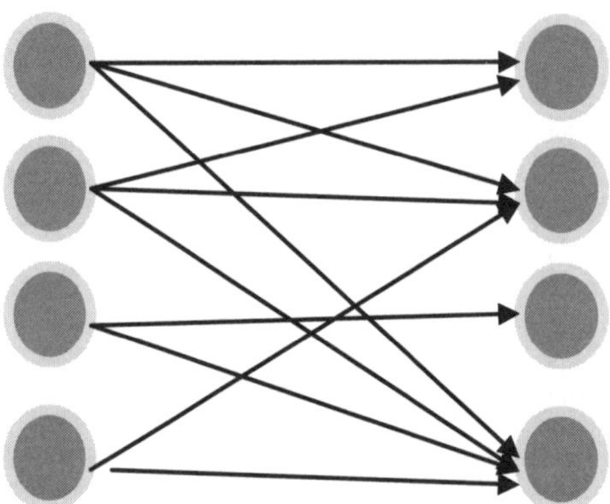

Figure 15.5 A set of hubs on left point to authorities on right (Kleinberg, 1999).

reinforcing, and hubs can serve to connect together different authority groupings within a specific subject area.

GOOGLE: AN EXAMPLE OF A LARGE-SCALE SEARCH ENGINE

Google is a leader among search engines; by 2005, Google was estimated to handle 45 percent of all Internet searching (Mills, 2005). Google is not just the name of a company, but a term used as a verb (to "google" something) as well as a trend ("googlization"). Google warrants a closer look because it is a recognized leader in the search marketplace, and as such, it frames the expectations of the public regarding interface, ease of use, and search efficiency. In addition, Google uses novel approaches to relevance ranking, including PageRank, an interesting application of link analysis.

Google History and Background

The success story that is Google is well-known. Developed in 1998 by Sergey Brin and Larry Page while they were graduate students at Stanford (Brin & Page, 1998), Google's search architecture utilizes a link-based retrieval model they had been working on since 1995 called PageRank (PR). The company name was derived from the word "googol" or 10^{100} (10 raised to the 100th power) (Brin & Page, 1998).

Google has become a Web phenomenon, handling about 543 million searches per day by 2007 (Smalera, 2007). Google has always strived to be the largest, most comprehensive of the Web indexes. The sheer volume of data that it stores is difficult to assess accurately, but as of mid-2007, data from Google itself led some experts to estimate it manages at least 20 petabytes of data on its servers; some reports speculate this figure could be as high as 200 petabytes (Smalera, 2007). A petabyte is about 1 million gigabytes, or about 1,000 terabytes. Numbers that big are hard to conceptualize, but to put this in perspective, consider that if a 30 gigabyte iPod can hold about 10,000 songs, a 1 petabyte iPod could hold about 300 million.

Google is impressive, but is it "smart"? Artificial intelligence (AI) has represented a "holy grail" of computing throughout its history, from the time of the proposed "Turing test" to the present. Traditional AI research has sought to create a "thinking" program that can interact with people (think of HAL in the film *2001: A Space Odyssey*), but much AI research has shifted focus to the relationship between embodiment and intelligence as needed in the field of robotics (Pfeifer & Bongard, 2007). Google is not an "intelligent" program by traditional AI standards, but even so, it can make inferences from its data. In a 2003 colloquium on data-driven textual and motion in graphics, Alexei Efros (2003) referred to Google as AI for the postmodern world, observing that whatever "intelligence" Google has is in the data itself, as represented in its index and the queries it receives. In this view, all questions have already been asked and answered; the challenge is not to create an answer, but to find one. Google's term spelling suggestions are from data associations and not a dictionary. When Google asks, "Did you mean. . .?" it reflects an inference that certain term combinations or spellings are much more common than others (Efros, 2003).

Google Infrastructure

The high level of search demand and the huge amount of data Google manages requires novel data management and parallel processing techniques. Google's data resides on about 200 server clusters in data centers around the world. Google's sophisticated networking software allows the use of relatively inexpensive PCs that have two dual-core processors, two hard drives, and cooling fans to dissipate heat (Barroso, Dean, & Hölzle, 2003). Each rack can hold up to 80 such machines, and parallel processing techniques allow the replacement of drives or whole PCs without interrupting service. Google depends on thousands of commodity class PCs with fault tolerant software as opposed to fewer high-end servers, a creative strategy that they have found to be a more economical approach to handle its enormous workload (Barroso et al., 2003).

Google Architecture

The decision to use commodity class PCs forced the developers to treat component failures as the norm as opposed to the exception. The resulting Google File System (GFS) economically handles the large-scale workloads but regularly and transparently repairs any damage such failure can cause to data integrity (Ghemawat, Gobioff, & Leung, 2003). Google runs three crawlers simultaneously that can crawl about 100 pages per second. Web documents are cached, assigned a document ID, and stored in compressed form in a repository. Document words, called occurrences or hits, are assigned a word ID to create a lexicon of over 14 million words. Information is stored about each hit, such as its position in the document as well as text decoration and capitalization. Links are extracted and stored in an anchors file, which allows further link analysis and weighting. This system, as diagrammed in Figure 15.6, is based on that presented by Brin and Page (1998).

Google and Relevance Ranking

Google's reputation and success is built largely on the efficiency of its relevance ranking of results. In addition to PageRank, which is discussed in some detail next, Google is also known to make use of other document features, such as text decoration. For instance, text in bold or in certain HTML fields is weighted more highly to reflect the emphasis given to the term by the document creator. Google also handles anchor text differently than some search engines. Instead of treating anchor text as other words in the document that are taken to represent the page they come *from*, Google treats anchor text as descriptive of the page the link *points to*. The creator of the page has actually already made that determination by choosing those words for the link; anchor text is therefore a form of human-assigned metadata for the

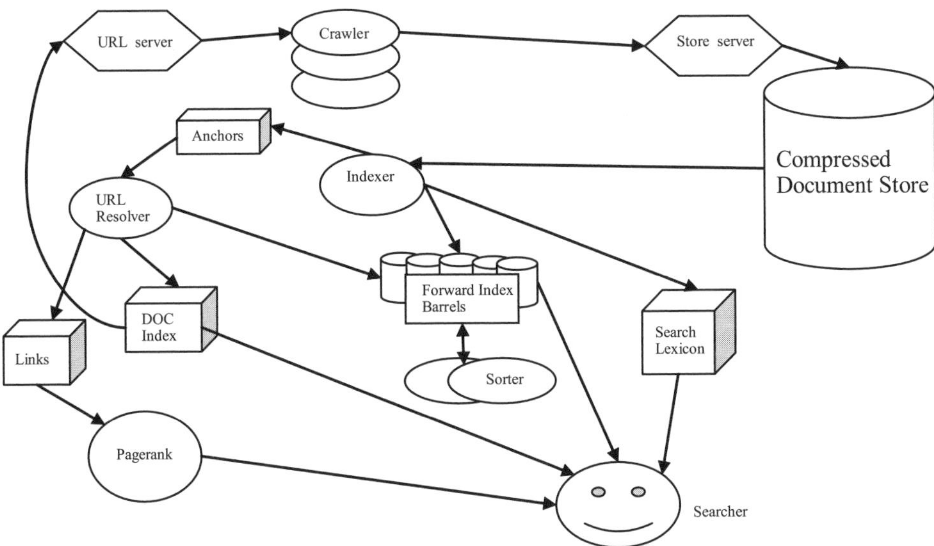

Figure 15.6 High-level view of the Google architecture as diagrammed by Brin and Page (1998). Multiple crawlers gather pages from lists of locations provided by the URL server, which are then sent to the store server and assigned a DocID, and a compressed form is saved in the document store/repository. The indexer uncompresses and parses the pages, and the terms, numbers of occurrences, and locations in the document are stored in "barrels" to form a sorted forward index. The indexer also extracts link information and stores it in the anchors file with the result that anchor text words in the forward index have pointers to the DocID of linked resource. The URL resolver uses the anchors file to store information about in-links and out-links to determine PageRanks. The extracted document words also form the lexicon of search terms for the searcher (Brin & Page, 1998).

linked resource. Another advantage of recognizing anchor text as unique is that links extend the coverage of the index to those sites, even if the Google Web crawler has not visited them. These features all contribute to Google's success, but their PageRank algorithm for ranking is its best-known feature and is discussed next.

Page Rank

On April 1, 2002, Google posted a description of their relevance ranking technology, described as "PigeonRank," which utilizes low cost "Pigeon Clusters" (PCs) (http://www.google.com/technology/pigeonrank.html). Of course, this was an "April Fool's Day" joke; Google does have a sense of humor. While this view is entertaining, PageRank does not have anything to do with pigeons. Google's PageRank algorithm utilizes link analysis for relevance ranking by viewing hypertext links as a "vote" for the importance of the pages linked to by the author making the link. Brin and Page (1998) describe PageRank as a representation of a hypothetical view of user behavior, described with the following scenario: Assume a Web user seeks a Web page only by browsing and following links but can never use the browser "Back" button. At any time, the user can decide to request a new random starting point for their browsing. The probability that the user visits a particular page is its PageRank; the probability that they request a new starting point is the damping factor used in the PageRank algorithm.

A simplified overview of the mathematics of this model is not too daunting and is sufficient for a basic understanding of how PageRank works. First, there are some terms to define. *PageRank* (PR) is the numeric ranking determined by Google for each page and used as a factor in relevance ranking; higher PR values imply higher relevance. A *backlink* is when a page has a link to it from another page. Brin and Page (1998) describe the algorithm as follows:

> We assume page A has pages T1 . . . Tn which point to it (i.e., are citations). The parameter d is a damping factor which can be set between 0 and 1. We usually set d to 0.85. There are more details about d in the next section. Also C(A) is defined as the number of links going out of page A. The PageRank of a page A is given as follows:
>
> PR(A) = (1-d) + d (PR(T1)/C(T1) + . . . + PR(Tn)/C(Tn))
>
> Note that the PageRanks form a probability distribution over web pages, so the sum of all web pages' PageRanks will be one. (p. 4)

There are some key observations from the previous mathematical expression that reflect what factors affect the PR of Page A. The PR of Page A is higher when:

1. There are many pages that link to it. The larger the set of pages T1–Tn is, the larger the summation of their collective contributions.
2. Each of individual contributions of pages T1–Tn to Page A's PR is higher when:
    a. They have fewer outgoing links, represented by the variable C in the denominator of each term. This means the value of a link to Page A is lessened when the page that links to it has a large number of links to other pages.
    b. They have high PR values themselves (a factor in the numerator of the each term in the summation).

However, the PR calculation also invites some questions. What is the *damping factor* shown by the variable *d*, and why is it usually set to 0.85? Moreover, even more puzzling, there is the apparent paradox of needing to know the PR of the pages that point to Page A before calculating its PR; how can those PRs be calculated if they too depend on calculating other PRs?

Of these questions, the damping factor issue is relatively straightforward. The variable *d* occurs in two places in this expression. It is in the first term of the formula where it is subtracted from 1 and occurs again when it is used in a product with the cumulative summation of all the PR terms. It is called the damping factor because when the summation of the terms is multiplied by *d*, it will reduce (or dampen) their total collective contribution. Its occurrence in the first term (1–d) has two effects: first, it means that even a page with no backlinks will have some PR; second, as noted in the quote from Brin and Page

(1998), it creates a probability distribution, which means that the sum of all PRs is 1. The value 0.85 as the damping factor has been determined by the developers to optimize the PR process.

As for the problem of calculating a PR that depends on calculating other PR values first, Brin and Page (1998) explain it as follows: "PageRank or *PR*(*A*) can be calculated using a simple iterative algorithm, and corresponds to the principal eigenvector of the normalized link matrix of the web" (p. 4). A discussion of eigenvectors or Markov chains is not essential to a "big picture" view; the simplified answer is that the formula starts with an estimated initial PR value, and with not too many subsequent iterations of the calculation, the values trend to an acceptably useful PR value (Rogers, 2002).

PageRank has proved to be effective in relevance ranking of retrieval sets, but it is also susceptible to manipulation, as demonstrated by the creation of link bombs. A *link bomb* refers to a coordinated effort to mislead the PR algorithm by deliberately creating links from certain words to a targeted page of interest. This technique is attributed to Weblogger Adam Mathes who created one in 2001 that placed a friend's Web page as the top retrieval for the search "talentless hack" (Tatum, 2005). A well-known example of link manipulation resulted in a Google search using the words "miserable failure" placing President George W. Bush's biography at the top of the retrieval set. Such manipulation does not take a large-scale effort; it is estimated this result may have taken as few as 32 (BBC News, 2003), and certainly no more than several hundred (Sullivan, 2004), pages submitted to Google with links to the Bush page using that anchor text with those terms. Google has since made changes to its algorithm to detect and prevent such manipulation of the PR rankings. To summarize, the main ideas in this discussion of link analysis are:

1. Citation analysis is useful in determining the importance and authority of sources, and this principle can be adapted to the hypertext nature of the Web.
2. The hypertext structure of the Web can be exploited algorithmically to provide numeric rankings that factor into a determination of relevance and/or authority.
3. There are different models for link analysis, two of which are HITS and PR.
4. HITS is primarily about identifying authorities and the hubs that interconnect them.
5. The calculation of Google PR for pages in a retrieval set is used in overall ranking. The PR of a given page is determined by both the number of pages that link to a page and the PR of those pages.

PEER-TO-PEER

Peer-to-peer (P2P) employs a distributed computing model for information seeking and represents an alternative to the large-scale, centralized indexes typical of most search engines. One implementation of peer-to-peer file sharing is the Gnutella software. Gnutella gained considerable notoriety with the Napster music sharing service, which after numerous legal challenges has become a fee-based service. Other similar services using this P2P model are Kazaa and LimeWire. Although these music distribution services have been one of the main uses of P2P, Gnutella P2P is an agnostic service; that is, the type of information requested or served does not matter (Ding, Nutanong, & Buyya, 2003). Therefore, P2P approaches are applicable to many types of file and information sharing, from simple text messaging and bookmark sharing to the shared computational activities of the "SETI at Home" project, which uses millions of personal computers to analyze radio telescope data for signs of extraterrestrial life.

In P2P, multiple computers running a common client can share tasks, messages, or search queries. A computer in the network sends a query to the computers in its immediate "neighborhood" of participating systems for processing, and each recipient performs a search of its local index. If the query is not answered, each computer in the initial neighborhood would pass it on to an ever-expanding network of participating systems. The number of hosts working on the search can become very large very quickly, and the larger and more diverse the network is, the higher the likelihood of finding an appropriate answer.

P2P information services are somewhat analogous to a party game where one person in a room can ask a question of the three people around them. If none of those three people knows the answer, they can each pass the query to the three people around each of them. If none of those nine additional people knows the answer, each of the nine can then query three more people in an ever-widening pool of potential sources of an answer, until eventually someone who knows the answer sends it directly to the person who started the process. The success of the game depends on the nature of the query, the number of people in the room, and the knowledge of the individuals present. There are many distributed search engines based on P2P, and the O'Reilly P2P site lists more than two dozen of them, including the Clip2 Distributed Search Solutions for technical data and research aimed at Gnutella developers and users and the Eikon prototype for distributed image search (O'Reilly Media, Inc., 2008).

CLUSTERING AND VISUALIZATION

The large retrieval sets returned for broad queries create the abundance problem alluded to earlier with the result that searchers are often drowning in information and starved for knowledge. One solution is the use of authority scores based on link analysis as previously described. However, even with good relevance ranking, retrieval sets are often large, and how the set is presented influences search success. A challenge for the user when a large set is retrieved is that the visual presentation of the set is often just a linear list of ranked results. Users often never see potentially excellent retrievals because they rarely scroll through more than the first few screens of results. Clustering technologies can provide visualization techniques that breakup a large set into a number of subsets representing useful categories.

There are services that provide clustered results that organize the search sets into a list of named category folders containing similar retrievals. An early clustering site was the Northern Light search engine, but it is no longer a free Web search service. Vivisimo, WebBrain, and Kartoo are other examples of search engines that combine the clustering of results along with visual displays that attempt to show the relationships among the categories. Sites of this type not only attempt to create a knowledge map of interrelated categories but also often can dynamically rearrange the display based on user input. The "WebBrain" and the metasearch engine "Kartoo" are highlighted here as examples.

WebBrain is a combination directory and search engine. The split screen display has a set of categories that rearrange themselves with topic selection. When the Web search option is used, the category display is organized around the search topics. Figure 15.7 shows the display when drilling down through "Recreation" and highlighting the subcategory "Outdoors." The visualization requires that the JavaVM has been installed with the browser.

The Kartoo visual display is Flash-based, so that software must be installed. Figure 15.8 shows the results of a query "gardening herbs." The Kartoo interface divides the screen vertically and lists topic folders on the left (this part of the display is reminiscent of the Northern Light category folders). The topic interconnections appear in the map area as the cursor hovers over a topic area.

Many library catalog systems are adding mapping features to assist with subject exploration. Visualization and topic mapping represent a promising approach in the battle against information overload. For example, in addition to a traditional search, I can elect to use a visualization tool when searching the local public library catalog. Figure 15.9 is a screen shot of the search "gardening" that shows related topics visually in a dynamic map that accompanies the result set.

SMART AGENTS AND PERSONALIZATION

The idea of "smart agent" software has been around for some time; generally, this refers to software that learns about your interests and can automatically do your bidding by running in the background, searching for new information of interest, and pushing it to you. Ideally, such a program could learn not just from you and your actions but also from other agent programs as well. Many such profile-based systems developed by libraries to anticipate client information needs precede the Web. Services such as selective dissemination of information (SDI) could provide academics with email updates with grant-funding opportunities or new research initiatives in areas of interest. Search engines and other Web technologies such as RSS now allow for much more sophisticated ways to anticipate content of interest to clients that can be "pushed" to them on a regular basis.

Web client–server cookie exchanges can be a simplistic automated form of this type of information update. Cookies serve as an HTTP "state object" used to maintain information about a transaction that is retrievable by the server that set them. When you log into your account in Amazon, the cookie exchange identifies you to the server, and you are welcomed with a list of

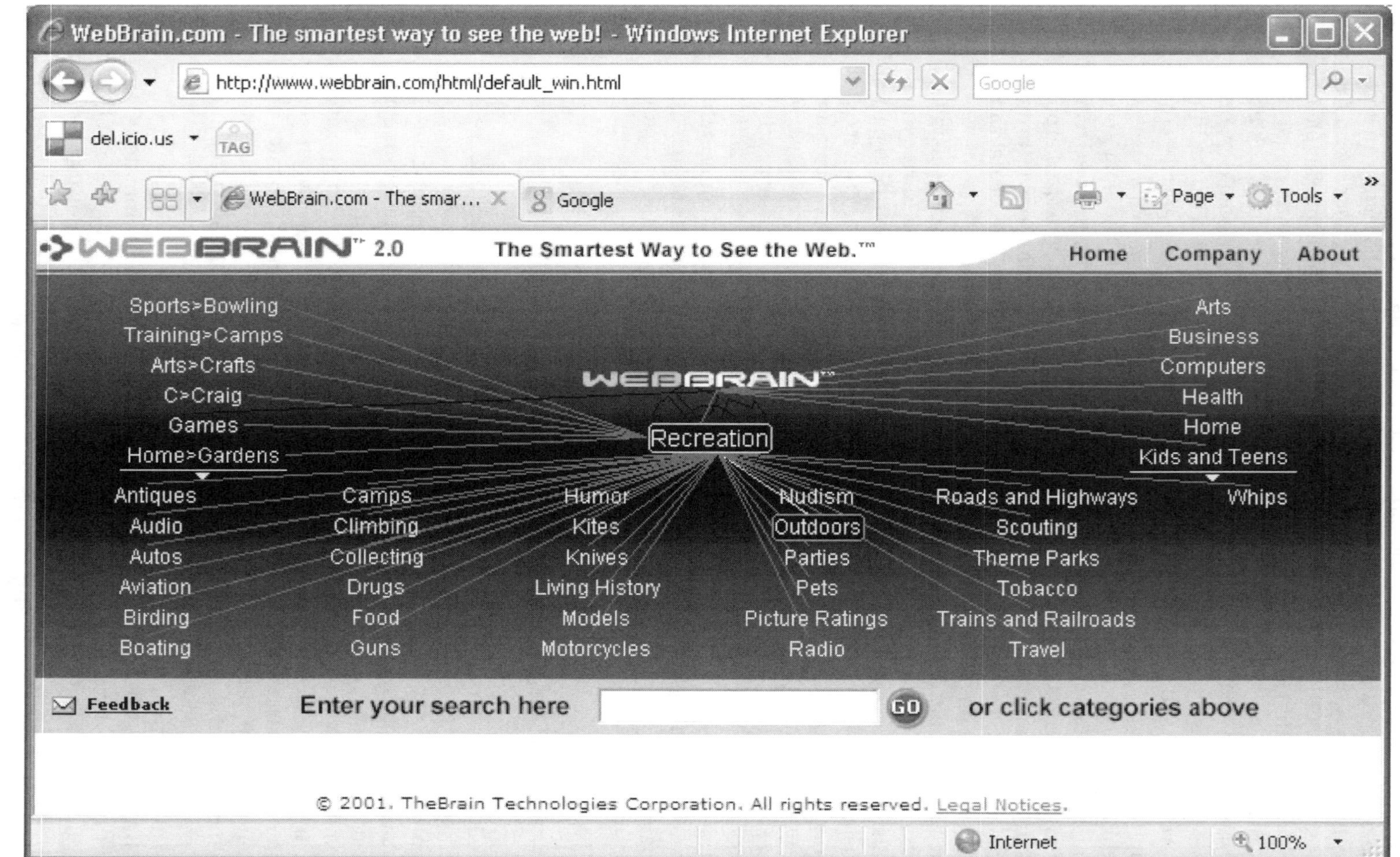

Figure 15.7 Screen shot of Webbrain after selecting the category "recreation" and highlighting "Outdoors."

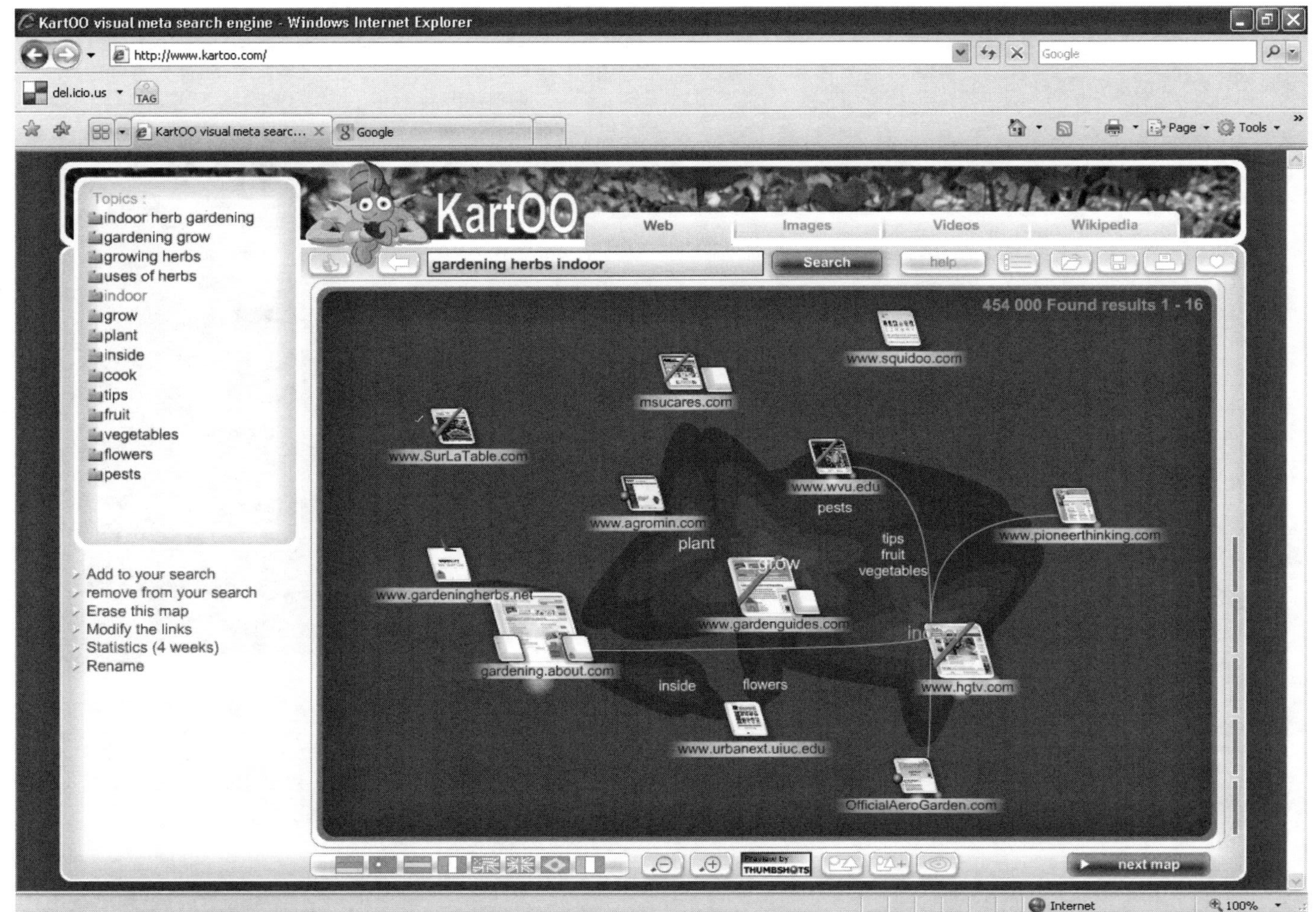

Figure 15.8 Screen shot of the Kartoo metasearch engine after a search for "gardening herbs" and highlighting the "Indoor" category.

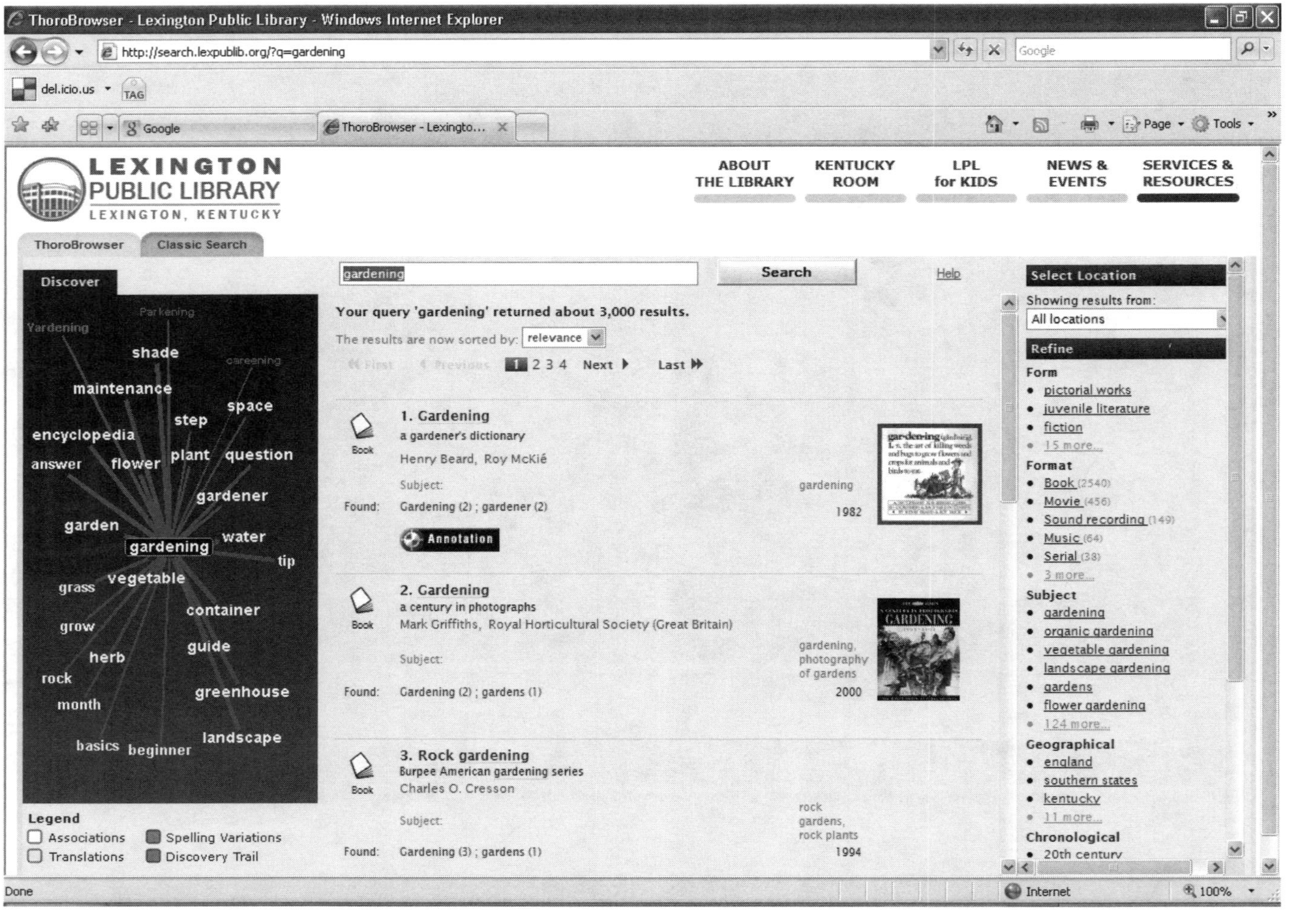

Figure 15.9 Screen shot of a public library search using visualization software.

suggestions of items thought to be of interest to you. These suggestions come from transactional information; consequently, it is not always very "smart" in its recommendations. For instance, if you recently bought gift books for others, the system assumes they reflect your personal interest areas for future shopping.

Personalization techniques have implications for Web search, and many services allow customization of search engine portals with a user profile such as the MyYahoo portal. Search engines can push information to a user based on a profile or automatically filter future search results based on known user interests, but there are privacy concerns raised by such techniques. The Electronic Privacy Information Center (EPIC, http://www.epic.org) has many resources on this issue. For instance, many are concerned with Google's retention of persistent identifiers, such as IP addresses and User IDs (EPIC, 2008). In addition to collecting these data, search engines could also view user profile information as a potential income stream, so there must be clear policies in place that control the use of such information. Information about user searches and its potential use has become a controversial political issue as both the U.S. and Chinese governments have sought information about searches done by users of these services (Associated Press, 2006; Klein, 2008).

COMPARISON WITH TRADITIONAL ONLINE SERVICES

It is informative to conclude this discussion of Internet search with a comparison of these free Web services with the traditional and highly structured online information systems, such as DIALOG and Lexis-Nexis. DIALOG was one of the first online database services used in libraries. The service dates to the 1970s and now provides access to nearly a thousand separate databases. Unlike the free content of the open Web, the company only provides fee-based searching, but the old axiom that "you get what you pay for" holds some truth for some information needs. Although the fee model for these services has not changed, the Internet has affected the cost of using these services. Prior to the Internet, part of the cost was just for the dialup telecommunication fee to make the connection; telnet and HTTP access have eliminated separate connection fees.

DIALOG ensures that the databases they provide have extensive quality control and are well-documented with database information sheets, referred to as "Bluesheets" because they were printed on blue paper. This creates a consistent search environment across all databases using either a single command-based or a graphical Web interface. Both interfaces allow for powerful, controlled searching of multiple indexes along with advanced Boolean set manipulation. In addition to natural language keyword searching with KWIC (keyword in context) display, many of these database indexes utilize a controlled vocabulary with an online thesaurus that facilitates its use. A summary comparison of search engines with DIALOG is in Table 15.1.

Free Web-based searching has changed how the public goes about looking for information and has given many people the impression that every kind of information they seek is easily findable with a Web search engine. However, given the issues explored in this chapter as well as the nature of the

TABLE 15.1 Comparison of Internet Search with DIALOG

Feature	Internet Search Engine	DIALOG
Query Terms	Typically natural language keywords	Both keyword and controlled vocabularies
Indexing	Typically a single index	Multiple indexes allow for more search options (author, personal name, descriptor, etc.)
Interface	Multiple approaches; dependent on the search engine	Single command or Web-based interface; common syntax across all databases
Advanced Search	Limited advanced search options that differ across many search engines	Many advanced search options (proximity searching, set manipulation, field restrictors, etc.)
Database Quality Control	Little to none	Rigorous
Database Organization	Little to none	Catalogued and described
Database Selection	Few options, perhaps restriction by domain or resource type	Hundreds of specialized databases with documentation and selection guidance; search single, multiple, or all databases.
Documentation	Little, often difficult to find	Complete; printed and Web-based

information gaps on the Web, it is clear that for some types of information seeking the fee-based online database services still have an important place. They provide access to specialized information not otherwise available, such as patent and trademark databases or legal information. The databases, rich feature set, and unified search interface available from services such as DIALOG, Lexis-Nexis, or Westlaw allow the expert searcher access to content and search options that is not possible with a general Web search.

SUMMARY

The opportunity and power of free Internet search has transformed both the Internet and its use for information seeking. During its relatively short history, Internet searching has gone from the simple VERONICA index of

Gopher servers to the Google index of billions of pages serving many millions of daily queries. The different types of queries people pose result in the duel problems of scarcity and abundance, and much of Google's success is due to the application of link analysis techniques to these problems. Large retrieval sets make finding the best items within the returned set an added challenge. The presentation of large retrieval sets with categorization and/or visualization techniques organize the items into meaningful subsets that enhance their usability. Personalization options can improve search effectiveness but pose potential privacy issues. Natural language query presentation is possible by matching previously asked search questions and subsequent retrieval selections but has not yet demonstrated the artificial intelligence needed for true human-computer conversation. A brief comparison of how the current Web search stacks up against searching older, more structured information systems such as DIALOG leads to the conclusion that although Web search has brought a universe of free information to the public, there are still some information needs that are better satisfied with these fee-based systems.

REFERENCES

Associated Press. (2006, January 20). Google won't hand over files. Retrieved October 1, 2007, from http://www.wired.com/politics/law/news/2006/01/70055.

Barroso, L. A., Dean, J., & Hölzle, U. (2003). Web search for a planet: The Google cluster architecture. *Institute of Electrical and Electronics Engineers (IEEE) Micro, 23*(2), 22–28.

Battelle, J. (2005). *The search.* New York: Penguin Group.

BBC News. (2003, December 7). "Miserable failure" links to Bush. Retrieved May 10, 2008, from http://news.bbc.co.uk/2/hi/americas/3298443.stm.

Bergman, M. K. (2001, September 24). The "Deep" Web: Surfacing hidden value. Retrieved October 1, 2007, from http://www.brightplanet.com/images/stories/pdf/deepwebwhitepaper.pdf.

Berners-Lee, T., Hendler, J., & Lassila, O. (2001). The Semantic Web. *Scientific American, 284*(5), 10.

Boutell.com. (2007, February 15). How many websites are there? Retrieved October 1, 2007, from http://www.boutell.com/newfaq/misc/sizeofweb.html.

Brin, S., & Page, L. (1998). *The anatomy of a large-scale search hypertextual Web search engine.* Paper presented at the Proceedings of Seventh World Wide Web Conference, Brisbane, Australia.

Broder, A., Fontoura, M., Josifovski, V., and Riedel, L. 2007. A semantic approach to contextual advertising. In *Proceedings of the 30th Annual international ACM SIGIR Conference on Research and Development in information Retrieval* (Amsterdam, The Netherlands, July 23–27, 2007). SIGIR '07. ACM, New York, NY, 559–566. DOI=http://doi.acm.org/lO.1145/l277741.1277837.

Chakrabarti, S., Dom, B., Kumar, S. R., Raghavan, P., Rajagopalan, S., Tomkins, A., et al. (1999). Hypersearching the Web. *Scientific American, 280*(6), 54–61.

Cheong, F. C. (1996). *Internet agents: Spiders, wanderers, brokers, and bots.* Indianapolis, IN: New Riders Publishing.

de Kunder, M. (2008, September). The size of the World Wide Web. Retrieved September 21, 2008, from http://www.worldwidewebsize.com.

Ding, C. H., Nutanong, S., & Buyya, R. (2003). *Peer-to-peer networks for content sharing.* Melbourne: The University of Melbourne, Australia.

Dogpile. (April 2007). Different engines, different results. Retrieved June 1, 2008, from http://www.infospaceinc.com/onlineprod/Overlap-DifferentEngines DifferentResults.pdf.

Efros, A. (2003). Data-driven texture and motion. In *University of Washington Computer Science and Engineering Colloquia.* The University of Washington. Retrieved October 1, 2007, from http://www.researchchannel.org/prog/displayevent.aspx?rID=3244&fID=345.

Electronic Privacy Information Center (EPIC). (2008, May 21). Congressman Barton urges scrutiny of Google's privacy practices. Retrieved June 1, 2008, from http://epic.org.

Garfield, E. (1972). Citation analysis as a tool in journal evaluation. *Science, 178*(4060), 471–479.

Ghemawat, S., Gobioff, H., & Leung, S.-T. (2003, December). *The Google file system.* Paper presented at the Proceedings of the 19th ACM Symposium on Operating Systems Principles, Bolton Landing, NY.

Gil, P. (2008, July). What is "The invisible Web"? Retrieved September 14, 2008, from http://netforbeginners.about.com/cs/secondaryweb1/a/secondaryweb.htm.

Gulli, A., & Signorini, A. (2005). *The indexable Web is more than 11.5 billion pages.* Paper presented at the WWW 2005, Chiba, Japan.

Hawking, D., & Zobel, J. (2007). Does topic metadata help with Web search? *JASIST, 58*(5), 613–626.

Jeanneney, J.-N. (2006). *Google and the myth of universal knowledge.* Trans. T. L. Fagan. Chicago: University of Chicago Press.

Kahle, B. (1997). Preserving the Internet. *Scientific American, 276*(3), 82–84.

Klein, N. (2008, May 29). China's all-seeing eye: With the help of U.S. defense contractors, China is building the prototype for a high-tech police state. Retrieved May 30, 2008, from http://www.rollingstone.com/politics/story/20797485/chinas_allseeing_eye.

Kleinberg, J. M. (1999). Authoritative sources in a hypertext environment. *Journal of the ACM, 46*(5), 604–632.

Langville, A. N. (2005). The linear algebra behind search engines. Retrieved October 15, 2007, from http://mathdl.maa.org/mathDL/4/?pa=content&sa=viewDocument&nodeId=636. Langville, A. N., & Meyer, C. D. (2006). *Google's PageRank and beyond: The science of search engine rankings.* Princeton, NJ: Princeton University Press.

Lawrence, S., & Giles, C. L. (1998). Searching the World Wide Web. *Science, 280*(5360), 98–100.

Lawrence, S., & Giles, C. L. (1999). Accessibility of information on the Web. *Nature, 400*(6740), 107–109.

Lawrence, S., Coetzee, F., Glover, E., Flake, G., Pennock, D., Krovetz, B., et al. (2000). *Persistence of information on the web: Analyzing citations contained in research articles.* Paper presented at the Conference on Information and Knowledge Management, McLean, Virginia.

Maze, S., Moxley, D., & Smith, D. J. (1997). *Authoritative guide to Web search engines.* New York: Neal-Schuman.

Mills, E. (2005, October 21). Google shares soar on hearty revenue report. Retrieved October 1, 2007, from http://news.com.com/Google+revenue+nearly+doubles/2100-1030_3-5905127.html.

Mowshowitz, A., & Kawaguchi, A. (2002). Bias on the Web. *Communications of the ACM, 45*(9), 56–60.

Notess, G. R. (2002, March 6). Little overlap despite growth! Retrieved October 1, 2007, from http://www.searchengineshowdown.com/statistics/overlap.shtml.

Online Computer Library Center (OCLC). (2002). Web characterization. Retrieved October 1, 2007, from http://www.oclc.org/research/projects/archive/wcp.

O'Reilly Media, Inc. (2008). Distributed search engines. Retrieved October 1, 2007, from http://www.openp2p.com/pub/t/74.

Pfeifer, R., & Bongard, J. C. (2007). *How the body shapes the way we think.* Cambridge: MIT Press.

Rainie, L. (2005, November 20). Search engine use shoots up in the past year and edges towards email as the primary internet application. *Internet and American Life.* Retrieved May 1, 2008, from http://www.pewinternet.org/PPF/r/167/report_display.asp.

Rogers, I. (2002). The Google Pagerank algorithm and how it works. *Google Pagerank whitepaper.* Retrieved October 10, 2007, from http://www.ianrogers.net/google-page-rank.

Smalera, P. (2007, September). Google's secret formula. *Conde Nast Portfolio,* 136–137.

Sullivan, D. (2004, January 6). Google's (and Inktomi's) miserable failure. Retrieved May 1, 2008, from http://searchenginewatch.com/showPage.html?page=3296101.

Sullivan, D. (2005, January 28). Search engine sizes. Retrieved October 1, 2007, from http://searchenginewatch.com/showPage.html?page=2156481#trend.

Tatum, C. (2005). Deconstructing Google bombs: A breach of symbolic power or just a goofy prank? *First Monday, 10*(10).

Vidmar, D., & Anderson, C. (2002). History of Internet search tools. In A. Kent & C. Hall (Eds.) *Encyclopedia of library and information science* (vol. 71, pp. 146–162). New York: Marcel Dekker, Inc.

Zillman, M. P. (November 24, 2007). Deep Web research 2008. Retrieved July 2008, from http://www.llrx.com/fea!IIres/deepweb2008.htm#Resources-Deep.

ADDITIONAL READING

Dornfest, R., Bausch, P., & Calishain, T. (2006). *Google hacks: Tips & tools for smarter searching* (3rd ed.). New York: O'Reilly Media, Inc.

Chapter 16

Libraries and the Internet: Learning from the Past, Exploring the Future

The introduction to this text asserted that the Internet has changed everything. While acknowledging this is perhaps an overstatement in the scheme of human history, it does seem reasonable to make this assertion in the context of libraries and their services. However, the predicted transformative power of the Internet did not begin to be realized until the emergence of the Web in the early 1990s. By the end of that decade, the information super highway metaphor of the pre-Web Internet with its focus on "getting connected" had given way to the power of hypertext and the search capabilities of the Web. In hindsight, it seems it was the Web, and not just the Internet, that changed the world. Now a new world-changing paradigm is emerging, that of Web 2.0, which according to some will inevitably evolve to Web 3.0. Web 2.0 has generated both hyperbole and genuine excitement; the challenge is to identify the trends that will emerge to form the framework of new library services from those that are merely passing fads. Each new phase of technological advancement is usually announced as a revolution. Some will not last; others represent an ongoing technological evolution as opposed to a revolutionary break with the past. When did Web 1.0 become Web 2.0? Obviously, this was not a discrete-time event; there was no announcement that Web 1.9 would rollover to Web 2.0 at midnight one day. In that sense, Web 1.0 will coexist with Web 2.0, Web 3.0, and, very likely, Web 4.0, however that will be defined.

Even without formal definitions, which are attempted later in this chapter, 2.0 has a powerful brand identity, a meme generically representing something modern, new, and improved. Web 2.0 supports or leads to business 2.0 or library 2.0. As will be discussed in this chapter, the transformative energy of Web 2.0 is not derived solely from the collaborative human activities it enables, but also from the morphing of the World Wide Web into the "World Wide Computer." Christensen (2003) describes innovations that can become "disruptive technologies," unleashing forces and opportunities that radically reshape the environment. He describes how entire industries have lost their market leadership by failing to recognize "the next great wave." The cumulative changes of Web 1.0 combined with Web 2.0 applications represent such a disruptive technology, and libraries are not immune to the forces Christensen describes. This adds some urgency to the dilemma of sorting out important trends from fads and presents the challenge of adapting to change while remaining true to the long-standing core values of librarianship.

Much of the perspective of this text is grounded in general Internet and Web 1.0 technologies, which are still relevant to the repositioning of the Web. While Web 2.0 allows much greater participation by those lacking the requisite technology expertise of earlier Internet activities, there is still a need for this expertise in the information professions. The backend technologies, databases, scripts, widgets, mashups, and content management systems used in Web 2.0 still require substantive technology knowledge and skills. Those with a deeper understanding of how these technologies work can advance the usability framework for others. One of the powerful outcomes of the developing Web 2.0 technologies is that by removing technology barriers it allows for expanded participation by those previously kept away by design or a lack of technical knowledge.

This concluding chapter is an opportunity to consider how the Internet, Web, and Web 2.0 have shaped, and continue to shape, the roles of librarians and libraries. The new roles and cultural shifts wrought by Web 2.0 are giving rise to the Library 2.0 model. These shifts are both exciting and disruptive as information professionals must reevaluate, and possibly relinquish, their traditional gatekeeper role and embrace a more participatory model. Some of the technologies that enable Web 2.0 have been addressed in other parts of this text; RSS, blogs, podcasts, and wikis are discussed in the chapters on TCP/IP, Internet protocols, Internet content, and Internet IR. These technologies, as well as some new ones and their applications, are considered holistically in this chapter through the Web 2.0/Library 2.0 lens.

Early in this text, the mnemonic of the "3 Cs," for *computers, connections,* and a *common language,* was used to define the Internet. Now a new "Rule of Cs" has emerged to describe the Web/Library 2.0 shift; Jenny Levine describes the "4 Cs" of Web 2.0 as *"collaboration, community, commons, and conversation"* (Stephens, 2007, p. 7). Web 2.0 has commanded a tremendous amount of attention, and because of its importance to libraries and their services, much of this chapter is devoted to it. This discussion begins by reviewing the relationship between libraries and the Internet as a prelude to discussing current trends. Table 16.1 summarizes the defining properties of the Internet over time.

THE INTERNET IN LIBRARIES: PRE-WEB

To those who grew up with the Web, often referred to as the Google generation or net generation (net gen), the early uses of the Internet probably seem quite primitive and not very exciting. The role of "Internet cheerleader" was a tough sell in the pre-Web environment; the command-based view of the

TABLE 16.1 A Summary of Internet Periods and Their Descriptions, Protocols, and Common Applications in Libraries

Internet Period	Descriptors	Technologies	Applications
Pre-Web (1969–1992)	• Command-based • Textual • Store and forward messaging	• Telnet • Gopher • Email • SLIP/PPP	• Connect to remote catalogs and databases • Email reference • Discussion lists
Web 1.0 (1992–present)	• GUI • Multimedia • Hypertext • Search/Pull/Static • Information silos • IM	• Browsers • Audio streaming • User-centered links • Google • HTTP file delivery	• Informational Web pages • Web delivery of databases/OPAC but no integrated one-search
Web 2.0 (~2004–present)	• Collaborative • Social • Interactive • Functional hybridization (Mashups) • Shared tagging	• Blogs • Wikis • Podcasts • Del.icio.us • Flickr • YouTube • Second Life	• Blogs for internal/external audience • Collaborative knowledge sharing • Virtual library
Web 3.0 (Now–future?)	• Semantic • "Intelligent" Web • Metadata • XML-based	• EAD • RDF • MODS/METS	• Archival finding aids • Metadata interoperability • METS/MODS

original Internet protocols was neither user-friendly nor intuitive, and there was a steep learning curve even for the tech-savvy user. Telnet connections to catalogs, the Online Community Library Center (OCLC), and database services such as DIALOG were useful to librarians and even some patrons, but they did not engage a mass audience. Connectivity was often problematic as there were few Internet service providers, and broadband was only available in the form of T1 or fractional T1 lines, which were often prohibitively expensive. Libraries debated the necessity and desirability of providing general Internet access to the public, as well as the many policy and use issues it introduced. Even those who favored providing Internet access as a key service often found they did not have the computers, infrastructure, or in-house expertise to deliver it; consequently, Internet access for the public was not common in libraries during this period.

WEB 1.0

As described in other chapters of this text, the emergence of the Web changed the Internet environment in significant ways and drove a reinforcing cycle of increased access and use. Viewed with a graphical browser, the Web was an immediate success, and traffic grew quickly; PC sales increased as did demand for bandwidth as the Web captured the attention of businesses and the public. The resulting dot com boom of the late 1990s drove huge investments in infrastructure that has made Internet access and increased bandwidth available throughout much of the United States. By the end of the decade, Internet access was a well-established service in libraries, schools, and most homes. U.S. Census data show the number of homes with computers grew from 15 percent in 1990 to 56 percent by 2001, and homes with Internet access in the United States went from 18 percent in 1997 to 54.3 percent in 2003 (U.S. Census, 2006). By the end of this period, 95 percent of public libraries report having Internet access as a service to their clients (Bertot & McClure, 2000). During this same period, the number of Web pages had grown exponentially; by 2000, Google reported an index of 500 million pages (Sullivan, 2005).

Vast amounts of content were added to the Web each year; the emergence of search engines facilitated access to Internet content and led to one of the major success stories of Web 1.0, the Internet search engine. The huge amount of content combined with powerful, free search engines changed how people used computers for information seeking. Searching has become a dominant activity of the Web, along with email (Rainie, 2005). Internet search engines not only provided viable alternatives to traditional sources of information but forever changed user expectations regarding the information provision role of libraries. Graphical browsers, such as Netscape and Internet Explorer, allowed users to access content through browsing or to facilitate searching. In many ways, searching represents both a defining characteristic and a technology of Web 1.0; the "pull" model for information access, where information is actively sought and requested, is a dominant theme of Web 1.0. Users formulated and submitted queries, resulting in lists of Web pages in the form of static HTML files, which could then be retrieved and displayed. To the majority of users, Google exemplifies the Internet search. Google is both the pinnacle of Web 1.0 technology and a model of Web 2.0 services, highlighting the sometimes-blurred boundaries between Web 1.0 and 2.0.

At its inception, Google laid down an implicit challenge to libraries in its mission statement "to organize the world's information and make it universally accessible and useful" (Google, 2008). This mission is very much the same as that of libraries, and the sense of competition has increased with the development of other Google services such as Google Books and Google Scholar. Studies of how people seek information show that the competition is not just an abstract concern but is very real. A 2002 Pew survey found 73 percent of college students seeking information reported using the Internet more than a library; only 9 percent used a library more than the Internet for information needs (Jones & Madden, 2002). A more recent report found 89 percent of college students begin their searching with a search engine compared to just 2 percent who start with a library Website (OCLC, 2006). The study also found 93 percent of these students report being satisfied or very satisfied with their

Internet searches compared to 84 percent reporting the same level of satisfaction for librarian-assisted searches. Other studies confirm the shift among many types of users from libraries to Internet search engines for information seeking. A British Library study concludes that university collections are not meeting the needs of the Google generation and could be "swept aside by history" unless they adapt and make closer links to Internet search engines (Gill, 2008, para. 1).

This shift in search behaviors and attitudes is occurring across many demographic groups. An illustrative example is from a recent interview on NPR "Morning Edition" about a young boy born with a deadly genetic disorder called Marfan syndrome and a doctor's search for new treatments. The doctor in the story had done research that suggested a drug that blocks a protein called TGF-beta could help this condition. The narrative continued:

> It generally takes years to develop a drug. But Dietz went to his computer, pulled up Google, and typed in "TGF beta-blocking drug." Up popped references to a drug called Losartan, which was on the market as a blood pressure medication but also happened to be very good at stopping TGF-beta. Dietz says it would have been hard to design a better drug. "Losartan has been used to treat tens of millions of people with high blood pressure," he says. "It's known to be an extremely safe and well-tolerated medication." (Kestenbaum, 2008, para. 11)

While anecdotal, it is informative that the doctor turned immediately to Google to find this information instead of a formal database such as PubMed. A preference for easily available sources such as peers is neither new nor unique (Coleman, Katz, & Menzel, 1957). Bates (2002) notes physicians often depend on sales representatives rather than the medical literature for new drug information. That such informal sources are generally preferred over more formal database sources for most queries is not surprising. Google, with its availability, convenience, ease of use, and seemingly relevant results, has become almost like a trusted friend for many.

The public sees little distinction between search engines and libraries, especially because Google offers additional research products and services and is engaged in large-scale digitization projects. However, where some see a threat, others see opportunity. Abram (2005) views the emergence of Google as healthy competition that will not only drive libraries in new directions but also make teaching roles even more important, especially in the context of information literacy. Jerilyn Veldof, director of the University of Minnesota Libraries undergraduate initiatives, also sees this as an opportunity, observing that "libraries are building a bridge between the Google paradigm these students are used to and a much more sophisticated research-library approach to information" (Coventry, 2006, para. 5).

Clearly, Web 1.0 and the Google generation's heightened expectations for convenience and ease of use of a search engine have created opportunities and challenges for libraries. The main public face of the library to these users is its Web page and its OPAC (Online Public Access Catalog), which is the main interface for access to its collections. It is inevitable that users compare their experience with library OPACs to their experience with using search engines. Two of the challenges faced by libraries in this comparison are: First, how to update and revitalize the library OPAC interface and its feature set to meet enhanced user expectations; and second, the structural need to develop effective metasearch capabilities for the array of heterogeneous databases to which they provide access.

The preference expressed by many users for Internet search engines to libraries is documented but the reasons for their preference is not always known. One important reason the libraries might be less used is that many users associate them exclusively with books. Items found in an OPAC search require additional effort to retrieve compared to the instant gratification of a search engine. It is reasonable to suspect some of the preference has to do with dissatisfaction with the OPAC experience when compared to using a search engine or to searching sites such as Amazon. In a study of academic library OPACs, Mi and Weng (2008) found that while user behavior and expectations have changed, many OPACs have not adapted to these new expectations. They identified interface issues such as confusing field labeling, displays of results that did not retain original search terms for possible modification, and failure to provide availability information with search results. Often the OPAC default search assumptions for term processing were not clear or required the use of explicit Boolean operators. In addition, they found a general lack of value-added elements users have come to expect such as text summaries, tables of contents, reviews, or links to vendors that provide those enhanced display services.

Some OPAC features do not always measure up to the Web 1.0 experience, let alone added Web 2.0 expectations. For instance, a useful service at our library allows requested books to be delivered within a day to a nearby campus location. To request this service, the patron must login with his name and a barcode, a unique number most users are unlikely to memorize. After that initial login, the patron barcode must be entered a second time when the delivery location is chosen. Further, if other books are requested during the same session, the barcode is required again for each book request, even though the user has already logged in. There is no “shopping cart” to save items as you search for other items, and no single “check out” to request delivery of all items to the desired location when the session is finished. The service is ostensibly designed this way for security reasons to prevent a stranger from making additional requests in someone else’s name if a user forgot to logoff at a public terminal. This scenario seems unlikely because many requests are made by faculty in their offices, and even if it occurred, the patron must still show his ID when the items are checked out at the receiving location. Compare this process to the Amazon experience: You login once, put items on a wish list or in a shopping cart, and check out everything together when finished. The repeated call for a barcode in the OPAC may seem like a minor inconvenience, but it is an example of how enhanced user expectations turn a desirable service opportunity into a potentially irritating one. OPAC issues sometimes are due to which features are enabled in the local configuration options, but many limitations are imposed by the vendor’s software design. Librarians have long been held captive by a limited set of programs capable of handling the many functions of an Integrated Library System (ILS). This is changing with the development of open source options such as Scriblio (http://about.scriblio.net/) and Evergreen (http://open-ils.org) that offer OPAC functionality with

2.0 features. Weber (2006) describes one library's experience in making this transition.

Another issue for OPACs is the frequent lack of metasearch options. The "Googlization" of searching has given rise to users who are less patient with the complex options that libraries offer and who prefer Google's simple "one box" search interface. The cliché that "only librarians like to 'search,' everyone else just wants to find" has more than a kernel of truth. Libraries must develop innovative technologies and standards to facilitate metasearch search capabilities across the large number of heterogeneous databases they manage to support a more seamless user experience. User and usability research suggests a need for a new generation of OPACs that are better at connecting users to the wide array of information sources and presenting the results in creative ways that meet user expectations. Coyle (2007) calls the Web 2.0 audience "User 2.0" and suggests new generation OPACs must go beyond 1.0 thinking to incorporate features enabling users to participate and add content and value to the experience. There are interesting models for the new generation OPAC; for example, LibraryThing (http://www.librarything.com/) is an online community catalog of 27 million books created by users with features such as tagging, shared recommendations, and blog connectivity.

WEB 2.0

Early references to a second generation Web appeared in the late 1990s in the context of the Semantic Web; a Web that would be based on XML such as that described by Bosak and Bray (1999). The Semantic Web, envisioned as a future "intelligent" Web, is now referred to as Web 3.0 in part because Web 2.0 has come to have a different meaning. Web 3.0 is discussed later in this chapter. There are various definitions and descriptions of Web 2.0; it seems to mean different things to different people in different contexts. Most definitions describe it as the collaborative, social, interactive, blogging, twittering, flickring, widget utilizing, mashup-driven Web that is collectively referred to as Web 2.0. Tim O'Reilly (2005) is credited with coining the term in 2003; he described it as:

> Web 2.0 is the network as platform, spanning all connected devices; Web 2.0 applications are those that make the most of the intrinsic advantages of that platform: delivering software as a continually-updated service that gets better the more people use it, consuming and remixing data from multiple sources, including individual users, while providing their own data and services in a form that allows remixing by others, creating network effects through an "architecture of participation," and going beyond the page metaphor of Web 1.0 to deliver rich user experiences. (para. 1)

Allen (2008) argues Web 2.0 is really a conceptual frame with technological, economic, philosophical, and user components. He observes that:

> Web 2.0 is a shorthand term for many different things, some in conflict, some overlapping but marked especially by the fact that they are ontologically non–compatible. In short Web 2.0 is about ideas, behaviours,

> technologies and ideals all at the same time. Moreover, its distinctive assertion of a change in state, from Web 1.0 (a term that was never used in any case) to Web 2.0, begs the question of the degree to which this change has actually occurred or may be occurring *because* of something new, or simply involves a re-expression of things previously understood as "the Web," but placed in a new arrangement or seen in a new light. (para. 4)

In the context of libraries, Web 2.0 thinking embodies all these facets: It is a technology, a philosophy, a business plan, a behavior, and a participatory model to engage users. This view of the Web led Michael Casey to coin the term "Library 2.0" and launch an associated blog in 2005 (Casey & Savastinuk, 2007). Again, the 2.0 brand applied to libraries is generally described rather than formally defined. Casey and Savastinuk suggest Library 2.0 is:

- A model for constant and purposeful change.
- Empowers library users through participatory, user-driven services.
- Through the implementation of the first two elements, Library 2.0 seeks to improve services to current library users while also reaching out to potential library users. (p. 5)

Note that technology is not an explicit element of their model. This is deliberate on their part—they acknowledge technology has an important role to play in developing services, but they emphasize that it is just a tool rather than an end in itself. However, this is a text on the technologies of the Internet, so an overview of the technology tools applicable to this model follows.

RSS Blogs and Podcasts

The blog, or the personal Web log, is made possible by the XML-based RSS (Really Simple Syndication) protocol. Blogs are essentially a personalized, interactive Web page that is easily updated and syndicated. Many sites such as WordPress.com and Blogger.com make it easy for anyone to start a blog. Blogs now reach a very wide audience; the Pew Internet and American Life Project estimated that by 2006, 39 percent of Internet users, or about 57 million American adults, read blogs, a significant increase from the previous year (Lenhart & Fox, 2006). More striking, they found that nearly 1 in 10 U.S. adult Internet users had a blog of their own. This same Pew study also reported demographic data showing that while the percentage of men and women bloggers was about the same, more than 54 percent of the respondents were younger than 30. The majority (89%) reported that blogging was a hobby. More than half were motivated by the desire for self-expression and sharing experiences as opposed to a journalistic agenda. For many, blogging is a component of other social networking activities; MySpace and LiveJournal topped the list of blogging sites. Sifry (2007) reports that the Technorati site tracks over 70 million blogs; they estimate that 120,000 new blogs are created each day and that the blogosphere has doubled in size in the four-year period between 2003–2007.

Although most blogs are just personal journals, they have also become a successful mainstream information outlet. A blog is essentially the sharing of one person's worldview. Many allow for and encourage varying degrees of participation by readers who wish to post comments. Blogs have become increasingly important to information professionals as both a source of information and a vehicle to share information within a group.

Blogs have found their way into libraries in a number of ways. Blogs are replacing discussion lists as the main venue for professional conversations, whether for professional development, communication with user groups, or as a news outlet. Blogs are quite versatile, allowing embedded elements such as chat, audio, video, and slideshows that are pulled from Flickr or YouTube. Blogs with such embedded content are being used in place of a traditional Website. Using a service such as FeedBurner.com, bloggers can offer an RSS subscribe option to readers that results in a Web-delivered targeted content stream that is easy to update and that has little of the technical or maintenance requirements of managing a Website. This is clearly appealing to many who do not have the resources or Web publishing skills to manage a full Web presence. Stephens (2007) identifies a number of value-added blogging activities for libraries, showcasing their use for readers' advisories, internal communication, and building interactive community-based Websites. RSS features can be added to catalogs so users can syndicate their search and receive notification when new items are added that match the search criteria.

Podcasts can be viewed as audio blogs. The term is from the words iPod and broadcast. Sometimes it applies to any downloadable MP3 file that can be put on an iPod or other MP3 player, but it generally refers to audio that can be syndicated and subscribed to, as with blogs. It is easy to create digital audio content; a number of media player programs as well as free tools such as the Audacity software are available that along with needed plugins, can create MP3 files of recorded audio. Podcasts not only allow anyone to create their own personal radio show, but they also have found many educational uses. For the iPod generation, a podcast is a possible way to deliver a lecture or audio program. Podcasting is becoming increasingly popular and Pew Research reports that 19 percent of Internet users have downloaded a podcast (Madden, 2008). The applications of this technology in libraries are numerous and include orientation tours, instructional audio on database searching, book or journal reviews, new book information, and events promotion (Jowitt, 2008).

Wikis

Wikis were discussed in Chapter 13, but obviously they are part of the Web 2.0/Library 2.0 discussion. The wiki, from the Hawaiian for "quick," is software that allows anyone to add or edit Web content without having to know HTML. Ward Cunningham is credited with both the idea of such a collaborative system and the name when he developed "WikiWikiWeb" in 1994 (Bishop, 2004). Probably the best-known example is Wikipedia (wikipedia.com), a collective encyclopedia built with the knowledge and expertise of the user community. Wikipedia has become a huge success—Nielsen Online reports that traffic to Wikipedia has grown nearly 8,000 percent over the last five years

(The Nielsen Company, 2008). Because of the wide subject coverage of Wikipedia, much of this traffic is due to referrals from search engines. This use of Wikipedia as a primary reference source is controversial because there is no assurance that all the information contributed by users is always accurate. In many ways, Wikipedia represents the crux of the broader dilemma faced by information professionals with many forms of participatory content creation enabled by Web 2.0, that is, the concern that the resulting resources may not be authoritative or appropriate. There are legitimate concerns about the lack of traditional gatekeepers to validate and control Wikipedia entries, and there are examples of content manipulation to promote a biased agenda, such as the evidence of corporate tinkering with entries for public relations purposes (Hafner, 2007). However, Wikipedia also reflects the tremendous power and self-correcting mechanisms of user-driven content systems. Errors are usually quickly detected, and studies comparing its content in specific disciplines with a traditional source have found it to be quite accurate. One study found the accuracy of science resources in Wikipedia compared favorably with those in Encyclopedia Britannica (Giles, 2005). Aside from the controversy surrounding the use of Wikipedia as a reference source, wikis are like blogs in that they present opportunities to build and share content in many forums, and their use is growing. Wikis are being used in libraries for internal knowledge bases to share best practices, for committee and meeting reports, to create specialized subject pages, to support course content, and for conference programming (Fichter, 2006). As with a blog, wikis can also engage the user community and record their input. Library applications of wikis as well as blogs could be to involve users in library planning or to build content resources in areas such as local history and genealogy. Such community involvement not only engages library users but taps into a huge pool of local experts to help develop a library resource.

Flickr, YouTube, and Shared Bookmarking

Flickr (www.flickr.com) is a photo-sharing site that is available for free with a Yahoo email account, making it easy to upload, tag, find, and share photographs with a private or public audience, depending on user preference settings. Flickr accounts can be used as a promotional tool or to involve library users in a collective project. Flickr has many educational uses; a recent Educause report describes an architecture class in which students went out into a city on a digital-photo scavenger hunt to gather images of architectural styles; the images were uploaded, tagged, and incorporated into the course (EDUCAUSE, 2008). Stephens (2007) describes some best practices for Flickr and libraries, including tailoring the profile appropriately for the intended use, tagging and organizing images, engaging the user community, and displaying the images on the Website via RSS feeds. YouTube (www.youtube.com), now owned by Google, is similar to Flickr but is for videos instead of photographs. It has become immensely popular, and librarians have used it for promotion and community engagement. Because YouTube allows users to post commercial television and movies in addition to personal videos, it has raised copyright issues and challenges. Media giant Viacom has filed suit against Google for copyright infringement (Neumeister, 2008).

Another highly touted tool is the shared bookmarking site del.icio.us (www.delicious.com). For anyone who has a large set of personal bookmarks and who wants to be able to access them from anywhere, this site is a boon. Bookmarking was a feature introduced with the first browsers to help users keep track of, and return to, sites they discovered. However, personal bookmarks may quickly grow into a huge set of links, and the tools for organizing and managing them in a browser are limited. The bookmark itself has little descriptive information other than the title of the page, which is sometimes not provided, so finding a desired bookmark is often a challenge. In addition, users with computers in different locations find they do not have access to all their collective bookmarks. However, with a free account on del.icio.us bookmarks can be set or imported from different computers to be organized and tagged with user-generated terms. Libraries are using shared bookmarks as an alternative to Web directories of selected resources on different topics. Web subject directories are common on many library Websites. However, they are a Web 1.0 strategy; a librarian would identify a site of interest and send it to the Webmaster, who would then include it with the next updates. Description of the subject link is limited, and access to it in the directory page is usually with an entry in an alphabetical list. Rethlefsen (2007) describes how shared library bookmarks allow this process to be streamlined by empowering librarians to quickly and easily post and tag interesting Web links they discover. Flexible tagging provides a rich natural language vocabulary making it more likely users will find a link on a topic they wish to explore. "Task tagging," a way to bundle links together for a specific audience or purpose, can facilitate better access to those resources; this grouping of bookmarks could even be done according to a traditional scheme such as Dewey classification.

Social Networking Services (SNS)

Social networking sites have become extremely popular, especially within certain demographic groups. A National School Board Association survey found that children and teens in the 9–17 year-old age range spend about as much time with online social networking (about 9 hours per week) as they do watching television (about 10 hours per week). Further, an astounding 96 percent of this age group report participating in some form of social networking technology (National School Boards Association, 2007). MySpace (www.myspace.com) and Facebook (www.facebook.com) represent two of the most popular sites; the tracking site Alexa reports they are respectively the sixth and eighth most visited Web destinations (Alexa.com, 2008). MySpace still has the most users, but Facebook, originally for college students but now open to all, is growing faster, doubling in size during 2007, while MySpace grew less at 28 percent (Brown, 2007). Now that Facebook has opened its doors to everyone, more than half of its 43 million members are not college students (Lyons, 2007).

These popular sites present an opportunity to connect with new users on their turf. Rapacki (2007) describes using a MySpace presence at the Wadsworth (Ohio) Public Library teen department as a means to engage teens in the community. The Hennepin County (MN) public library (http://www.myspace.com/hennepincountylibrary) uses MySpace for a similar purpose. Facebook has been used by university libraries to connect with students, but the terms of use agreements for these services sometimes conflict with library goals. These sites are designed for individual personal use, and some social network sites prohibit or limit institutional accounts not associated with a single user (Greenwell & Kraemer, 2007). In addition to outreach, social networking has many internal professional applications for advancing career opportunities, from acting as an online rolodex to making new connections. Some sites, such as LinkedIn (www.linkedin.com), focus on a professional audience and are marketed as a networking tool to support career goals.

Instant Messaging (IM) and Twitter

These applications fall under the wide Web 2.0 umbrella, but instant messaging (IM) and chat applications have been around for some time. IM is less formal and more immediate than email and has much of the appeal of text messaging. America Online (AOL) offered an early IM client as a service to customers, which is now branded simply AIM. Yahoo IM and Windows Messenger are other IM options. IM has been used in libraries for reference chat service for almost as long as email has, and clients such as Trillian allow chat to take place across competing services (Ciocco & Huff, 2007).

Twitter is described as a form of microblogging; the messages are limited to 140 characters and can be sent via the Web, IM, or mobile phone. Twitter describes its service as a way to send updates to those who care about all the little things in your life as they occur; it is the chat equivalent of a quick, casual "what are you up to" conversation you might have with friends. Twitter describes itself as the medium of choice for updating friends and family about your everyday life in the time between your emailing and blogging activities. This form of ongoing interactive messaging has limited appeal to some; not everyone has a need to share these details of their life, but Twitter, like email and chat, could be used to provide brief informational services in the form of online reference as have email and chat. Some of these various messaging functionalities are being integrated into single client solutions; for instance, Microsoft has introduced Office Communicator, a client program to integrate messaging functions within Office and Outlook. It promises to integrate messaging with your contact list, allow rich IM content from Office applications, support PC to PC phone connections, and enable multiparty conversations with IM, phone, or video conferencing.

Tagging

It is apparent that there is significant functional overlap among many of these technologies. SNS sites may offer blogs, photo sharing, and RSS capabilities. One of the common threads for many Web 2.0 technologies is the potential for user-generated tags for content description. This empowers users, and they seem to embrace these capabilities to create descriptive access points that work for them; 28 percent of Internet users report tagging activities used to categorize online content such as photos, news stories, or blog posts (Rainie,

2007). Tagging with unrestricted term vocabulary results in a *folksonomy*, a hybrid of *folk* and *taxonomy* (Peters & Bell, 2008). Folksonomies are unrestricted user generated vocabularies that enable a "group think" approach to describing content. This process can result in a large set of assigned terms, which are often represented as a tag "cloud." The cloud visualization can indicate term frequency by the size of words in the cloud; the larger the size of the word, the more commonly it was assigned by users to describe the content. Users often have a number of options for providing content description; in addition to tagging with words or phrases, they may post full reviews or generate numeric ratings. Such reviews have proved to be very popular within many consumer sites; the ability to hear about actual user experiences with a product has become an equally useful source of information to traditional review sources.

However, given librarians' long history of creating controlled forms of content description many have understandably mixed feelings about fully embracing user-generated metadata. It is one thing to let people tag their own photographs, but it is something else to permit users to add descriptive tags to traditional catalogs. What does this mean for all the high-quality metadata that has been created through years of effort? Would users overwhelm record displays with tags that add little descriptive value? It is true that some user tags such as "cool" are of limited value, but it is likely that the expansion of descriptors used could be useful by permitting terms that users prefer, especially about new topics. In addition, data mining techniques can exploit useful patterns in the collective tag wisdom of users resulting in better application of tag clouds to IR. Even though librarians justifiably defend formal metadata as a means to enhance access to resources, there is evidence that alternate approaches can provide as good or better search results. Hawking and Zobel (2007) examined queries of a university Website utilizing subject metadata and found metadata-enabled searching actually underperformed when compared to queries using anchor text. One reassuring aspect for librarians is that user tagging and traditional controlled vocabularies are not mutually exclusive strategies; allowing user tagging in an OPAC does not mean the other forms of value-added metadata must be abandoned. However, it does force librarians to reconceptualize information systems and view the world more from the "user 2.0" perspective.

Mashups

The term *mashup* comes from disk jockeys and musicians who create new compositions by "mashing" together other songs (Purvis, Sambells, & Turner, 2006). Mashups add functionality to a site by making use of an API (Application Program Interface). A common example of a mashup is the extensive use of the Google Maps API to overlay a new application on a site. Many sites have incorporated this functionality; for example the Zillow real estate service (www.zillow.com) allows searching for homes for sale in a neighborhood or city and then displays them on a Google map with stickpins. There are many possibilities, for instance, restaurant or consumer review sites could display the physical locations associated with the review. Libraries could do a similar mashup connecting OCLC WorldCat with mapping to show locations of nearby libraries holding an item of interest. Google Map applications can be created with PHP and Ajax programming, but you can discover how to create maps without programming on the wayfaring site (www.wayfaring.com), which allows users to create and save customized maps they can link to later (Purvis et al., 2006).

Virtual Reality and Second Life

Virtual reality (VR) environments have also received considerable attention, and many libraries and schools are exploring Second Life (SL), operated by Linden Labs, as a way to extend their reach into the virtual world. SL is a multiuser virtual reality environment, referred to as a MUVE (Multiuser Virtual Environment). Second Life (www.secondlife.com) allows users to join without cost. You must create an avatar, which is a digital representation of yourself, and attend a virtual orientation to learn how to move about, after which you are free to explore its world. SL has its own economy, based on "Linden dollars," and people can earn and spend this currency through their virtual activities in SL. Avatars can be customized, have wardrobes, move by walking or flying, and most importantly, interact with other avatars. Interaction typically is through keyboard chat features, but voice chat communication is also possible. Many users get very involved with this virtual world, buying and selling real estate, or starting virtual business ventures.

Linden Lab reports there are 13.8 million users of SL, and during one week in May 2008, 458,000 had logged in (Second Life, 2008). The reported total user population is impressive, but the one-week login data reflect only 3.3 percent of the entire reported population. Even when the recent login period is extended to a two-month look back period, only about 8.3 percent of the SL population logged in during that time. Shirky (2006) believes that many people sign up to check out SL but do not return. This suggests that articles that promote it as the next "big thing" are based on total SL population data and do not factor in the churn rate, which refers to those who try it once and do not return. Second Life evolved from the MUD (Multi User Dungeon/Dimension) programs that also gave rise to various gaming environments such as World of Warcraft. Modern gaming worlds are known as MMORPGs (Massive, Multiplayer, Online Role-Playing Games). However, SL is not actually a game; by most standards, a game has points, levels, or other goal-oriented activities generally lacking in SL. Second Life is just that—a virtual life that can be experienced and explored.

Many libraries and universities have decided to create or explore a presence in SL to reach this audience of virtual clients or to enhance their real life services. Calongne and Hiles (2007) report that more than 100 universities have a presence or meet classes in SL. There is an "information island" in SL where virtual libraries have been established, presuming that participants in SL need, want, and will use library services. The Alliance Library System began exploring SL for its 259 member libraries in April 2006 and within a year had developed the Second Life Library, called the Info Archipelago (Bell, Pope, Peters, & Galik, 2007). They report 5,000 avatar visits per day to this location, although it is not clear what portion of these visits are targeted ones or just counts of avatars. In some demonstrations of SL library programs, the only nonlibrarian visitors seem to be simply lost, and their only questions were for directions to other places; further studies of library use by the SL community are needed to reveal more about the value and use of SL library efforts.

SL is described as "free," but there are costs. Land ownership requires a membership with a monthly fee; in addition, Linden dollars are needed for various other activities in SL. The exchange rate is about 1 dollar to 200 Linden dollars. Software must be downloaded and installed; while this is available at no cost, many users experience hardware and configuration issues that must be resolved. Once the software is working, a significant amount of bandwidth is required to support virtual life activities. It is conceivable that organizational networks would find this activity problematic on a large-scale; a cost/benefit analysis is called for before a major commitment is made by an organization to its widespread use. Demonstrations of SL are available for those interested in getting a feel for the experience without joining or installing client software (Mason, 2006).

In addition to costs, SL is an uncontrolled environment, which raises potential liability issues for public entities such as schools and libraries. All users must agree to Linden Lab's terms of use, which gives them the right, but not the obligation, to resolve conflicts or harassment allegations. A library or university presence is an extension of the organization, yet it is operating in a world they do not control. An example: Shortly after the shootings at Virginia Tech, an avatar visiting Ohio University's SL campus virtually fired at other avatars causing much distress among other users. Other problems could arise in the form of sexual harassment or cyber-bullying. There are questions about controversies that could ensue from requiring that class activities take place in SL (Bugeja, 2007). Carnevale (2007) asks if colleges can afford to police online worlds if real world problems occur. Some universities, including my own, have posted policies that ask visitors to abide by real-world campus and classroom rules and etiquette; the policy states that students and visitors will be held to the established "real life" student code of conduct, which raises some interesting enforcement scenarios. No matter what policies are in place, SL does attract some who will not be deterred by requests for appropriate behavior. Harassing behaviors are part of the "griefer" subculture that goes back to the late 1990s to describe antisocial behaviors in multiplayer games (Dibbell, 2008). Examples of "griefing" behavior include players attacking their own teammates or repeatedly attacking a novice player who is many levels below the griefer's level. Their motives might be to disrupt the game, to drive new participants away, or just to be a nuisance in a way that their peers find amusing. The culture has found its way into SL, and there are notorious examples of their actions, such the disruption of a virtual CNET interview by dropping phalluses on the virtual stage or vandalizing candidate John Edwards virtual campaign headquarters (Dibbell, 2008).

So is SL the next big thing? Some predict VR will be the future of the Web (Bell et al., 2007). However, there are doubters, and their concerns go beyond just possible liability issues. As a disclaimer, I am not an active Second Lifer. It is not that I am disinterested; it just does not pass my personal cost/benefit threshold yet. It is also worthwhile to consider that the technological landscape is littered with previously predicted revolutionary technologies. For example, Gopher, once cutting edge, is now just a footnote to the Web. The Virtual Reality Modeling Language for creating 3-D worlds emerged in 1994 as another candidate for the next big thing, but most net gens have probably never heard of it. Another relevant example was the predicted application of MOO (MUD Oriented Object) software for creating text-based VR environments with chat features that became available in the 1990s. Its uses were interesting but revealed limitations that may be pertinent to some aspects of SL. One problem with MOOs was the limitation of typing chat within a group setting; it is difficult to synchronize the conversational flow by typing responses because by the time a thoughtful response was ready the conversation had often moved on to another topic. The development of voice chat options in MUVEs may address this limitation, but much of the interaction still requires keyboard chat. A bigger issue for some was the "game" aspect of the software used to create the virtual meeting space. Participants walked into a virtual building, rode a virtual elevator, and had to locate a virtual meeting room, all of which seemed to add little value to the experience and were a distraction to the work at hand. Some of the applications of SL seem to add similar overhead for getting to the resource or the learning experience. Do these examples imply these technologies were not important in their time or that they should not have been on a trend-spotter's radar? No, it just means that sometimes in all the excitement and media attention surrounding something new, a technology may have as much hype as substance. Obviously, SL is much more sophisticated than those primitive MOO programs, but whether you walk or fly to the meeting or class in SL, there is an added effort associated with the experience of simply getting into the world and to your place of virtual interaction, to say nothing of the effort to initially create and fashion your avatar.

Nonetheless, there are committed people engaged in serious efforts to explore SL to support professional activities and educational opportunities. As noted earlier, my university has a SL island and even allows students to apply for small grants of Linden dollars to support SL educational expenses. Professional associations such as the Special Libraries Association and the American Library Association have a presence in SL and use it for professional development and conferences. The virtual interaction among avatars is a potentially exciting form of group interaction that makes new educational environments possible to support learning, at least for users amenable to the MUVE experience. The game-like features and avatar customization of SL might be very appealing and engaging to net gens and some users but less so to others. This is not to suggest that SL is a "virtual emperor with no clothes" but only that more time and study are needed before a judgment can be made about its true potential for such activities. Even if SL as it exists does not become everything its promoters suggest, other virtual environments specifically tailored to educational applications are being developed and experience gained with SL will be useful preparation for that future.

The World Wide Computer

One of the disruptive aspects of Web 2.0 is the notion of the Web as a platform for delivering applications. Carr (2008a) and others describe how the

World Wide Web is becoming the World Wide Computer. He compares this transition to an earlier disruptive technology: that of electric power at the turn of the twentieth century. Initially, that industry was centered around supporting onsite power generation by selling components and expertise needed for industries to produce the power they needed. As the electric power grid developed, it replaced the need to duplicate generating capacity at each site. The parallel with computing is intriguing and compelling; companies are finding less need to build, support, and develop customized computing and data storage solutions if they can be accomplished more efficiently via the Web. This scenario of computers using network applications sounds vaguely familiar to those who recall the "thin client" model of the mid-1990s. Thin clients referred to network computers that could be stripped of most peripheral devices and would pull smaller, more nimble Java applications from a server. Cheap PCs, user attitudes, limited bandwidth, and few network applications prevented this model from taking hold then. However, Web 2.0 technologies and services are converging with shifting user attitudes to a tipping point in favor of this paradigm. The success of sites such as Flickr for photographs and del.icio.us for storing bookmarks proves users are comfortable with the idea that their content can be stored remotely, and the seamless integration of Web technologies and broadband Web access into computing life makes the distinction between local and remote locations insignificant.

Many companies are approaching their computing needs in a similar fashion, and not just for storage. Cloud computing, also called utility computing or Hardware as a Service (HaaS), makes it possible to rent virtual machines and data centers as a Web service. Companies such as Amazon created a huge infrastructure to support its own business activities; they now find they can sell some of this capacity as a service. Amazon CEO Jeff Bezos compares generating your own computing capacity to generating your own electricity (Reiss, 2008). The availability of cloud computing permits entrepreneurs to start a business without the capital required to build their own infrastructure. However, there is a tradeoff with cloud computing just as there is with electric power: If the grid fails, your systems go down with it, so some local backup systems remain necessary.

CRITIQUES OF WEB 2.0

Critics of Web 2.0 are not necessarily antitechnology Luddites and contrarians; there are thoughtful perspectives and cautionary views that should not be summarily dismissed. Zimmer (2008) notes that there are unintended consequences to Web 2.0 technologies:

> Web 2.0 also embodies a set of unintended consequences, including the increased flow of personal information across networks, the diffusion of one's identity across fractured spaces, the emergence of powerful tools for peer surveillance, the exploitation of free labor for commercial gain, and the fear of increased corporatization of online social and collaborative spaces and outputs. (para. 2).

Certainly, privacy issues arise in many facets of Web 2.0. Every service you sign up for requests and stores personal information and has unfettered access to the content users produce or store. Privacy concerns seem to have a generational component; for that matter, many Web 2.0 services appear to have varying levels of appeal to different age groups. This could relate to a lack of technology skills to use the service, but it could also have more to do with how different personalities and age groups view communication and personal space. Younger audiences appear to be much more comfortable with sharing vast amounts of personal information via social networks, while others find such public venues uncomfortable or invasive. In the pre–cell phone world, it was not uncommon for some telephone customers to pay extra fees not to be listed in a directory to protect their privacy; such an individual would seem an unlikely user of MySpace. In addition to privacy concerns, some users, probably more so in older demographic groups, might believe that social networking sites simply do not offer a service they desire or that is worth the investment of time. Lyons (2007) describes his experience with Facebook in a way that may resonate with others in his over 40 demographic:

> But the weird side of Facebook is that, while loads of oldsters are jumping on board, the site still looks and feels like a place for kids. There's a big emphasis on figuring out what kind of person you are and how many friends you have and which ones are your best friends forever. . . . It's as if two very different tribes were trying to inhabit the same space. I sometimes get the creepy feeling that we oldsters are barging into some college party where we don't belong and trying a little too hard to look like we're having fun, like the sad middle-age guys in the movie Old School who attempt, pathetically, to recapture their college days. (p. 68)

Similar reasons could apply to the use or nonuse of IM or Twitter; avoidance may have nothing to do with technological comfort or ignorance of its availability but might simply reflect the lack of a perceived need for that type of brief, immediate communication with others. After all, there are still people who do not have or want cell phones and wonder who everyone else needs to be constantly talking to as they walk and drive.

Another concern Web 2.0 brings to the fore is the displacement of the gatekeeper role of older media and its replacement by the "cult of the amateur." Tenopir (2007) discusses Web 2.0 critic Andrew Keens' book on this topic and finds some kernels of truth in his concern that reliable accurate information is being overwhelmed by unfiltered, unattributed, and unvetted sources or, in Keens' words, "digital narcissism." However, Tenopir notes that quality still matters, and she takes Keens' message to be "buyer (reader) beware"—a sensible proposition that also reinforces a professional role in promoting information literacy skills.

Other critics observe that while pervasive technology can connect people as never before, people are more alienated than ever. Turkle (2007) develops this theme along several lines. She describes the tyranny of devices that require constant attention, taking time away from other forms of reflection or face-to-face interaction. People interrupt face-to-face conversations to answer a cell phone call or text message. Children grow up tethered to parents and peers by cell phones, and the emphasis on "bite size" messages and instant replies preclude responses that are more thoughtful and reflective. Second Life allows a loner not to be alone but lacks the demands and rewards of genuine intimate friendships. Social networking entertains but can distract the young from real-world action requiring their actual engagement. Even Web 2.0 guru Tim O'Reilly (2006) has expressed concerns about the dark side of these technologies; he listed three of his concerns in a speech at the University of California School of Information:

> First, privacy. Collective intelligence requires the storage of enormous amounts of data. And while this data can be used to deliver innovative applications, it can also be used to invade our privacy. . . .
>
> Second, concentration of power. While it's easy to see the user empowerment and democratization implicit in web 2.0, it's also easy to overlook the enormous power that is being accrued by those who've successfully become the repository for our collective intelligence. Who owns that data? Is it ours, or does it belong to the vendor? If history is any guide, the democratization promised by Web 2.0 will eventually be succeeded by new monopolies, just as the democratization promised by the personal computer led to an industry dominated by only a few companies. . . . Don't just take for granted that technology will bring us a better world. We must engage strenuously with the future, thinking through the dark side of each opportunity, and working to maximize the good that we create while minimizing the harm.
>
> Third, greed. Web 2.0 has ignited a new feeding frenzy among venture capitalists and entrepreneurs. It's perhaps too early to call it a bubble, but once again, enormous fortunes are being created by people with little more than a bright idea and an instinct for how to harness the power of new technology. (para. 39–42)

Concerns about the negative impact of technology on culture and people are not new; in hindsight, some appear to have been exaggerated and others may just reflect generational shifts. Carr (2008b) raises interesting questions in his observation that the technologies and media we use can shape how we read and think, and wonders "Is Google making us stupid?" However, counterarguments certainly can be made that highlight the positive outcomes possible from the knowledge sharing, connectivity, and communication that these technologies promote. The global connections enabled by Web 2.0 technologies could translate into broader awareness and commitment to solving real-world problems. Children may be reading fewer traditional materials, but they are reading and writing a great deal online. Not all tethering connections to children result in intrusive helicopter parents but instead can result in closer bonds and more open communication between parents and children. Nonetheless, like most technologies that have come before, there are tradeoffs associated with their use, and both sides of the conversation have merits.

WEB 3.0

As Yogi Berra would say, predictions are hard, especially about the future; I would add "and especially hard when talking about technology." However, with the emergence of Web 2.0, it is naturally predicted that Web 3.0 is just around the next virtual corner; in fact, many assert Web 3.0 is already here. As with Web 2.0, views differ on the nature and definition of Web 3.0, or even if discussions of the future of the Web should be framed in this numerically sequenced way. One view of Web 3.0 describes it as primarily a virtual reality-based Web (Bell et al., 2007). More often Web 3.0 definitions are aligned with the view of Web founder Tim Berners-Lee, who describes it in terms of the Semantic Web (Shannon, 2006). Other descriptions of this view refer to Web 3.0 as the worldwide database; some anticipate the data-driven Semantic Web combined with "smart agent" technologies as the path to a future Web that will become a form of artificial intelligence. An interesting demonstration of the capabilities being ascribed to Web 3.0 and the earlier discussion of the Web as a platform is the Zcubes Website (http://home.zcubes.com). This site offers a Web-based platform with over 2,000 features for seamless browsing, searching, editing, drawing, and content creation by dragging and dropping parts from other sites to publish to the Web or in email. It is illustrative of things to look forward to on the Web.

SUMMARY

The statement by Farkas (2007) that "now is an amazing time to be a librarian" summarizes the feeling of many in the profession (p. 43). There are new tools that can be used to enhance library online services and engage users in new forms of participation and content development. The Internet and Web in all its forms enables many exciting possibilities, while simultaneously presenting significant challenges. A major challenge is the difficulty of keeping up with new trends and technologies, while also heeding O'Reilly's advice for "thinking through the dark side of each opportunity" (2006, para. 43). Services must embrace the new without abandoning traditional functions and audiences. In their discussion of Library 2.0, Casey and Savastinuk (2007) quote a library manager who reminds us that "though many library users have needs that have changed in step with technological innovations, many have not, and we do a disservice to those patrons if we focus exclusively on keeping up with technological innovation" (p. 6). Therefore, librarians must strike a delicate balance between being a trend-spotter/cheerleader and a skeptic, exploring new technologies for their own sake but ultimately focusing on the value-added benefits of their use. Purportedly there is a Chinese curse that says, "may you live in interesting times." Clearly, these are interesting times to be in the information professions.

REFERENCES

Abram, S. (2005). The Google opportunity. *Library Journal, 130*(2).

Alexa.com. (2008). Top sites. Retrieved May 1, 2008, from http://www.alexa.com/site/ds/top_sites?ts_mode=global&lang=none.

Allen, M. (2008). Web 2.0: An argument against convergence. *First Monday, 13*(3).

Bates, M. J. (2002). *Toward an integrated model of information seeking and searching (Keynote).* Paper presented at the Fourth International Conference on Information Needs, Seeking and Use in Different Contexts, Lisbon, Portugal.

Bell, L., Pope, K., Peters, T., & Galik, B. (2007). Who's on Third in Second Life? *Online, 31*(4).

Bertot, J. C., & McClure, C. R. (2000). Public libraries and the Internet 2000: Summary findings and data tables. *National Commission on Libraries and Information Science.* Retrieved October 15, 2007, from http://www.nclis.gov/statsurv/2000plo.pdf.

Bishop, T. (2004, January 26). Microsoft Notebook: Wiki pioneer planted the seed and watched it grow. Retrieved October 2007 from http://seattlepi.nwsource.com/business/158020_msftnotebook26.html.

Bosak, J., & Bray, T. (1999). XML and the second-generation Web. *Scientific American, 280*(5), 89–94.

Brown, E. (2007, December 10). Smiles, everyone. Retrieved May 15, 2008, from http://www.forbes.com/business/forbes/2007/1210/066.html.

Bugeja, M. J. (2007). Second thoughts about Second Life. *Chronicle of Higher Education, 54*(3), C2–C4.

Calongne, C., & Hiles, J. (2007, April 17–19). *Blended realities: A virtual tour of education in Second Life.* Paper presented for the 12th Annual TCC Worldwide Online Conference Voyaging into a new era! Retrieved June 3, 2008, from http://etec.hawaii.edu/proceedings/2007/calongne.pdf.

Carnevale, D. (2007). Colleges find they must police online worlds. *Chronicle of Higher Education, 53*(45), A22–24.

Carr, N. (2008a). *The big switch.* New York: W. W. Norton & Company.

Carr, N. (2008b, July/August). Is Google making us stupid? *Atlantic,* 56–63.

Casey, M. E., & Savastinuk, L. C. (2007). *Library 2.0: A guide to participatory library service.* Medford, NJ: Information Today.

Christensen, C. M. (2003). *The innovator's dilemma: The revolutionary book that will change the way you do business.* New York: Collins.

Ciocco, R., & Huff, A. (2007). Mission IM-possible: Starting an instant message reference service using Trillian. *Computers in Libraries, 27*(1), 26–31.

Coleman, J., Katz, E., & Menzel, H. (1957). The diffusion of an innovation among physicians. *Sociometry, 20*(4), 253–270.

Coventry, M. (2006). Libraries for a new generation: Getting the net gen on the right information highway. *UMN News.* Retrieved October 1, 2007, from http://www1.umn.edu/umnnews/Feature_Stories/Libraries_for_a_new_generation.html.

Coyle, K. (2007). The library catalog in a 2.0 world. *The Journal of Academic Librarianship, 33*(2), 289–291.

Dibbell, J. (February, 2008). Griefer madness. *Wired, 16,* 90–97.

EDUCAUSE. (2008). 7 things you should know about Flickr. Retrieved May 30, 2008, from http://net.educause.edu/ir/library/pdf/ELI7034.pdf.

Farkas, M. (2007). Balancing the online life. *American Libraries, 38*(1), 42–45.

Fichter, D. (2006). Using wikis to support online collaboration in libraries. *Information Outlook, 10*(1), 30–33.

Giles, J. (2005). Internet encyclopedias go head to head. *Nature, 438,* 900–901.

Gill, J. (2008, January 17). Researchers' web use could make libraries redundant. Retrieved May 1, 2008, from http://www.timeshighereducation.co.uk/story.asp?storycode=400168.

Google. (2008). Mission statement. Retrieved May 1, 2008, from http://www.google.com/corporate.

Greenwell, S., & Kraemer, B. (2007). Social networking software follow-up: Facebook and MySpace (and more). *Kentucky Libraries, 71*(4), 11–15.

Hafner, K. (2007, August 19). Seeing corporate fingerprints in Wikipedia edits. *New York Times,* p. 1.

Hawking, D., & Zobel, A. J. (2007). Does topic metadata help with Web search? *JASIST, 58*(5), 613–626.

Jones, S., & Madden, M. (2002, September 15). The Internet goes to college. *Internet and American Life Project.* Retrieved October 2007 from http://www.pewinternet.org/pdfs/Pip_College_Report.pdf.

Jowitt, A. L. (2008). Creating communities with podcasting. *Computers in Libraries, 28*(4), 14–15, 54–16.

Kestenbaum, D. (2008). Old drug offers new hope for Marfan Syndrome. Retrieved May 30, 2008, from http://www.npr.org/templates/story/story.php?storyId=90257827.

Lenhart, A., & Fox, S. (2006, July 19). Bloggers: A portrait of the internet's new storytellers. Retrieved October 1, 2007, from http://www.pewinternet.org/pdfs/PIP%20Bloggers%20Report%20July%2019%202006.pdf.

Lyons, D. (2007, October 29). Party crashers. *Forbes, 180,* 68–70.

Madden, M. (2008, August 28). Podcasts proliferate, but not mainstream. Retrieved September 27, 2008, from http://pewresearch.org/pubs/941/podcasts-proliferate-but-not-mainstream.

Mason, P. (2006, January 5). Do avatars dream of electric racoons? *As part of Newsnight's Geek Week, business correspondent Paul Mason and presenter Jeremy Paxman broadcast TV's first ever face-to-face studio session from inside the computer game Second Life.* Retrieved June 2, 2008, from http://news.bbc.co.uk/2/hi/programmes/newsnight/4583924.stm.

Mi, J., & Weng, C. (2008). Revitalizing the library OPAC: Interface, searching and display challenges. *Information Technology and Libraries, 27*(1), 5–22.

National School Boards Association. (2007). Creating & Connecting: Research and guidelines on online social—and educational—networking. Retrieved June 2, 2008, from http://www.nsba.org/SecondaryMenu/TLN/CreatingandConnecting.aspx.

Neumeister, L. (2008, May 27). Google backs video sharing on YouTube Viacom suit says it violates copyrights. *Lexington Herald Leader,* p. D5.

The Nielsen Company. (2008, May 14). Wikipedia U.S. Web traffic grows 8,000 percent in five years, driven by search. Retrieved June 10, 2008, from http://www.nielsen-netratings.com/pr/pr_080514.pdf.

Online Community Library Center (OCLC). (2006, June 1). OCLC reports on college students' library perceptions. Retrieved May 1, 2008, from http://www.libraryjournal.com/info/CA6340281.html.

O'Reilly, T. (2005, October 1). Web 2.0: Compact definition? Retrieved October 1, 2007, from http://radar.oreilly.com/archives/2005/10/web-20-compact-definition.html.

O'Reilly, T. (2006, May 14). My commencement speech at SIMS. Retrieved June 2, 2008, fromhttp://radar.oreilly.com/archives/2006/05/my-commencement-speech-at-sims.html.

Peters, T., & Bell, L. (2008, April 11). Trends, fads or folly: Spotting the library trends that really matter. Retrieved April 15, 2008, from http://www.collegeofdupagepress.com/library-learning-network/soaring-to-excellence-2008/spotting-the-library-trends-that-really-matter/.

Purvis, M., Sambells, J., & Turner, C. (2006). *Beginning Google maps applications with PHP and Ajax; From novice to professional.* Berkeley, CA: Apress.

Rainie, L. (2005, November 20). Search engine use shoots up in the past year and edges towards email as the primary internet application. *Internet and American Life.* Retrieved May 1, 2008, from http://www.pewinternet.org/PPF/r/167/report_display.asp.

Rainie, L. (2007, January 31). Tagging play: Forget Dewey and his decimals, Internet users are revolutionizing the way we classify information—and make sense of it. *Pew Internet & American Life Project.* Retrieved May 30, 2008, from http://pewresearch.org/pubs/402/tagging-play.

Rapacki, S. (2007). Why teens need places like MySpace. *Young Adult Library Services, 5*(2), 28–30.

Reiss, S. (2008, May). Planet Amazon. *Wired, 16,* 88–95.

Rethlefsen, M. L. (2007). Tags help make libraries DEL.ICIO.US. *Library Journal,* 26–28.

Second Life. (2008, May 28). Economic statistics. Retrieved May 29, 2008, from http://secondlife.com/whatis/economy_stats.php.

Shannon, V. (2006, May 24). A "more revolutionary" Web. Retrieved May 1, 2008, from http://www.iht.com/articles/2006/05/23/business/web.php.

Shirky, C. (2006). Second Life: A story too good to check. Retrieved June 4, 2008, from http://www.valleywag.com/tech/second-life/a-story-too-good-to-check-221252.php.

Sifry, D. (2007, April 5). The State of the live Web, April 2007. Retrieved May 1, 2008, from http://www.sifry.com/alerts/archives/000493.html.

Stephens, M. (2007). *Web 2.0 & libraries, part 2: Trends and technologies* (Report). Chicago, IL: American Library Association.

Sullivan, D. (2005, January 28). Search engine sizes. Retrieved October 1, 2007, from http://searchenginewatch.com/showPage.html?page=2156481.

Tenopir, C. (2007). Web 2.0: Our cultural downfall? *Library Journal, 132*(20), 36.

Turkle, S. (2007). Can you hear me now? *Forbes.com.* Retrieved June 4, 2008, from http://www.forbes.com/forbes/2007/0507/176_print.html.

Weber, J. (2006). Evergreen: Your homegrown ILS. *Library Journal, 131*(20), 38–41.

U. S. Census. (2006). Computer and Internet use in the United States: 2003. Retrieved October 1, 2007, from http://www.census.gov/population/pop-pro file/dynamic/Computers.pdf.

Zimmer, M. (2008). Preface: Critical perspectives on Web 2.0. *First Monday, 13*(3).

ADDITIONAL READING

Information Behaviour of the Researcher of the Future. Retrieved February 1, 2008, from http://www.bl.uk/news/pdf/googlegen.pdf.

Miller, W., & Pellen, R. M. (Eds.). (2005). *Libraries and Google.* Binghamton, NY: Haworth Information Press.

O'Reilly, T. (2005, September 30). What Is Web 2.0: Design patterns and business models for the next generation of software. Retrieved May 1, 2008, from http://www.oreillynet.com/pub/a/oreilly/tim/news/2005/09/30/what-is-web-20.html.

Scholz, T. (2008). Market ideology and the myths of Web 2.0. *First Monday, 13*(3). Retrieved from http://www.uic.edu/htbin/cgiwrap/bin/ojs/index.php/fm/article/view/2138/19454.

Silver, D. (2008). History hype and hope: An afterword. *First Monday, 13*(3). Retrieved from http://www.uic.edu/htbin/cgiwrap/bin/ojs/index.php/fm/article/view/2143/1950.

Appendix
The Binary Machine

BINARY NUMBERS

To understand why the computer is a binary machine, it is necessary to review binary numbers and Boolean logic. A firm understanding of these basic concepts is essential to a number of topics throughout this text, such as IP addressing, subnet masks, the ASCII byte streams used in all Internet protocols, and the encoding schemes used to handle binary file formats.

Number Systems: Base 10, Base 2, and Base 16

People are most familiar with the decimal (base 10) numbering system and instinctively understand the value of decimal numbers. The comfort level with this system is due to a variety of cultural, political, and biological factors (for instance, people have 10 digits to help with counting; U.S. currency uses decimal thanks to Alexander Hamilton). A number system uses symbols (digits) to represent values and assigns different meanings to the digits depending on their *position* in the number. It is possible to have numbering systems that ignore "place." Simple counting systems such as groups of five slashes (four vertical with a fifth drawn through the others) or even more complex Roman numerals, do not use column place in this way, but Western numbering does. Base-10 numbers require 10 digit symbols and a shared understanding that the position of the digit reflects some power of 10 as the column value. The 10 digits are 0–9 (remember that zero is a perfectly good number!) When you view a base-10 number such as 7,826 it is immediately parsed without much thinking as 7 thousands, 8 hundreds, 2 tens, and 6 ones. That parsing presumes, however, this is a base-10 number; to be more complete when writing this number, technically information about its base with the subscript (10), as in $7{,}826_{(10)}$ should be provided. Many numbering systems are possible in addition to base-10, and they are all equal in the sense that any value can be represented in them. The difference is only in the column values and the number of digits used.

The 10 symbols required for base-10 numbers present an engineering problem to the designers of computing systems. A device that discriminates 10 different levels of magnetic charges and associates each of them with 10 different digits is hard to build. It is, however, relatively easy to create devices that can discern two different states, such as a switch that is on or off, or the presence or absence of a charge, and associate each state with the digits 0 or 1. This is why the binary (base-2) numbering system is a great fit for computers. Only two digits are required (0 and 1), and the column position values are based on powers of 2. Table A.1 shows a base-10 example that analyzes the number $7{,}826_{(10)}$

To determine the value this number represents, note that the position of the digit adds a factor of 10 to the column value. Binary numbers work the same way. For example, try to convert the binary number $100101_{(2)}$ (the subscript tells you not to view this as a base-10 number) to decimal. Table A.2 shows this number's value.

The binary number 100101 is equivalent to decimal 37. Using the same approach you could reverse the process to determine that the decimal number 7,826 is equal to the binary number 1110 001110110. It is apparent from this exercise that although the total values are the same, it takes a longer number to express a given value in binary compared to base-10; this makes sense, as you see that each column "packs more punch" with base-10. Note, too, that binary is hard for people to read, and to make the long 12-digit base-2 number more readable, a 4-bit portion is separated from the 8-bit portion. Putting a group of 8 bits together is significant as this octet represents a *byte*, which in turn is usually associated with a single character in various data representation schemes such as ASCII (the 4-bit portion is half a byte or a *nibble*).

Another numbering system that is important in computing is the hexadecimal numbering system (abbreviated as hex), which is base 16. Base 16 requires 16 digits; 0–9 gives 10, but then there are no more numbers. However, because these are just symbols that are associated with a value, any symbol can stand in for a number. Hex uses the letters a–f for the needed six addi-

TABLE A.1 A Base-10 Number

Power of 10	10^3	10^2	10^1	10^0
Column value	7x1000	8x100	2x10	6x1
Number	7	8	2	6

Column position values are based on powers of 10; starting at the far right, the exponent is zero. The exponent value is incremented by one with each column move to the left. Note that any number raised to the zero is one, and any number raised to the one is the number itself.

TABLE A.2 Binary Number 100101

Power of 2	2^5	2^4	2^3	2^2	2^1	2^0
Column value	1x32	0x16	0x8	1x4	0x2	1x1
Number	1	0	0	1	0	1

Note that the column values are all powers of 2 where the exponent value starts with 0 at the far right and is incremented by 1 with each column to the left.

TABLE A.3 Hex Numbering Compared to Base 2

Power of 16	16^5	16^4	16^3	16^2	16^1	16^0
Value	1,048,576	65536	4096	256	16	1
Power of 2	2^{20}	2^{16}	2^{12}	2^8	2^4	2^0

tional digits (for 11, 12, 13, 14, and 15). Because base 16 numbers use 16 as the base, the value of each column moving to the left increases very quickly, as shown in Table A.3.

This rapid increase in column values with hex makes representing very large numbers very compact. Also, from the comparison with base 2, note that the hex column values map directly to base 2 column values if each base 2 column exponent value is incremented by 4 ($2^4 = 16$); this makes the conversion between binary and hex slightly easier than the conversions to decimal.

Data Representation Codes

From the discussion so far, the following conclusions can be made:

- There are many ways to represent a value.
- Computers only use binary numbers, but people prefer not to work with these very long numbers; they are usually converted to base 10 or base 16 to simplify their notation for our use.
- The same value expressed in binary requires a longer number (i.e., more digits) than when the same value is expressed in either base 10 or base 16.

The problem of how to represent character text in computers was address early in the development of digital computer systems. In the nineteenth century, Samuel Morse addressed a similar problem for the telegraph technology of that era. Morse code used dots and dashes (essentially a binary code) to represent all the characters of the Western alphabet. The ASCII (American Standard Code for Information Interchange) serves as a standard code for interpreting computer text formats. The code designers needed to define how many bits are required to identify all the possible characters in the Western alphabet. There are 26 letters, and each has upper and lowercase forms. There is also a need for punctuation characters and perhaps special symbols (such as $, %, @, etc). In a code with just two states (0 or 1), the number of unique values is dependent on how many digits long the code can be. A code that is just three digits long can have eight (or 2^3) possible values: 000, 001, 010, 100, 011, 110, 101, and 111. A heuristic can be deduced that the number of possible values (or addresses) is 2 raised to a power that is equal to the number of bits long the code is. Standard ASCII uses 7 bits, making it possible to represent 128 (or 2^7) different symbols. Extended ASCII uses all 8 bits of a byte, allowing for 256 symbols. This is more than adequate for the Western alphabet, but not for many other character sets. Unicode comes in 16- and 32-bit versions; with 16 bits, 2^{16} or 65,536 code values are possible.

Binary Addressing Schemes

Computer and network systems use binary numbers to uniquely address elements such as RAM addresses, MAC codes for network interface cards, and IP addresses for Internet hosts. The same simple rules apply; binary numbers are used for all such addresses, and the number of possible addresses depends on the length of the permitted address number in bits. IPv4 uses 32-bit addressing, which means the theoretical limit for these addresses would be at most 2^{32}, or just over 4 billion (it turns out that there are additional constraints on these addresses as discussed in Chapter 4). MAC addresses use a 48-bit number, usually displayed in a hex format for a more compact representation.

BOOLEAN LOGIC

The other reason computers are binary machines is that they depend on a binary logic system called Boolean logic, developed by George Boole in 1847, thereby enabling librarians to start using Boolean logic in their searches! Of course, those IR applications actually came much later, but Boolean searching is a convenient example to demonstrate this algebraic system.

A search using two terms, for instance “cat” and “dog,” could be combined with Boolean operators. A Boolean AND means a retrieval takes place only when both terms are in a record, with a Boolean OR, either term (or both) is sufficient to result in a retrieval. This is represented algebraically as a logic truth table for the Boolean operators AND, OR, and NOT. Instead of words, truth tables use numbers to represent the operands. The Boolean AND results are shown along with the Boolean OR in Table A.4. Table A.5 shows the Boolean NOT results.

The Boolean AND looks like the arithmetic operation of multiplication, the OR looks like the arithmetic operation of addition, and Boolean NOT is an inverse function. This simple algebraic system is the foundation of the logic gates built into the circuitry of a computer. This logic system is explained in other areas of this text, such as in the discussion of subnet masks.

TABLE A.4 The Boolean AND and Boolean OR Truth Tables

AND table			**OR Table**		
Operand	**Operand**	**Result**	**Operand**	**Operand**	**Result**
0	0	0	0	0	0
0	1	0	0	1	1
1	0	0	1	0	1
1	1	1	1	1	1

TABLE A.5 The Boolean NOT Operation

Operand	**Result**
0	1
1	0

Glossary

absolute reference: Reference that unambiguously defines a location, such as a complete URL of an Internet resource.

addressing granularity: The level at which index terms are tracked in a document; terms can be associated with just a document ID, a block within a document, or the exact word position within the document.

algorithm: A series of steps by which a problem can be solved; usually used in the context of programming directives.

aliasing: A distortion or artifact of the sampling process when converting analog data to digital.

amplitude modulation: When information is added to a carrier signal through signal modulation.

anti-aliasing: A technique to compensate for aliasing by eliminating distortion. Graphics programs use this feature to smooth out the edges of images and text.

applet: Java programs called within a Web page, retrieved, and then run within the browser by the Java VM.

array: A type of variable that stores multiple values in a tabular form.

Archie index: Short for "archives," it was developed at McGill University and was the first widely used Internet index; it provided access to files stored on anonymous FTP sites.

ARP (Address Resolution Protocol): A broadcast network message that seeks a MAC address associated with an IP address.

ARPANET (Advanced Research Projects Agency Network): A network initiative supported by DARPA. It was the first packet switching data communications network and gave rise to the modern Internet.

ASCII (American Standard Code for Information Interchange): A text code that uses 7 or 8 bits to represent textual data. Standard 8-bit ASCII can represent 256 different symbols.

associative array: An array is a way to store multivalue variables using a two-column table. The left column is a series of string names that makes up the array index.

asymmetric: In the context of connection technologies, the difference between upstream and downstream bandwidth that makes a connection asymmetric.

authorities: In the HITS model, authorities are pages with a high number of in-degree links.

bandwidth: The capacity of the medium to carry a signal.

binary: Base 2 numbering that uses only zeros and ones.

bitmap images: See raster graphic.

block-level elements: In HTML, elements that are always rendered on a new line in the browser display.

blogs: From the words Web and log or a "weblog." A personal narrative intended to be syndicated using RSS.

Boolean logic: An algebraic system developed by George Boole in 1847 that uses binary operands and three operators: AND, OR, and NOT. It is the foundation of computer logic gates and is also used as an IR model.

BOOTP: A protocol used to assign an IP address with a MAC address. In BOOTP, the computer booting up on the network broadcasts a request message with its MAC address, and the BOOTP server responds with the IP address as well as other network configuration information that is held in its database.

bridge: A device connecting two different network segments at the OSI data-link level.

broadband: A generic term used for the various high bandwidth connection technologies.

browser: The client software developed to retrieve and display Web pages.

bus: A circuit path that connects devices within a computer or over a network.

byte boundary: A subnet mask that "borrows" a full byte of the available host bits.

cache: A dedicated memory area for data or instructions used to speed access to the information.

CBIR (Content-Based Information Retrieval): When programs attempt to use the actual content of the file to perform retrieval instead of metadata associated with it. Examples are image and audio retrieval systems that attempt to match content patterns.

circuit switching: A communication strategy in which direct circuit connections are made between nodes.

client-side: An approach where any needed processing takes place in client software running on a local computer as opposed to on a server.

color depth: The number of bits used to represent colors in graphics; typically ranges from 8 to 32 bits.

compiled program: A program that requires a separate action on the written code that converts it into machine language. The compiled version is an executable file.

concatenate: A way to add or combine text strings; it is frequently used in scripting.

cookies: A persistent client-side state object, originally developed by Netscape to compensate for the statelessness of the Web.

CSMA/CD (Carrier Sense, Multiple Access with Collision Detection): The Ethernet technology for managing packet traffic and potential collisions.

CSS (Cascading Style Sheets): A style language supported by the W3C that allows separation of content and presentation in HTML.

dataflow diagrams: A process-centered modeling technique used in systems analysis.

DBMS: For database management system; a program or collection of programs for storing and retrieving information.

deprecated: In HTML, tags that are no longer supported in the standard.

descriptive markup: Markup that identifies a function or style instead of specific formatting; for instance, the use of the <em> </em> tag for emphasis, but without defining specifically how that will be displayed in every client view.

DHCP (Dynamic Host Configurations Protocol): A protocol that dynamically assigns an IP address to the host for that session; the IP address is "leased" for a period by that host, but once it expires or is released, a different address might be assigned for future sessions. It is similar to BOOTP in that it uses an exchange of broadcast messages between the host and some server.

digital: Information that is represented in binary form; as 0s and 1s.

directory tree: The hierarchical structure created on disk drives to organize and collocate files.

dithering: When a nonsupported color is specified in an image but is unavailable to a browser. The browser substitutes a similar available color, often with inconsistent or poor results.

DNS (Domain Name System): A hierarchical system of servers maintaining a database of names and addresses providing these lookup services; this is how IP addresses are associated with a URL.

DNS lookup: What happens with every Web client–server interaction that references a URL; the translation of the URL into a numeric IP necessary for packet addressing.

DOM (Document Object Model): An object-centered view of a page and its elements.

dot notation: The convention that identifies an object within an object hierarchy, such as "document.banner," or a method, such as "document.write." In CSS and scripting the dot notation is used for creating classes.

dot pitch: A function of display hardware that refers to the distance between pixels measured in millimeters.

DPI (Dots Per Inch): A measure of display or print resolution.

driver: Software that mediates between an operating system and some device or client program.

DSL (Digital Subscriber Line): A digital telephone technology that has most of the advantages of ISDN for lower costs and faster speeds. DSL dedicates part of the available bandwidth to support an analog voice signal, which allows simultaneous computer and voice connection. It is a generic term for a large variety of specific standards that fall into one of two basic types: symmetric, where the upstream and downstream speeds are the same, and asymmetric, where they are different.

DTD (Document Type Definition): In markup languages, a model for a specific class of documents. Part of the SGML specification, it is a language for defining markup elements, their attributes, and their relationships.

EA address: An Ethernet address; a 48-bit number that is a specific type of MAC address identifying a node on an Ethernet network.

element: In markup languages, elements are associated with the components of a document or their attributes and are defined by tags.

embedded styles: Style information that is included within an HTML container.

entity relationship (ER) diagrams: A modeling technique used in systems analysis that identifies entities, their attributes, and their relationships. ER diagrams use a standardized set of symbols to represent the components of a database and the cardinality of the relations.

enumerated array: In scripting, an array is a way to store multivalue variables using a two-column table. The left column is a sequence numbered list that comprises the array index.

Ethernet: A data communication network standard that defines a packet type, error controls, and wiring standards. Robert Metcalfe developed the first Ethernet specification at Xerox PARC (Palo Alto Research Center) in 1973. This was revised in 1982 and released as Ethernet II by Digital Equipment Corp, Intel, and Xerox. It was adopted by IEEE (Institute of Electrical and Electronics Engineers) with the release of the 802.3 standard for CSMA/CD networks. Ethernet specifies packets (called frames) as well as wiring standards.

event handlers: In scripting, event handlers are associated with functions or other script commands; they are some event such as a mouse over, mouse click, or a page load that can precipitate an action.

false hits (or drops): In IR, a retrieved item that is deemed nonrelevant; the term comes from early IR systems that used notched cards to represent metadata. The cards representing a document collection could be physically manipulated to segregate a retrieval set in a way that caused potentially relevant records to drop; nonrelevant retrievals were therefore "false drops."

federated search: In the context of library systems, a metasearch capability that permits a search to be broadcast to the many separate databases within a collection.

folksonomy: A hybrid of *folk* and *taxonomy* that are unrestricted user-generated vocabularies resulting in a "group think" approach to describing content.

FQDN (Fully Qualified Domain Name): A name associated with a particular machine or host at a domain.

frequency modulation (FM): Where a source modulates the frequency of a carrier wave to allow the transmission of information.

FTP (File Transfer Protocol): The TCP/IP protocol developed specifically to upload or download files via an Internet connection.

function: In scripting, also called a *subroutine* or *procedure*, it is a set or block of instructions that execute together to yield a single result; these blocks can be reused in a modular fashion throughout a program.

gopher: Developed at the University of Minnesota, it was a menu-based client–server protocol for access and delivery to information resources.

hacks: In security, a hack is an attack; in scripting or CSS, it usually refers to an unusual or inelegant solution to some programming problem.

hexadecimal: Base 16 numbering system commonly used to represent large binary numbers, mostly for human convenience. For instance, a 48-bit Ethernet address can be expressed as a 12-digit hexadecimal number. Because 16 digits are needed, the letters a–f are added to the set of 0–9 digits available for base 10 numbers.

homonyms: Refers to words that are either pronounced or spelled the same but have distinct meanings. For instance, a "router" could be a network device or a woodworking tool.

HSL (Hue, Saturation, and Lightness): A color model recognizing that people see hues of color, not mixes of the three additive primary colors. Hue refers to the color's place on the spectrum, represented on a scale of 0–255. Saturation values refer to the clarity of degrees of hue; lightness refers to how light or dark the color appears.

HTML (Hypertext Markup Language): Developed by Tim Berners-Lee, HTML is a text-based standard that defines the tags needed for document structuring and presentation on the Web.

HTTP (Hypertext Transfer Protocol): The protocol that controls the client–server interactions and communication streams for the delivery of content from a Web server to a browser.

hub: A network device that forwards packets to every other device connected to it.

hypertext reference: In HTML, the anchored hypertext reference that creates links within Web pages to other documents or locations.

ICMP (Internet Control Message Protocol): Another type of datagram carried in an IP packet just as UDP or TCP packets are; it is used for error checking between gateways and hosts and between different hosts at the Internet layer for error reporting and routing decisions.

image maps: The process of identifying shape coordinate areas in an image and associating them with separate URLs.

in-degree/out-degree: In link analysis, the number of links pointing to a page, or the number of links to other sources within a particular page.

inline: In HTML, inline elements are rendered on the same line; they do not force a line break. If they do not fit on a line, they will wrap across the screen onto a new line.

instance document: In XML, a document created according to the rules of some specific markup language.

Internet: The global network of computer networks that uses TCP/IP for data communications.

intranets: An internal or local network based on TCP/IP.

inverted file: Also an inverted index or an inverted index file; a structure that results in an index listing items from some field with links to the documents or record where the terms appear and perhaps to their specific location within each document.

invisible Web: By definition any Internet content that is unavailable to search engine spider harvesting is considered "invisible." It includes content that is dynamically generated, protected by a firewall or the robot exclusion protocol, or within file formats harvesting programs cannot process.

IP address: The logical address associated with some Internet node using either IPv4 or IPv6. Address classes have been established, and organizations are assigned a class in the domain registration process. The IP address space assigned to an organization is handled internally by associating device MAC addresses with available IP addresses or through dynamic IP address assignment.

IP packets: The packets specified by TCP/IP that move data from one host to another.

IR (Information Retrieval): As described by Korfhage (1997, p. 324), IR is "the location and presentation to a user of information relevant to an information need as expressed by a query." Essentially, IR systems function as an intermediary between information resources and a user's information need.

IRC (Internet Relay Chat): A real-time Internet connection used for chat sessions.

ISPs (Internet Service Providers): The companies that provide access to Internet services for the public through dialup or broadband options.

link bomb: The deliberate manipulation of the Google PageRank algorithm by making links to specific phrases to cause unusual retrieval results for a search.

logical markup: See descriptive markup.

loopback address: The IP address 127.0.0.1 that is used for testing TCP/IP installations.

lossy compression: A file format that can have data loss with the compression algorithm; JPG is an example of such a format.

MAC (Media Access Control) addresses: A hardware identifier for a network device; for Ethernet networks, this is the Ethernet address. MAC addresses are mapped to IP addresses for Internet hosts.

Macro viruses: Viruses written in the Visual Basic scripting language used by Microsoft for application macros. VB Macros make it possible for data files to carry a virus.

malware: A generic term used to describe any of the programs designed to annoy, damage, or otherwise invade your computer, including viruses, worms, and Trojan horses as well as various types of spyware and adware.

markup languages: Text-based languages that use special or reserved text characters to convey structural or presentational information to a parsing program.

mashups: Hybrid functionalities made possible through shared APIs, such as the use of the Google Maps API to add map functions to a Website.

metasearch: A simultaneous search of multiple databases or search engines.

MIME (Multipurpose Internet Mail Extensions): The automated encoding scheme that facilitates the transfer of binary information in an ASCII text representation; for instance, MIME enables binary file email attachments.

mobile malicious code: Any program that moves from computer to computer via a network that is intentionally designed to modify a computer system without the user's consent.

modem: A modulator/demodulator, a device that allows a computer to connect to other computers via an analog telephone line.

MUVE (Multiuser Virtual Reality Environment): A virtual world, such as Second Life, that is shared by multiple simultaneous users.

namespace: In XML, a way to define a vocabulary that can then be shared with other markup languages.

NAT (Network Address Translation) Protocol: A way to manage the correspondence between public and private network addresses; it is like a proxy server acting as an intermediary for the packet streams.

net neutrality: A policy issue that determines how packets are treated; with net neutrality, all packets are equal, and no packets are given "priority" status on the Internet over others.

NetBIOS (Network Basic Input/Output System): Network ports used for functions such as file and printer sharing.

node: In networks, each connected device is a node. In XML, the hierarchical tag structure is also referred to as a node tree, and each element is a node.

normalization: A formal process based on relational database theory to test data structures to ensure the database integrity.

octal values: In the context of UNIX file permissions, octal values are a shorthand way to refer to the eight different combinations of read, write, and execute permission that are possible.

octet: A byte value in an IP address; 8 bits of the 32 bits used in IPv4.

open source: Community-based software development that is free to download and adopt. Developers have access to the source code and are free to extend the software and support other users.

P2P: For peer-to-peer—a direct connection between two computers in which there is no central server and little needed hardware as with a direct connection between the two computer Ethernet ports with a crossover cable. In the context of the Internet, it refers to file sharing networks enabled by software such as Gnutella to facilitate data exchange between to nodes.

packet encapsulation: When the datagram of a packet is another packet; packets nested within packets. For instance, an IP packet typically carries a TCP or UDP packet in its data segment.

packet switching: A data communication strategy where information is broken up into small, discrete packets with a source and a destination addresses. The packets are transmitted over a network along with lots of other unrelated packets headed toward their destination.

packets: The datagrams that result when data is broken up into discrete chunks, labeled and addressed, and sent out over a network.

PageRank: The algorithm developed by Google founders Sergey Brin and Larry Page that uses link analysis to contribute to a relevance measure.

parameter: something that a command or function is to act upon; parameters can be passed to commands or functions.

physical markup: See procedural markup.

ping: A utility run from a command prompt on Internet-connected hosts; it forms a message based on an ICMP echo request directed to a host to see if it is "alive."

pipelining: In HTTPv1.1, a method that permits multiple requests to be processed simultaneously.

pixel: A contraction of the two words *picture* and *element;* it refers to a single dot on a display, the number of which is determined by the resolution setting.

polysemy: Refers to one word that may have related but quite distinct meanings depending on the context, such as the term *mouth,* which could be a body part or the end of a river.

port: A communication channel; it might be associated with a physical device, such as a USB or parallel port for a printer, or a logical port, such as the assignments made by TCP/IP.

portal: In the context of Web design, a portal is considered a site that acts as the primary entry point for the Internet activities of users.

precision: In IR, precision is a performance measure that is based on the proportion of relevant retrievals within a search set.

probabilistic: One of the classic IR models that attempts to algorithmically estimate the probability that a retrieval is relevant to a query.

procedural markup: In HTML, markup that describes the exact appearance or function of an element, such as using the bold tag to add formatting to text.

protocol: The set of rules for device and data communication.

proxy server: A host that stands in as a proxy for another host's Internet activities; it serves as an intermediary for the packet streams. They are used to authenticate users to a service and to restrict or filter Internet access.

raster graphic: A format where shapes are approximated by filling in squares within a grid.

recall: A performance measure that is based on the number of relevant retrievals in a set compared to the total number of relevant documents in some corpus. Determining that total is problematic outside of IR test bed environments.

relative reference: In HTML, referencing some other resource on the same server with an anchor or image tag by providing only the information needed to locate that file relative to the location of the referring file in the directory tree.

resolution: There are various contexts for this term—*monitor resolution* refers to two different measures: The vertical resolution is the number of rows of pixels on the screen, and the horizontal resolution is the number of intensity changes permitted across each row of pixels. Therefore, the vertical resolution is the number of pixels in a screen column, and the horizontal is the number of pixels in a row across the screen. *Bit resolution* is the number of pixels used to create the image. Print resolution is DPI setting for the output.

root element: In markup languages, the root element is the top-level element that by definition has no parent element; it is a starting tag not nested within any other tag. A defined root element is required by a DTD.

router: A device designed to forward packets between networks or segments. Routers use IP addresses and a subnet mask to determine if the packets are destined for a location within the network or for some outside Internet destination.

RSS (Really Simple Syndication or alternatively, Rich Site Summary, or RDF Site Summary): An XML-based protocol that enables a variety of syndicated feeds of blogs or podcasts.

schema: In the context of database systems, a schema is developed from the process of system analysis and the modeling of the database; the schema reflects the structure of a database and helps visualize or describe its organization.

scripting languages: A lightweight form of programming where textual commands are interpreted by some operating system or parsing program.

segments: Subsets of the nodes managed as a group within the larger network.

servlet: A Java application that runs on a server in an assigned servlet container.

SSID (Service Set Identifier): A network identifier that provides a minimum level of access control to a WLAN but is not highly secure because it is not encrypted and is often automatically assigned.

SGML (Standard Generalized Markup Language): A meta-language derived from GML that specifies how to create markup languages. Developed as an ANSI standard in 1983, it became an ISO standard in 1986 and is the foundation of HTML.

SIP (Session Initialization Protocol): A form of instant communication over a client–server Internet connection.

SLIP/PPP (Serial Line Internet Protocol/Point-to-Point Protocol): Protocols that assign an IP address to a host via a dial-up connection. SLIP is an older standard that does not have the compressions and error checking that PPP does.

SMTP (Simple Mail Transfer Protocol): The TCP/IP client–server protocol that supports email.

SOAP (Simple Object Access Protocol): W3C describes SOAP as an XML-based mechanism for exchanging information in a decentralized and distributed environment.

spam: The generic term for unwanted and unsolicited mail. The term is from the classic Monty Python restaurant skit where all the breakfast options included varying amounts of the processed meat known as SPAM™, whether the customer wanted it or not.

splash page: An initial Website page designed to catch the attention of a visitor.

SQL (Structured Query Language): A standardized command-based language for querying relational databases.

statelessness: The lack of an ongoing stateful connection between client and server. The HTTP protocol was developed for single communication events between client and server ending with the closing of the connection; because no record of the transaction is kept by the server the condition known as *statelessness* results. With a stateless protocol, there is just one transaction per connection, and multiple separate connections are needed to retrieve a page if multiple files such as images are associated with it.

stickiness: The degree to which a Website is designed to retain users.

stopwords: Words in documents such as articles, prepositions, and conjunctions that are deemed meaningless as index terms.

streaming: A client server strategy for delivering multimedia over the Internet that delivers content at a data rate that matches the available bandwidth, allowing continuous playback.

subnet: A network management strategy that separates nodes into separate groups, which are created by "borrowing" some of the bits reserved for host ID to extend the network ID portion.

subnet masks: Generically, a mask refers to the idea of hiding something to isolate one element of interest; a subnet mask is a number used to isolate the network or host portions of packet addresses to enable routing decisions.

subroutine: See function.

switch: A network device similar in function to a hub that serves as a network connection point for many devices. Switches use the MAC addresses associated with the frames (Ethernet packets) and filter the packet streams, but unlike hubs, switches forward packets only to the device with the correct address.

synonymy: Means that many terms can represent the same concept; synonyms are different words with similar meanings (e.g., automobile or car).

tags: In the context of markup languages, tags are used to identify elements by using reserved text. In HTML and XML, tags are identified by the use of the less than and greater than signs.

TCP/IP (Transmission Control Protocol/Internet Protocol): The packet switching technology used to support all Internet activities.

telnet: An Internet protocol that facilitates a real-time connection between two Internet hosts.

term stemming: In text processing, stemming refers to truncating a term to its root.

term weights: In text processing, weights can be assigned to terms in addition to simply tracking the presence or absence of a term. Term frequency, position, field location, or decoration can all be incorporated into weight calculation.

topology: The physical layout of the wired connections in a network. Common topologies are:

bus: Where each node comes off the connecting backbone wire in a linear series.

mesh: Where every node is connected to every other node, ensuring direct communication between every pair of devices.

peer-to-peer: A connection between two computers with no central server. A direct connection between the two computer ports.

star: Where wires to nodes radiate out from a central server.

token ring: Where computers are connected together in a circular arrangement, and a special packet, called the *token,* moves around to each node and determines what device can send data.

tree: A hybrid of a bus and a star, with potentially multiple stars coming off a central bus.

Trojan horse: As the name implies, Trojan horse programs are imposters; they claim to be something good but are, in fact, malicious. They depend on misleading the user to run them, and this misrepresentation is their defining characteristic. Unlike worms, they are nonreplicating, and unlike viruses, they do not infect other files. Nevertheless, if they succeed in tricking the user to run them, they can serve as an entry point for a future attack.

typography: How text characters appear when printed on a page or screen; typography is expressed as different fonts and sizes.

UDP (User Datagram Protocol): A packet type used to carry IP data when reliable delivery is not a priority. UDP is an alternative packet type that does not have the built-in error checking and acknowledgement features of TCP that ensure the integrity of the delivered data. UDP is primarily used for streaming protocols where speed is prioritized and packet delivery acknowledgement is unnecessary.

URI (Universal Resource Identifier): The unique identifier for a point of contact on the Internet.

URL (Uniform Resource Locator): The standard Web page locator as approved by the IETF; it includes a protocol, FQDN, and filename and location on a Web server.

vector images: Graphics where shapes are determined by applying mathematical formulas instead of filling in squares on a grid.

VERONICA (Very Easy Rodent-oriented Net-wide Index to Computer Archives): An early automatically generated searchable index for Internet Gopher resources; only the terms in the menu items were indexed—the full text was not.

virus: A form of malicious mobile code; executable code that acts as either a file infector or a boot sector infector.

VoIP: Voice over IP is a TCP/IP alternative to POTS for telephone service.

VPN (Virtual Private Network): A strategy to extend an address space by the creation of a virtual, secure "tunnel" through which authentication data and private network traffic can pass, allowing a remote user to access their organization's network from the outside.

WAN (Wide Area Network): A collection of local area networks.

Web (World Wide Web): The part of the Internet utilizing the HTTP protocol and results in a global hypertext database of information resources, many of which are in HTML format. Developed by programmer Tim Berners-Lee at CERN, it was first publicly demonstrated during the Hypertext '91 Conference in San Antonio Texas.

Web 2.0: Coined by Tim O'Reilly of O'Reilly publishing, Web 2.0 is the view of the Web as a platform, delivering useful applications and enabling a more dynamic, interactive, and participatory Web.

Web 3.0: Viewed as the evolution of the Web into an intelligent, Semantic Web that makes extensive use of XML and metadata to facilitate program-to-program communication as well as enhanced intellectual access to resources.

Wi-Fi (wireless fidelity): An IEEE standard for wireless connectivity by way of a broadcast signal using WAP (Wireless Application Protocol).

wiki: A collaborative software tool, developed by Ward Cunningham. The name is from the Hawaiian for "quick" and refers to software enabling anyone to add or edit Web content without having to know HTML or any details about the hosting platform. Wikis have become an important source of Internet-based reference, such as the online encyclopedia at Wikipedia.com, but they also present opportunities to build and share collaborative content in other contexts, such as internal knowledge-bases or other collaborative projects.

World Wide Web Consortium (W3C): The coordinating standards body that oversees Web development.

worm: Often lumped together with Trojans, they are somewhat different in action. Worms can turn computers into "zombie" spambots and cause thousands of replicated copies of itself to be sent out over a network and take part in "denial of service" attacks. They can infect local files and cause the afflicted host to lose data or crash.

WYSIWYG (What-you-see-is-what-you-get): When a program displays a final presentation view of a document; for instance, an HTML editor that instead of displaying code, shows how a browser would render the document.

WWW: See Web.

XHTML: HTML that is compliant with the more strictly enforced rules of XML.

XML (Extensible Markup Language): A lightweight meta-language derived from the SGML standard that has been optimized for the Web.

Bibliography

56 K Info. (2007). *Technical support.* Retrieved May 1, 2008, from http://home.core.com/web/technicalsupport/library/56kinfo.html.

Abram, S. (2005). The Google opportunity. *Library Journal, 130*(2).

Adobe.com. (2008). SWF technology center. Retrieved May 1, 2008, from http://www.adobe.com/devnet/swf.

Afergan, M., Darnell, R., Farrar, B., Jacobs, R., Medinets, D., Mullen, R., et al. (1996). *Web programming desktop reference 6-in-1.* Indianapolis, IN: Que Corporation.

Alexa.com. (2008). Top sites. Retrieved May 1, 2008, from http://www.alexa.com/site/ds/top_sites?ts_mode=global&lang=none.

Allen, M. (2008). Web 2.0: An argument against convergence. *First Monday, 13*(3).

American Library Association's (ALA) Presidential Committee on Information Literacy. (2006, July 24). Final report. Retrieved May 18, 2008, from http://www.ala.org/ala/acrl/acrlpubs/whitepapers/presidential.cfm.

Anderson, C. (2004, October). The long tail. *Wired Magazine, 12,* 170–177.

Arick, M. R. (1993). *The TCP/IP Companion: A guide for the common user.* Boston: QED Publishing Group.

Arnold, B. (2008). Sizing the web: Domains, sites, hosts. Retrieved May 1, 2008, from http://www.caslon.com.au/metricsguide1.htm#domains.

Associated Press. (2006, January 20). Google won't hand over files. Retrieved October 1, 2007, from http://www.wired.com/politics/law/news/2006/01/70055.

Baeza-Yates, R., & Ribeiro-Neto, B. (1999). *Modern information retrieval.* New York: ACM Press.

Barroso, L. A., Dean, J., & Hölzle, U. (2003). Web search for a planet: The Google cluster architecture. *Institute of Electrical and Electronics Engineers (IEEE) Micro, 23*(2), 22–28.

Bates, M. J. (2002). *Toward an integrated model of information seeking and searching (Keynote).* Paper presented at the Fourth International Conference on Information Needs, Seeking and Use in Different Contexts, Lisbon, Portugal.

Battelle, J. (2005). *The search.* New York: Penguin Group.

Bawden, D. (2007). Information seeking and retrieval. *ALISE, 28*(2), 126.

Baxter, G., & Anderson, D. (1996). Image indexing and retrieval: Some problems and proposed solutions. *Internet Research, 6*(4).

BBC News. (2003, December 7). "Miserable failure" links to Bush. Retrieved May 10, 2008, from http://news.bbc.co.uk/2/hi/americas/3298443.stm.

BBC News (2007, May 14). Web 2.0 "neglecting good design." Retrieved October 1, 2007, from http://news.bbc.co.uk/2/hi/technology/6653119.stm.

Bell, L., Pope, K., Peters, T., & Galik, B. (2007). Who's on Third in Second Life? *Online, 31*(4).

Bergman, M. K. (2001, September 24). The "Deep" Web: Surfacing hidden value. Retrieved October 1, 2007, from http://www.brightplanet.com/images/stories/pdf/deepwebwhitepaper.pdf.

Berinstein, P. (1999). Do you see what I see? Image indexing for the rest of us. *Online, 23*(2), 85–88.

Bernard, M., Mills, M., Peterson, M., & Storrer, K. (2001). A comparison of popular online fonts: Which is best and when? *Useability News, 3*(2).

Berners-Lee, T. (1999). *Weaving the Web: The original design and ultimate destiny of the World Wide Web by its inventor.* New York: Harper Collins.

Berners-Lee, T., Hendler, J., & Lassila, O. (2001). The Semantic Web. *Scientific American, 284*(5), 10.

Bertot, J. C., & McClure, C. R. (2000). Public libraries and the internet 2000: Summary findings and data tables. *National Commission on Libraries and Information Science.* Retrieved October 15, 2007, from http://www.nclis.gov/statsurv/2000plo.pdf.

Bhola, J. (2002). *Wireless LANs demystified.* New York: McGraw-Hill.

Bishop, T. (2004, January 26). Microsoft Notebook: Wiki pioneer planted the seed and watched it grow. Retrieved October 2007 from http://seattlepi.nwsource.com/business/158020_msftnotebook26.html.

Black, P. E. (2006). Dictionary of algorithms and data structures [online]. Retrieved September 13, 2008, from http://www.nist.gov/dads/HTML/invertedFile Index.html.

Black, P. E. (2008). Dictionary of algorithms and data structures [online]. Retrieved September 13, 2008, from http://www.nist.gov/dads/HTML/invertedIndex.html.

Black, U. (1999). *Advanced Internet technologies.* Upper Saddle River, NJ: Prentice Hall.

Bosak, J., & Bray, T. (1999). XML and the second-generation Web. *Scientific American, 280*(5), 89–94.

Boutell.com. (2007, February 15). How many websites are there? Retrieved October 1, 2007, from http://www.boutell.com/newfaq/misc/sizeofweb.html.

Bray, T., Paoli, J., Sperberg-McQueen, C. M., Maler, E., Yergeau, F., & Cowan, J. (2006). Extensible markup language (XML) 1.1 (2nd ed.). Retrieved May 1, 2008, from http://www.w3.org/TR/xml11/#sec-xml11.

Brenner, S. E., & Aoki, E. (1996). *Introduction to CGI/PERL.* New York: M&T Books.

Brin, S., & Page, L. (1998). *The anatomy of a large-scale search hypertextual Web search engine.* Paper presented at the Proceedings of Seventh World Wide Web Conference, Brisbane, Australia.

Broder, A., Fontoura, M., Josifovski, V., & Riedel, L. (2007). A semantic approach to contextual advertising. *ACM SIGIR International Conference on Research and Development in Information Retrieval,* 559–566.

Brown, E. (2007, December 10). Smiles, everyone. Retrieved May 15, 2008, from http://www.forbes.com/business/forbes/2007/1210/066.html.

Bugeja, M. J. (2007). Second thoughts about Second Life. *Chronicle of Higher Education, 54*(3), C2–C4.

Burd, B. (2001). *JSP: JavaServer pages.* New York: M&T Books.

Bush, V. (1945, July). As we may think. *Atlantic Monthly, 176,* 101–108.

BytePile.com. (2002, October 19). DSL categories. Retrieved October 1, 2007, from http://www.bytepile.com/dsl_categories.php.

Calongne, C., & Hiles, J. (2007, April 17–19). *Blended realities: A virtual tour of education in Second Life.* Paper presented at the 12th Annual TCC Worldwide Online Conference Voyaging into a new era! Retrieved June 3, 2008, from http://etec.hawaii.edu/proceedings/2007/calongne.pdf.

CalTech Information Technology Services. (2003, January 6). NetBIOS blocked at campus border. Retrieved August 1, 2003, from http://www.its.caltech.edu/its/security/policies/netbios-block.shtml.

Canavan, J. (2007, February 13). W32.Swen.A@mm. Retrieved May 1, 2008, from http://www.symantec.com/security_response/writeup.jsp?docid=2003-091812-2709-99&tabid=2.

Carnevale, D. (2007). Colleges find they must police online worlds. *Chronicle of Higher Education, 53*(45), A22–24.

Carr, N. (2008). *The big switch.* New York: W. W. Norton & Company.

Carr, N. (2008, July/August). Is Google making us stupid? *Atlantic,* 56–63.

Case, D. O. (2007). *Looking for information: A survey of research on information seeking, needs, and behavior* (2nd ed.). New York: Academic Press.

Casey, M. E., & Savastinuk, L. C. (2007). *Library 2.0: A guide to participatory library service.* Medford, NJ: Information Today.

Castelli, V. (Ed.). (2002). *Encyclopedia of library and information science* (Vol. 71). New York: Marcel Dekker, Inc.

Chakrabarti, S., Dom, B., Kumar, S. R., Raghavan, P., Rajagopalan, S., Tomkins, A., et al. (1999). Hypersearching the Web. *Scientific American, 280*(6), 54–61.

Chan, L. M. (2007). *Cataloging and classification: An introduction* (3rd ed.). Lanham, MD: The Scarecrow Press, Inc.

Charles, G. T., Jr. (1997). *LAN blueprints.* New York: McGraw-Hill.

Cheng, H.-L., & Rasmussen, E. M. (1999). Intellectual access to images. *Library Trends, 48*(2), 291–302.

Cheong, F. C. (1996). *Internet agents: Spiders, wanderers, brokers, and bots.* Indianapolis, IN: New Riders Publishing.

Chien, E. (2001). Nimda mass mailing worm. Retrieved August 1, 2003, from http://www.symantec.com/security_response/writeup.jsp?docid=2001-091816-3508-99.

Chowdhury, G. C. (1999). *Introduction to modern information retrieval.* London: Library Association Publishing.

Christensen, C. M. (2003). *The innovator's dilemma: The revolutionary book that will change the way you do business.* New York: Collins.

Chu, H. (2003). *Information representation and retrieval in the digital age.* Medford, NJ: Information Today.

Ciocco, R., & Huff, A. (2007). Mission IM-possible: Starting an instant message reference service using Trillian. *Computers in Libraries, 27*(1), 26–31.

Cisco Systems. (2008). Simple Network Management Protocol (SNMP). In *Internetworking technology handbook.* Retrieved May 1, 2008, from http://www.cisco.com/en/US/docs/internetworking/technology/handbook/SNMP.html.

CNET Wireless Resource Center. (2008). 3G. Retrieved October 1, 2007, from http://www.cnet.com/4520-7363-6361076-4.html?tag=wrc.ln.

Clark, T. M. (1999). *Teach yourself Paint Shop Pro 5 in 24 hours.* Indianapolis: SAMS.

CNET Wireless Resource Center. (2008). 3G. Retrieved October 1, 2007, from http://www.cnet.com/4520-7363-6361076-4.html?tag=wrc.ln.

CNET Wireless Resource Center. (2008). Wi-Fi. Retrieved October 1, 2007, from http://www.cnet.com/4520-7363_1-6361076-3.html?tag=wrc.mn.

Cohen, F. B. (1994). *A short course on computer viruses* (2nd ed.). New York: John Wiley & Sons.

Coleman, J., Katz, E., & Menzel, H. (1957). The diffusion of an innovation among physicians. *Sociometry, 20*(4), 253–270.

Comer, D. E., & Stephens, D. L. (1991). *Internetworking with TCP/IP Volume I: Principles, protocols, and architecture* (2nd ed.). Englewood Cliffs, NJ: Prentice Hall.

Comer, D. E., & Stevens, D. L. (1991). *Internetworking with TCP/IP Vol II: Design, implementation, and internals.* Englewood Cliffs, NJ: Prentice Hall.

Coventry, M. (2006). Libraries for a new generation: Getting the net gen on the right information highway. *UMN News.* Retrieved October 1, 2007, from http://www1.umn.edu/umnnews/Feature_Stories/Libraries_for_a_new_generation.html.

Coyle, K. (2007). The library catalog in a 2.0 world. *The Journal of Academic Librarianship, 33*(2), 289–291.

Davis, M. E., & Phillips, J. A. (2006). *Learning PHP and MySQL* (1st ed.). Cambridge: O'Reilly.

Deep, J., & Holfelder, P. (1996). *Developing CGI Applications with Perl.* New York: John Wiley and Sons.

de Kunder, M. (2008, September). The size of the World Wide Web. Retrieved September 21, 2008, from http://www.worldwidewebsize.com.

Dibbell, J. (February, 2008). Griefer madness. *Wired, 16,* 90–97.

Dillon, M., Jul, E., Burge, M., & Hickney, C. (1993). *Assessing information on the Internet: Toward providing library services for computer-mediated communication.* Dublin, OH: OCLC Online Computer Library Center, Inc.

Ding, C. H., Nutanong, S., & Buyya, R. (2003). *Peer-to-peer networks for content sharing.* Melbourne: The University of Melbourne, Australia.

Dornfest, R., Bausch, P., & Calishain, T. (2006). *Google hacks: Tips & tools for smarter searching* (3rd ed.). New York: O'Reilly Media, Inc.

EDUCAUSE. (2008). 7 things you should know about Flickr. Retrieved May 30, 2008, from http://net.educause.edu/ir/library/pdf/ELI7034.pdf.

Efros, A. (2003). Data-driven texture and motion. In *University of Washington Computer Science and Engineering Colloquia.* The University of Washington. Retrieved from http://www.researchchannel.org/prog/displayevent.aspx?rID=3244&fID=345.

Electronic Privacy Information Center (EPIC). (2008, May 25). Congressman Barton urges scrutiny of Google's privacy practices. Retrieved May 1, 2008, from http://epic.org.

Fahey, M. J., & Brown, J. W. (1995). *Web publisher's design guide for Windows.* Scottsdale, AZ: Coriolis Group.

Farkas, M. (2007). Balancing the online life. *American Libraries, 38*(1), 42–45.

FCKeditor. (2008). The text editor for the Internet. Retrieved October 1, 2007, from http://www.fckeditor.net.

Ferris Research. (2008). Industry statistics. Retrieved May 1, 2008, from http://www.ferris.com/research-library/industry-statistics.

Fichter, D. (2006). Using wikis to support online collaboration in libraries. *Information Outlook, 10*(1), 30–33.

Fitzgerald, M. (2004). *XML Hacks: 100 industrial-strength tips & tools.* Beijing: O'Reilly.

Flynn, R. R. (1987). *An introduction to information science.* New York: Marcel Dekker.

Friedman, T. L. (2005). *The world is flat: A brief history of the twenty-first century.* New York: Farrar, Straus, and Giroux.

Garfield, E. (1972). Citation analysis as a tool in journal evaluation. *Science, 178*(4060), 471–479.

Ghemawat, S., Gobioff, H., & Leung, S.-T. (2003, December). *The Google file system.* Paper presented at the Proceedings of the 19th ACM Symposium on Operating Systems Principles, Bolton Landing, NY.

Gil, P. (July 2008). What is "The invisible Web"? Retrieved September 14, 2008, from http://netforbeginners.about.com/cs/secondaryweb1/a/secondaryweb.htm.

Giles, J. (2005). Internet encyclopedias go head to head. *Nature, 438,* 900–901.

Gill, J. (2008, January 17). Researchers' web use could make libraries redundant. Retrieved May 1, 2008, from http://www.timeshighereducation.co.uk/story.asp?storycode=400168.

Gilroy, A. A., & Kruger, L. G. (2006). Broadband Internet regulation and access: Background and issues. Retrieved October 1, 2007, from http://usinfo.state.gov/infousa/economy/technology/docs/60574.pdf.

Goodrum, A., & Spink, A. (2001). Image searching on the Excite Web search engine. *Information Processing and Management, 37,* 295–311.

Google. (2008). Mission statement. Retrieved May 1, 2008, from http://www.google.com/corporate.

Graham, I. S. (1996). *The HTML sourcebook* (2nd ed.). New York: John Wiley & Sons.

Graves, M. (2002). *Designing XML databases.* Upper Saddle River, NJ: Prentice Hall.

Greenwell, S., & Kraemer, B. (2007). Social networking software follow-up: Facebook and MySpace (and more). *Kentucky Libraries, 71*(4), 11–15.

Grimes, R. A. (2001). *Malicious mobile code.* Cambridge, MA: O'Reilly and Associates.

Gulli, A., & Signorini, A. (2005). *The indexable Web is more than 11.5 billion pages.* Paper presented at the WWW 2005, Chiba, Japan.

Hafner, K. (2007, August 19). Seeing corporate fingerprints in Wikipedia edits. *New York Times,* p. 1.

Harms, D. (2001). *JSP, servlets, and MySQL.* New York: M&T Books.

Harold, E. R., & Means, W. S. (2002). *XML in a nutshell* (3rd ed.). Beijing: O'Reilly.

Harris, R. (2007, June 15). Evaluating Internet research sources. Retrieved October 1, 2007, from http://www.virtualsalt.com/evalu8it.htm.

Hawking, D., & Zobel, J. (2007). Does topic metadata help with Web search? *JASIST, 58*(5), 613–626.

Heilmann, C. (2006). *Beginning JavaScript with DOM Scripting and AJAX: From novice to professional.* New York: Apress.

Heise Security. (2008, January 15). Quantity of malware booms. Retrieved May 1, 2008, from http://www.heise-online.co.uk/security/Quantity-of-malware-booms—/news/101764.

Hoffer, J. A., Prescott, M. B., & McFadden, F. R. (2002). *Modern database management* (6th ed.). Upper Saddle River, NJ: Prentice Hall.

Hofstetter, F. (2005). *Internet technologies at work.* Burr Ridge, IL: McGraw-Hill

Holman, B. K., & Lund, W. (1997). *Instant JavaScript.* Upper Saddle River, NJ: Prentice Hall.

Holzschlag, M. E. (1998). *Web by design: The complete guide.* San Francisco: Sybex.

Horrigan, J. (2007, February). Wireless Internet access. *Internet and American life project.* Retrieved March 26, 2008, from http://www.pewinternet.org/pdfs/PIP_Wireless.Use.pdf.

Information behaviour of the researcher of the future. Retrieved February 1, 2008, from http://www.bl.uk/news/pdf/googlegen.pdf.

Jamsa, K., Lalani, S., & Weakley, S. (1996). *Web programming.* Las Vegas, NV: Jamsa Press.

Jeanneney, J.-N. (2006). *Google and the myth of universal knowledge.* Trans. T. L. Fagan. Chicago: University of Chicago Press.

Jones, S., & Madden, M. (2002, September 15). The Internet goes to college. *Internet and American Life Project.* Retrieved October 2007 from http://www.pewinternet.org/pdfs/Pip_College_Report.pdf.

Jowitt, A. L. (2008). Creating communities with podcasting. *Computers in Libraries, 28*(4), 14–15, 54–16.

Jupiter Media. (2005). Jupiterresearch forecasts broadband's rise to dominance, increasing from 32 million U.S. households in 2004 to 69 million in 2010. Retrieved October 2007 from http://www.jupitermedia.com/corporate/releases/05.06.02-newjupresearch.html.

Kahle, B. (1997). Preserving the Internet. *Scientific American, 276*(3), 82–84.

Kaplenk, J. (1999). *UNIX system administrator's interactive workbook.* Upper Saddle River, NJ: Prentice-Hall.

Kaspersky Lab. (2008, April). Kaspersky Lab forecasts ten-fold increase in new malware for 2008. Retrieved May 1, 2008, from http://www.kaspersky.com/news?id=207575629.

Kestenbaum, D. (2008). Old drug offers new hope for Marfan Syndrome. Retrieved May 30, 2008, from http://www.npr.org/templates/story/story.php?storyId=90257827.

Kientzle, T. (1995). *Internet file formats.* Scottsdale, AZ: Coriolis Group.

Kiernan, V. (2005). Missing the boat, or penny-wise caution? *The Chronicle of Higher Education, 51*(27), A33–35.

Klein, N. (2008, May 29). China's all-seeing eye: With the help of U.S. defense contractors, China is building the prototype for a high-tech police state. Retrieved May 30, 2008, from http://www.rollingstone.com/politics/story/20797485/chinas_allseeing_eye.

Kleinberg, J. M. (1999). Authoritative sources in a hypertext environment. *Journal of the ACM, 46*(5), 604–632.

Kleinrock, L. (1996, August 27). The birth of the Internet. Retrieved October 1, 2007, from http://www.lk.cs.ucla.edu/LK/Inet/birth.html.

Korfhage, R. R. (1997). *Information storage and retrieval.* New York: Wiley & Sons.

Kozierok, C. M. (2005). *The TCP/IP guide.* Retrieved June 1, 2006, from http://www.tcpipguide.com/index.htm.

Krohl, E. (1994). *The whole Internet: Users guide and catalog.* Sebastopol, CA: O'Reilly and Associates.

Kroski, E. (2007, April 2). Information design for the new Web. Retrieved October 1, 2007, from http://infotangle.blogsome.com/2007/04/02/information-design-for-the-new-web.

Lancaster, F. W. (1979). *Information Retrieval Systems: Characteristics, testing, and evaluation.* New York: John Wiley.

Langville, A. N. (2005). The linear algebra behind search engines. *Journal of Online Mathematics and its Applications (JOMA).* Retrieved October 15, 2007, from http://mathdl.maa.org/mathDL/4/?pa=content&sa=viewDocument&nodeId=636.

Langville, A. N., & Meyer, C. D. (2006). *Google's PageRank and beyond: The science of search engine rankings.* Princeton, NJ: Princeton University Press.

Lawrence, S., & Giles, C. L. (1998). Searching the World Wide Web. *Science, 280*(5360), 98–100.

Lawrence, S., & Giles, C. L. (1999). Accessibility of information on the web. *Nature, 400*(6740), 107–109.

Lawrence, S., Coetzee, F., Glover, E., Flake, G., Pennock, D., Krovetz, B., et al. (2000). *Persistence of information on the web: Analyzing citations contained in research articles.* Paper presented at the Conference on Information and Knowledge Management, McLean, Virginia.

Leary, M., Hale, D., & Devigal, A. (1997). *Web designer's guide to typography.* Indianapolis, IN: Hayden Books.

Lehnert, W. (2002). *The Web Wizard's Guide to HTML.* Boston: Addison-Wesley.

Leiden, C., & Wilensky, M. (2000). *TCP/IP for dummies* (4th ed.). Foster City, CA: IDG Books Worldwide Inc.

Leiner, B. M., Cerf, V. G., Clark, D. D., Kahn, R. E., Kleinrock, L., Lynch, D. C., et al. (1997). The past and future history of the Internet. *Communications of the ACM, 40*(2), 102–109.

LeJune, U. A. (1996). *Netscape and HTML Explorer.* Scottsdale: Coriolis Group.

LeMay, L. (1997). *Teach yourself Web publishing with HTML 4* (2nd ed.). Indianapolis, IN: SAMS.

Lenhart, A., & Fox, S. (2006, July 19). Bloggers: A portrait of the Internet's new storytellers. Retrieved October 1, 2007, from http://www.pewinternet.org/pdfs/PIP%20Bloggers%20Report%20July%2019%202006.pdf.

Lie, H. W., & Bos, B. (1999). *Cascading Style Sheets, designing for the Web.* Reading, MA: Addison Wesley.

Loshin, P. (1999). *IPv6 clearly explained.* San Francisco: Academic Press.

Lyons, D. (2007, October 29). Party crashers. *Forbes, 180,* 68–70.

Madden, M. (2008, August 28). Podcasts proliferate, but not mainstream. Retrieved September 27, 2008, from http://pewresearch.org/pubs/941/podcasts-proliferate-but-not-mainstream.

Martin, D., Prata, S., Waite, M., Wessler, M., & Wilson, D. (2000). *UNIX primer plus* (3rd ed.). Indianapolis: Sams.

Mason, P. (2006, January 5). Do avatars dream of electric racoons? *As part of Newsnight's Geek Week, business correspondent Paul Mason and presenter Jeremy Paxman broadcast TV's first ever face-to-face studio session from inside the computer game Second Life.* Retrieved June 2, 2008, from http://news.bbc.co.uk/2/hi/programmes/newsnight/4583924.stm.

Maze, S., Moxley, D., & Smith, D. J. (1997). *Authoritative guide to Web search engines.* New York: Neal-Schuman.

McCall, T. (2007, December 17). Gartner survey shows phishing attacks escalated in 2007; More than $3 billion lost to these attacks. Retrieved May 1, 2008, from http://www.gartner.com/it/page.jsp?id=565125.

McClelland, D., Eismann, K., & Stone, T. (2000). *Web design studio secrets* (2nd ed.). Foster City, CA: IDG Books.

Meadow, C. T., Boyce, B. R., & Kraft, D. H. (2000). *Text information retrieval systems* (2nd ed.). San Diego, CA: Academic Press.

Meloni, J. C. (2000). *PHP fast & easy Web development.* Roseville, CA: Prima Publishing.

Mi, J., & Weng, C. (2008). Revitalizing the library OPAC: Interface, searching and display challenges. *Information Technology and Libraries, 27*(1), 5–22.

Microsoft.NET. (2008). Overview. Retrieved October 1, 2007, from http://www.microsoft.com/net/Overview.aspx.

Miller, J. B. (2003). PC security in a networked world. *Kentucky Libraries, 67*(4), 18–22.

Miller, J. B. (2006). The Internet has changed, like, everything. *Kentucky Libraries, 70*(2), 4–6.

Miller, W., & Pellen, R. M. (Eds.). (2005). *Libraries and Google.* Binghamton, NY: Haworth Information Press.

Mills, E. (2005, October 21). Google shares soar on hearty revenue report. Retrieved October 1, 2007, from http://news.com.com/Google+revenue+nearly+doubles/2100-1030_3-5905127.html.

Molyneux, R. E. (2003). *The Internet under the hood: An introduction to network technologies for information professionals.* Westport, CT: Libraries Unlimited.

Morville, P. (2005). *Ambient findability.* Sebastpol, CA: O'Reilly Media, Inc.

Mowshowitz, A., & Kawaguchi, A. (2002). Bias on the Web. *Communications of the ACM, 45*(9), 56–60.

Nahorney, B., & Gudmundsson, A. (2003). Symantec corporation security updates Sobig page. Retrieved August 2, 2003, from http://www.symantec.com/security_response/writeup.jsp?docid=2003-081909-2118-99&tabid=2.

National School Boards Association. (2007). *Creating and connecting: Research and guidelines on online social—and educational—networking.* Retrieved June 2, 2008, from http://www.nsba.org/SecondaryMenu/TLN/CreatingandConnecting.aspx.

National Science Foundation. (2005, September 28). The launch of NSFNET. Retrieved October 1, 2007, from http://www.nsf.gov/about/history/nsf0050/internet/launch.htm.

Neumeister, L. (2008, May 27, 2008). Google backs video sharing on YouTube Viacom suit says it violates copyrights. *Lexington Herald Leader,* p. D5,

A new wave. (2002). *The Economist, 362*(8256), 68.

Nielsen, J. (2003, June 30). Information foraging: Why Google makes people leave your site faster. Retrieved October 1, 2007, from http://www.useit.com/alertbox/20030630.html.

Nielsen, J. (2006, April 17). F-shaped pattern for reading Web content. Retrieved May 1, 2008, from http://www.useit.com/alertbox/reading_pattern.html.

Nielsen, J. (2008, April 28). Right-justified navigation menus impede scannability. Retrieved May 1, 2008, from http://www.useit.com/alertbox/navigation-menu-alignment.html.

The Nielsen Company. (2008, May 14). Wikipedia U.S. Web traffic grows 8,000 percent in five years, driven by search. Retrieved June 10, 2008, from http://www.nielsen-netratings.com/pr/pr_080514.pdf.

Norman, D. (2007). Simplicity is highly overrated. Retrieved October 1, 2007, from http://www.jnd.org/dn.mss/simplicity_is_highly.html.

Norton, P., & Nielson, P. (1992). *Inside the Norton antivirus.* New York: Brady.

Notess, G. R. (2002, March 6). Little overlap despite growth! Retrieved October 1, 2007, from http://www.searchengineshowdown.com/statistics/overlap.shtml.

OfficeTeam. (2006, January). We never talk anymore. Retrieved October 1, 2007, from http://www.officeteam.com/portal/site/ot-us/template.PAGE/menuitem.f641a8b96a6cc83772201cb202f3dfa0/?javax.portlet.tpst=2bc7e8a2726625787220 1cb202f3dfa0&javax.portlet.prp_2bc7e8a27266257872201cb202f3dfa0_releaseId=1601&javax.portlet.prp_2bc7e8a27266257872201cb202f3dfa0_request_type=RenderPressRelease&javax.portlet.begCacheTok=com.vignette.cachetoken&javax.portlet.endCacheTok=com.vignette.cachetoken.

Online Computer Library Center (OCLC). (2002). Web characterization. Retrieved October 1, 2007, from http://www.oclc.org/research/projects/archive/wcp.

Online Community Library Center (OCLC). (2006, June 1). OCLC reports on college students' library perceptions. Retrieved May 1, 2008, from http://www.libraryjournal.com/info/CA6340281.html.

O'Reilly, T. (2005, September 30). What Is Web 2.0: Design patterns and business models for the next generation of software. Retrieved May 1, 2008, from http://www.oreillynet.com/pub/a/oreilly/tim/news/2005/09/30/what-is-web-20.html.

O'Reilly, T. (2005, October 1). Web 2.0: Compact definition? Retrieved October 1, 2007, from http://radar.oreilly.com/archives/2005/10/web-20-compact-definition.html.

O'Reilly, T. (2006, May 14). My Commencement speech at SIMS. Retrieved June 2, 2008, from http://radar.oreilly.com/archives/2006/05/my-commencement-speech-at-sims.html.

O'Reilly Media, Inc. (2008). Distributed search engines. Retrieved October 1, 2007, from http://www.openp2p.com/pub/t/74.

Pepus, G. (2007). Smart image and video search. *KM World, 16*(6), 6–9.

Peters, T., & Bell, L. (2008, April 11). Trends, fads or folly: Spotting the library trends that really matter. Retrieved April 15, 2008, from http://www.collegeofdupagepress.com/library-learning-network/soaring-to-excellence-2008/spotting-the-library-trends-that-really-matter/.

Pfeifer, R., & Bongard, J. C. (2007). *How the body shapes the way we think.* Cambridge: MIT Press.

The PHP Group. (2008, June 6). History of PHP and related projects. Retrieved June 9, 2008, from http://us2.php.net/history.

The PHP Group. (2008, June 8). Predefined variables. Retrieved October 1, 2007, from http://us3.php.net/variables.predefined.

The PHP Group. (2008). Using register globals. Retrieved October 1, 2007, from http://us3.php.net/manual/en/security.registerglobals.php.

Powell, T. A. (2003). *HTML and XHTML: The complete reference.* Emeryville, CA: McGraw-Hill/Osborne.

Powers, D. (2006). *PHP Solutions: Dynamic Web design made easy.* New York: Springer-Verlag.

Purvis, M., Sambells, J., & Turner, C. (2006). *Beginning Google maps applications with PHP and Ajax; From novice to professional.* Berkeley, CA: Apress.

Quantity of malware booms. (2008, January 15). Retrieved May 1, 2008, from http://www.heise-online.co.uk/security/Quantity-of-malware-booms—/news/101764/from/atom10.

Rainie, L. (2005, November 20). Search engine use shoots up in the past year and edges towards email as the primary internet application. *Internet and American Life.* Retrieved May 1, 2008, from http://www.pewinternet.org/PPF/r/167/report_display.asp.

Rainie, L. (2007, January 31). Tagging play: Forget Dewey and his decimals, Internet users are revolutionizing the way we classify information—and make sense of it. *Pew Internet & American Life Project.* Retrieved May 30, 2008, from http://pewresearch.org/pubs/402/tagging-play.

Rapacki, S. (2007). Why teens need places like MySpace. *Young Adult Library Services, 5*(2).

Ray, E. T. (2003). Learning XML. Sebastopol, CA: O'Reilly.

Reiss, S. (2008, May, 2008). Planet Amazon. *Wired, 16,* 88–95.

Rethlefsen, M. L. (2007). Tags help make libraries DEL.ICIO.US. *Library Journal,* 26–28. Retrieved May 1, 2008, from http://www.gartner.com/it/page.jsp?id=565125.

Riccardi, G. (2003). *Database management with Web site development applications.* New York: Addison Wesley.

Rob, P., & Coronel, C. (1997). *Database systems: Design, implementation, and management* (3rd ed.). Cambridge, MA: Course Technology.

Rockwell, W. (2001). *XML, XSLT, Java, and JSP: A case study in developing a Web application.* Indianapolis, New Riders.

Rogers, I. (2002). The Google Pagerank algorithm and how it works. *Google Pagerank whitepaper.* Retrieved October 10, 2007, from http://www.ianrogers.net/google-page-rank.

Rorissa, A. (2007). Benchmarking visual information indexing and retrieval systems. *Bulletin of the American Society for Information Science and Technology, 33*(3), 15–17.

Rosenfield, L., & Morville, P. (1998). *Information architecture for the World Wide Web.* Sebastopol, CA: O'Reilly.

Rubin, A. D., Gerr, D., & Ranum, M. J. (1997). *Web security sourcebook.* New York: John Wiley and Sons, Inc.

Ruby on Rails. (2008). Web development that doesn't hurt. Retrieved October 1, 2007, from http://www.rubyonrails.org.

Russo, P., & Boor, S. (1993, April 24–29). *How fluent is your interface? Designing for international users.* Paper presented at the INTERCHI '93, Amsterdam, The Netherlands.

Salton, G., & McGill, M. J. (1983). *Introduction to modern information retrieval.* New York: McGraw-Hill.

Schneider, G. M., & Gersting, J. L. (2000). *An invitation to computer science.* Pacific Grove, CA: Brooks/Cole.

Scholz, T. (2008). Market ideology and the myths of Web 2.0. *First Monday, 13*(3).

Schrock, K. (1998). 5 W's for evaluating Web sites. Retrieved October 1, 2007, from http://kathyschrock.net/abceval/5ws.htm.

Schwartz, B. (2005). *The paradox of choice: Why more is less.* New York: Harper Perennial.

Second Life. (2008, May 28). Economic statistics. Retrieved May 29, 2008, from http://secondlife.com/whatis/economy_stats.php.

Shafer, D. (1996). *JavaScript & Netscape wizardry.* Scottsdale, AZ: Coriolis Group Books.

Shannon, C. (1949). Communication in the presence of noise. *Proceedings of the Institute of Radio Engineers, 37*(1), 10–21.

Shannon, V. (2006, May 24). A "more revolutionary" Web. Retrieved May 1, 2008, from http://www.iht.com/articles/2006/05/23/business/web.php.

Sheldon, T. (2001). DSL (Digital Subscriber Line). *Tom Sheldon's Linktionary.* Retrieved January 27, 2006, from http://www.linktionary.com/d/dsl.html.

Shirky, C. (2006). Second Life: A story too good to check. Retrieved June 4, 2008, from http://www.valleywag.com/tech/second-life/a-story-too-good-to-check-221252.php.

Sifry, D. (2007, April 5). The State of the live Web, April 2007. Retrieved May 1, 2008, from http://www.sifry.com/alerts/archives/000493.html.

Silver, D. (2008). History hype and hope: An afterword. *First Monday, 13*(3).

Simoneau, P. (1997). *Hands-on TCP/IP.* New York: McGraw-Hill.

Sloan, S. (2006, February 19). Inklings of change—inside the potential sale of Knight Ridder: Industry pressures, technology advances put print journalism and Herald-Leader at a crossroads. *Lexington Herald Leader,* p. A16.

Smalera, P. (2007, September). Google's secret formula. *Conde Nast Portfolio,* 136–137.

Smeaton, A. (2007). TRECVid-Video evaluation. *Bulletin of the American Society for Information Science and Technology, 33*(3), 21–23.

Sophos, Inc. (2002, May 1). Melissa worm author sentenced to 20 months. Retrieved May 1, 2008, from http://www.sophos.com/pressoffice/news/articles/2002/05/pr_uk_20020501smith.html.

Sophos, Inc. (2008). JDBGMGR hoax. Retrieved May 1, 2008, from http://www.sophos.com/security/hoaxes/jdbgmgr.html.

Sperberg-McQueen, C. M., & Thompson, H. (2000, April). W3C XML Schema. Retrieved September 27, 2008, from http://www.w3.org/XML/Schema.

Stelter, B. (2008, June 15). Internet providers clamp down on users' time online. *Lexington Herald-Leader,* p. A7.

Stephens, M. (2007). *Web 2.0 & libraries, part 2: Trends and technologies* (Report). Chicago, IL: American Library Association.

Storey, T. (2005). The long tail and libraries. *OCLC Newsletter, 268,* 6–10.

Strom, E. (1998). *PERL CGI programming: No experience required.* San Francisco: Sybex.

Sullivan, D. (2004, January 6). Google's (and Inktomi's) miserable failure. Retrieved May 1, 2008, from http://searchenginewatch.com/showPage.html?page=3296101.

Sullivan, D. (2005, January 28). Search engine sizes. Retrieved October 1, 2007, from http://searchenginewatch.com/showPage.html?page=2156481#trend.

SVG Working Group. (2003, January 14). Scalable vector graphics (SVG) 1.1 specification: W3C Recommendation. Retrieved May 1, 2008, from http://www.w3.org/TR/SVG.

Talbot, D. (2008, May/June). Where spam is born. *Technology Review, 111,* 28.

Tang, A., & Scoggins, S. (1992). *Open networking with OSI.* Englewood, NJ: Prentice-Hall.

Tatum, C. (2005). Deconstructing Google bombs: A breach of symbolic power or just a goofy prank? *First Monday, 10*(10).

Tennant, R. (2002). The digital librarian shortage. *Library Journal, 127*(5), 32.

Tenopir, C. (2007). Web 2.0: Our cultural downfall? *Library Journal, 132*(20), 36.

The Text REtrieval Conference. (2007, August 8). Overview. Retrieved May 1, 2008, from http://trec.nist.gov/overview.html.

Tittel, E., Price, S., & Stewart, J. M. (1997). *Web graphics sourcebook.* New York: Wiley & Sons, Inc.

Trend Micro (2008, January). Malware today and mail server security. *A Trend Micro White Paper.* Retrieved May 1, 2008, from http://www.emediausa.com/FM/GetFile.aspx?id=8541.

Turkle, S. (2007). Can you hear me now? *Forbes.com.* Retrieved June 4, 2008, from http://www.forbes.com/forbes/2007/0507/176_print.html.

Unisys. (2008). LZW patent information. Retrieved September 19, 2008, from http://www.unisys.com/about__unisys/lzw.

U.S. Census. (2002). Census data on disabilities. Retrieved September 30, 2007, from http://www.census.gov/hhes/www/disability/sipp/disab02/awd02.html.

U.S. Census. (2006). Computer and Internet use in the United States: 2003. Retrieved October 1, 2007, from http://www.census.gov/population/pop-profile/dynamic/Computers.pdf.

U.S. Census. (2008, May 15). Quarterly retail e-commerce sales. Retrieved May 22, 2008, from http://www.census.gov/mrts/www/ecomm.html.

Vidmar, D., & Anderson, C. (2002). History of Internet search tools. In A. Kent & C. Hall (Eds.), *Encyclopedia of library and information science* (vol. 71, pp. 146–162). New York: Marcel Dekker, Inc.

Vlist, E. v. d. (2001, October 17). Using W3C XML schema. Retrieved October 10, 2007, from http://www.xml.com/pub/a/2000/11/29/schemas/part1.html.

W3C. (1998, October 1). Document Object Model (DOM) level 1 specification. Retrieved October 10, 2007, from http://www.w3.org/TR/REC-DOM-Level-1.

W3C. (2000, May 8). Simple Object Access Protocol (SOAP) 1.1. Retrieved October 10, 2007, from http://www.w3.org/TR/2000/NOTE-SOAP-20000508/.

W3C. (2001). Semantic Web activity. Retrieved October 1, 2007, from http://www.w3.org/2001/sw.

W3C. (2004, February 10). RDF primer. Retrieved October 10, 2007, from http://www.w3.org/TR/REC-rdf-syntax.

W3C. (2007, July). WCAG 2.0 Web content accessibility guidelines update. Retrieved May 1, 2008, from http://www.w3.org/WAI/EO/Drafts/wcag20pres/wcag2intro20070725.doc.

W3C. (2008). Cascading style sheets home page. Retrieved May 2, 2008, from http://www.w3.org/Style/CSS.

W3C. (2008). Document Object Model (DOM). Retrieved October 1, 2007, from http://www.w3.org/DOM.

W3C. (2008, April 27). The extensible stylesheet language family (XSL). Retrieved May 1, 2008, from http://www.w3.org/Style/XSL.

W3C. (2008, May 26). Scalable vector graphics: XML graphics for the Web. Retrieved June 10, 2008, from http://www.w3.org/Graphics/SVG.

W3Schools. (2008). CSS tutorial. Retrieved May 2, 2008, from http://www.w3schools.com/css/default.asp.

W3Schools. (2008). Introduction to XML schema. Retrieved October 1, 2007, from http://www.w3schools.com/schema/schema_intro.asp.

Watkinson, J. (2000). *The art of digital audio* (3rd ed.). Oxford: Focal Press.

Weber, J. (2006). Evergreen: Your homegrown ILS. *Library Journal, 131*(20), 38–41.

Wellman, S. (2007, December 5). Drudge Report goes mobile. Retrieved May 19, 2008, from http://www.informationweek.com/blog/main/archives/2007/12/drudge_report_g.html.

Wells, J., Lewis, L., & Greene, B. (2006). *Internet access in U.S. public schools and classrooms: 1994–2005.* Washington, D.C.: U.S. Department of Education.

White, M. (2000, February 2). Loans.com latest web name to make millionaire of seller. *Herald-Leader,* p. C2.

Wilson, T. D. (2000). Human information behavior. *Informing Science, 3*(2), 49–56.

Wisniewski, J. (2008). The new rules of Web design. *Online, 32*(2), 55–57.

Wolf, G. (1995, June). The curse of Xanadu. *Wired, 3,* 137–202.

Wong, Q. (2008, May 1). WiMax to widen Net access: New device more powerful, secure than Wi-Fi. *Lexington Herald-Leader,* p. A3.

Wrolstad, J. (2004, September 10). FCC: Broadband usage has tripled. Retrieved May 2007 from http://www.newsfactor.com/story.xhtml?story_title=FCC—Broadband-Usage-Has-Tripled&story_id=26876.

XML Guild. (2007). *Advanced XML applications.* Boston, Thomson.

Yaneza, J. L., Thiemann, T., Drake, C., Oliver, J., Sancho, D., Hacquebord, F., et al. (2008). 2007 threat report and 2008 threat and technology forecast. Retrieved May 1, 2008, from http://us.trendmicro.com/imperia/md/content/us/pdf/threats/securitylibrary/tre_threat_report.pdf.

Yang, K. (2005). Information Retrieval on the Web. In B. Cronin (Ed.), *Annual review of information science and technology* (vol. 39, pp. 33–80). New York: ASIST.

Yott, P. (2005). Introduction to XML. *Cataloging & Quarterly, 40*(3/4), 213–235.

Young, M. L. (2002). *Internet: The complete reference* (2nd ed.). Berkeley McGraw-Hill Osborne.

Zakon, R. (2006, November 1). Hobbes' Internet timeline. Retrieved May 1, 2008, from http://www.zakon.org/robert/internet/timeline/.

Zeller, T., Jr. (2005, February 1). Law barring junk e-mail allows a flood instead. *New York Times*, p. A1.

Zimmer, M. (2008). Preface: Critical perspectives on Web 2.0. *First Monday, 13*(3).

Zipf, G. K. (1949). *Human behavior and the principle of least effort; an introduction to human ecology*. Cambridge, MA: Addison-Wesley.

Index

About the Author

JOSEPH B. MILLER earned a BS degree in biology from the University of Minnesota and worked for a number of years in both biochemistry and plant pathology research programs at the University of Kentucky prior to his current career in library and information science. He received his MSLS degree from the University of Kentucky in 1992 and accepted a faculty appointment at the University of Kentucky in 1993, serving in several appointments. Since 2003, he has held the rank of Associate Professor in the School of Library and Information Science and serves as Coordinator of Computing Services for the school. He devotes the majority of his efforts to teaching technology courses in the SLIS curriculum, managing technology resources and the delivery of technology workshops to librarians throughout the state. Mr. Miller has published work in both biology and library science. He is a member of the Beta Phi Mu Honorary Society and the recipient of several awards, including the SLIS Melody Trosper Award (1992) and the College of Communications and Information Studies Excellence in Teaching Award (2000). He is also active in a number of professional organizations and is a past president of the Kentucky chapter of the Special Libraries Association.

Recent Titles in Library and Information Science Text Series

Basic Research Methods for Librarians
Ronald R. Powell and Lynn Silipigni Connoway

Library of Congress Subject Headings: Principles and Application, Fourth Edition
Lois Mai Chan

Developing Library and Information Center Collections, Fifth Edition
G. Edward Evans and Margaret Zarnosky Saponaro

Metadata and Its Impact on Libraries
Sheila S. Intner, Susan S. Lazinger, and Jean Weihs

Organizing Audiovisual and Electronic Resources for Access: A Cataloging Guide, Second Edition
Ingrid Hsieh-Yee

Introduction to Cataloging and Classification, Tenth Edition
Arlene G. Taylor

Library and Information Center Management, Seventh Edition
Robert D. Stueart and Barbara B. Moran

The Collection Program in Schools: Concepts, Practices, and Information Sources, Fourth Edition
Kay Bishop

Children's Literature in Action: A Librarian's Guide
Sylvia Vardell

The School Library Media Manager, Fourth Edition
Blanche Woolls

Young Adult Literature in Action: A Librarian's Guide
Rosemary Chance

Introduction to Library Public Services, Seventh Edition
G. Edward Evans and Thomas L. Carter